BOAT TRAINS

THE ENGLISH CHANNEL AND
OCEAN LINER SPECIALS

To my family of girls who have provided a constant stream of encouragement whilst researching and writing this book.

BOAT TRAINS
THE ENGLISH CHANNEL AND OCEAN LINER SPECIALS

History, Development and Operation

MARTYN PRING

PEN & SWORD
TRANSPORT
AN IMPRINT OF PEN & SWORD BOOKS LTD.
YORKSHIRE - PHILADELPHIA

First published in Great Britain in 2020 by
PEN AND SWORD TRANSPORT
An imprint of
Pen & Sword Books Ltd
Yorkshire - Philadelphia

ISBN 978 1 52676 192 7

Typeset in 10.5/13.5 pt Palatino
Typeset by SJmagic DESIGN SERVICES, India.
Printed and bound in India by Replika Press Pvt. Ltd.

Pen & Sword Books Ltd incorporates the Imprints of Pen & Sword Books Archaeology, Atlas, Aviation, Battleground, Discovery, Family History, History, Maritime, Military, Naval, Politics, Railways, Select, Transport, True Crime, Fiction, Frontline Books, Leo Cooper, Praetorian Press, Seaforth Publishing, Wharncliffe and White Owl.

For a complete list of Pen & Sword titles please contact

PEN & SWORD BOOKS LIMITED
47 Church Street, Barnsley, South Yorkshire, S70 2AS, England
E-mail: enquiries@pen-and-sword.co.uk
Website: www.pen-and-sword.co.uk

Or
PEN AND SWORD BOOKS
1950 Lawrence Rd, Havertown, PA 19083, USA
E-mail: Uspen-and-sword@casematepublishers.com
Website: www.penandswordbooks.com

Contents

Acknowledgements

Childhood memories abound for a lifetime. An organised school trip to Southampton Docks in the last throws of the Atlantic liner age left a huge impression on me. But this was no ordinary trip as four primary schools in north Bristol banded together to charter a train that would take us to the south coast port, and a highly memorable trip that was to include afternoon visits to Bucklers Hard and Beaulieu. But to me as a railway-mad youngster this was no ordinary train; we were on a boat train. On reaching Southampton we left the main line, entered the dock estate and in a slow meandering craw, the then world's greatest vessels suddenly came into view – *Queen Mary*, *United States*, the lavender coloured hulls of smaller Union Castle liners and other passenger ships were on top of us, and could be seen so clearly through wide carriage windows prompting a long-held fascination in the role of boat trains. Later visits to Dorset and Weymouth's diesel hauled Channel Islands' boat trains trundling through the town's back street merely fired the imagination.

Having written the earlier text 'Luxury Railway Travel: A Social and Business History', I was left with a wealth of unused material. The idea of embracing this around cross-channel and ocean liner services provided the perfect opportunity to encapsulate everything as a companion volume wrapped around the notion of exploring 'boat train' travel. This title, therefore, covers English Channel ports and routes as well as others around Britain responsible for handling ocean liners. Apart from blue water traffic, one of the most visible aspects of boat train provisioning was of services operating in perfect harmony in Britain and on the Continent at the same time. The routes to northern European cities and south to the French Riviera, Switzerland and Italy have been at the forefront of traveller interest ever since railways and steamers first started working in tandem.

There were many intriguing research investigations. Many of the themes present have required the able assistance of many people who have helped shape this text. Mary S. Lovell's knowledge of the Riviera's glamour set was particularly insightful as she kindly pinpointed me towards the direction of Winston Churchill's regular 1930s soirees aboard the Côte d'Azur trains. In this context I should also like to thank Heidi Egginton at the Churchill Archives, Churchill College, Cambridge University who authenticated the Mary Penman extract. Jim Davies at British Airways Speedbird Centre Archives and Museum generously provided me with a transcript of an employee's reminiscences of the Pullman flying boat train. Likewise, the team at SNCF/French Railways Society and Beth Ellis, Curator, Digital Collections & Web Editor, P&O Heritage Collection for their expert contributions. I am greatly indebted to my commissioning editor John Scott-Morgan, Campbell McCutcheon and William Miller for reading a first draft. Campbell and Bill Miller's contributions were uniquely invaluable drawing together the maritime elements into this branch of railway history exploration.

Image research took me in many different directions, particularly with regards to how boat trains interacted with railway company, shipping lines and port owner operations. To this end, I'm very grateful for the assistance of a wide range of people who helped including Felicity Jones and Elaine Arthurs from the curatorial team at STEAM – Museum of the Great Western Railway who helped with the identification of several GWR boat train images. Similarly, Peter Rance and Laurence Waters for their GWR picture research, and for permission to use the American Pullman image material taken from an original brochure housed at the Great Western Trust, Didcot Railway Centre. Continuing the GWR theme Andy King, Senior Curator for social, industrial and maritime history at Bristol Culture, M Shed Museum, Gerald Nichols for their Bristol and Avonmouth Docks historical images as well as Alan Kittridge for his GWR and Plymouth Docks material. Ian Collard for his LMS and British Railways Riverside Station and Liverpool Pier Head shots, Michael Bunn and Bram van der Velden, Photographic Archivist at the French Railways Society, Ludo Beckers of the Red Star Museum in Antwerp for the Belgian Red Star Line boat train image, Maria Newbery, Curator of Maritime & Local Collections and Joanne Smith, Archivist at Southampton City Council, Paul Chancellor at the Colour Rail Library for his exhaustive research and suggestions of boat trains, David Davison in Dublin for Father Browne *Titanic* related photographs, Paul Smith, who was company archivist at Thomas Cook, Mike Phipp, aviation writer for his Imperial Airways Pullman image, Richard Moulton at Tuck DB, Peter Waller at Online Transport Archive, Tom Gillmor, Mary Evans Picture Library, Tony Hillman of Southern Railway Publicity, http://www.srpublicity.co.uk, John Clarke at Railway Wonders of the World, Jane Skayman, archivist at Mortons Media Group who run *The Railway Magazine Archive*, Justin Hobson from Science and Society Picture Library at the Science Museum Group, London and the research team at the National Railway Museum York and finally Arnaud Droits et Photothéque, Wagon-Lits-Diffusion. Lastly special thanks to Dr Richard Furness who again has provided me with a batch of high-quality railway posters from his matchless Poster to Poster book series. All have contributed greatly to supplying distinctive visual material recording such an eventful and colourful period of combined rail and sea travel.

Whilst every effort has been taken to research and interpret events correctly, I am sure there may be errors and omissions for which I take full responsibility. I would be delighted to hear from readers of any comments and suggestions they may have. Please contact via info@martynpring.co.uk

Foreword

Paul Atterbury

My first experience of boat trains came when I was a nine-year old train spotter, standing on the platform at Surbiton station and watching Weymouth-bound Channel Island expresses going past. My second, soon after that, was leaving Victoria with my mother on a boat train bound for Dover, at the start of a visit to northern France. There were no Pullmans, but it was a fitting boat train, and very exciting for a small boy, as were the big blue Wagon Lits carriages and the massive steam locomotive waiting for us in Calais.

My last boat train experience was in Weymouth in 1987, watching the Channel Islands train winding its way along the crowded quays to the Harbour station. I was about to move to Dorset, and was just in time to see this important, and just surviving, bit of railway history.

The boat train has a special place in the complex story of railway travel, combining as it does high romance and drama with an efficient and integrated transport system. It is an important setting for hundreds of books and films, and it is also the story of international politics before the age of the jet plane. When the boat train concept was developed in the late nineteenth century, it brought together luxury, modernity, speed and practicality with the new sense of internationalism. Ships and trains expanded horizons and diminished borders and boundaries. The idea was very simple: fast trains, often equipped with dining facilities, should run directly to and from special harbour and quayside stations so passengers could be transferred seamlessly to and from the waiting ships, unencumbered by their luggage. It helped, of course, that most of the ships on the shorter cross-channel routes were owned and operated by railway companies. Like many simple ideas, it was very successful and by the Great War an extensive network of boat trains was in operation, connecting cities and harbours throughout Europe and in many parts of the world. One of my favourite LNWR postcards, shows three very smart ladies taking tea in the Salon de Luxe on the American Express from Euston to Liverpool. After the

First World War the network was massively expanded, thanks to the wartime experience of having to move vast armies and their equipment quickly and efficiently by train and boat. In Britain, the 1920s and 1930s were the age of the named train, and many of those names reflected their maritime destinations and routes. Through the Second World War and the 1950s this integrated train and boat relationship continued to flourish and then, with the rise of private car ownership and modern air travel, the boat train idea declined and slowly died. Its time has passed.

In the late 1980s we had a house in Dieppe, and we sometimes travelled from London Victoria to Newhaven on an ordinary suburban electric train that was still listed on the destination board as a boat train. When we arrived at Newhaven, this train still ran into the special platform, then called Newhaven Marine, but previously called East Quay or Harbour Boat Station, and not to be confused with Newhaven Harbour station. At that point Dieppe still had a Gare Maritime on the quayside, and from here the train for Paris set off along the esplanade. Boat train stations were special places only served by special trains, and it is good to remember them: Folkestone Harbour, at the end of that steep slope and viaduct across the water, Dover Marine, a magnificent terminus station now used as a car park, Southampton Terminus for Docks, still visited occasionally by special trains, and many others, all distinct and memorable in their own way. We should not forget the vanished ones: Blackfriars, the starting point for boat train journeys to destinations across Europe, still carved in stone, and Port Victoria, whose scant remains on the end of the Isle of Grain speak of failed endeavour and misplaced ambition.

It is strange that so little has been written about the boat train, bearing in mind its place in the history of politics, romance and efficient international modern travel. So, this book is a timely, and essential addition to the railway history shelf.

Dorset, April 2020

Introduction

The venerable 'Boat Train' is a specific railway phenomenon variously described as 'a train that regularly carries passengers between a city and port' or 'a train scheduled to take passengers to or from a particular ship'. Boat train operations involve well-tested procedures in harbours and ports as train carriages arrive at station termini or alongside ships on quay sides allowing passengers (and freight) to continue journeys with a sea crossing before disembarking and boarding another train to a final destination. In a few circumstances this still continues to be the case, but with trains bringing dwindling numbers of foot passengers to ferry terminals some services are rendered uneconomic and a poor shadow of previous glories. Yet for a century and a half, the boat train was an integral component of combined rail and sea operations before the car, modern roll-on roll-off (ro-ro) ferries and the dominance of air travel took primacy. As a travel function, the boat train was not unique to these islands, but as a result of geography, they were a common sight on British, Irish and European routes as well as truly establishing itself into railway promotional literature and tradition. Such a text obviously bestrides the nautical sector. From mid-Victorian times, maritime developments were immense, as ships provided international passengers with ocean liner, cross-channel and short-sea travel opportunities. Progress unquestionably exercised influence on railway companies and in their dedicated boat train operations. Some elements of seafaring activity, particularly in relation to steamer and ferry operations and port and harbour ownership, were railway subsidiary operations, but the sum of the whole represented a tale of considerable efforts made by many travel organisations delivering what is described today as joined-up thinking and practice.

Despite the visibility of steamship technology progress and its rapid development in scale during the second half of the 1800s, the role of the boat train is a serious topic few railway, social and travel historians have addressed in any detail. Following initial research, it became apparent this project could not be covered adequately in a single volume. This edition therefore covers ports in southern England where boat train movements were common, as well as international ports where their operations were a key factor of transoceanic travel. Some liner ports not on the south coast were also used extensively for cross-channel operations across the Irish and North Seas forming separate titles in due course. The boat train, therefore, is one of the most compelling examples of rail-based operations since it provides a unique transport solution moving passengers from mainline railway stations to vessels and also envelopes all aspects of catering, hospitality and travel promotion lending to some of the most iconic and memorable examples of luxury rail travel ever constructed. Part of the boat train's innate appeal is that it combines both rail and sea journey experiences. Offering a unique historical perspective that charts a course through the past 150 years of the modern industrial age, boat trains were assured special social markers melding the link between rail/sea/rail transit. Whilst the travelling experience improved steadily for everyone in the second half of the Victorian era, boat train passengers, for many years, were left with a curious choice of first, second or third-class carriage travel according to individual requirements and pocket. But at the top end of the market in first-class, the inclusion of Pullman stock on boat trains in some cases meant the payment of a supplementary fare was not always welcomed by passengers.

Britain's dominant position in commerce and empire building during the second half of the nineteenth century saw swift growth of international trade and in the numbers of people travelling overseas. To cater for developments, two particular types of boat train emerged for both business and passenger needs; one serving travellers on channel crossings from the British Isles to the Continent, Scandinavia and Ireland, and a second providing specialist train services for blue water ocean going ships. From the 1870s boat trains were indelibly linked to the arrival of modern steamships, whether they were carrying passengers on cross-channel steamers, an intermediate class of vessel used for short-sea crossings such as on the North Sea or progressively on large ocean liners. Another element which transformed steamers was the progressive move from paddle to twin screw propulsion. On a daily basis with an ever-increasing number of incoming and departing ships, British ports were busy places.

On demand boat trains became a regular feature of railway and port landscapes by the 1890s as Britain's imperial tentacles spread around the globe. In addition, dedicated continental boat trains were part of the age's travelling pulse as many specific services were required for Mediterranean ports with ships heading to India, the Far East and Australasia. Train services to and from western French ports, reduced considerably the number of days passengers had to traverse the changeable and potentially dangerous North Atlantic seas. Furthermore, with Central and South America maritime routes, Spanish and Portuguese port departures minimised the endurance of tropical heat and equatorial sea passage before cabin windows bigger than portholes, open promenades, and by the mid-twentieth century, air conditioning became the norm in cabins and staterooms on passenger liners. In more recent years, sea facing balconies are now the standard cruise ship experience. Something else also impacted on the dynamics of boat train operations in this period was the allure of Mediterranean sunspots, and the emergence of an embryonic warm weather cruise tourism industry.

In January 1891 Hamburg America Line's (HAPAG) founder and general manager Albert Ballinn, spotted a gap in the sea-borne travel market by utilising a liner lying idle in the winter for a Mediterranean pleasure trip ultimately opening up a completely different business opportunity for shipping lines and railway companies. The vessel *Augusta Victoria* set sail on a two-month cruise around the Mediterranean shores. A few years later in February 1895 the journey of Red Star liner *Friesland* on a voyage from New York to the Holy Land, became the setting for the first detailed recording of life on board and the cruise experience. For upscale travellers, the boat train became an integral travel component of line-voyages and specialist ocean cruising arrangements. Ballinn was a key influencer of developments; within two decades he had become one of Germany's leading industrialists. As a shipping magnet noted as an expeditious leader of first-class travel and service culture, he outrivalled many competitor shipping lines with his prestigious trans-Atlantic liners, boat-trains operating to and from North Sea ports to Berlin, and in the development of class-leading hospitality and restaurant operations. He was well connected too. Historian Andrew Roberts records Ballinn knew the boat-loving Kaiser well, and on the eve of the Great War dined with Winston Churchill in last ditch attempts to prevent a Franco-German conflict which ultimately dragged in Britain.[1] Churchill, with aristocratic acquaintances and open access to business leaders, was a character who loved the good things in life, and in becoming a notable supporter of civilised passenger transport. For him first-class travel on the cream of trans-Atlantic liners like *Majestic* and premier mainline rail expresses across Britain and Europe became par for the course during his long life.[2]

Nothing new perhaps, but such events represented a node in time where untainted pleasure-seeking travel spaces fused with business and politics. Ocean-going travelling palaces and the railway carriage with their exquisite first-class saloon and dining car offerings from the many pre-grouping British and European railway companies and specialist organisations provided highly attractive venues, mirroring London, Paris and Berlin's best hotels and clubs as places to smooth political manoeuvrings, to facilitate business deals or sometimes combining both. By Edwardian times they were the undoubted beacons of glamour and an age that exuded exclusivity and selectivity. Impossible to quantify but the cumulative loss of many important and influential menfolk on *Titanic, Empress of Ireland* and *Lusitania* may have dented many an organisation's progress. In addition, the Great War impacted significantly on Britain and Germany's merchant marine. Britain lost two super-liners and a succession of smaller liners sunk by U-boat torpedoes and mines, whilst Germany's trio of luxury vessels were subsequently taken as reparations by Cunard, White Star and United States Line for war-time losses.

Wherever ocean steamships were to be found, accompanying boat trains wound their way, sometimes rather fast, between main-line London termini and ports. Yet there was an unmistakable thrilling association to them. A special representative of the *Pall Mall Gazette* noted American boat expresses in Britain had long enjoyed the standing of being the fastest trains in the world.[3] The presence of gilded visitors from across the pond did much for the reputation of these special services; travel writers were equally at home in their praise of the ocean boat train's charm and distinctive qualities:

> Join the special boat express leaving Waterloo Station every Wednesday morning, which in less than two hours after will be threading its way through the marvellous network of lines in Southampton Docks, passing vessels of enormous dimensions which seem to sink into insignificance when compared with the appalling magnitude of the White Star liner (*Adriatic*) towering above the train as it draws up alongside. Quickly and methodically passengers and baggage are soon aboard, and the diminutive tugs

begin to accomplish the seemingly impossible, and the leviathan of great tonnage is moved slowly away from its moorings, to the accompaniment of the cheers of those who have come to bid farewell to friends en route to the other side of the world.[4]

Adriatic was the fifth vessel of what might be termed the 'Twentieth Century' series.

Boat train operations at the turn of the twentieth century reflected normal railway company practice in this country. But the three-class structure echoed demands of European travellers criss-crossing the English Channel and the North Sea who were far more familiar with the triplicate travel strands, and more importantly, from a commercial perspective, reflected the class-structures and facilities accorded to passengers travelling on liners. On ocean going ships, a second-class designation, particularly for trans-Atlantic crossings, was a relatively new phenomenon as shipping lines identified a new constituent of middle-class prosperity in both the Old and New World made up of professional and well-educated passengers, wishing to tap into the trappings of more civilized travel but choosing to travel less expensively.[5] And this would include a new breed of skilled artisans such as Cornish tin miners many of whom travelled second-class; the most successful returned home, from time to time, as Atlantic commuters.[6] Whereas the North American trade was of vital importance, some shipping lines with long-distance vessels heading to India, the Far East and Australasia carried a combination of first and third-class, eliminating the second-class passenger designation (others offered an exclusive first-class only provision). Comparably, the Aberdeen Line, for instance, is an example of a small number of shipping firms who carried just third-class passengers, but in a degree of comfort undreamt of at the end of the Victorian era.[7] Edwardian travellers had a bewildering choice of ocean passage.

Railways, as a whole, mirrored societal landscapes found at sea. From the early 1900s dominant themes of speed, size and extravagance were driven by the competitive nature of shipping lines' operations allowing for the first time the social space and amenities for passengers to really appreciate voyages in all weathers (except for winter storms of the Atlantic and Pacific), where the types of facilities, the quality and presentation of food on offer, and in time, the range of recreational activities afforded passengers became important travel considerations. R.A. Fletcher writing in *Travelling Palaces: Luxury in Passenger Steamships* published by Sir Isaac Pitman & Sons in 1913, captured much of how the combined travel industry operated in the early years of the twentieth century, providing us with a concise summary of the kinds of facilities premier-class passengers availed themselves:

> The accommodation on the great steamships is unrivalled by nineteen out of twenty first-class hotels ashore, whether in the gorgeousness of the surroundings which are so characteristic of some steamships, the culinary delicacies supplied at their tables, the thousand and one little details introduced to add to the comfort of the passengers and the luxury of the furnishings, or the attendance.[8]

Steamers and accompanying boat trains were the only means of international travel from the British islands prior to the arrival of commercial flight. By the mid-1990s, however, the opening of the Channel Tunnel provided a fixed link between Britain and France. The year 2019 saw the twenty-fifth anniversary of journeying to the Continent on Eurostar – operations effectively masterminding the passing of scheduled and leisure boat trains (*VSOE/Orient Express*). Ferries – previously referred to as cross-channel steamers and short-sea crossing vessels in the non-oil age – delivered the means for international travel; the net result of this association was that the boat train became an intrinsic element of a combined rail/boat/rail travel experience connecting ports, principal cities and national capitals. In France a few historic boat trains connecting with cross-channel steamers were redirected to the capital and new services created to the south of the country and elsewhere. The day-time departure of the *Côte d'Azur Express* in 1904 was a case in point as it was deliberately planned to coincide with the previous London night-time boat train arrivals.[9] Whilst technically not boat trains in the strictest sense of the term, a number of these trains are included in the narrative since they are so indelibly linked to the collective travel experience, and there is acceptance of the growing importance of European capital cities in the development of routes and individual tourist plans and itineraries. As shall be seen, the carriages of Wagons-Lits, French, and in time, German railway companies established high thresholds; their exquisite, luxurious coaches attached to inter-war boat trains were simply the way to travel. This marked a process that had begun a hundred years earlier, as historians Dr Richard Mullen and Dr James Munson observed in their 2009 book, *The Smell of the Continent: The British Discover Europe*, where British Continental visitors had assumed international travel should be conducted 'in "comfort" as prerogative of their success and as an essential ingredient of civilisation'.[10]

Where the boat train ends and where special rail tourist services begin is another area of the travel conundrum. Within this grove can be found international sleeper services; boat trains and sleepers were often combined together and no-where was this more evident than in the opening up of Canada at the end of the Victorian era. Canadian Pacific's massive combined railway and shipping operations worked hand-in-glove providing integrated facilities across the Atlantic, the Pacific and the vast interiors of the British dominion. The company's trans-Continental railroad between Montreal and Vancouver had been completed in the late 1880s, offering a quicker alternative for the movement of freight and passengers from the Far East, reaching Britain and Europe quicker than by Suez Canal transit. Although the shipping line was a Canadian company, their blue water operations, nonetheless, were registered in, crewed, and run from Britain. At the turn of the twentieth century, the London & North Western Railway (LNWR) was certainly reaching out to the potential of the Canadian travel market. *The LNWR Officers' Committee Minute Book* of July 1900 reported that the

> The Battersby Tourist Agency, consisting of Mr. Norman L. Lusher and certain members of the late Mr. D. Battersby's family, have been appointed to succeed the latter as representative of the London and North Western Company's interests in Canada, subject to the supervision of Mr. Wand, the Company's general agent for America and the Dominion, on the same terms as to remuneration that the late Mr. Battersby received.[11]

In March 1908, the British connection allowed LNWR to announce details of special passenger arrangements made with Canadian Pacific to offer integrated luxury train and steamer services crossing the Atlantic, Canada and the Pacific so that Japan could be reached in just twenty-two and half days. *The Railway Magazine* carried an editorial feature under a heading of 'A Railway Across the Sea' of a 'new and striking poster just issued by the London

REDUCED FACSIMILE OF THE LONDON AND NORTH-WESTERN RAILWAY'S NEW "EUSTON AND JAPAN" PICTURE POSTER.

Reduced facsimile of an LNWR poster carried by *The Railway Magazine* in March 1908 was an attempt to illustrate the colossal mileage involved in reaching Japan involving two sets of ocean liners and dedicated boat trains. The luxurious facilities of both company's trains were a key feature in persuading travellers to use the combined travel facility. Shortly to depart from Platform 6 at Euston, the company's Canadian Pacific special boat train is shown around 1909. Whilst the service operated with full-catering operations, little extras for the five-hour journey to Liverpool could be bought including a Nestle chocolate vending machine seen here to the right-hand side of the station platform. Various combinations of carriage stock would be employed including *American Special* stock to attract high-end Edwardian travellers keen on discovering the world. (*Above*: The Railway Magazine Archive; *Below*: NRM/SSPL)

and North-Western railway, advertising the all-British route from England to Japan *via* Liverpool, Montreal and Vancouver'.[12]

Another Canadian combine, the Canadian National Railway attempted similar integrated international transport and travel solutions, establishing a new trans-Atlantic shipping line operating to and from Bristol Avonmouth in the years before the Great War. Whilst China and Japan could be embraced from Canada, they could also be reached via the Hook of Holland and eastern European routes consideration of the Trans-Siberian Railway where Peking (Beijing) could be reached in thirteen days and Tokyo in fifteen days.[13] Russia in the last quarter of the 1800s had undergone a railway-building boom brought on by the country's defeat in the Crimean War.[14] Whilst the easterly Trans-Siberian line was quicker than by sea, days of monotonous and comparatively slow rail travel progress across the Russia's vast expanses and harsh terrain hardly endeared the route as an enlightening luxury experience; the sheer scale of the lands flummoxed many traveller expectations. The route was chiefly used by the country's small affluent aristocracy and by foreign diplomats, but little used for security reasons for goods and freight traffic.[15]

The boat train's association with transoceanic travel, sometimes conveying hundreds of people in separate boat train portions to awaiting ocean-going liners, was a precursor to a very specific entry into railway lexicon. At the top end of the market, boat trains personified indulgence rail travel creating the first and last stages of a unique travel experience. Boat train images – sometimes with first-class passengers in trains made up entirely of luxury Pullman style carriages – alongside iconic named cross-channel steamers, and some of the world's greatest liners ever built are with us forever. This book captures the elements that made up a luxurious travel dimension, but the prism of investigation also takes in the other end of the spectrum. In many ways the boat train was a miniature version of society demonstrating the shocking divisions between rich and poor at the turn of the twentieth century. Whilst some services undeniably conveyed the world's elite, at the other end of the scale dedicated third-class boats trains always departed far earlier than their first and second-class combinations to arrive first at port destinations and awaiting liners, so these passengers could embark on vessels before the elite passengers arrived.

Some railway companies and shipping lines even tried to classify these operations as a form of 'fourth-class': emigrant passengers were squashed in boat trains with hard-seated carriages providing only the most basic of amenities. Typically, this was the scene awaiting Europe's dispossessed as they were ferried to an improved life (yearned for, but not always guaranteed) in the New World and beyond. Squalor was ever present on special third-class boat trains as Europeans escaped impoverished existences. Most of the dedicated stock – the London & South Western Railway (LSWR), for instance – had specialist carriages that could be hired by other railway companies, but had to be fumigated and hosed-down after every journey made.[16] They were the railway equivalent of the steerage-class passenger transit, but R.A. Fletcher suggested there had been great improvements in the class of persons who travelled third-class. He noted:

> Most British (shipping) lines will not carry emigrants from Central Europe because of their dirty habits. This may seem unkind, but if you were to see the disgusting condition of some of the men and women who come from that part of the Continent, you would not wonder at the restriction but would be surprised that they were ever allowed to enter a railway train – even a fourth-class continental – for a seaport or were allowed to embark.[17]

Before the Great War, Britain's unique first and third-class railway passenger classification had been around for roughly forty years, and some of the country's best-known boat trains reflected normal railway practices carrying first and third-class carriages, as was found on LNWR's *American Special* boat trains post 1912. Much improved facilities in third-class together with the rise in social standing of many international travellers, rendered the necessity of second-class rail travel almost obsolete. When the South Eastern and Chatham Railway (SECR) unveiled their new Pullman stock for Continental boat train services in 1910, the final brake carriage painted in the same livery as the Pullman cars, contained just one compartment allocated to second-class travellers.[18]

Aside passenger, dining and kitchen carriages – sometimes in set formations – the boat train's unique combinations required the assistance of powerful locomotives to move considerable amounts of mail, small parcels and passengers' heavy handfuls and trunks of luggage. These were contained in a variety of accompanying named vehicles: baggage cars, stowage cars, general utility vans (GUVs), full and corridor brake carriages, guards' vans or, as in

France with carriage vans known as fourgons, with designs and formats varying according to railway company practice. The GUV in its many forms was a key element in moving passenger luggage for many years. Apart from domestic postal matters, into this mix could be included the rapid transit of international mail to Europe and overseas. Fletcher's observations captured the commercial mood in the years leading to the Great War. He concluded:

> As matters stand now, the mails from America may be landed at Queenstown, or Fishguard, or Plymouth, or Southampton, according to the steamer by which they are conveyed. The latest arrangement (1913) permits of a mail being delivered in London and certain provincial towns in less than seven days of its departure from New York City; it arrives on a Friday night and is distributed on Saturday morning, and replies can be sent to catch at Queenstown the mail steamer sailing from Liverpool on the Saturday afternoon. Not a moment is wasted.[19]

With returning liners landing mail in England, the Great Western Railway (GWR) played an influential role. Their *Ocean Mails* services collected mail and passengers at Plymouth, Fishguard and Bristol Avonmouth. Likewise, the LNWR had important responsibilities for co-ordinating the shipment and reception of mail traffic at Holyhead, Liverpool and working with Irish railway company partners to and from Queenstown (Cobh). The profitability of mail traffic though was questioned in some quarter as Fletcher expressed:

> The amount of remuneration offered by the postal authorities to the steamship companies for the conveyance of the mails seldom leaves any profit to the company for the work, and some contracts, or mail carryings without contract, have resulted in a dead loss to the carriers.[20]

On some international routes, a mail contract could underpin the viability of setting up particular shipping services. For instance, in 1901 the British government paid the Imperial Direct Line an annual subsidy of £20,000 (and a similar figure to the Jamaican authorities) to carry the West Indian mails from Bristol Avonmouth. On large British registered trans-Atlantic liners, an 'ocean post office' or 'sea post office', similar to a land-based post office, were included in roomy compartments on vessels to expedite the delivery of mails to and from New York. This had become well-accepted practice and conducted in areas on steamers holding around 1,000 bags of mail equal to about three or four staterooms. From the late 1880s, these initiatives were copied by American, German and, in time, French shipping lines.[21] Mail contract arrangements, though, differed between railway companies and steamship owners – by the eve of the Great War the railway companies had had the best part of seventy-years' experience in handing postal arrangements. Boat trains such as the *Irish Mail* collected mail from trackside apparatus along the route from Euston to Holyhead destined to all corners of the globe in specialist self-contained carriages known as the Travelling Post Office (TPO).[22] Aside from TPO non-stopping arrangements, boat trains were also used to carry bullion and other precious metals. The conveying of such cargo involved the building of specialist bullion wagons attached to fast-transit rail services and delivered to high-security areas on ships. As nineteenth-century maritime writer John Gould noted, 'In these days of heavy gold shipments, the specie-room on the steamship is a very important institution. It is located in an out-of-the-way place amidships, under the saloon. Few of the passengers know of its existence, or the valuable treasure that is carried across the ocean with them'.[23]

This all came about as the result of the Great Gold Robbery hullabaloo of 15 May 1855. Gold bars and coins in sealed boxes wrapped with iron bars disappeared from safes on board the guard's van of the South Eastern Railway (SER) boat train en route to Folkestone, Boulogne and Paris. Extensive investigations by both British and French authorities – each unsurprisingly blaming the other – concluded the heist could not have taken place at either port or aboard the cross-channel paddler, or prior to the arrival of the secured boxes at London Bridge station, but was likely to have taken place on board the train. Quite naturally railways/railroads provided the backcloth for literary mystery and film intrigue. In 1903 *The Great Train Robbery* was an American silent film believed to have been inspired by an earlier stage play and the 1900 train robbery committed by Butch Cassidy; it was widely accepted by the academic film community as using ground-breaking editing techniques in the creation of a recognizable form of Western films. In later years Michael Crichton in Britain used the boat train Great Gold Robbery as the subject for a bestselling 1975 novel. Three years later the author used the Victorian era location by adapting the book to film; Crichton himself directing and writing the screenplay for *The Great Train Robbery*. The successful 1978 film starring Sean Connery, Donald Sutherland and Lesley-Anne Down still regularly does the rounds of terrestrial television screenings.

If sophisticated theft was not enough, then passenger demise provided another strand of railway mystery story. As Martin Edwards observes, 'Trains and rail travel have long provided evocative settings for tales of murder and mayhem and succeeding generations of crime writers have made ingenious use of them.'[24] Hardly surprising the 1912 short-story murder mystery *The Case of Oscar Brodski* featuring Richard Austin Freeman's Dr John Thorndyke medical detective character, used the Amsterdam boat train and the North Sea steamer crossing as a backcloth to the novel. Later in 1940, a compartment on a Channel Islands Waterloo bound boat train became the setting for Miles Burton's – better known as John Rhode – murder unknown in the detective novel *Death on the Boat Train*. Before all of this, Charles Dickens had introduced the notion of the boat train to a wider public. In 1851 he rode 'the wave of modernity' on the South Eastern Railway's (SER) new Paris service.[25] On another occasion on 9 June 1865, Dickens was a passenger in the last carriage of the 2.38 pm boat train from Folkstone. The train was derailed in a serious accident at Staplehurst with loss of life. Having survived the derailment, he gained great credit valiantly attempting to help fellow travellers from upturned carriages which had fallen beside the tracks. The news of the accident which had included one of the country's best-known authors received considerable newspaper attention.

There is little surprise that the boat train should be indelibly linked to travel writing over the years, conjuring a yearning to visit foreign places. Some out-and-out cross-channel boat trains covered considerable distances. GWR's Birkenhead Woodside terminus station, one of Merseyside's two waterside terminals, was the commencement point for a Folkestone and Dover boat train. Woodside, within sight of Liverpool Riverside across the Mersey, and a significant place of interest in our story, offered travellers a wealth of colour in post-war years – LMS red, Great Western chocolate and cream and Southern green rarely found anywhere else in the North West. According to the *Liverpool Echo*'s transport and travel writer Rex Christiansen, 'the Southern presence was explained in Western Region timetables with chocolate coloured covers, which I always felt were intended to give passengers an appetite for travel!'[26]

The views of British ports would be one of the last sights emigrants would see before embarking on their new lives. This always made fascinating press material even as late as the mid-1950s. The *Belfast News-Letter* reported on two well-dressed young sisters from the city at Waterloo, clutching their dolls with them, boarding a Southampton boat train linking with a migrant ship heading to Australia.[27] The boat train was always good fare for newspapers. The *Sunderland Echo* reported on General Wilfred Kitching, international leader of the Salvation Army, who was photographed with his wife aboard a Southampton boat train leaning out of a carriage window, having just returned in the liner Queen Elizabeth from a tour of America.[28]

But it was the notion of the 'celebrity' conjuring powerful images and stories over the years. The first-class boat train with its array of influential people in the public eye was music to the ears of newspaper editors. From late-Victorian times, theatre performers moved regularly between London and New York. The nature of their work required less stressful ways to travel but this was not always guaranteed as the boat train had to keep to time. *The Stage* observed that even celebrities of the day were afforded no special favours as 'special boat trains and trans-Atlantic liners have a habit of waiting for no one'.[29] Thespian Dame Alice Ellen Terry, a leading British Shakespearean actress who later turned to touring and lecturing, almost missed her boat train for departure to Australia. In April 1914 *The Shipley Times and Express* reported on the event:

> Miss Ellen Terry left London yesterday morning for Tilbury to embark in the Orient line steamer *Omrah* for Australia, where she is to give her series of lectures on Shakespeare's heroines. A number of friends came to St. Pancras to see her off, including Sir Herbert and Lady Tree, Mr. Edmund Gwenn, and Miss Minnia Terry, and [at] 10.15 there was a crowd of about fifty standing round the special carriages reserved for her. At 10.30 when the signal was given for the train to leave, Miss Terry had not arrived, and her friends were leaving the platform when she was seen rushing through the hall of the booking-office. There was no time for any formal leave-taking, and just had time to step into her carriage and shake hands with three or four friends when the train moved out of the station.[30]

In a few short years, the leading lights from the silver screen would also be added to the elevated position of almost missing a ship's departure:

> When Miss Greer Garson, the film actress, lost the *Normandie* boat train at Waterloo Station on Saturday, she was driven to Southampton in a fast car by Mr Percy H. Mosely, of Lansdown House, Berkely, Square, London. Here [picture of her] Greer thanking and saying good-bye to Mr Mosely as she boarded the liner's tender at Southampton Docks.[31]

Shipping lines (and railway companies often working in tandem) were never shy of generating publicity. They would regularly release passenger information lists in the sure-fire knowledge that it was the perfect mechanism to garner a few extra press column inches, especially if it involved personalities; the role and timings of boat trains and ocean liners were never far from shared view. Maritime writers Robert McDougall and Robin Gardiner captured the sentiments precisely:

> Captains of liners, particularly during the interwar years, pandered to every whim of their famous passengers. The line that attracted the most celebrities could rely on many more ordinary first-class bookings from mere mortals wishing to bathe in the stars' reflected glory, so the practices were encouraged by the owners.[32]

The Manchester Courier commented on one major Edwardian luminary who just happened to be the biggest female entertainer in Britain:

> Among the departures from Euston yesterday by the boat train for the White Star liner *Cedric* were Mr and Mrs Alec Hurley, the lady being better known as Miss Marie Lloyd. A large crowd, including music-hall representatives, gathered on the station to bid farewell to the popular couple. Miss Marie Lloyd said she was confident of success 'over the water.'[33]

Whilst America's plutocrats were not exactly media celebrities of their day, their trans-Atlantic shenanigans pandered to the newspaper gallery. The boat train played its full part when White

Star Line issued a press release surrounding an incident which forced its new liner *Olympic* to return to port. The *Northern Whig* was amongst a host of newspapers reporting on the exploits of one of Manhattan's elite millionaires:

> Mr E.P. Sheldon, president of the United States Trust Company, of New York, landed from the *Olympic* near noon, engaged a special train at a cost £78 plus first-class fare, and left Southampton at 12.33 in an effort to reach Liverpool in time to catch the *Adriatic*, due to sail at 6.30 p.m. for New York. The journey was 260 miles, and the railway authorities would not guarantee to cover it under six hours. This would bring Mr. Sheldon to the Liverpool Riverside station three minutes after the *Adriatic* had left, but like a good sportsman he took the off-chance of the train being able to save enough time on the journey to enable him to reach the liner a minute or two before she cast off. Mr. Sheldon successfully accomplished his task but was lucky to do so. He did not reach Liverpool Riverside station until 6.39, the liner, however, was delayed by the luggage, the last pile of which was being swung on board when Mr. Sheldon's special train steamed into the station. The last two and a half miles of the journey on the Dock Railway occupied seventeen minutes, as a great portion of the distance had to be traversed at a speed not exceeding four miles an hour, with a railway official walking in front of the engine. As the train steamed into the station its solitary passenger was standing at the window with his hand gripping the handle of the door. He jumped out before the train had quite pulled up and was hurried through the bridge on to the landing stage and up the gangway on to the steamer. A few minutes later the vessel was sailing on her way to New York. Mr. Sheldon declined to make any statement to the Press representatives beyond the remark 'If I had missed the ship, I should have had to wait ten days.'
>
> There were nine other passengers from the *Olympic* on board the *Adriatic*, they having left the damaged liner on Wednesday night by tug, and travelled to Liverpool by the ordinary boat train from Euston yesterday afternoon.[34]

The boat train, before the jet aircraft's arrival, also played an essential role in sporting affairs with the transportation of players, sports equipment, kits, specialist clothing, and personal luggage trunks in dedicated and secure brake vans for overseas cricket and rugby tours which could last months. The MCC South African winter tour in October 1956 was no exception as the tour party left aboard a Union Castle liner arriving in Cape Town some two weeks later.[35] One group of companions that had to endure a more stressful start to their international steamship voyage, but also somewhat fortunate, was the Tottenham Hotspur football team who missed their boat train from Waterloo. They had to board the liner that was taking them from Southampton to the Argentine from a tugboat and some distance downstream in the Solent.[36]

Rail and sea travel were not always positive experiences, especially for children and their accompanying parents. Never far from minds was the seasickness malady, and for some the prospect of the boat train, a channel crossing or long-drawn-out ocean travel brought undiluted thoughts of misery ahead of any holiday break or voyage. Pharmaceutical companies sensed a business opportunity and by the mid-1950s had tackled these problems head on. Kwells, whose promotional strapline was 'prevent travel sickness', coupled together this little ditty courtesy of their copy-writers:

The journey is now over,
the passengers descend
From Channel boat at Dover,
from boat train at Ostend
You can tell by the expression
(for expression always tells)
Those who travelled in depression
And those that took their KWELLS.[37]

Whilst the pharmaceutical sector might have had an answer, shipping lines, too, ventured an excuse based on the quality of food they provided on board liners, citing many passengers were not used to sophisticated culinary presentation. A humorous observation stated they 'simply eat too much on voyages causing attacks of biliousness!'[38]

International traveller numbers had grown significantly by late-Victorian times, particularly in relation to Europe as travel had become easier, quicker and safer over the years. Interest in overseas destinations, ocean and rail travel and indeed a connected level of enthusiasm associated with novel, magazine and newspaper reading was now deep rooted. The end of the Napoleonic Wars saw an increase in the numbers of travel-books, guides and articles published, influencing fearless British travellers embarking on Continental ventures, many still influenced by Byron's romanticised writings.[39] By the mid-nineteenth century, ocean steamer stateroom libraries were well stocked. In time on the biggest of liners this would include the ship's daily newspaper facilitated by the latest developments in wireless communication. But not so on short sea crossings where passengers organised their own reading material. From the end of the 1800s, commercial organisations such as W.H. Smith had come a long way. Willian Henry Smith had acquired his first LNWR book selling concession at Euston station in 1848 and established over 1,000 station bookstalls selling a variety of cheaply priced novels, some marketed by publishers as 'railway editions' specifically for reading on trains (and cross-channel steamers). They also carried of many specialist magazines and publications providing distinctive literary, illustration and progressively photographic views of the world all distilled into informed traveller guides. A concise short story format was made for railway journeys and sea crossings. In June 1907, *The Daily Telegraph* observed the emergence of something they described as 'the bookstall maiden'. This, they noted, was 'a novelty, and a novelty of a pleasing type'. It was an experiment at local and provincial railway stations 'where the business is not sufficient to justify the employment of a male clerk, and where, on the other hand, it is too important to be left to the charge of boys'. They went on, 'hers is not dull, monotonous round. Moreover, it gives opportunity for the display of business ability and for self-culture, under, for the most part, agreeable circumstances' free from the factory, office or the workshop. Merchandising came to the fore: 'Space is limited, and the wares must be distributed in the most economical and attractive fashion. The newest novel must be well to the front' whilst 'magazine literature must be given its share of space, and the ever-increasing army of newspapers must be placed as to be immediately accessible'. *The Telegraph* ventured 'certain modern bookstalls are not content with food for the mind. A space is devoted to chocolate and other confections favoured by railway travellers.' At the same time as we have seen the chocolate vending machine became a familiar sight on station platforms. Within this framework the bookstall maiden being well-read held an influential role in being able to talk about the latest developments in the world and recommending appropriate travel reading. *The Telegraph* commented 'as the population grows, and the school master gets more and more abroad, so does the demand for newspapers and magazines advance'.[40]

Continental travel was excitement personified; setting foot on European soil represented the first stage of an international excursion. Channel ports with direct rail links to London had been set in stone since 1847, opening a new chapter in tourism travel fulfilling Victorian 'innovation, comfort and speed' cravings.[41] Ninety years later, the same longings still applied. *Railway Wonders of the World*, a consumer railway publication from the mid-1930s recorded:

> There is a tremendous attraction about Continental travel. There is the experience of a real thrill brought about by the first landing on a foreign shore, by hearing another language, by eating different food, by seeing strange sights, and by thus beginning a holiday that, in every sense of the world, a 'change'.

For late-Victorian artists and photographers, the grandeur of boat trains provided a commanding visual resource. Combined, they distilled powerful imaginings of life where shipping lines, postal authorities, government agents, railway companies and travel packagers worked hand in glove providing totally integrated transport services. Leaving the British Isles, connecting cross-channel steamers and awaiting trains ensured passengers were left with distinct travel memories. The boat train which had evolved at a befittingly elegant pace was now suddenly in the shop window of luxury travel experiences. And many of these iconic trains explored sported the most memorable of names. In the golden age of international rail travel and named boat trains, services such as the *Blue Train/Le Train Blue*, *Golden Arrow/Flèche d'Or* and *Night Ferry/ Ferry du Nuit* summoned distinct images of glamour becoming familiar icons to British, Continental and American travellers alike.

Unquestionably, there was a relationship between money and the ability to travel calibrated by social distinction. To some extent, organised travel with agents providing hospitality coupons had overcome some of the practicalities of overseas expeditions, but for the independent visitor, considerable pre-planning was required for travel arrangements. From the second half of the nineteenth century, the ability of international tourists visiting the Old World and for Britons and Europeans visiting the Americas to pay for

Dover's Shakespeare Cliff was originally constructed by South Eastern Railway forming part of the Folkestone Harbour branch connection linking London with Dover Marine and its surfeit of cross-channel steamers. Over the years Farthingloe's twin-track rail tunnel entrance was often used by railway photographers to record Continental boat train traffic. Almost two generations apart, the 1950s Britannia hauled Pullman *Golden Arrow* mirrors the pre-grouping positions of the SECR 4-4-0 locomotive boat trains. (*Above left*: Lens of Sutton Association; *Above right*: John Scott-Morgan Collection; *Below*: J&C McCutcheon Collection)

goods and services in local currencies was pivotal to the quality of the visitor experience. Bank archivist Dr John Booker says it is 'one branch of the history of travel which has been largely overlooked, perhaps because it straddles a kind of no-man's-land between banking and tourism. This neglected area is the provision of travellers' money.'[42] Straightforward and timeless money advice was a theme picked up as long ago as 1855 by Karl Baedeker in his Paris guide recounting 'The first, second and third most important thing in travel is money. With money, most other deficiencies may be remedied.'[43]

The boat train's allure contributed significantly to an international travel culture. For global travellers, the boat train was the both the beginning and end of voyages as steamships sailed the Atlantic Ocean and to the widest corners of the British Empire and its many colonial interests. Between the late-Victorian years and the outbreak of the Great War, international shipping lines and especially the railway companies with their interconnected grand hotel and cross-channel steamer services, all played crucial roles in the execution of seamless payment systems facilitating the expansion of travel and the quality of the experience they afforded to international tourists. The appearance of the traveller's cheque in 1891 provided easier tourist payment mechanisms to secure ready money in local currencies, but all coinciding with major technological and service developments that delivered more comfortable ways to travel whether on rail, at sea or on land.[44] This also led to other travel enhancements. The period before the Great War was one of great cooperation between railway companies, shipping lines and port authorities. Their combined workings all helped to preserve Liverpool as one of the country's leading passenger liner ports. Cunard's passengers crossing the Atlantic heading for England, for instance, could buy train tickets for LNWR trains on board ship, all helping to form an important first impression of the efficiency of British life. For upscale visitors, it was indicative of what might be expected of their stay in the Old World. In addition, a mechanism existed through the Railway Clearing House where 'through' tickets could be purchased by those passengers wishing to travel to other destinations other than directly to London.[45]

The booking in of travelling trunks for incoming and outgoing passengers by railway companies was based on the American railroad model where such transit arrangements for travellers coming to Europe had been in place for some time. European railway companies and shipping lines followed with the practice. Norddeutsche Lloyd (NDL) on crossings from New York to Germany initiated similar arrangements with German railway companies from the late 1870s.[46] The French too operated comparable arrangements where luggage on a French Line ship could be checked in for delivery to any part of the country. Such activity was typical of an emerging service culture that permeated pre-grouping railway companies and shipping lines. The numbers of American tourists coming to Britain and Europe at the turn of the 1900s expanded significantly; for those firms involved in all aspects of luxury travel operations this was a highly productive period. Yet this was not just one-way traffic as increased numbers of Britons from the ever-expanding ranks of Victorian bourgeoisie were resolved to visit overseas. The tide of travel fashion had moved on; no longer simply a case as soon as the London season was over of society's cream heading en masse towards the countryside or the mountains, but now a more adventurous cohort intent on discovering what the New World had to offer. Major cities such as New York and Chicago and the opening up of California held an endearing fascination. People like people they see in themselves; many trans-Atlantic steamers were packed to the brim in first and second-classes, representing a step in the transformation of the floating palaces into a turn of the century tourist Mecca. This inordinate privilege has a new customer base as a hundred years on, the focus of lavish tourism flows may have shifted to Asian customers and real-time payment systems managed by exclusive financial institutions, but the same dimensions still apply.

The nature of travel has changed significantly, and in particular, with individual modes of transport. By the late 1950s the jet airliner reduced journey times, compared to traditional turboprop airliners, by up to 50 per cent, and thus began a process where the ocean liner was surpassed and therefore passenger demand for boat trains. In 1958 the British Havilland Comet 4 and the American Boeing 707 became the backbone of the Atlantic crossing. Cross-channel ferries from the 1960s increasingly became no-frills set-ups adapted for the needs of commercial vehicle freight transport operations and the private car affording passengers a degree of transport independence that had begun in the 1930s. Boat trains, whilst still not completely outmoded, lost their travel grandeur. Certainly, from the end of the nationalised railway era, Britain's surviving boat train services were a poor reflection of their former selves.

CHAPTER 1

Victorian and Edwardian Travel Progress

Port and Harbour Development

Harbours and ports were deeply connected to all forms of maritime transport, be they cross-channel steamers, short-sea crossing vessels or large ocean-going ships. In some ports it was a combination of all three shipping forms. From 1870 onwards British North American ocean liner traffic had been largely concentrated at Liverpool. Indeed, up until the 1950s the city was for the best part of a century Britain's busiest port. Described as the 'first port in the world', its reputation garnered in Victorian times as the only deep-water haven on Britain's west coast. It assumed the status as the dominant embarkation point for North Atlantic passenger and freight business ably supported by a fast-developing railway infrastructure. This included the construction of three superb city railway hotels establishing high-quality accommodation standards for international travellers as well as dedicated boat trains delivering passengers to Liverpool's quayside. In 1899 author Stephen Crane acknowledged for his short stories, told US readers Liverpool was 'the beginning of an important sea path to America' whilst likening the terminus hotel as 'an institution dear to most railways in Europe'.[1] Unsurprisingly, Liverpool was accorded the 'Gateway to the West' but access to the city port was not always a unified travel experience.[2] Up until the early 1890s passengers and their luggage had to board and disembark liners from Mersey river tenders.

This in part led Inman Line, led by James Spence and Edmund Taylor, uprooting and relocating to Southampton's deep-water port facilities in February 1893. The loss to Liverpool of a major shipping line was intense. William B. Forwood in his book *Reminiscences of a Liverpool Shipowner, 1850–1920* published by Henry Young & Sons in 1920 described the transfer in characteristic terms, 'the old Inman Line, loved by Liverpool people for their handsome ships with their overhanging stems and long graceful lines, is now only a memory'.[3] Yet trans-Atlantic business was brisk as later in the year the company's four major vessels – *City of Paris*, *New York*,

Chicago and *Berlin* – were used by *The Polytechnic Touring Association (PTA)* members travelling to and from New York on organised tours to the Chicago World's Fair.[4] Some years earlier in 1886, Inman had been bought by US-owned International Navigation Company (INC) with the shipping operation destined to become a major player on the North Atlantic travel scene, cementing a key business relationship with Southampton's railway owners. Steel construction had almost entirely substituted iron in liner construction making them considerably lighter and more durable. Furthermore, safer twin screw propulsion had generally replaced single-screwed vessels; these combined developments providing continuous improvements in Atlantic Ferry steamship travel. American shipping lines had begun to mount serious competition with frequent and regular crossings taking on established British and German shipping firms. Inman Lines *City of New York* and *City of Paris* pair had their names shortened to *New York* and *Paris* with a new American pennant. These Atlantic greyhounds put in consistent high-speed crossings attracting a strong customer following.

In this period, there were nine major liners providing regular passenger services between Britain and New York including American Line's two premier vessels, Cunard's *Etruria* and *Umbria* and White Star's *Majestic* and *Teutonic*. These liners typically had provision for around 500 and 600 first-class passengers as shipping lines started to place greater reliance on the comfort of saloon traffic rather than in shipping numbers in steerage-class. American Lines parent company INC invested in two new state of the art steamers weighing in at just under 12,000 tons – *St. Paul* and *St. Louis* – providing a premium weekly service between Southampton, Cherbourg and New York. Whilst American Lines might be described as the new kids on the block (they had only begun running services between Philadelphia and Liverpool in 1873), and at the time without government mail contracts, but they now had a quartet of quality liners, renowned for some of the best first-class staterooms working the Atlantic Ferry incorporating modern conveniences of combined bathrooms and toilets. These vessels, later supported with US mail subsidies, provided real competition to British and German companies.

Such was the commercial pressure now being applied to Liverpool, together with increased passenger mutterings at the level of inconvenience with five-hour train journeys between Euston and the River Mersey, Cunard gave due consideration to move as well.

By the new century, rapport between LSWR and American Line matured to a point where special dedicated boat trains known as the *American Line Express* ran between Waterloo and Southampton Docks overlapping with arriving and departing liners. In 1901 LSWR adapted three–five coach sets of *American Eagle* stock for the company's prestige passengers. Carriage superintendent W. Pantner converted his earlier opulent *Eagle* carriages providing gangway coach connections, a restaurant car and installing a kitchen in full-length brakes at one end of the boat train. Later a LSWR *American Line Express* in July 1906 was involved in an horrific accident as a boat train from Plymouth, travelling at considerable speed, derailed approaching the station at Salisbury. The death count involving well-known American citizens was high as the first two of three passenger coaches (all first-class) at the front of the train were smashed to oblivion. Later in October of that year, public relations were in full flow as Mr P.E. Curry, manager of the American Line at Canute Road, Southampton made a donation to the Salisbury Infirmary for their kind and willing assistance made during the terrible railway disaster. (NRM/SSPL)

However, the threat prompted the Mersey Docks & Harbour Board to make significant port improvements in double-quick time. Dredging the river and extending the existing Prince's landing stage allowed liners to moor alongside the quayside. Other facilities were constructed including new stores facilities at the Prince's Half-Tide Dock entrance and the construction of a railway terminus at the landing stage and connection of railway lines across the dock estate on to the LNWR rail network. The result was a brand-new complex built in only fifteen months. Liverpudlians accorded the new liner facilities with different names - New Pier Head and Atlantic Station before Liverpool Riverside became the official name. The liner and railway complex saw its first official customer with White Star's *Germanic* on 1 June 1895. Due to line weight restrictions shunters based at Edge Hill would bring boat trains in and out of Riverside. At busy times LNWR boat trains would terminate at Lime Street about a mile from the landing stage greatly inconveniencing many international travellers. Ironically, it was not until March 1950 the position was totally resolved when the swing bridge at Prince's Half-Tide Dock was rebuilt to a new design. Strengthening the dock infrastructure allowed mainline locomotives to haul boat trains through to the quayside thus eliminating the need for Edge Hill shunters. The magical sound of a London, Midland and Scottish Railway (LMS) Stanier whistle could now be heard alongside modern ocean liners.

At the end of the nineteenth century Britain's harbours and ports were busy places leading to intense rivalry, which according to Fletcher, was 'to provide the most attractive facilities for the great steamships, and the railway companies, many of which are interested financially in the development and success of this or that port, second most ably the efforts of the port authorities and the steamship companies to save time and money and increase their own revenue'.[5] Liverpool maintained its status as Britain's major destination gateway, but its dominance was already under threat as port developments at Southampton afforded passengers easier and quicker access to the capital. There was also a perception, whether rightly or wrongly, that because Southampton was owned by LSWR, the railway company had its fingers firmly on the pulse of developments whereas Liverpool was rather slower to make improvements. Yet attention returned to Liverpool where shipping line executives held considerable sway in local affairs. Boat expresses were naturally a common site sight and acknowledged as a vital component of the city's port traffic. White Star Line owner Thomas Ismay was a director of LNWR; his appointment created a series of interlocking directorships for the two companies establishing a trend whereby shipping lines and Britain's main railway operators became closely entwined.[6]

Victorian shipping line conventions spilled over to the boat train. The etiquette of sailing-ship days, where ship owners introduced

This combined LNWR and White Star poster by an unknown artist epitomises the external promotional relationship of the two organisations at the beginning of the twentieth century in seeking out high-valued business and leisure customers. It illustrates a well-dressed male passenger, carrying the obligatory suitcase and umbrella, whilst striding across a White Star graphic image centred in the middle of the North Atlantic with geographic contours of the US and Canada to one side and Britain, Ireland and the continent of Europe on the other. These countries were the movers and shakers of international business at the time. The importance and role of Liverpool as a shipping line centre with frequent and convenient LNWR train services to Liverpool Exchange and boat trains to Riverside is quite clearly shown and probably dates the poster before White Star's decision to move its premier liner operations to Southampton and a closer relationship with LSWR. (NRM/SSPL)

their most important first-class passengers to the captain, lived on in a new form. Fletcher noted.

> Now the custom is to run a special train from London to the nearest station to the ship, to notify all the saloon passengers the time of its departure, and for a representative of the company to travel on the train with them. This gentleman, often one of the partners or managing owners, will escort the distinguished travellers on board and introduce them to the captain.[7]

This was certainly the position with the provision of American boat trains where representatives were on hand to meet the travelling needs of their most valued of customers, many of whom were frequent trans-Atlantic travellers. *Titanic's* departure was a case in point as the LSWR threw caution to the wind maximising the publicity value of the ship's short-lived status as the largest and most spectacular of all ocean liners as well as the great and the good of international passengers. Whilst it would be the best part of another century before modern marketing paradigms of customer care and frequent flyer incentives became the norm, their routes can be traced back to the Edwardian era. Nothing it appears in travel business is completely new.

Aside Liverpool's dominance, there were other British ports: Plymouth, due to its westerly proximity, offered competition as a port of call and for the all-important mail drop, and a role the mighty Great Western Railway (GWR) employed significant power; Bristol, Glasgow and London held a fair share of trans-Atlantic passengers in later years although in the new Avonmouth port's case, it was predominantly cargo liner traffic. But it was to be Southampton that ultimately dominated passenger port proceedings becoming the country's premier liner terminal. The port's progress was ably supported by LSWR, and its successor at railway grouping Southern Railway, as the port owners. Both companies oversaw significant expansion of commercial freight and passenger interests over their operational lives before the port entered state ownership in 1947. Britain's pre-grouping railway companies were the means to deliver and return large numbers of passengers to liner ports so their interaction with shipping lines, port authorities and, to a lesser extent, the Admiralty was vital for all parties' commercial interests and specifically in delivering a trouble-free passenger experience. Because of its dominant position in western heartlands, GWR had always assumed the automatic right to influence passenger shipping developments to the Americas.

Despite noteworthy aspirations, Bristol and the building of new docks at Avonmouth hardly registered with emerging liner business until the turn of the twentieth century. However, the far south-west of Wales was considered to be slightly different although the Great War ultimately conspired against it. By constructing a new deep-water harbour at Fishguard, the company's reasoning was that it could not only consolidate its position with southern based Irish Sea crossings, but also attempt to tap into burgeoning liner traffic with a harbour designed to accommodate three large liners at a time. This all came at considerable cost for the Great Western estimated at just short of £1 million.[8] GWR eventually purchased the moribund North Pembrokeshire & Fishguard Railway and the interests of the people behind the Fishguard Bay Railway & Pier Act in 1898. Together with the Irish Great Southern and Western Railway (GSWR) and the Fishguard & Rosslare Railway, a decision was taken jointly to build two new harbours with connecting railway heads for steamer ferry traffic between Britain and Ireland. Aside cross-channel operations, the Great Western's intention was to coax Cunard and White Star - the two-leading ocean liner shipping lines on the North Atlantic run – from their existing home bases at Liverpool as Fishguard was some forty miles nearer to New York than any other British port. Plans to develop what would be later described as an 'Ocean Terminal' with passenger facilities comparable to Southampton unfortunately did not materialise.

Events on England's south coast were changing rapidly at the turn of the twentieth century. The port of Southampton had come into railway company ownership when the LSWR bought the facilities from the Southampton Dock Company for a figure of £1,360,000 in 1892. The company had been involved in a fierce competitive battle with the GWR to secure passengers and commercial traffic from liners stopping at Plymouth Sound, but the company's acquisition of the port provided new secure deep-water access. LSWR over the next three years invested £2 million in port infrastructure, and by the mid-1890s Southampton was in the enviable position of being the preferred home port or port of call to many shipping lines including the American Line. *The Railway Magazine* described the handover of the port to LSWR, and the company's fulfilment of its obligations to the powerful US shipping line in less than five years, in most glowing terms. 'A new order of things, amounting positively to a physical revolution, has been established in the port since the transference of the dock property was effected.'[9]

Over the next twenty years the city established itself as the principal competitor for liner traffic mostly at the expense of Liverpool. Southampton undoubtedly had a winning hand since it possessed the benefit of a double tide – courtesy of the geographical shape of the Solent and of the flows from the Rivers Test and Itchen, strategically closer to London (circa one and half-hour railway journey time), and in a far better position to service European passengers travelling further afield from Germany, the Netherlands, Belgium as well as those liners using the Normandy ports of Cherbourg and Le Havre. In addition, by 1900 it was able to offer passengers dedicated station access and close proximity to a fully modernised luxury hotel costing the railway some £30,000 in development.[10] Apart from international liner traffic LSWR also operated from the port its own fleet of fast cross-channel steamers to France and the Channel Islands providing well-off overseas travellers with a network of routes, shipping lines and a host of related ancillary travel services. Advertising was pitched at prosperous customers. LSWR showcased the company's night-time route crossings on a new generation of comfortable, luxurious mail steamers. As with three routes to Scotland, reaching the French Riviera and Italy could now be accommodated via a third alternative London, Southampton, Havre and Paris route involving several railway company partners.

From the 1890s HAPAG and NDL possessed fleets of smaller liners making regular North Atlantic crossings principally to provide German and eastern European emigration to the United States. The German lines used Southampton as a port of call and on east bound journeys stopping at Plymouth. In fact, in the years before the Great War, NDL used these English stops to take on the railway companies targeting travellers by promoting their quartet of trans-Atlantic vessels as alternatives to cross-channel steamers 'providing fast and luxurious travel to France and Germany in ocean liners'.[11] Ironically, it was both GWR and LSWR's fast and efficient boat train services that made this facility an attractive option. Passenger traffic volumes increased significantly largely on the back of North Atlantic liner traffic. Both HAPAG and NDL financed investment earned largely from profitable emigrant business to provide first-class passengers with grandiose facilities that enabled the two to tap into an increasingly wealthy American cohort.

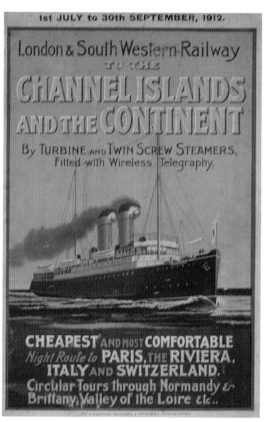

This fascinating LSWR poster by Douglas Snowden in 1910 illustrates to great effect the integrated nature of cross-channel travel in the late-Edwardian period. Guaranteeing connections between boat and train was pivotal to the success of the Southampton and Havre night-time route. Interestingly, *The Riviera* as a destination creeps into the London and Paris headline as PLM and Wagon-Lits services to the Azur coast included morning departures from Paris that timed with incoming boat trains. The same themes are present in the company's 1912 Continental Handbook. (*Above right*: Southern Railway Publicity)

The luxurious facilities of Cunard and White Star's express liners which personified the Edwardian era mirrored society on both sides of the Atlantic. Dr Richard Davenport-Hines describes 'first-class life on *Titanic*' as 'a microcosm of New York life that Caroline Astor devised, and which the Astors' hotels turned into a rich, sumptuous spectacle'.[12] In 1893 a twenty-year process of travel gentrification between Britain and the United States, where Southampton was placed at its heart, began when American Line's steamer *New York* first docked at the port this cementing a long-standing relationship between LSWR and the American steamship company. This expansion would later include the intrusive activities of financier John Pierpont Morgan, who was scheduled to play a pivotal role shaping shipping line affairs with the acquisition of the British White Star via his International Mercantile Marine (IMM) conglomerate or popularly known in the press as the Morgan combine. In Britain, the P&O Company's sixty-second annual general meeting regarded the multinational organisation (without actually naming it) as a meddlesome aggressor putting the Empire at risk. The chairman's 1902 address noted 'It should be the interest of the Government to prevent the P. and O. Company falling into the hands of some American octopus.'[13] Despite public protestations, White Star's corporate takeover was viewed with dismay but in the end the power of money held sway as the company's majority shareholding was held by a relatively small number of well-connected and pivotal industrialists including Lord Pirrie of Hartland & Wolff, (the company's Belfast shipbuilders) and the Ismay family. The affair was bitterly contested in many British quarters with considerable media disquiet regarding the actions of American capitalists. Sir Ernest Cassel was purported to have intervened on behalf of King Edward VII in an attempt to prevent acquisition, although a concession was made to keep the company's ships on the British register. Perhaps a signpost of future shipping industry events was the official opening of Liverpool's Riverside landing stage in July 1895 when John Pierpont Morgan was a prominent passenger on the first public train arriving at the port?[14]

Southampton though had a strong card hand to play. Major ports worked closely with the shipping lines to create the necessary on-site supporting infrastructure for the smooth running of operations and the range of landside facilities to provide for a rapid turnaround of liners. With White Star moving to the port, LSWR was required to develop a completely new dock system to service the massive new Olympic class liners. The railway company erected a terminal, cargo sheds, dedicated warehousing for luggage and the development of hotel accommodation. The five-star South Western Hotel opened in 1912 was built for the needs of affluent incoming and departing passengers, their families or well-wishers and located a short distance from the new Ocean Dock. The hotel also had its own rail link allowing *White Star Express* titled boat trains, which ran for the first time in 1908, together with other relief boat train services with a totally integrated facility appealing to discriminating first-class passengers. McDougall and Gardiner set the scene. 'The railway terminal, actually on the dockside and at the same level, meant that passengers never had to carry luggage far or up a steep gradient, as they had to at Liverpool. Passengers could get on a train in London and get off again alongside the ship they were to sail in.'[15] Whilst Liverpool might have argued differently, Southampton provided a seamless luxury travel facility indicating the port had well and truly arrived. LSWR's port initiatives were many and varied and included a new laundry facility as part of site development. The requirements of individual shipping lines varied but Cunard and White Star, as a matter of company policy, ran their own laundries. They were essential components forming just one cog in a massive mechanism needed to turn around liners on the Atlantic Ferry in a day and half timeframe. *The Globe* ran an interesting feature entitled 'Cleaning up after a trip across the sea' noting.

> When the ocean liner has docked and its passengers have all passed down the gang plank, the work of the officers and crew is not, as might be supposed, at an end for that trip. Indeed, it is then that the real drudgery of the ship's people begins, for between the docking and the departure the big craft must be thoroughly overhauled and cleaned from stem to stern, inside and out. Moreover, this task must, generally speaking, be accomplished within the limited period of 36 hours.

Depending on the number of passengers, Cunard's *Lusitania* and *Mauretania* might generate up to 80,000 articles of linen that had to be washed, dried and returned to the ship in the same manner as would be expected of a first-class hotel ashore. Similarly, passengers in second-class would expect clean tablecloths and serviettes for each meal. Even in third or steerage-class table linen might be changed two or three times per week. Cabins also generated huge amounts of fresh laundry; sheets, quilts, blankets, pillowcases and clean towels. According to *The Globe*,

> It becomes necessary to count, sort, and check some 35,000 pieces of linen. No linen, however, is ever washed aboard. It is placed in sacks containing each from 200 to 250 pieces and sent in waggons to the laundry. Upon its return to the ship there again occurs the tedious task of counting, sorting, &c.

The article went on:

> Every sheet, towel, tablecloth found to be worn to any applicable degree is immediately discarded, for no "rags" are tolerated on a first-class liner. During the course of one trip a liner will use something like 300 Turkish towels alone and as many as a thousand smaller ones for the first-cabin passenger alone.

Yet the position was rather different in steerage as the publication observed:

> Cleaning is conducted along somewhat different lines. Everything that might be damaged by water is taken out of the steerage quarters and the hose is brought into play. Then the whole steerage is scrubbed down.[16]

Liner crossings filled to the rafters with passengers and bad weather crossings also exacerbated the volume of soiled linen, so a precision support industry was required and one where the dockside railway played a pivotal part in proceedings. Liners involved in perhaps two- or three-month voyages to India, the Far East and Australasia though were equipped with on-board laundries. All support infrastructure was absolutely necessary as many liner fleets progressively became intimately involved in cruise operations. Whilst much activity was posted around Liverpool and Southampton, it would in time impact on just about every British port of substance.

Ballinn's dabbling at the end of the Victorian era set off a chain of events that shaped a rapid advance in what is today acknowledged as 'cruise tourism'. The word, of Dutch and French origin, crept into the English language during the nineteenth century, and in similar circumstances, mirrored the acceptance of tourism into the lexicon. Shipping lines experimented with new ideas to fully utilize and maximise the usage of vessels. A new form of ocean travel – short duration warm weather cruises – appeared involving popular destinations around Britain and Ireland and the waters of southern Europe and Scandinavia, as well in time, less familiar destinations further afield. British and Continental shipping lines tested new formats creating life pleasures at sea with itineraries made up of interesting and convenient places to visit, by and large within a steamer's night-time sea passage. For the most part of the nineteenth century ships were far from purpose-built for cruising and were taken out of normal line-voyage requirements when business was quieter especially across the winter months. P&O Steam Navigation Company (P&O) first offered a deep-water Mediterranean cruise in 1844 calling at the antiquities of Malta, Greece and its islands and Constantinople in the Ottoman Empire. The first conversion of an existing vessel took place in 1881 when the shipping line's vessel *Ceylon* was refitted as a full-time cruise vessel by the Oceanic Yachting Company claiming to be the first ship to cruise around the world.

Because Britain and Ireland were islands with a long-established maritime tradition, it was evident its coast lines, harbours and ports should become the focus of cruise tourist activity. Around the British Isles, and in particular cruising off Orkney and Shetland were some of the earliest examples of planned cultural and heritage-based sea tours. Similarly, the North Sea was considered a key centre of activity as steamers visited Norway, its fjords and the northern Islands providing almost unlimited daylight in the summer months. The Northern Lights became a tremendously popular destination with a variety of shipping lines operating services. In time and further afield, the West Indies, the Bahamas and Cuba became favoured winter resorts for the well-heeled with a variety of lines from the 1890s providing regular services from America's eastern seaboard, Britain and Europe. Amongst the more adventurous members of the leisured classes, these alternative destinations acquired significant followings, but the early stages of cruise industry development were largely confined to British and German shipping lines. Britain's pre-grouping railway companies also acclimatised to cruise business opportunities. Liverpool's Booth Line, well known for its Royal Mail steamers regularly sailing to the northern Brazilian state of Para and to Manaus, 1,000 miles up the Amazon River, expanded its fleet to include the provision of substantial passenger liners. In 1903, the company started carrying tourists to Lisbon and Madeira with combined Great Northern Railway and Booth Line posters promoting tours to Portugal and Spain from £12 to £20 with packages that included first-class facilities, hotels and travelling expenses.

The French were slow off the mark developing cruising - their first four-stacker trans-Atlantic liner did not materialize until 1914: French shipping firms, using smaller ships, preferred to concentrate activities around the Mediterranean promoting the assurance of their cuisine. Nevertheless, cruising in its different forms was an embryonic business and a comparatively luxury market; long-distance cruising and voyages of discovery restricted to the wealthiest of clients. The notion of passengers becoming 'pleasure seeking travellers', using ships as floating hotels moving from one destination to another had yet to be fully appreciated by the biggest shipping company managers' who still viewed line-voyages, the Atlantic Ferry and Britain's Empire territories as their main sphere of activity. Smaller shipping lines and travel agents were far more adept, however, recognizing enterprising business opportunities for what today is referred to as the short-break cruising format. In August 1910 Cruising Co. Ltd chartered Union Castle's *Dunottar Castle* for a series of Mediterranean itineraries with *The Bystander* magazine advertising copy quoting the vessel was 'the only large steamer 100 A1 at Lloyds' entirely devoted to pleasure cruises.[17]

The Royal Mail Steam Packet Company had built up a considerable merchant fleet ship during the Edwardian period moving its home base to Southampton; by 1908 summer week-end trips to France were offered.[18] Irish travel writers also latched on to a new trend of using trans-Atlantic liners to attract visitors to the Continent, and to Ireland, and in direct competition to established railway company cross-channel operations such as GWR and GSWR's new facilities at Fishguard and Rosslare. A syndicated feature appearing in the *Tyrone Courier* and *Belfast News-Letter* amongst others noted

> The excellent facilities offered to the holiday-maker anxious to reach the holiday haunts of Ireland or the historic points in Brittany or Normandy, by alighting at either Cherbourg or Queenstown, will undoubtedly come for a large share of patronage, which will be sustained by the experience of comfort and glimpse into new features of life which travel under such conditions possess.[19]

Whilst northern cold-water destinations were popular in summer, the Edwardian period also saw significant developments in warm weather cruising less than a decade after the modern loo and bathrooms appeared in first-class suites on vessels deemed appropriate for cruising. Such facilities were considered essential to attract the right type of customer. The Orient Lines vessel *Ophir* was a luxury ship popular with passengers attaining a label of the *Queen* of the Indian Ocean. She was converted in 1901 to become the royal yacht again setting a seal of approval for new forms of transport activity. In 1913 the *Victoria Luise* became the first liner to cruise the West Indies and considered to be a milestone in the industry as the former *SS Deutschland* was refurbished into a dedicated top-end one-class cruise ship. The number of private bathrooms was doubled, passenger capacity reduced, the vessel became slower for passengers to appreciate island hopping settings (and more economical for its operators) but also repainted in white designed to help keep the ship cool in the heat of the Tropics. Shipping lines now had their eyes on more organized forms of cruise tourism as Cunard's *Franconia* and *Laconia* were introduced in 1911 and 1912 respectively as the shipping line's first dual-purpose intermediate sized cruise ships. These vessels operated on the Liverpool and Boston route in the winter whilst employed on cruise duties for summer months. Viewed together these events are highly symbolic in the longer-term development of upscale cruise tourism and the inter-connected role of the boat train.

Port locations and their proximity to large populations shaped the shipping industry. Whilst Southampton was undoubtedly closer to the capital than Liverpool, London would not be completely outdone as a passenger port as expansive facilities along the Thames were of vital importance to the nation's economic well-being. London's inner-city waterfront was an extremely important conduit but during the late 1800s, the amount of cargo handled by the port expanded significantly forcing commercial activity to drift eastwards down river. Port facilities sprawled as bigger ships required deep water access as well as land as trade in commodities created new processing industries. There were complications, too, due to competing interests as the East and West India Docks Company and its rival the London and St. Katherine Dock Company competed for domination. As a result, there was no specific focal centre for passenger liner and ferry traffic until new docks were constructed at Tilbury heralding a modern passenger steamship era for the capital. *Caledonia* which had entered service in 1894 was the first P&O vessel to use Tilbury Dock in 1903 and operating twenty-eight day summer cruises to the North Cape, Spitzbergen and the Fjords aboard their cruising yacht 6,000 ton *Vectis*, whilst Canadian Pacific – a fast growing commercial enterprise at the time – operated some of its London based liners from 1904. Several smaller shipping lines like National, Hill and Wilson Line also used London. In 1909 a degree of consolidation occurred as The Port of London Authority (PLA) was created sucking in the new port at Tilbury as well as upstream waterside docks. In time, Tilbury would become the capital's main liner embarkation point but until the post First World War period, shipping lines particularly those providing steamers to the Orient and the Pacific such as Shaw, Savill and Albion forced to use a variety of dock locations for passenger liner services. These included George V and the Royal Albert Docks amongst others.

Without a primary focus, London's port facilities lagged a long way behind those at Liverpool and Southampton presenting shipping lines with practical difficulties. Dockside facilities were simply not conducive to handle large volumes of liner traffic. P&O toyed with the idea of relocating from London to the south coast as early as 1902. Discussions with the LSWR were said to have been particularly cordial and advanced. Southampton, in fact, in its early years as a commercial port, was used by the company as its home port up until 1881. A Press Association report stated:

> Upon enquiry at the London offices of the P. and O. on Tuesday, it was stated that up to present it had not been definitely decided to remove the company's business from London to Southampton. In shipping circles, however, the return of the P. and O. Company to Southampton was regarded by many as highly probable. There is a disposition to regard the imperfections of the London docks as fully admitted, and the accommodation afforded by the Royal Albert Dock being insufficient for the large new boats which will shortly be delivered to the P. and O. Company's order, the vessels must be taken elsewhere.[20]

In the end P&O decided, announcing at its 1902 annual general meeting, not to split its mail contracts with Southampton (noted by the chairman as the 'finest passenger port in the United Kingdom') whereby it kept its mail and passenger business together at Tilbury and its cargo operations in the Albert Dock.[21] Yet the capital's inadequacies simply did not disappear since London possessed not one single passenger-embarking or landing stage that was close to a railway line forcing customers of shipping firms to put up with tiresome connections. Hansom cabs had to negotiate less than salubrious East London districts to reach dock gates. By late-Victorian times, many shipping lines using London realised the amenities they offered first, and second-class passengers was complete nonsense which risked damaging their business integrity since the capital was now home to a succession of lavish new hotel establishments. Fletcher summed up the position effortlessly:

> Some-day London may wake up and provide herself with the facilities which many of her citizens have urged so pertinaciously, but until then she will retain the reputation of being the most uncomfortable large port in the United Kingdom at which to land or embark.[22]

Whilst P&O sided with Tilbury in the pre-war years, its overall facilities were less than ideal for international passengers as they had to walk along an unsheltered road between the railway station and the dockside even though the port was the nearest of all cross-channel ports to London. However, this was about to change as the company, which ultimately had a long association with Tilbury Docks, built dedicated berths in 1916 specifically for its use although in later years this was broadened to include other shippers. From the 1920s the port's commercial position improved substantially offering shipping lines an attractive passenger and cargo point due to its proximity to the capital and with it came a succession of medium sized vessels using the facilities. On the back of these developments, traffic volumes increased and with it the completion of a new Tilbury Riverside station. In the 1930s Orient Line regarded Tilbury as its big liner home port whilst in 1939 Cunard White Star decided to make London as home for their new 34,000-ton liner *Mauretania*.[23] Similarly, White Star's *Georgic* was the largest motor ship to regularly use the Thames Estuary. Passengers could now enjoy a short boat train journey from the capital taking just forty-five minutes placing the St. Pancras and Tilbury service on a more equal footing to the sub-two-hour Southampton jaunt.

Whilst some of these developments were in the future, progress towards the end of the nineteenth century in more luxurious forms of rail travel could not have existed without similar advances taking place on the sea. And again, this in turn could not have existed without significant port infrastructure projects as the size and scale of ocean liners took enormous strides. In Britain, Europe and the United States there were major efforts to revamp existing ports as they underwent significant expansion. Bigger harbours, deeper quaysides with cranes and a wide range of support facilities were required to accommodate ever-increasing giant leviathans.

Extensive new construction took place with myriad partners largely facilitated by railway companies, shipping lines, local authorities and private investment. Port development included the building of quay side railways, hotels and cargo warehousing to target profitable and prosperous passengers looking for the quickest sea routes to the United States, Canada and other parts of the globe. Passenger ports, especially in the summer, were hectic places. Regular luxury cruising might still be on the horizon, but the first seeds had been sown. Scotland was not the only long-distance domestic destination under the gaze of Britain's embryonic travel industry. Increasing numbers of travellers found their way to Europe – Britain was perceived as an expensive place to holiday in comparison to Europe – as British railway companies introduced their own high-end mail steamers with awaiting train connections at destination ports. The lure of the Continent took great hold as the country's railway companies from the mid-Victorian period were free to develop their own cross-channel steamer operations: They soon found a willing market place as Dr Simon Heffer detected 'the upper classes, anxious to avoid the influx of working-class holidaymakers (at traditional resorts), began to take their holidays abroad, helped by Bradshaw's international timetable and European train travel'.[24] Mullen and Munson took a similar view echoing 'travel very quickly became the fashion for those who could afford it and, with each passing year, more could do so'.[25] Yet this increasingly involved an invasion of the middle and lower-middle classes; by the 1880s the idea of the honeymoon abroad had taken root driven by motivations to visit 'famous cities, buildings, scenery and works of art'.[26]

Britain and Europe's railway networks, coupled to increasingly sophisticated railway company and travel agent marketing literature, ensured the lure of mysterious foreign travel and new places of discovery was now just a day's travel away. *The Clifton Society* newspaper reported on a 1906 paper given by Mons Albert Sartiaux, chief engineer of the French Northern Railway who ventured on the prospects of a Channel Tunnel between the two nations; they noted on 'the familiar legend as to Englishmen's fondness for travel' with 1.2 million crossing the English Channel annually.[27] By 1908, SECR were tapping into this mushrooming market developing a range of Continental excursion tickets covering Boulogne, Calais, Ostend, Brussels, Amsterdam, The Hague and other Dutch towns. Further afield these arrangements

S. E. & C. R. Dover Boat Express.   No. 270.

SECR's Dover boat expresses were a favourite subject for railway photographers in the early years of the twentieth century. The inclusion of specialist cars for traveller luggage were of particular interest giving the boat train a very distinguishing and camera-friendly look. (*Above and below*: J&C McCutcheon Collection)

extended to Paris, the Riviera resorts of Cannes, Nice, Monte Carlo and Mentone and Switzerland.[28] Calais and Boulogne had grown enormously in Victorian times. Harbour improvements in 1876 ensured around a quarter of a million passengers could simply step on to a boat train on the jetty bound for Paris.[29] By 1881 sleeping cars were added to the Calais-Paris line.[30] Aided by a relentless flow of independent day-trippers and weekend guests staying in new, large hotels organised by travel agents, French coastal resorts grew.[31] Indeed, the overwhelming attraction of Paris would come to the fore courtesy of Nord's railway links to the capital from the coastal resorts. Paris had in effect become a British day-tripper market whilst establishing itself as the *first* destination for international travellers.[32] Whilst the French were relatively late starters developing a national railway network of repute, it was far from one-way traffic where Britons, and increasing numbers of Americans headed off to France and the Continent; the French themselves were ingrained travellers. Mons Sartiaux speculated 'With the tunnel, London and Paris would be only five hours apart, and traffic would be tripled within a few years.'[33]

Talk of tunnel boring under the English Channel had reached fever pitch in the years before the Great War. A *Bystander* editorial in its January 1914 French Riviera Supplement ridiculed retired admirals' poo-pooing the idea:

> We want that Tunnel (*c'est le tunnel qu'il nous faut*) because we want to get quicker out of England; we want, once we've settled in a train at Charing Cross or Victoria, to be able to remain in it till we reach Paris, Nice, or Bâle, or Biarritz, or Blazes. We want to avoid not so much the sea-sickness, which probably, as the Admirals say, does us good, but the bother of being trained and detained, boarded and unboarded, baggaged, unbagged, and then rebaggaged: to be able to get to our France, not merely rid of our francs. We want, oh! Admiral, to de-insularise ourselves, and if you want to convince any breathing soul that danger of invasion is likely to lie in the mouth of a "Chunnel" that could be blown to smithereens or flooded by the pressing of one of Winston's buttons, then tell it, Sir, to your Marines.[34]

What was often neglected was the considerable level of travel taking place between northern France and Germany, Belgium and the Netherlands brought about by the nineteenth century's huge

Whilst the prospect of a Channel Tunnel was mere conjecture, railway companies relied on traditional poster advertising to promote key messages. Produced for the summer season of 1914, this SECR poster demonstrates the lengths pre-grouping railway companies would go emphasising the quality of their joined-up travel services. Nowhere was this more apparent than on short-sea crossings, and in SECR's case, the range of London stations it had at its disposal for the convenience of cross-channel passenger traffic.

economic and technological changes. At the top of the travel market, this was driven by a cosmopolitan pan-European multi-lingual cultural elite, devoid of national boundaries, extending from London to St. Petersburg. This was a world where the individual mattered, and not the country of birth. Yet there was also a certain degree of national protectiveness and one-upmanship taking place. Railway writer Andrew Martin in his 2017 book, *Night Trains: The Rise and Fall of the Sleeper* detected these sentiments in Baedeker's 1904 Paris British visitor guide noting of French trains 'The carriages are inferior to those in most other parts of Europe … Before starting, travellers are generally cooped up in the close and dusty waiting rooms.' The generality of Parisian railway restaurants are 'dear and often poor'.[35] Similarly, NDL, targeting prosperous American visitors to Germany, extolled the standards of their regional railways emphasising the quality of its second-class carriages to be better than first-class in England.[36] From a British perspective this was grossly unfair because by the turn of the century, a good number of British railway companies such as the Midland Railway and the London, Brighton & South Coast Railway (LBSCR) had teamed up with the American Pullman Company providing passengers with a new level of comfortable deluxe train travel and experience. Improved travelling facilities could be found in Britain and indeed across the civilised world. Mark Twain was far more accommodating of the fast-developing Italian railway system, and in particular at the quality of its magnificent station buildings but baffled as to how a 'bankrupt government' could 'have such palatial railroad depots' which he likened to being sufficiently clean to eat from. He perceived:

> As for the railways – we have none like them. The cars slide as smoothly along as if they were on runners. The depots are vast palaces of cut marble, with stately colonnades of the same royal stone traversing them from end to end, and with ample walls and ceilings richly decorated with frescoes. The lofty gateways are graced with statues, and the broad floors are all laid in polished flags of marble.[37]

Over longer distances sleeping cars became an integral feature of boat train business especially for Ireland bound services, and on demand ocean liner expresses which could turn up in port at any time. North Atlantic crossings in winter could be horrendous experiences with many passengers disembark steamers at the earliest opportunity; Plymouth did very well with both the Great Western and LSWR scraping over commercial opportunities. As an island nation, the boat train had been a feature of railway life since the mid-nineteenth century performing several unique functions as they serviced discrete markets with cross-channel steamers, but also larger ocean-going passenger ships. Harbours and ports developed to convey imports and exports of raw materials such as coal and for the transportation of mail, parcels, bullion and other manufactured goods from the workshop of the world. But it was the movement of passengers and the development of linked port railway systems that provided the stimulus for European and international travel. Boat trains were pivotal for the short-sea crossings between Britain and the Continent.

European boat train travel had begun in earnest with the South Eastern Railway (SER) who as long ago as 1851 inaugurated the first dedicated Paris bound boat train service. Before the construction of deep-water harbours, English Channel boat trains ran on flexible schedules determined by the tides. Boat trains could be late nonetheless; Charles Dickens was once recorded being caught in a snow drift for four hours aboard a Holyhead service before the locomotive was eventually dug out. Boat trains encapsulated a social structure straddling society in its widest context. Whilst there were always luxury sections of boat trains, and in time dedicated Pullman boat trains for both ocean going and cross-channel services, they reflected a three-class passenger construction mirroring the class structures of many shipping lines but also ticketing arrangements still common on the Continent. The three-tier ticket designation on boat trains lingered on in Britain until the post-war period when the traditional three-class ticket label eventually disappeared on 3 June 1956. Third-class services were officially predesignated as second-class and this classification continued until 11 May 1987 when British Rail termed second-class as 'standard-class'.

As noted, the last decade of the 1800s, saw continual improvement in the quality of carriage stock and, for the first time, Britain's railway companies, most notably the LNWR, the LSWR and to a lesser extent the GWR, took cognizance of the importance of first-class passengers arriving from the United States. The Great Western were slower to respond, but then it had had its hands tied for several years reacting to and integrating standard gauge practices to its former broad-gauge network. However, from around the end of the decade the company too was fast developing business opportunities. Conditions and facilities aboard the liners was improving with a succession of fast new vessels traversing the North Atlantic – the Blue Riband was constantly changing hands. The 1889 Paris Exposition was a huge inducement for Americans (and for all tourists) to travel on a grand scale. By the following year, New York port authorities estimated at least 80 per cent of the 99,189 first or second-class passenger arrivals in the city were of people returning home.[38] American commentator William Rideing in 1890 provided greater clarity to the spread of shipping activity already taking place on the Atlantic trade: 'Nearly two thousand trips were made from New York alone to various European ports' resulting in 'about two hundred thousand cabin passengers were carried to and fro'.[39] And importantly, this excluded emigrant traffic from Britain, Ireland and Europe landing in the United States. At the turn of the twentieth century it was estimated nearly 80,000 Americans were living or on extended visits to London, Paris and Berlin. Apart from desires to visit Europe's heritage hotspots, this growth was fuelled by an US infusion with a Continental cultural elite. Professor Orlando Figes captures the sentiment suggesting the impact of railway development was transformational bringing about an upheaval in 'sense of time and space' powering 'the international circulation of European music, literature and art' bringing 'about a revolution in the cultural marketplace'.[40] Not just confined to Europe this included an affluent metropolitan class of New York, Boston and Chicago, who courtesy of new fast steamships criss-crossing the North Atlantic, were increasingly charmed on their soil by visiting arts performers. Unsurprisingly, European culture formed part of the itinerary playing fields.

By late-Victorian times most British railway companies had for the most part defined their passenger offer by way of the first or third-class structure. Three-class arrangements still existed on a few train services and on Continental and ocean boat trains. Yet within these complexities a luxury travel product in Britain had yet to be fully defined; enhanced customer travel facilities were still rather limited, and only really changed markedly during this period.

Certainly, prior to this period there was a perceived hospitality service gap in terms of standards and pricing between English and American hotels and well-recorded by travellers from across the Atlantic, yet by the Edwardian age this had narrowed significantly as railway hotels in London were deemed some of the best in town. But the real transition started with the arrival of the *grand* hotel which represented a remarkable shift in the US and Europe's hotel-keeping industry, and with it an all-encompassing service offer. By the early years of the 1900s, the grand hotel market was characterised by properties owned by moneyed individuals and managed by accomplished hoteliers. American writer Blanche McManus observed the changes since they not only appealed to an English demand for comfort, but to the American who demanded luxury.[41] In her book *The American Woman Abroad* (Dodd, Mead and Company, 1911) she writes strikingly how new London and Paris hotels much appealed to her fellow countrymen contending:

> The lavishly convenient American way of living has had much to do with the change that has come over the European caterer to the foreigner. Now that he has learned the trick and is working on his own account, adapting it to his needs, even though the pace be slow, it is still evident that it has come as a result of a first desire to please an American clientele. The patriotic Frenchman dramatically points to the big hotels which have gone up in Paris during the last few years, and exclaims, 'It is for you Americans that these luxurious establishments have been built; it is you who are coming here in our midst and demoralising our own people with your dollars.'

Notwithstanding hospitality developments taking place in Britain and Europe, the spread of mass consumption ultimately led to the evolvement of an 'American style of hotel-keeping and management' that was to become so well-engrained. Like London, Paris also had its spread of majestic railway hotels. Marketing writer Mark Tungate observes, 'most historians agree that the boom of the grand hotel was concurrent with the birth of the industrial age, when steam not only created the new rich, but got them moving'.[42] West End's grand hotel and department store fortresses were like magnets to wealthy overseas travellers. An early form of retail or shopping culture was pervasive as special malls and arcades of individual shops appeared in prosperous districts, but it was to the multifaceted department store that most visitors turned to. In 1907, Harrods arranged to price everything in their windows both in sterling and in dollars in view of the large influx of US visitors expected for the summer season.[43]

Unsurprisingly these developments spilled over into the railway industry. Some companies such as the Midland and the London, Brighton & South Coast Railway Company (LBSCR) had made headway with respective Pullman offers, but to some extent there were still too many vague notions of what constituted quality and luxury, and how this might fit with first-class on-board dining and sleeping arrangements. Inertia varied from one railway company to another, whose managements pondered over the expense of investing in new products and services. Up until then nothing really offered in Britain by railway companies was on the scale of the Pullman Company's US or, indeed, Wagon-Lits' European operations; the two specialist organisations had things very much their own way. This had come about as a result of the highly competitive nature of Britain's railway system, the way the railway companies conducted their business, and in some companies a general management malaise, indifference or even intransigence, all exacerbating the problems of understanding what a first-class provision was. Britain's mainstream railway companies now, however, started to plug the gap by offering their own interpretations of luxury rail travel. And some very successfully too. Pullman's ideas were brazenly copied by British carriage manufacturers such as the Metropolitan Carriage & Wagon Co Ltd. Highly comfortable and symbolic first-class saloons appeared on SER's prestige coastal services helping initiate a trend whereby railway companies on both sides of the English Channel took the provision of luxury rail facilities as a means of securing best fare-paying passengers.[44] In time this would become the province of Pullman and Wagon-Lits almost entirely as the two organisations worked hand in glove with railway companies developing prestige routes and services. The boat and the *American* trans-Atlantic narrative were now essential components in this parade.

On observing cross-channel developments some operators like LSWR, the Metropolitan Railway and LBSCR kept a watching brief preferring to mine the potential of regular home-based business travellers. LBSCR though did have the foresight to recognise its Brighton Pullman stock could be utilised for Newhaven boat trains, but by and large commuter traffic in and around London and other major cities, represented a lucrative first-class segment to be fully exploited. But with an explosion in the growth of international business, this cohort was considered the most likely to take Continental business trips wallowing in the delights of Paris and other European capitals. Other companies, conversely, were more experienced in providing the types of facilities prosperous travellers wanted. LNWR, GWR and LSWR provided ocean liner boat trains meeting the approval of their major shipping line partners by attracting the growth of inbound American tourists. Of the main boat train routes, Liverpool and other west coast routes had been quicker in adopting eight-wheeled bogie carriages offering passengers a more comfortable ride.[45] By the 1900s, Great Eastern (via Harwich), SECR and LBSCR were offering far superior cross-channel services linking London directly with Wagon-Lits' Continental operations. Wagon-Lits also set up shop in London with an office at 20 Cockspur Street prompting a spurt in growth and development of luxury rail travel, as railway managers for the first time really had a fuller appreciation of the demands of the segment by beginning to really understand the growth potential of 'travelling for pleasure', and the value of the business and tourist market where often the two combined.[46] As such ideas surrounding the destination, the itinerary and the tourist were taking greater hold in the British Isles. Within railway circles, this represented a completely new subset of activity.

In mainland Britain, the tourism areas of Scotland, the Lake District and North Wales together with other remote geographical areas blessed with natural beauty such as the West Country were written about extensively attracting greater numbers of people eager to explore and experience established and new tourist trails. The imagining of awaking next morning on one of the Anglo-Scottish sleeping expresses to the Scottish Highlands created strong imagery which leading railway companies exploited by the end of the Victorian period. Apart from longer railway journeys, crossing the Atlantic by steamers were important places for the gestation of imagination helping to dispel the problems of being contained within the confines of a ship for the best part of a week. Travel opened inspirational possibilities beyond the confines of the ship's space providing an appeal and sense of puzzlement that grew steadily with travellers. There was something magical about the south-west of England whose land mass was often the first sight for Plymouth and Southampton stops. Cornwall had been the last part of England to be connected to the national railway network. This, perhaps, a blessing in disguise as international travellers suddenly discovered its delights aided by ingenious GWR promotional material finding its way on to Atlantic steamers.

The county, together with neighbouring Devon, possessed relative benign climates, so by late-Victorian/Edwardian times, south-west resorts progressively took the role of mid-winter alternatives to the Azur coast. Some independent travellers also using Plymouth liners, would similarly spend a day or two in the south-west with family and friends helping to explain a degree of under-utilisation of London boat trains provided by both GWR and LSWR. In the nineteenth century significant numbers of Cornish people moved to America with one enterprising Brooklyn establishment the Star Hotel dedicated to looking after its émigré brethren.[47]

Britain's ordered class system, which some commentators argued the railways perpetuated in ways other transport forms did not, ensured a valuable stream of tourists who could afford intercontinental travel. This relatively new phenomenon was not confined just to Britain as in the United States a veritable new industry emerged through the entrepreneurial activities of individuals, railroads and latterly financial institutions endeavouring to manage travel services for the well off. British railway companies were not the only organisations involved with European travel. The running of the then highly successful Thomas Cook organisation by 1899 was administered by the third generation of family members. In earlier years travelling abroad was considered an adventure, and even Cook's commercial prowess could not mask some of the practical difficulties accompanying international travel. The richest of customers had to conform and make do with what was on offer. But by now Thomas Cook ran many of its ancillary services; its Nile steamers were considered the most luxurious on the river with much effort taken up with the marketing and promotion of globetrotting expeditions.

There were other enterprising British firms specialising in overseas rail travel. Dean & Dawson, founded as a partnership in the 1870s, had by the eve of the Great War offices in the Strand and Piccadilly and were expanding their luxury travel operations to include tours to the Riviera, the Swiss and Italian Lakes, Egypt and the Holy Land.[48] Similarly, the American Express Company followed its prosperous customers across the North Atlantic in their quest for adventure, new discoveries and the promotion of their travel facilities (cheques) through a variety of agencies in London, Liverpool, Paris and Bremen.[49] By 1909 not only had the company West End offices, they had permanent branches at Liverpool and Southampton, the main British embarkation ports, but also

By the early 1900s, collaboration between railway companies, port authorities and travel companies were deep-rooted affairs. International travellers simply expected more. This example of Cook's and SECR joint poster advertising emphasised the first stage of coordinated boat train and cross-channel steamer services that ensured a seamless cross-channel travelling experience from Britain to just about anywhere in the world. Cook's worked with a variety of pre-grouping railway companies to promote their travel services.

Paris, working with a variety of partners overseeing the stays of American tourists in the French capital, and the cities of Bremen and Hamburg home to the main two German shipping lines.[50] American Express initiated marketing relationships with two of Morgan's shipping line conglomerate – the American Line and Red Star. Despite undoubted tourism sector progress, James C. Fargo, the company's President disliked intensely the use of organised travel visits from outside the company's offices.[51] But by this time, the American Express Company had its foot through the door on this side of the water forming correspondent arrangements with leading banks in Scotland, France, Austria, Germany, Italy, the Netherlands, Norway and Sweden and all representing countries where large numbers of emigrants had made their way to new lives. The company in addition formed an association with French bank Credit Lyonnais, creating outlets across Europe in Brussels, Madrid, Geneva, St. Petersburg as well as the eastern Mediterranean antiquities of Constantinople, Smyrna, Alexandria and Cairo and all destinations that were regularly serviced by Wagon-Lits and the Thomas Cook organisation.[52] The prospect of organised or individual planned international rail and sea travel had never been easier. The PTA with its primary focus on promoting 'affordable' travel to London's newly educated white-collar community, also ensured the boat train was an integral element for visiting France, Ireland, Norway and Switzerland.[53]

The end of the nineteenth century brought about a significant expansion of international tourism and in the numbers of new modern steamers, especially those operating on North Atlantic routes. William Smith, a British traveller of some repute, suggested crossing the Atlantic was no longer the ordeal it once was in his book *A Yorkshireman's Trip to the United States and Canada*, Longmans, Green and Co., 1892. Aboard the White Star steamer *Majestic,* he recorded the voyage as a 'very ordinary experience and a run over to the States will soon be thought of no more consequence than was a journey from Yorkshire to London fifty years ago, when the intending traveller to the South made his will, and in other ways settled his world affairs, before starting on his three days' journey by coach to the great metropolis'.[54]

Similarly, Dr Neil Matthews records the writings of the London Polytechnic community involved in a trip to the 1893 Chicago World Fair. 'Americans in particular – for being in such a rush that modern transportation had to take risks in order to meet the greater expectations of speedy travel', describing 'Lightening express trains across continents and racers upon the oceans are necessities of the day.'[55]

Chiming with similar sentiments *The Illustrated Sporting and Dramatic News* enthused:

> To a great number of intending travellers, the means and cost of a journey or voyage are matters of importance. The steamships of the different companies are sufficiently luxurious to satisfy anyone, and nowadays a run across to America and back is well within the grasp of any one with a fortnight at his disposal.[56]

Within a decade, further capacity was seen on the Atlantic Ferry with the introduction of swift new 'travelling palace' super-liners together with the experiences Cunard, White Star and other shipping lines brought so characterising the period before the Great War. Fletcher notes the combination of speed and facilities expected by premier-class passengers, and in particular Americans:

> There is no denying that there is a public demand for greater speed, and that companies which can place the greatest steamships on their service and give them the greatest speed, and equip them with the most luxuries, however superfluous most of them may be to the majority of the passengers, will receive the greatest and most profitable patronage.[57]

Maritime developments surrounding speed and facilities were extended to land. D.T. Timins in a review of railroad travel in America for *The Railway Magazine* commented,

> Our American cousins are fond of flaunting the glories of their wonderful trains before our eyes in a way which would lead one to naturally suppose that a library, observation car, barber's shop, typewriter etc, were to be found in every train throughout the entire continent.[58]

This, of course, was not the case with all US railroad (and British railway) experiences, but Americans nonetheless were used to high-quality travelling standards. The domestic US market was also served by Pullman's key competitor Wagner, but as a business they did not venture beyond their home territory. It was into this modern new upscale travelling community British railway companies were expected to do their bit. However, the three leading boat train providers operated in parts of the country where Pullman, (a name familiar to many well-read and travelled Americans), did not provide catering and travelling services to incoming passengers. The American traveller market, whilst lucrative, could be difficult to manage as they were as a rule well-educated, worldly-wise but finicky requiring close attention to detail. They were part of an increasing band of prosperous travellers who were the new-found wealth constituting what would be described as the first wave of the 'Americanisation of London society'.[59] *The Exeter and Plymouth Gazette Daily Telegram* newspaper reported on ocean steamer business, 'The prospect which was held out at the beginning of the season of an enormous influx of American visitors to Europe is in a fair way to be realized. We are told that between 1,200 and 1,500 cabin passengers set sail last week – as many as 600 on Saturday alone.'[60] Similarly, *The Western Times* noted several years later, 'The season now fast waning has been prolific in American visitors who have provided a harvest for the hotels, the *Victoria* having had as many as 250 at a time, and 130 arriving on occasion by a single train.'[61]

Despite the Prince of Wales wallowing with a new band of US plutocrats, Queen Victoria was a potent tourism attractor for many wealthy Americans. A form of 'Victorian Grand Tour' around London emerged as American visitors took in the Tower of London, Windsor Castle and Hampton Court whilst staying in the capital.

Handling US tourists was big business. Newspapers across the land reported on the success of the 1905 summer holidays quoting 'an expert estimate that before the season closes, American visitors will have spent £4,000.000 in Europe'.[62] The *Daily Telegraph's* American correspondent noted one well-known international traveller in particular heading to Britain in 1907. 'New York', according to genial writer Mark Twain, 'is an energetic place, but all the vitality one has in his body is required for London'.[63] Such endorsements were important since they would ultimately contribute significantly to hotelier, retailer, shipping line and railway company commercial successes. Not surprisingly, many Americans preferred to travel in ways they were familiar with. The first dedicated luxury and open style first-class carriages and dining saloons appeared during this period specifically tailored for visiting US citizens. Little wonder, the term 'American' would appear in the title of these specialist ocean liner boat trains. Such was the scale of the American 'Army of Invasion', it was estimated by the outbreak of the Great War some 150,000 US travellers were arriving annually.[64] Other sources put this figure higher since Atlantic Ferry passenger capacity had increased significantly in the years before the Great War with the emergence of the super-liner classes, access to other New England and Canadian port destinations and increased competition for American traffic from European shipping lines. Had *Titanic* not succumbed to an iceberg, first-class provision might have been even greater.

Edwardian Britain saw the foreshadows of today's consumer society; the emptiness and shallowness of spending of money purely for show was ridiculed by some members of New York's so-called *Four Hundred Club*, a gathering of women from America's new wealth. Moreover, at the turn of the twentieth century the marketplace for luxury travel products began to converge as new standards of customer service permeated businesses across Britain, Europe and the United States. Hospitality for the first time became a 'respectable industry' as travel organizations pandered to the needs of the super-rich and their corporate businesses who could change travel plans at a moment's notice simply demanding the very best amenities and service wherever they went. Nothing unusual in this even a century later, but historian Richard Davenport-Hines observed 'immediacy was a keynote of the Edwardian mood' demonstrating 'an impatience that had been unknown twenty years earlier'.

Such petulance did save lives: Last minute booking changes invariably meant a few first-class passengers missed *Titanic's* maiden voyage. One poor soul though missed the ship's departure only to go down with the *Lusitania* several years later. Edwardian upper classes were entranced by period super-liners and the accompanying palatial surroundings of boat train carriages that got them to and from port. For the super-rich, transport aboard ships and special 'American' boat trains were designed in such a way that made life feel perfectly normal and a natural extension of privileged lifestyles. On most of the new super-liners, the ship's superstructure was allocated to the needs of first (and second-class) passengers to create a travelling experience that was not like going to sea at all. Many would be oblivious to poor wretches hidden beneath them in steerage; but despite the magnitude of *Titanic's* sinking, in time portrayed as a look-back to the shattering of Edwardian theatrical splendour, ship-board trans-Atlantic life did continue much in the same way in the months following the headlines. First-class cabins placed amidships provided quiet and comfortable spaces that could be enjoyed in solitude and an escape from the constant scrutiny and rituals of the goldfish bowl. Perchance a time for much needed reflection? Gazing out to sea observing the panorama of constantly changing sea conditions had its limitations but book in hand from well-stocked libraries, listening to the ship's orchestra, using the gymnasium, swimming pool, writing or sending wireless telegraphy messages, simply playing cards and board games or conversing with fellow wanderers as well as attending the rituals of prescribed meal times was a means to while away the hours. In most conditions, crossing the pond in either direction was achieved in less than a week. For many the meeting of new souls in the confines of the different liner surroundings – even sister ships could be completely different reflecting the up-to-the-minute design trends – was a labour of love.

Dover Straights Services

The English Channel ports at their shortest crossing had been linked by rail connections on both sides of the water since the 1840s. The journey between London, Paris and anywhere beyond in the mid-nineteenth century was long-winded and cumbersome taking the best part of a half a day's travelling time. Dover was reached in 1844 whilst Folkestone – a new port developed from a former silted-up harbour by the South Eastern Railway (SER) – a year earlier. The twenty-one miles between Dover and Calais had been used by cross-channel shipping for many years to cater for the time-honoured London stagecoach route and because of its strategic position, Dover was shared with the Royal Navy. The commercial harbour was reached by two competing routes; one being the SER and the other with the London, Chatham & Dover Railway (LCDR) each originating from different London stations but converging at Dover's Admiralty Pier. Both the SER and the LCDR would ultimately merge. Nonetheless, the English Channel ports were extremely busy with regular steam packet services – the SER being one of the early railway company pioneers having run the first day trip to France on 14 June 1843. On the French side by mid-century, Compagnie des Chemins de Fer du Nord (Nord) had connected Paris to the Channel ports of Boulogne, Dunkirk and Calais where steamers took just three hours to reach the English coast.[65]

Aside freight movement cross-channel traffic was made up of several elements of passenger traffic, workers, excursion or day trippers looking for adventure, and a thriving tourist market driven by rich Victorians ready to discover Europe at leisure. In April 1849, northern based excursion agent Henry R. Marcus publicised cheap excursions to Paris and Brussels. His marketing devices were information pamphlets containing 'things to do' and 'places to stay' all targeted at what would be described today as the budget end of the market. By 1848 regular sailings were taking place between Folkestone and Boulogne supported by the construction of the Pavilion Hotel providing passengers with a much-appreciated facility. Steam propelled paddle steamers were the notable feature in early years exercising considerable influence on the development of cross-channel travel trade as vessels progressively became bigger and faster. Paris, with its wealth of royal palaces and beauty spots, was a cultural magnet for weekend trippers. What is often overlooked is how important European travel became for Victorian travellers.

In 1851 the SER inaugurated a new Paris bound boat train service where for first-class passengers several carriages would include washbasins and chamber pots. Two years later railway companies were provided with the necessary statutory powers to run steamships although it would not be until the early 1860s before they exercised greater influence over cross-channel affairs.[66] The harbour at Ramsgate with its Dunkerque crossing also provided a commercial shipping resource supported by LCDR, but despite its association as a chief embarkation point during the Napoleonic Wars, it remained as a secondary resource for cross-channel passenger shipping for much of the nineteenth and twentieth centuries. The port played a subservient role to Dover and Folkestone and thus remains outwith the boat train story. Despite some pooling the south-east railway companies operated their own cross-channel steamer services to France and the low countries such as the Dover-Ostend route. On French routes, travellers were presented with considerable choice with embarkation points including Dover, Folkestone and Newhaven, which was reached by the railway in 1847, the Brighton Railway thus initiating regular Dieppe sailings.[67]

To the observer, it may appear odd that SER and LCDR company management did not pick up on the idea of providing better services for their Continental steamships and boat trains much earlier than they did. Both companies, however, embarked on a programme of providing new cross-channel paddlers from the 1860s, and from the early 1880s LCDR provided the first recognised 'modern' paddle steamer. This was driven by increased tourist demand as the British middle-classes – the richest in Europe - had stronger desires to travel than their European counterparts. By 1869 the number of English Channel crossings had reached 345,000.[68] Those pursuing a mischievous strand, might suggest the two railway companies spent too much time bickering with each other, rather than keeping an eye on emerging tourism trends, which as a result of their endeavours had made foreign travel easier and more affordable.[69] Despite the numbers, the notion of travelling in style to Europe did not become the norm until much later in the Victorian era, notwithstanding the undoubted expansion of passenger traffic brought about by the introduction of faster and more efficient screw-driven steamers propelled by compound machinery which gradually replaced paddlers in the later part of Victoria's reign.[70] Even the mighty Midland Railway offered special fares to Scotland's elite on its Settle and Carlisle route providing inclusive hotel accommodation coupons for the 1878 Paris Exhibition.[71] The Midland Railway did not possess any direct cross-channel arrangements itself – it did dabble with ideas of using its Somerset and Dorset joint line to run a fledgling service with partners from Poole – but like most major British railway companies at the time, went on to set up correspondence offices in Paris to attract both prosperous French travellers to its network and to tap into commissions for through rail and steamer ticketing arrangements to the capital and also south to the Riviera. Dover Pullman Express boat trains were operated by both companies between 1882 and 1884 whilst elite train services known as *Club Trains* linking London to Paris were introduced by LCDR and SER in 1889 to coincide with the Paris International Exhibition (Monsieur Eiffel's new tower was unveiled) with two separate trains to Dover departing and arriving at different London terminuses.[72]

The LCDR train was known as *The Paris Limited Mail* whereas the SER *Club Train* had two luxury American style saloons and a fourgon owned and supplied by Wagon-Lits with the company providing a first-class service described as 'a good club standard' of accommodation.[73] These services, however, were withdrawn on 30 September 1893 as they were not a commercial success due to the two railways' competing offers, the requirement to pool their Continental receipts and the still somewhat primitive and exposed Dover maritime facilities. Wagon-Lits regrouped to mainland Europe, but the precedent had been set to utilise luxury Pullman carriages in boat train formations dictated by a growing market. By the end of the nineteenth century the English Channel ports were major confluence points: SER provided Royal Mail Continental steamer services for Dover and Calais, Ostend and Folkestone to Boulogne.[74] The twice daily Dover and Ostend mail packets were considered the fastest on the channel connecting with important mail trains from Brussels and Cologne first established in the mid-1870s.[75] The Belgian government in 1886 attempting to meet increase passenger demand, introduced new paddlers *Prince Albert* and *Ville de Douvres* making the Dover-Ostend service a thrice-daily run. By 1888 two new Belgian sisters - *Princesse Henriette* and *Princesse Josephine* - had joined cross-channel tussles, marking Belgium's entry into the high-quality and luxury end of the market.[76] In 1893 *Leopold II* and *Marie Henriette* became the last Belgian paddlers operating on the Ostend-Dover service.[77]

The SER was now running better quality coaches for its premier English Channel services introducing Pullman type carriages. In 1891 the company ordered six American Pullman style cars initially to run on the loading gauge restricted Hastings line. Known as Gilbert cars, they were acquired in knocked-down form from the Gilbert Car Manufacturing Co. of Troy, (Pullman's great American rival), and then reassembled at SER's works in Ashford. The train was branded the *American Car Train* sporting spacious

Aside Belgium's routes across the North Sea to Harwich, Dover and Ostend since mid-Victorian times had been an important conduit for cross-channel mail. In 1846, the Belgian government initiated its own steamboat services and by 1862 had taken sole responsibility for the mail service between the two countries. Thus began a long-term association where up-to-date connecting boat and mail trains together with cross-channel vessels were a prominent feature as demonstrated in these two postcard images from the turn of the twentieth century. (*Above and below*: J&C McCutcheon Collection)

accommodation and quality interiors that were not matched by any other railway company at the time, but most importantly from a passenger perspective, there was no supplementary fare payable. In 1896 the Hastings Gilbert cars were extensively rebuilt with enclosed corridor connections, electric lighting and more modern-looking windows.[78] Likewise, SER introduced two large paddle packets – *Duchess of York* and *Princess of Wales* – in the mid-1890s. The latter was employed on the Boulogne service connecting with a new Paris express boat train. Chemin de fer du Nord (Nord) built two cross-channel paddlers – *Le Nord* and *Le Pas de Calais* – for the early morning Dover-Calais departure (under the 1896 mail agreement between Britain and France) being the only cross-channel paddle steamers constructed in France. *Mabel Grace* was SER's last paddler ordered just before the LCDR merger.[79]

The SER acquired home-built luxury corridor coaches for its boat train service to Folkestone which was then extended in September 1897 along the coastline to Dover and known as the *Folkestone Vestibuled Limited*. Both trains were painted in crimson lake livery embellished in gold leaf and a style decoration borrowed from Pullman. The luxury Hastings train continued until the turn of the century, but the route proved uneconomic with the rake broken up to run individually or in pairs with many other important SER trains including morning boat trains, and in so doing, much improving the popularity of the Folkestone-Boulogne crossing.[80] With merger, some of the carriage stock formed part of a new train called the *American Corridor Train* and with it received a new makeover. *The Folkstone Herald* waxed lyrical about the addition:

> This truly magnificent train has just come out of 'dock' from the Ashford works, and it may fairly be stated it is spick and span as could be desired. The upholsterers have done their work well – so well in fact that the cars present a picture of refined taste. With the exception of the various royal trains in Europe there is nothing better in England than this. The train is luxuriousness itself, and Folkstone should feel itself highly pleased to be served daily by such a train. But how is it supported? Certainly, people will not make journeys for the sake of the thing, but it is a matter for much regret that the 'corridor' is not better patronised. There is no doubt about it, the Amalgamated Companies are running the train at a dead loss during these winter months. We often hear of the sins of omission and commission of the Company,

826   THE SKETCH.   Dec. 23, 1896

COMFORTABLE CHRISTMAS TRAVELLING.

The travelling public in general, and that section of it in particular whose business or pleasure takes them to Hastings, should be grateful for the American Car train recently inaugurated by the South-Eastern Company. The new train makes only one trip a-day, leaving Hastings in the morning, London in the afternoon; but, judging by the manner in which its comforts have already been appreciated, more trains of a similar kind will be put into use on this system as speedily as they can

A DINING-CAR.

be built. Two most palpable gains in these dark and chilly days are the electric light which illumines each of the six carriages—two first-, one second-, and three third-class—and the hot-water pipes which warm them. In the important consideration of oscillation, the new train leaves on cause for complaint, for, although the weight of each carriage is only about half of that of the heaviest car in use in America, still, it is heavier by four tons than the English "bogie" saloon, and, as proved by experience, it travels with greater steadiness. Nor does its length, which is fifty as against the ordinary forty-four feet, prevent it from going smoothly round the curves or accomplishing the journey of fifty-nine miles between Cannon Street and West St. Leonards within an hour and a half.

Again, although a first-class passenger can perambulate, thanks to the flexible vestibules of leather and latticed steel, throughout the entire length of the train, while the third-class traveller has three carriages—some hundred and fifty feet—in which to roam, the English idea of seclusion has not been forgotten. About one-half of one of the first-class carriages forms a spacious and elegant ladies' saloon, while the seats in the third-class have been so arranged that two friends can sit together, while the lonely or unsociable passenger can have a seat all to himself—an arrangement unknown in the American "day-coach" which may be said to correspond with our third-class accommodation. Although there is only one rate of fare in America, it is impossible to travel with any degree of comfort there, unless you pay extra for a seat in a Pullman or Wagner Palace Car. No "day-coach" in America is so commendable as the third-class saloons on this new train. The general scheme of decoration is lighter and brighter than is generally the case; excellent lavatory compartments and smoking-rooms are provided on each carriage, and the cuspidor so indispensable in America—even in the fashionable "Congressional Limited," which runs between New York and Washington—is a very rare commodity in the English train, and is difficult of discovery because it only exists, in the disguise of a footstool, in the smoking-rooms!

While on the question of railway improvements, I must refer to the two new dining-cars which the Midland Company are to place in the London and Manchester express service on the first day of the New Year. Built in the company's Derby workshops, they are designed to give the greatest ease, comfort, and safety possible to passengers, whether travelling at a low or a high rate of speed. The bodies of the carriages, which are sixty feet long, eight feet wide, and eight feet high, rest upon bogie trucks with six pairs of wheels. A number of india-rubber springs of a new type are also interposed between the under-frame and the body of the car, the complete structure being so arranged as to minimise vibration and irregularities of motion. The floors, sides, and roofs have been built up with felt, indiarubber, hair, and vulcanite between the timbers, for the purpose of absorbing or preventing the conduct of sound and deadening the noise and rattle which usually accompany locomotion by rail; and to further this object the side and top windows are double glazed with plate glass. The decoration, which has been carried out by Messrs. Gillow, of Lancaster, introduces a new departure in railway upholstery. Each car is lighted by means of compressed oil-gas (each lamp having four jets), and is warmed by hot water from the engine, the heat radiating from a brass grill. A ladies' and a gentlemen's lavatory is also provided at each end of the car.

"A DOLL'S HOUSE."

Mr. Labouchere is certainly a very wonderful man. He seems equally at home in the character of defendant in a libel suit, and in acting as Providence to the thousands of hapless little mortals who, but for his efforts on their behalf, would spend a very cheerless Christmas in workhouse, poor-school, or hospital. You would have been very much struck with that if you had seen the Albert Hall last week, converted for the nonce by the readers of *Truth* into a magnificent doll's house. All day long a well-dressed Lilliputian crowd stood fascinated before the serried rows of dolls—dolls in every conceivable attire, dolls with "a past," dolls with a present—and looked with wondering eyes on this densely populated patch of Toyland.

The quaint little figures had about them a curious historical charm, reflecting as they did not only the modes of the moment, but also the leading topics of the day. Thus, cheek by jowl with a battalion of stalwart soldiers stood a squadron of sturdy sailor-boys; a row of Salvation Army lasses seemed to implore the attention of the waxen-faced worldlings whose elaborate costumes were in their way miracles of ingenuity and taste. The great ones of every side of life were represented. There were Li Hung Chang and Mr. Gladstone, surrounded by his family, including, of course, Miss Dorothy Drew, in that memorable meeting of the Grand Old Men at Hawarden. Little Miss Labouchere herself sent a Mistress of the Hounds in scarlet bodice and dark-blue habit. Miss Marie Corelli sent Little Jessamine Dale from "The Mighty Atom." Stageland was represented by the lovely Lohengrin in his gorgeous armour, and by "Charley's Aunt," who expired (at the Globe Theatre) a night or two after the show; and by "The Gay Parisienne," whose vagaries were varied by Miss Peggy Pride *vice* Miss Louie Frevar; and again by pretty Pitti Sing, who still charms Savoyards. There were dolls representing pictures by Millais and Kate Greenaway; others figuring as Truth, as Charity, or the Queen of the May; in fact, the dwellers in that great doll domain would have needed a directory all to themselves—those Pierrots, nurses, Watteau beauties, Tars and Tommies, who stood pertly in their rows.

Having seen them all, who could declare that the art of plain-sewing is lost? Among the thousands of dolls shown, scarce one but has had lavished on it rows of exquisite stitchery, and it must be no easy matter to decide as to which among the exhibits most deserve the prizes provided by the editor of *Truth*. The record as to the number of dolls dressed is held by Mrs. Alexander and Miss Rawson, who sent three hundred each.

As in former years, a prominent feature in the exhibition was a glass case containing eleven thousand newly minted sixpences. These coins, the gift of an anonymous donor, have become a recognised feature, and the giver evidently realises vividly what kind of present appeals most to the childish mind. Mr. Tom Smith was represented by twenty-three thousand crackers. Indeed, not the least interesting portion of the show were the cleverly arranged groups of miscellaneous exhibits, which formed a very varied background to the long lists of the dolls themselves.

The editor of *Truth* started his Toy Fund and Doll-Dressing Competition some seventeen years ago, and at the first exhibition, which was held, by the way, at the editorial offices in Queen Street, the number of exhibits was under a thousand. This year the total

LI HUNG CHANG'S VISIT TO HAWARDEN.
Designed by Miss Teresina Hardaway.

reached nearly thirty thousand, including the four thousand dolls every one of which was specially dressed for the show. The new sixpences first appeared on the programme in 1883, and they have never failed since. The mere business of arranging the distribution of the toys must be no light matter, and Mr. Labouchere is heartily to be congratulated on the thoroughly effective fashion in which he has organised this most important and least-known side of the work.

With notable developments taking place in carriage construction during the 1890s, it was noticeable pre-grouping railway companies should find a receptive home with upscale titles to announce enhancements to the quality of new stock running on their routes. The notion of the American day-coach entered the railway and press vocabulary, and in a few short years, the term would be synonymous with high-class boat trains designed for first-class passengers spilling off Atlantic liners. (Illustrated London News Ltd/Mary Evans) but who will say there is not enterprise here? The authorities at London Bridge deserve the utmost credit for this enterprise, and it is for the public – so far as it lies in its power – to do all it can to maintain the service. Brilliantly lighted, comfortably warmed, and a maving alcove of cosiness, the 'corridor' has become one of the institutions of Folkestone. A journey to town, too, is made the more enjoyable by the courteous attention of the conductors, who are ever ready at the service of the 'voyagers'.[81]

Prior to amalgamation, LCDR was running alternative boat train services from Victoria to Dover. The company had a complicated development history especially in its early days and generally hampered by a shortage of money. Vicissitudes, nonetheless, by 1861 both SER and LCDR were running boat trains to Dover. The Chatham Company or Railway as company was also known was operating in a highly competitive market. By and large SER tended to carry more passengers than its rival resulting in a certain degree of resentment at board level. This remained at the heart of the two companies for many years having been forced to agree to an imposed Continental Agreement in 1865 (made retrospective to 1863) when LCDR took a share of mail train traffic, forcing the two organisations to pool arrangements for Continental passengers.[82] Following resumption of normal cross-channel transit after the end of Franco-Prussian hostilities, a significant increase in passenger traffic was seen. LCDR in 1874 experimented with six-wheeled sleeping cars whilst in July 1884 the company borrowed a Pullman car from LBSCR promoting a *Dover Pullman Boat Train* and effectively the first footings for elegant travel connecting with Wagon-Lits' recently launched *Orient Express* service from Paris. In 1892 LCDR acquired some of the former Midland Pullman drawing-room parlour cars to use on its cross-channel boat train. Impressively titled the *Dover Continental Pullman Boat Express*, the Pullman initiative only ran for two years, but coincided with the introduction of the company's new steamer *Invicta*, a vessel combining speed with luxury and raft of new facilities including promenade decks, electric lighting, and a first-class saloon with dedicated refreshment bar.[83]

By the late 1800s, Dover and Folkestone were key points for onward journeys in France and to the south of Europe. Both Calais and Boulogne were the arrival and departure points for many Wagon-Lits pan-European railway services as the company

CHARING CROSS STATION. FOLKESTONE EXPRESS.

S 5400   S.E.& C. RAILWAY PIER AND HARBOUR STATION, FOLKESTONE.

SECR Continental boat trains and cross-channel steamers featured prominently in a series of early-1900s postcards. The first from Tuck shows an SECR *Folkstone Car Train* from around 1906 at Charing Cross station. The company's specialist cars were later taken over by the Pullman company, and in 1919, the brake cars were rebuilt as parlour cars *Thistle* and *Albetross* with full length clerestories but seen as a design overhang of the Victorian and Edwardian era. A more modern approach to the Continental boat train is illustrated in the second SECR postcard image from a painting by F. Moore (a collective name given to a studio of artists operating in the early years of the twentieth century) of no. 145 4-4-0 Class locomotive heading up a port service. Distinctive 'Birdcage' brake coaches designed by Harry Wainwright and built at Ashford works, formed a recognisable sight in the early years of the merged company's mainline service operations. The third image shows the SECR railway pier and harbour station at Folkestone. The birdcage is again evident on the rear right-hand carriage. (*Opposite above*: Tuck DB; *Opposite below*: NRM/SSPL; *Above*: J&C McCutcheon Collection)

expressively expanded its many dedicated luxury catering and sleeping-car trains to connect with London boat trains. The British side too saw positive developments as the SER and the LCDR ultimately amalgamated as one new organisation.[84] The benefits of not competing on duplicate boat train services was clearly talked about in the press to the benefit of shareholders providing them with increased returns across the two rail businesses.[85] On New Year's Day in 1899 a newly merged company, the SECR Management Committee was created removing wasteful and damaging competition between the two previous companies that was so unpopular with travelling passengers. The combined organisation would ultimately seize luxury train operation opportunities full-heartedly, but it would be the best part of a decade before this was fully realized with a totally reinvigorated Pullman Company under British ownership.

To some extent this is somewhat surprising since many pre-grouping railway companies had upped their ocean special services, especially in dealing with prestige liner traffic, and those operating short-sea crossing and boat trains across the North Sea. Pre-grouping railway companies progressively turned towards marketing collaboration with shipping lines. LNWR pitched itself with a certain degree of panache as by early years of the new century, the company had Holyhead boat trains of a similar quality standard to its premier Anglo-Scottish expresses. For Holyhead ocean liner duties LNWR could also call upon its specialist Liverpool boat train stock.

Elsewhere, there were progressive carriage developments involving boat train operations. LSWR had dedicated open-style American boat trains, the Great Eastern Railway (GER) had bespoke first and third-class restaurant carriages for its Harwich North Sea crossings and the LBSCR ran Pullman cars for its Newhaven-Dieppe cross-channel sailings. Yet despite competitor activity the new SECR organisation was relatively slow off the mark developing comparable services; despite the Dover Straights being relatively close to London, reachable by rail in a shade under two hours and with a company track record of reasonably rapid boat trains having serviced Admiralty Pier since the late 1880s.

Dover was lagging behind competition. It was almost fifteen years before the port started to attract regular liner traffic. In 1903 HAPAG ships began to call at the port to and from Germany, followed in the next year by Belgium's Red Star Line as well as other shipping firms.[86] The decision to use Dover was a sound decision: Antwerp liners would stop at the port for British passengers before commencing their westbound North Atlantic crossings. The company issued a succession of marketing material including posters and postcards to promote its regular weekly service on the Antwerp, Dover and New York route much in conjunction with SECR and targeted at British and American audiences. On eastbound voyages, Red Star in April 1905 started to issue circular tickets from Dover. Embarking on one of their liners, passengers could spend at least ten hours on board during the Antwerp run. Belgian State

An LNWR American Boat Special calls at Holyhead, rather than Liverpool, connecting with a White Star liner. To shorten railway journey times, both American Line and White Star started to call at the North Wales port, where the railway company retained a major interest, reducing the distance from Liverpool by seventy-four miles and sea time by a further three hours. Holyhead was always associated with busy Anglo-Irish sailings, and by this time, the North Wales region had become a major tourism destination in its own right, but also as a convenient link for an Irish diaspora who had made it in the United States intent on visiting the old country. Yet like Cunard's short-lived Fishguard stopover, the port's potential as an international liner port was curtailed by the Great War. Holyhead, ever since, has remained the most important Irish Sea port providing the shortest crossing to Dublin's conurbation. (NRM/SSPL)

Railways' boat trains met passengers for the return to Dover via Brussels and Ostend. The cost of the first-class package was £2 10s inclusive.[87] Around 1909, SECR responded to customer demands (and LBSCR competition from around the corner at Victoria), by ordering six first-class *British* style buffet and parlour carriages from the Pullman Company. Pullman writer Antony Ford makes the observation 'the extraordinary extent to which luxury travel had progressed following the acquisition of the English Pullman Company in 1907, by Mr Davidson Dalziel, M.P. for Brixton, as he then was, Chairman of the Pullman Company and President du Conseil of the Wagon-lits Company, is perhaps a matter of some surprise to the average person'.[88] Dalziel's intervention though was crucial in founding a brand that became synonymous with British luxury train travel, and forever closely associated with the country's premier boat train services. From the 1880s a big luxury market fermented established from a Pullman boat train footprint.

Whilst both the SECR and Red Star invested considerable resources in their efforts to promote Dover as a trans-Atlantic

Little surprise the Red Star Line and the newly merged SECR railway company should not promote the Dover to New York route to British audiences. SECR already operated luxury Continental bound boat trains, including a Pullman provision, so the relationship with Red Star seemed a natural extension to business affairs to attract prosperous passengers. This 1912 poster suggests the Belgian shipping line saw themselves as a major player on the North Atlantic scene (being part of the IMM consortium) with a quartet of medium-sized steamers providing regular Saturday departures. In the same year, the Red Star liner *Finland* made front page news taking 164 US athletes to the Stockholm Olympic Games.

Although the company was American owned, it played on its distinctive cultural links to set itself apart from other French, German and British shipping firms. Red Star liners compounded the boundaries of European society by reflecting the social divides found elsewhere in Britain and America – their first-class facilities were still small, contained worlds – but they played to the gallery with a more relaxed travelling style including a fondness for evening entertainment and a diverse international food and drink cuisine offered to guests. Aside more prosperous travellers, Red Star Line, as well as their French counterparts (German lines HAPAG and NDL had acquired a rather tarnished reputation for their steerage-class passenger facilities) would also take its share of emigrant business across the Atlantic to New York, Philadelphia, and later, to Canada. Typical of boat train arrivals is this emigrant train pulled by a Belgian locomotive at the Rijnkaai station in Antwerp. (*Opposite*: NRM/SSPL; *Above*: Collection City of Antwerp, MAS) liner port, the position was not to last as IMM, as a policy decision consolidated its shipping operations preferring to use Southampton with its critical mass of customer focused railway company owned facilities. Dover's position as a blue water passenger embarkation port disappeared for the best part of ninety years, until the end of the twentieth century when the UK and the British Isles as a destination itself became one of largest cruise markets in the world.

To those SECR customers in the know, they simply would not have been amazed at the quality of travelling developments taking place in the years before the Great War. The *Southern Belle* was now in full flight which included individual Pullman cars added to LBSCR's Newhaven boat trains. But a fully-fledged Pullman boat train on the shortest crossing between Britain and the Continent was something new. When SECR's Pullman cars entered service in March 1910 they ran in the company's own crimson-lake (maroon) livery. The boat expresses were typically hauled by Wainwright D and later rebuilt 4-4-0 E1 class locomotives and run with dedicated pair sets (to create a four car Pullman train) and composite second and third-class brakes or as buffet-parlour pairs sandwiched between a head and tail of ordinary non-corridor stock. As Bucknall commented the new Pullman cars 'were a great success and at once became a lasting component of the leading boat train services to both Folkestone and Dover'.[89] By the eve of the First World War much of the intensively used SECR Pullman stock had seen better days. The fleet of fifteen cars was withdrawn and placed in storage for the duration of hostilities before being sold to the Pullman Company in 1919, partially refurbished and returned for operation. There were other new Pullman cars entering the company's carriage fleet, but the company maintained a policy of having permanently fixed first, second and third-class boat train Pullmans with standard stock. In the years before grouping SECR offered eight separate trains for boat train duties continuing this practice into the Southern years. The routes to Dover would not change until the post-war period when SECR boat trains started to use the old SER route but using the LCDR part of London Victoria station – shared with the LBSCR – becoming the preferred starting point with longer platforms. Gradual improvements followed although journey times could take much longer as boat trains had to take circuitous and slow routes in some cases. Despite handicaps passengers were prepared to put up with mild inconvenience.

On sea there were also rapid developments. SECR began promoting its London to the Riviera service as 'the only route

These two atmospheric postcard images highlight SECR Kent boat trains in similar port surroundings. No. 160 and no. 157 (shown in another image) were frequent cross-channel boat train performers. In the more populated shore-side setting, a lack of motorised vehicles probably dates the image from the early 1900s. (*Above and below*: J&C McCutcheon Collection)

with a sea passage of 1 hour'.[90] *The Queen* was introduced in June 1903 was the first cross-channel ship with steam turbine propulsion ushering in a new era of fast and efficient vessels. By 1911 a raft of new turbine steamers entered operations on the narrow routes of the English Channel. On SECR's Dover-Calais run, *Riviera* entered service in June 1911 with *Engadine* appearing in in September. The latest steamers complemented the company's new Pullmans. Before the First World War, the company ordered another batch of geared turbine steamers for the Dover-Calais route. *Biarritz* and *Maid of Orleans* after war-time duties were eventually released around 1920.

Newhaven Services

Throughout the Victorian period, the port of Newhaven was not part of the Continental 'sampler or excursionist' market. Despite being considered the less expensive of cross-channel boat train lines, Newhaven-Dieppe, since the mid-1850s, had established itself as a preferred route attracting a superior Continental traveller. For a start, it offered an integrated port and rail facility; customs and passport offices formed part of the London & Paris Hotel situated alongside the station halt with its direct access to daily steamer crossings.[91] In 1862 Thomas Cook concluded a deal with Brighton company launching new Parisian and Swiss expeditions the following year.[92] At the same time LBSCR together with Compagnie des Chemins de fer de l'Ouest (CF de l'Ouest), often referred to as l'Ouest or the Ouesté Railway, who covered the western part of France, were granted powers to operate their own Newhaven-Dieppe ships. By the 1870s, the route had become popular with international travellers as the two companies took delivery of a succession of paddle steamers.[93] Two new paddlers – the last of their type – were ordered by the company in anticipation of extra business for the 1889 Paris Exhibition; this proving a sound business decision as the event attracted an extra 107,500 tourists, and a figure in terms of visitor numbers, holding up well in following years.[94] By the late 1880s, LBSCR's engrained relationships challenged the south-east port routes offering faster cross-channel steamer crossings in less than three and a half hours but also trialling new screw propulsion. *Seine* was the first French-built screw-driven steamer, incorporating a more modern look with a cruiser type stern, coming onboard in August 1891. Similarly, *Seaford* completed in the summer of 1894, was LBSCR's first screw-driven vessel but she had a short life having been rammed and sunk in fog by a French ship in August 1895. A replacement vessel *Sussex* quickly followed the next year.[95]

In addition to well-appointed ships, by utilising its Brighton Pullman cars on boat trains, LBSCR could harness the potential of tapping into lucrative passengers who were prepared to pay extra for the privilege of refined services. From the early 1890s the company increased its Brighton line Pullman car fleet and was in the enviable position of deploying specialist Pullman cars for many years on its premier Newhaven operations. LBSCR in order to attract custom offered 'a series of tours to the South of France and Italy at exceptionally low fares' for the Riviera Season via their Newhaven-Dieppe route.[96] All of this effort hardly surprising since the Riviera, next to Paris, was the most popular French destination for British travellers.[97]

From the end of November 1904 LBSCR and PLM trialled a daytime through carriage service to Paris connecting with Riviera expresses at Gare Lyon. The scenic Dieppe-Paris route was considered to be particularly attractive affording passengers a 'most picturesque railway journey through the glorious valley of the Seine, and also of the grand old Norman city of Rouen'.[98] LBSCR's cross-channel steamers made rapid advances sealing the crossing between the two ports in a little over three hours. The company introduced its first steam turbine vessel *Arundel* in June 1900 complementing its *Sussex* and *Brighton* vessels, and a second triple-screw turbine steamer

LBSCR H1
4-4-2 Class no. 40 is hauling a Pullman four car Newhaven boat train at Balham in the years before the First World War. LBCR's livery matched its *Southern Belle* Brighton Pullman service in contrast to SECR's crimson lake Pullman liveried Continental boat trains. (STEAM)

Dieppe by mid-decade. The Newhaven-Dieppe route now operated with a class steamer fleet reflecting the quality of its Pullman boat train rail connections, and in position to mount a serious assault on the first-class traveller market.

Quite naturally fierce rivalries existed amongst pre-grouping railway companies and on both sides of the channel. The order of the day for increasingly adept organisations was to galvanise new business opportunities by utilizing their rail networks for greater passenger usage. The provisioning of elite and superior first-class passenger rail/sea/rail services were set to become important elements of pre-grouping railway company operation in the years up to the Great War. Mid- and western channel routes though had some downsides because of longer sea crossings. In rough weather, fast steamers carrying mail contracts were known not to hang around, and a pleasant travelling experience could not always be guaranteed.

LBSCR was adept at partnering with French railway companies. The old l'Ouest organisation, despite being financially strapped, worked hard with LBSCR to promote the London Victoria, Newhaven, Dieppe and Paris Gare St. Lazare axis. l'Ouest had two principal Paris stations at St. Lazare and Montparnasse providing routes to Normandy and Brittany. In January 1909 the company was absorbed into the Chemins de fer l'État (ETAT) and the first round of French railway state-ownership. The company was often referred to as Réseau de L'État, the State Network, whilst in the British press the new organisation was referred to as the French State Railway or simply ETAT. By the eve of the First World War, the sea passage between Newhaven-Dieppe took a shade under three hours for the sixty-four-mile crossing representing the shortest route between London and Paris. A day-time transit between the two capital cities took eight hours with the company providing restaurant corridor trains between Dieppe and Paris. Around 1913 the route was shortened by twenty miles with the construction of a line via Pontoise instead of the old route through Rouen.[99]

LBSCR and ETAT introduced three turbine steamers (the first by a French company) for the joint Newhaven-Dieppe route. *Newhaven* was delivered in May 1911; *Paris* was added as another turbine steamer but introducing a thoroughly modern looking image with the first cross-channel steamer to incorporate a cruiser stern in December 1911, whilst *Rouen* was added in September 1912.

Newhaven-Dieppe's cross-channel steamers mirrored LBSCR's Pullman approaches applying a similar level of quality to the interior of their steamers. *The Tatler* reported on the most comfortable of travel facilities:

> The *Rouen's* fine saloons have been most luxuriously fitted and furnished, a special feature being the beautiful inlaid woodwork which has been introduced into the scheme of decoration. The seats and the berths have been upholstered in red plush, and the effect produced is both striking and artistic. The saloons and cabins are steam-heated and electrically lit and the ventilation is carried out on the latest principles, electric fans being introduced into all the cabins.[100]

Arrangements had been put in place by LBSCR and ETAT to implement further accelerations to services, but these were to be held up by war.[101] Earlier in 1907, l'Ouest had introduced an upscale traveller train de marée (boat train) to complement LBSCR's long-established use of Pullman stock for its Newhaven boat trains which continued up until grouping.[102] LBSCR heavily promoted the region's picturesque qualities described as 'delightful Normandy scenery' that brought tourists 'into communication with the holiday resorts of Western France, some fashionable and gay, others quiet and modest. Dieppe is a first-class sea-side resort, offering the visitor the best of bathing and amusements, including a first-class casino and golf links'. The Normandy coast also offered English visitors alternative and quieter coastal resorts, pleasant holiday places as well as inland of Dieppe a 'wealth of delightful country scenery'.[103]

Innovation was a key theme amongst Edwardian railway operators with the Brighton company co-operating with French railway partners to provide circular tours covering Brittany and the historic Loire Valley. The station at St. Lazare became a kind of destination in its own right due to its proximity to the homes of French impressionist artists who used its moody location for inspiration. The station had a reputation as a place of pilgrimage for artists awed by the station roof's filtered light and its bellowing wafts of locomotive steam and smoke.[104] But it was the French capital's other main line termini and their access to the warm weathers of the south of France and Spain attracting most railway passenger focus.

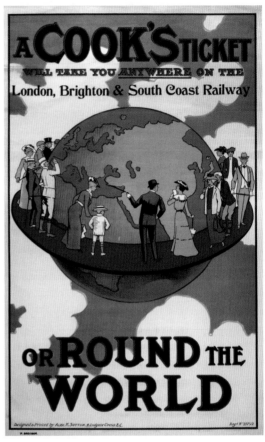

The first of the two Thomas Cook and LBSCR posters from 1904 demonstrates the partnership arrangements made to secure prosperous travellers to visit the well-worn tourists haunts of the Riviera and Italy. The second poster is a perfect example of the approaches adopted by international tourism providers at the time, as demonstrated with the earlier SECR poster. 'Phileas Fogg and Passepartout's' adventures, some thirty years earlier, had been well and truly engrained in travel culture by the early twentieth century. Thomas Cook was well positioned to co-ordinate such travel schedules around the globe with its own ticketing and hotel coupon arrangements. (Thomas Cook)

Southampton Services

Cross-channel passengers also had mid-channel choices with LSWR providing Cherbourg and Le Havre French services and to the Channel Islands. *Normandy* and *Brittany* were the company's first commissioned paddle steamers in 1863–64. Waterloo based LSWR had a long-established track record of running premier class expresses for its Southampton (and later Plymouth) ocean express boat trains since this period. On developing cross-channel traffic, the company was mindful of the value of LBSCR's part Pullman hauled Newhave-Dieppe service in attracting high-end customers. LSWR which had provided a basic form of service to Le Havre since around 1847, countered in the early 1890s, utilising new ocean liner carriages for its Southampton crossings providing prosperous passengers with improved facilities at a port it owned. Not content with a time-honoured expertise of running ocean boat trains, LSWR in late-Victorian times was able to mount a serious assault on mid-cross-channel steamer traffic with more efficient triple-expansion engine screw-driven steamers.[105] An impressive looking Continental booking office building including a separate Transit Shed was also built in the outer dock providing vessels fast access to the Itchen and Southampton Water. Cross-channel services were greatly improved as the company introduced *Columbia* and *Alma* to its Le Havre service whilst *Frederica* was returned to Channel Islands duties raising the competitive bar with GWR.[106] With the combined operations, LSWR according to the *Bournemouth Guardian* offered the 'best and most comfortable boats'.[107] By the 1894 summer season, LSWR operated an accelerated and improved daily service to the Channel Islands with new steamers *Lydia* and *Stella*. In promoting the company's 'Royal Mail Route', advertising extolled all-in-one travel arrangements noting 'Express Boat Trains are taken direct into the Southampton Docks alongside the Steamers and their luggage placed on board without any trouble or additional expense.'[108]

In July 1898 LSWR introduced *Vera* as a spare vessel for their Le Havre and Channel Islands services. Railway companies started to mirror maritime developments taking place with large ocean-going vessels, as better propelled, faster and more efficient steamers worked the channel crossings in tandem with speedier and more frequent boat trains. Until late-Victorian times, cross-channel steamers were not large, characteristically around 1,500 tons, and prone to the stormy waters of the English Channel. Typically, *Princess Ena* which appeared in 1906 operating on the Southampton-St. Malo route, but by September 1910 she was joined by LSWR's new generation of turbine steamers when the *Caesarea* was introduced following with *Sarnia* in April 1911. Travel advice trips contained tips on how to avoid falling out of bunks on night crossings, but the company's next batch of turbine steamers were especially designed for night passages. The company's *Normannia* and *Hantonia* entered service in 1912 replacing the 1894 *Alma* and *Columbia* pair. Southampton, one of Britain's three great ocean ports, it connected with liners leaving France with a direct night-time Le Havre service served by a fast, late evening London boat train departure as well as providing a direct link from the port to Paris which appealed to many travellers from the Midlands and the north of England without having to incur an additional overnight's port accommodation. LSWR's turbine steamers possessed 'cabin de luxe' accommodation which also appealed to Cook's upscale customers.[109] Whilst France

The Channel Islands poster acknowledges they were not just a British preserve, but a popular destination amongst French travellers. With the islands' close proximity to the European mainland, the company was able to use its coastal ports partnering with CTN to maximise upscale holiday excursion traffic.

7. **Les Chemins de Fer Français** (Ouest-Etat)
Le 8103 — Transatlantique Paris-Cherbourg de la Cᵗᵉ Internationale des Wagons-Lits - Machine Nº 230.160

Photo Logan

The publishing house Neurdiein, based at 44 Rue Letellier in Paris, were arguably the largest producer of postcards in France. Its distinctive trademark was ND Phot with the company behind many shots of classic French expresses. The first photo shows one of ETAT's luxurious boat trains in Ouest livery running with Wagon-Lits restaurant cars taken in 1908. The second image also Ouest liveried 2818 - serie 2701/2820 built in 1908 shows the locomotive hauling a *Train Transatlantique* deluxe carriage boat train. These express services were used for Cherbourg liner arrivals and departures and for meeting LSWR's premier Southampton cross-channel steamers. In the years before the First World War combined LSWR/ETAT trains were pretty luxurious affairs noting both regular trans-Atlantic traffic – many liners calling at both Cherbourg and Southampton – and also for principal cross-channel passenger steamers. (*Above and below*: French Railways Society)

LES GRANDS TRAINS FRANÇAIS
11   Chemins de fer de l'Etat.
Train transatlantique Paris-Cherbourg. — ND Phot.

undoubtedly had its attractions, so did the Channel Islands. The combined ETAT rail organisation with direct Paris links had the islands in its sights, promoting destinations in Normandy, further west in Brittany as well as running ocean liner boat trains in and out of Cherbourg.

Before the Great War, LSWR ordered a pair of new steamers for the Southampton-Channel Islands service. Due to war-time necessities only one vessel was built. *Lorina* was finally released by the Admiralty as a troopship entering service with Southern Railway livery some five years after she was ordered. Crossing the Channel would have to be put on the back burner for the duration of the war. LSWR and Thomas Cook promoted its cheapest and most comfortable night route aboard the well-appointed Le Havre triple-screw turbine mail steam ships. For British and American visitors, the Thomas Cook organisation was particularly adept at meeting the needs of a discriminating audience. Normandy's resorts were now extensively promoted in the summer months and part of this early tourist packaging similarly included working closely with the Thomas Cook organisation with the initiation of collaborative advertising. Part of the material would be promoted as LSWR but using the same stock images would also be branded Thomas Cook representing particularly good examples of early joined up marketing.

In 1913 with the addition of a publicity machine based next door to general manager Herbert Walker's office, LSWR 'immediately initiated an attractive and intelligent programme of tours in northern France'.[110] The French Channel resorts of Deauville, Trouville and the Normandy coast and countryside attracted large numbers of bourgeois visitors from Britain, Europe and the New World in the in the late nineteenth century. They would be drawn to Normandy by the international appeal of French artist Claude Monet whose powerful impressionist work characterised the region's verdant pastures. Normandy was reflected in imagination and reality; his visual imagery extolling luxury and exclusivity in typically Gallic sceneries making the north-west region of France a popular tourist destination appealing to a new, predominantly conformist tourist. Coastal resorts progressively found themselves as bastions and enclaves of upper middle-class respectability driven by a steady tourist flow, stimulated by the combined promotional efforts of both shipping lines and railway companies. The latter did much to link Paris and the regional centres to Monet's Normandy as the railway had reached the coast in 1871.[111] Large numbers of 'elite and professional visitors' were ready to immerse themselves in the region's famous landscapes becoming one of tourism's first orchestrated 'theme parks' where a destination construction of illusion and reality wrestled along with each other. Indeed, the land surrounding Monet's Giverny garden was doctored to avoid the railway's intrusion. Robert Herbert captured the mood and tourist gaze admirably describing Monet's subjects as becoming 'integrated with images of nature as park-land, that is, as vacationland'.[112]

LSWR provided a Southampton to Cherbourg service three days per week – two in winter – as well as dedicated freight only sailings for diary and vegetable goods. Cherbourg though never achieved the same inter-war prominence as Le Havre as it was twice as far away from Paris. However, despite the distance, Cherbourg had considerable liner traffic in the late nineteenth century. It addition, it was the preferred cross-channel port for Queen Victoria. Making her first visit to Lucerne in Switzerland in August 1868, Victoria and her family crossed the English Channel on the royal yacht and then took the Imperial train to Paris – the city she had first seen in 1855 and had dubbed 'the most beautiful and gayest of cities'. As Duff records 'to this route she remained faithful for the rest of her life' conferring on the port 'great respectability'.[113] The following day the royal party left Paris aboard the Imperial train again for the 323 mile journey over Chemin de Fer de l'Est metals to the Swiss border.[114]

Despite LSWR's reduced sailing schedules the Cherbourg route attracted considerable numbers of tourists attracted to western Normandy pursuing specialist holidays such as individual and group sketching parties and rambling. Aside Cherbourg large numbers of tourists were drawn to Brittany's upscale destinations using LSWR's Southampton to St. Malo sailings. The region formed a great holiday ground for the fashionably inclined, but was a cost-effective destination attracting boat loads of adventurous tourists – men and women –armed with their bicycles. A small sum could go a long way for a holiday vacation of a month or two in the land of the Bretons, described as a 'race of hardy agriculturalists and fisher folk'. Brittany was also seen as a seductive but primitive place as represented in a far more unsophisticated pre-industrialised age by Paul Gauguin's new impressionist and simplistic art styles. Whilst Normandy had its smart seaside resorts of St. Malo, Paramé and Dinard together with the far west's isolated settlement of

Pont-Aven with its rustic artists' colony, fuelled by strong cider and cheap rooms, was considered an ideal and appealing journey's end for British tourists. One Irish visitor described the Breton town with its American expats community of painters as resembling 'a gigantic studio'. The region, however, in time slowly succumbed to tourism development. Denis Donoghue writing in *The Railway Magazine* captured something of the period noting the region's health-giving potential and its 'light hearted gaiety, the merry children digging in the golden sand, the jolly bathers splashing in the waves, and the universal holiday "atmosphere" captivate the visitor's fancy immediately'.[115]

Cross-channel business was brisk. *The Railway Magazine* commented on 'the rapidly growing number of people who annually leave home for a sojourn abroad'.[116] Social historian Professor Harold Perkin similarly concurred with overseas travel trends by stating in 1913 that 'over three quarters of a million Britons left the country for Europe, most of them middle-class tourists going on holiday'.[117] Growth in the number of foreign trips was aided by a continuing decline in the birth rate amongst the middle-classes leaving more money (and time) for life's luxuries.[118] Post-war, crossing the channel became a smart affair again providing ample room for Continental service extensions by the early 1920s. And with grouping a new smart image prevailed as Southern Railway adopted the LSWR green livery for carriages, whilst the wooden sides of the former SECR Pullman cars, like their LBSCR brethren, were painted in umber with cream upper panels.[119] The company in July 1925 also unveiled their new King Arthur Class locomotives to the press – their largest locomotives yet – designed for hauling prestigious Continental boat trains.[120]

Weymouth Services

Further along the coast, Weymouth's cross-channel operations had a long and protracted history involving a variety of parties including the local municipal authority responsible for the harbour, rival LSWR operations and the Weymouth & Channel Islands Steam Packet Company Limited who ran the Royal Mail Packet Service. In 1889, the Great Western took over the service with the first sailing to the islands on 21 July, together with a commitment to provide new steamers replacing ageing Steam Packet paddlers. Thus, began an era of a thoroughly modern service where harbour facilities were vastly improved including the construction of a new landing stage, dredging providing deeper water access for new vessels and an efficient passenger transfer mechanism between ships, boat trains and the rest of the railway system. GWR offered a direct Paddington-Weymouth route, with the company's new trio of twin-screw vessels – *Lynx, Antelope* and *Gazelle* (known as *Lynx* class steamers) – and cut three hours off total passage time to the islands. A direct Bristol boat train was also offered with connections to Trowbridge and Swindon, but this was eventually suspended some years later through lack of demand.[121] The new steamer *Lynx* made her inaugural run from Weymouth on Sunday, 4 August 1889 described as an historic event, since it was serviced by the first boat train to use the Harbour Tramway. The train departed London at 9.15 the previous evening arriving at the new Quay station on time.[122] Improved services were required since visitor interest in the Channel Islands was growing. Ward and Lock produced a series of travel brochures including an 'Illustrated Guide to, and Popular History of, the Channel Islands' in the 1880s. The aim, simply, was 'to increase this appreciation and to furnish the tourist with such information as shall enable him to utilise his time in the islands to the best advantage'.[123]

With longer sea-time operations from Southampton to the Channel Islands (and St. Malo), LSWR came under considerable competitive pressure from GWR, even though their operations were long-established. In fact, LSWR had been instrumental in new developments introducing the first screw propulsion steamer *Diana* in 1876, and with *Dora* in 1889, the first vessel to be driven by a triple-expansion engine and lit by electricity.[124] Channel Islands rivalry between the two railway companies was now widespread leading to a succession of new steamers crossing the western channel. As previously noted, LSWR ordered a trio of fast new cross-channel ships – *Frederica, Lydia* and *Stella* – delivered in 1890 whilst the Great Western countered the next year ordering *Ibex* to match LSWR's new trio of vessels. Thus, according maritime historian B.L. Jackson, *Ibex's* arrival in September 1891 'added to the competition, each company improving its train service or clipping a few minutes off the voyage'.[125] The Great Western kept a close brief on LSWR's Southampton cross-channel steamer traffic. By running a competitor steamer route from Weymouth, GWR was able to introduce two new vessels designed specifically for daylight services. *Roebuck* and *Reindeer* were added to Channel Islands operations in May and June 1897 respectively with both vessels being improved versions of the earlier *Ibex*.

By the end of the Victorian era, Great Western's Weymouth-Channel Islands provisions had a succession of specially designed express steamers operating across the western channel. *Roebuck* and *Reindeer* possessed 150 first and seventy-six second-six passenger berths.[126] First-class saloons and sleeping accommodation amidships were fitted with electric lighting designed according to the *Isle of Wight Times* to provide 'passengers with the maximum of comfort'.[127] An improved Paddington boat train service also came in the summer of 1897 with services departing London at 8.50 am and arriving at Weymouth Quay at 1.10 pm. Following rapid transit of passengers and cargo, the steamer sailed just twenty minutes later.[128] Passenger numbers undoubtedly increased providing Great Western with an advantage over its LSWR rival. An end to an unofficial 'Race to the Islands' came in March 1899 with the *Stella* disaster when the LSWR vessel struck Auguiere Rock on the Casquets in patchy fog with the loss of 105 lives.

From 1 October 1899 there was an amalgamation of interests as GWR and LSWR decided on running a joint service. B.L. Jackson takes up the story:

> During the summer each company would run six times a week: from Southampton by night and by day from Weymouth with both companies sailing to the mainland by day. Tickets would be interchangeable, and the gross receipts (less deductions) would be placed in a common fund and divided.

Over the winter months the GWR and LSWR would run only on three nights a week from the mainland and alternate days from the islands.[129]

Whilst cross-channel sea racing might be over, in the early 1900s the Great Western put considerable efforts to improving its West Country permanent way. Speeded-up services also had a beneficial knock on as new express trains ran to meet Weymouth steamers. *St. James's Gazette* reported in July 1901:

> The train leaving Paddington at 9.35 am arrived at Weymouth Junction in three hours and 33 minutes, averaging about 48 miles an hour, exclusive of stoppages, for the whole journey. This particular train is run in connection with the boat service to the Channel Islands, and yesterday the Great Western steamer *Ibex* made the passage. In this connection it may be stated that the

Great Western and the South-Western Companies are sharing the cross-Channel traffic between them, and that during the summer months the Great Western boats will cross during the day and the South-Western during the night.[130]

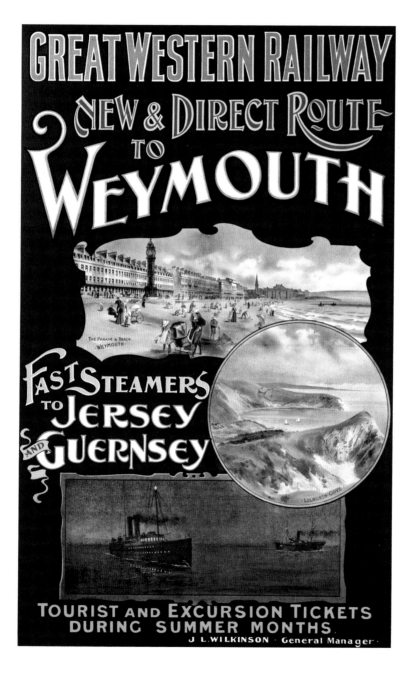

This unsigned poster from 1905 indicates the marketing efforts behind the Great Western's attempts to cultivate Channel Islands summer-time visitors to its Weymouth based steamers. Aside dedicated boat trains providing direct access to Paddington, GWR also leveraged its famous *Cornish Riviera Limited* for cross-channel duties with carriages at the rear of the train slipped for Weymouth and the Channel Islands.

This was all aided by the attractiveness of Weymouth as a holiday resort. GWR actively promoted the destination in upscale press publications at the turn of the twentieth century as the English Naples. Stopping at Weymouth for a day or two became an intrinsic part of a Channel Islands visit and all part of the company's business strategy (like in Cornwall) to encourage travel within Britain rather than visiting overseas.

Plymouth Services

Whilst Plymouth's primary role was the development of international liner traffic, Great Western with its Millbay resources, offered the potential of cross-channel traffic especially with Brittany, a region geographically and culturally remote but a destination that had much in common with Cornwall. GWR felt it could complement its *Cornish Riviera* offer with a distinctive and mystical landscape in France. Furthermore, Brittany as a Celtic language speaking region offered period travellers a foretaste of a fascinating destination. The company established a Plymouth route to Brest and also stops at other smaller harbours around western Brittany providing a passenger and cargo capacity especially for agricultural produce finding a ready-made English market. This had come on the back of a short-lived Plymouth, Channel Islands & Brittany Steamship Co. operation, which introduced a twin-screw vessel *Channel Queen* carrying around 100 passengers for a Plymouth-Guernsey-Jersey-St. Brieuc service in September 1895. Unfortunately, the ship hit rocks on 1 February 1898 with the loss of twenty-one lives.[131] New facilities came on stream at Plymouth in 1903 as a new pontoon was built allowing passengers better access to GWR's French steamer services.[132] By May 1909 the company was actively promoting holiday traffic to Brest with its fast Plymouth boat trains and accompanying steamer crossings. The GWR produced accompanying literature drawing on close parallels between Cornwall and France's most western region. As railway historian Dr Alan Bennett echoed:

> Overall, Cornish and Breton landscapes and cultural traditions bore close resemblances, thus the iconography and thematic structure of the literature, legend and artwork reflected shares perspectives best expressed in the celebrations of their antiquities, dramatic coastal cliff-scapes and the numerous fishing communities.[133]

In a modern context, period travel literature portrayed Cornwall and Brittany as destinations with complementary attributes. Land's End – Pointe du Raz and St. Michael's Mount – Mont Saint-Michel (technically in Normandy) became similar tourism hot spots but shared similar visitor qualities. Both regions were alluring and mysterious places but, most importantly, very accessible. Notwithstanding traveller demand, there were other commercial forces at play behind GWR's investment at building passenger and freight business in Brittany as the port authorities at Brest in the pre-war years were making significant overtures to shipping lines to attract trans-Atlantic liner mail and passenger traffic planned at the expense of Cherbourg and Le Havre. Such moves, it was envisaged, would enhance visitor interest in western districts and would offer an alternative (if longer) route to the French capital. This was based on thinking around Normandy where trendy coastal resorts had grown immensely in popularity, particularly amongst upscale visitors from both sides of the Atlantic during the Edwardian period.[134] Brittany, on the other hand, offered potential tourists an appealing destination with an opportunity for the broadening middle-classes to experience new sights and to sample pastoral and nostalgic rural representations less likely to be seen in other parts of France. From GWR's perspective Brittany provided alternative travel opportunities utilising existing services but despite its best endeavours everything did not go to plan. The company produced an arresting poster for the Plymouth and Brest steamer service based on a painting by Dorothy George of two Breton girls clothed in national costumes which according to Wilson was considered as 'particularly charming' standing out from the rest of period publicity material.[135] However, by around 1911 a Plymouth-Nantes operation, which had been transferred from Weymouth, together with the Plymouth-Brest service had ceased due to lack of trade.

In the later years of Victoria's reign there was a significant expansion in what could be broadly termed as the luxury train express. In Europe this was traced back to early 1880s where they not only linked capital cities, but from this book's perspective in a profusion of boat train services providing direct links to the Continent from Britain. There were many British visitors who originated their journeys in London and then crossed the English Channel or the North Sea by steamer using a variety of routes. At the time, there were also correspondingly increased numbers of American citizens disembarking from a profusion of Atlantic liners at French, Belgian, Dutch and German ports. Whilst Pullman might have struggled to gain a foothold in Britain, it faced an uphill task in Europe as a series of luxury train operations were recognised by an enterprising and wealthy Belgian engineer and train enthusiast George Nagelmackers who founded Compagnie Internationale des Wagon-Lits (CIWL) in 1872. Often a shortened form was used for English speaking audiences – the International Sleeping Car Company – but in time Wagon-Lits and CIWL became the adopted trading names. For the purpose of this book Wagon-Lits is the preferred company description rather than CIWL. Nagelmackers, like Midland Railway's James Allport, had spent several years in America observing Pullman's operations at close hand and keen to bring the same standards of refinement to a patchwork of countries, states and railway systems criss-crossing Europe. His first luxury train offering were coaches initially used on local train services between Paris and the spa resort of Ostend, and then Cologne to Vienna. Company operations grew so by 1883 his company would become the driving force behind what was to become the Continent's most famous, legendary and indulgent train. He retained a particular affiliation to Ostend aided by SER's Dover and Belgian cross-channel steamers. This really established the town placing it on the tourism map alongside other French northern seaside towns as alternative fashionable places to be seen in summer 'frequented by the aristocracy and occasional royalty' whilst 'attracting a wealthy clientele from all over Europe'. The resort became a bustling leisure centre with a new built infrastructure of luxury hotels, restaurants, casinos, concert halls, parks and promenades. Professor Orlando Figes in his book The Europeans (2019) described Ostend 'as one of those seaside towns once made fashionable by emperors and kings but democratized by the railway'.[136] Ostend and Brussels had been reached by railway in 1838 being the first Continental railway to be impacted by British tourist travel.[137] The slightly cooler temperatures to be found on the northern coasts were appealing to women at the time.

With much activity focused on the French capital, the route between Paris, Munich and Vienna developed into one of the busiest forcing railway companies to innovate offering dining and sleeping cars and thus removing the necessity for meal stops and improving journey times. Into this grove stepped Nagelmackers whose company created the legendary luxury train known as the *Orient Express* where fact, fiction and folklore were always closely entwined. By the end of the nineteenth century affluent American tourists were arriving in their droves aboard the Atlantic Trade's 'floating palaces' stepping off at a succession of British and European ports. By the early 1900s, the American Express Company had begun to develop a network of offices in European capitals to cater for their prosperous clients who wanted to explore the mysteries of the Continent in a degree of comfort and style and prepared to pay for the privilege of so doing. Nagelmackers latched on to these opportunities by creating a moving hotel on wheels copying designs and services offered by Europe's grandest land-based hotels. Wagon-Lits did not care to replicate the designs of the American Pullman cousins with their large open seating areas but preferred to modify carriages to appeal to the tastes of well-to-do European travellers. Such were their standards they appealed to royalty, the rich, famous and the glamorous alike representing a first age of the VIP and the modern spectacle of celebrity culture. In 1892 the company expanded its Paris-Istanbul franchise building the Pera Palace Hotel in Istanbul followed by a second, the Therapia Summer Palace, through a subsidiary business operation that brought in a succession of other luxury hotels, all coming under the Nagelmackers' organisational umbrella and proving very nearly to be his undoing. By 1895 the Cimiez Riviera Palace Hotel was eventually opened, setting a seal on hospitality led operations. Naturally all of these advances seeped into boat train development.

CHAPTER 2

The Inter-War Years: A Golden Age of Travel

Dover Straights Services

At the beginning of the inter-war period well-established and regular combined ferry and railway operations between Britain, France and Belgium had been in place for over seventy years with pre-grouping railway companies doing their best to provide better and speedier cross-channel experiences. As we have seen first-class services were also founded to convey prosperous passengers with better travelling experiences as could be enjoyed elsewhere in Britain. By the twentieth century there were consistent demands for more luxurious cross-channel boat trains particularly as embarkation points were overcrowded. This included the existing station facilities on Dover's Admiralty Pier which was prone to closure during heavy seas. SECR in 1906 submitted plans to build a new station terminus on reclaimed land on the pier's north side. The reclamation project is said to have been one of the great civil engineering projects before the Great War. When legislation to form Southern Railway was introduced in 1921, it was logical for the new organisation to base their south-east boat train/ferry operations at Dover; the Straights provided the shortest Continental cross-channel crossing plus had the benefit of a spanking new enclosed railway terminus.

Author Andrew Martin says whilst 'Southern trains may not have travelled over long distances; they could take a running jump at the sea.'[1] And this the company most certainly did as they consolidated their London based boat train operations at Victoria – the station terminus provided up to seven weekday services linking England, France, Belgium and the Netherlands. Aside Dover-Calais and Dover-Ostend, Southern managed other southeast cross-channel routes from Folkestone-Boulogne and Folkestone-Flushing, Newhaven-Dieppe and western channel crossings from Southampton to Cherbourg, St. Malo and Channel Islands routes. New boat train carriage stock known as the 'Continentals' appeared in 1921 on the Straights routes equipped with Pullman gangways as

Dover Marine railway station opened for civilian use in January 1919, although it had been used for military traffic during the First World War. Built on a twelve-acre reclaimed site, the terminus station comprised a cavernous steel and glass roof some 800 feet in length with two 60-foot wide concrete island platforms. Station signage was in both English and French. The second image shows the intricate line arrangements into the new station complex. (*Above and below*: J&C McCutcheon Collection)

SECR were of the view that Pullman car usage would continue with the merged organisation. In fact, the inclusion of two Pullman cars in the rake (depending on seasonal traffic) was often standard practice in order to match Wagon-Lits luxury boat train departures on the other side of the channel. By late 1923 two more eight-coach boat trains appeared and quickly painted in the new Southern Railway green livery to showcase the company's new prestige vehicles. With grouping new railway owned tonnage appeared on the English Channel with *Isle of Thanet* and *Maid of Kent* operating on the Dover

This 1920s poster with artwork designed by Alfons Marchant for Belgian State Railways promoted European travel via Dover showcasing one of the organisation's new modern steamers. The three-hour sea journey made Dover-Ostend an attractive post-war route with tourists keen to see the places of recent conflict; nearby Nieuwpoort was the starting point of the line of trenches from the North Sea to Switzerland. Belgian State Railways saw an opportunity to attract excursionists to its landmarks and popular tourist destinations by promoting quick passage on the Dover-Ostend Royal Mail Route. The country was also convenient for many Continental travellers heading elsewhere in northern Europe. The second images show the ninth edition of Southern Railway's Belgium guidebook produced by Southern Railway in the early 1930s concentrating on the coastal resorts. (*Above left*: NRM/SSPL; *Above right*: Southern Railway Publicity)

Straights from 1925. The French introduced two new vessels to the Dover Straights – *Côte d'Azur* in 1930 and her sister *Côte d'Argent* – both ships looking remarkably similar to Southern's new *Isle of Thanet* pair. By 1932, the Belgian government also had four new ships for the English Channel – *Prinses Astrid*, *Prince Leopold*, *Prince Charles* and *Prinses Josephine Charlotte* – all operating predominantly from Dover.

The years between the wars could be described as the golden age of luxury train travel where 'power, speed and glamour' were closely embedded themes.[2] Whilst the period was particularly characterised by Southern, Nord and Wagon-Lits establishing London and Paris premier cross-channel services, similar developments were taking place elsewhere on the Continent with the introduction of many new upscale Continental trains all with a raft of appealing titles — named trains in the 1930s epitomised luxury travel becoming successful marketing tools for their operators and especially those by the flamboyant Wagon-Lits and MITROPA firms. In the inter-war years both companies worked with a variety of railway operators to revive and launch new Continental trains dovetailing with British cross-channel operations. Virtually, almost every European capital could be reached in a twenty-four-hour period by train connections. However, competition between mainline railway operators and nascent civil aviation carriers intensified. In Europe, long-distance train travel was very well-known but the need to introduce faster trains and non-stop services to counter air transport competition was clearly evident with PLM in France pottering with diesel and steam options.[3] By the 1930s air competition began to impact at the top end of the passenger market with Berlin's Tempelhof, one of the busiest airports in Europe, handling some fifty flights per day.[4]

Under Southern Railway management, substantial railway travelling improvements were undeniably made, impressing even the most sceptical of commentator or journalistic hack. *Railway Wonders of the World*, a railway enthusiasts' publication from the mid-1930s noted:

What an extraordinary revolution has taken place in railway travel in the south-east of England in the last twenty years! At the beginning of the present century the South Eastern and London, Chatham and Dover lines were the butt of every humourist who wanted to make capital out of our railways. For slow, late and uncomfortable running the South Eastern was held on all hands to have few rivals, and not, it must be admitted, without some reason; but to-day all that is totally changed. On such trains as the 80-minute Folkestone expresses … you may witness some of the fastest railway travel in England. Up-to-date Pullman cars and comfortable corridor coaches make up the trains and you can have meals and light refreshments brought to you wherever you sit.

Southern Railway's Victoria Continental headquarters backed up their operations with a swath of representative offices across Europe during the inter-war years. The Visit London poster produced in 1929 has a timeless and endearing quality, and clearly demonstrates the scope the company went to attract international visitors on to its range of cross-channel services.

Whilst railway amalgamation created a certain degree of route consolidation, by 1933 when this Southern Railway poster was created, competition between the company and its arch-rivals was intense. Artwork produced by Patrick Keely clearly demonstrated how close London and Paris were to each other, as well as the breadth of Southern's reach across the English Channel to Belgium and France and to destinations further afield. (NRM/SSPL)

It was not just British mainline railway companies and their Continental partners organising international passenger services. Travel operator Thomas Cook maintained a long and highly successful association with Wagon-Lits going back to the foundation of luxury Continental trains. The relationship between the two travel organisations went back as far as 1883 when Wagon-Lits inaugurated the *Orient Express* service, ultimately cementing a merger on 8 February 1928 when Thomas Cook began a journey with successive new twentieth-century corporate owners such as Ernest and Frank Cook, grandsons of Thomas Cook, unexpectedly sold the family business to Wagon-Lits for £3.5 million.[5] The acquisition was described in official channels as a 'fusion of interests' but within the Cook organisation many regarded the move as an abdication of responsibility and snuffing-out of tradition as some forty of their offices closed through duplication as the two most important travel agencies of their time merged parts of their respective operations. Yet synergies between luxury travel operators were there to be exploited especially with potential tourist customers from the top end of the social scale. When Thomas Cook moved to their new Mayfair Berkeley Street head office in 1926, part of the fifth floor was rented to the Pullman Car Company who were responsible for the building's management dining-room.

Pullman was to enjoy a renaissance in the 1920s with their position as a mainstream supplier of luxury rail travel facilities working closely with both LNER and Southern Railway with new routes and services. Wagon-Lits with their upscale hotel network carried over 2 million passengers per annum by the time of the Cook purchase.[6] All three companies enjoyed close connections at board level where a certain logic to lever brand interactions wherever possible pervaded thinking although how successful these were with old-school working practices and a certain rubbing between Cook and Wagon-Lits in Europe remains open to interpretation. In the boom years, Wagon-Lits had ordered too many carriages and during the slump of the 1930s was left with rolling stock in excess of its immediate requirements.[7] Greater utilisation of second-class Pullman cars on the Continent was a mechanism Wagon-Lits looked to increase its traffic exploiting Cook's knowledge of international operations, overseas destinations and its well-upholstered middle-class customer base. One particular example was Cook's Egyptian operations where the company's knowledge and expertise went back to the mid-nineteenth century. As Dr Piers Brendon notes

Wagon-Lits 'were anxious to fill their new-Pullman and sleeper trains (the Birmingham-built *Star of Egypt* and *Sunshine Express*) to Luxor and Asyut'.[8]

The Dover Straights also marked the beginning of other ventures for Southern, particularly in its quest to balance international boat train workloads with year-round revenues. For the young and fashionable there were winter alternatives to the Riviera. The mountains of Switzerland, and to a lesser extent Austria, where the Tyrol was still considered fashionable, beckoned as they increasingly turned attentions to Alpine winter sports. The ancient arts of skating, curling, the more modern forms of bobsleigh and three and four-man tobogganing at the up-to-the-minute resorts of Davos, Gestaad and St. Moritz – with its infamous run first developed in the 1880s – together with the Norwegian importation of skiing became vogue. In a few short years a growing love of downhill skiing had grown enormously, and by the 1936 Winter Olympics had become a competition event. The delights, thrills and spills of daredevil winter sports became highly popular amongst English holidaymakers in the mid-1920s, as highlighted by *The Sphere's* columnist Charles W. Domville-Fife. He noted St. Moritz's famous Cresta Run, together with other Alpine resorts, catering for a smart set were managed by specialist clubs with a fair share of expatriate and resident English colony members.[9]

Switzerland's tourist infrastructure had begun with the railway age; their railways were one of the first tourist agencies to place bilingual officials at major stations. By mid-century images of Swiss mountain scenery were firmly planted in British travellers' minds, rising to new heights as Dr Arnold confirmed Switzerland is to England, what Cumberland and Westmorland are to Lancashire and Yorkshire and the general summer touring place.[10] As Mullen and Munson commented: 'The British devotion to Switzerland brought benefits for the whole continent since it was the Swiss who began a new, and cleaner, era in hotel life.'[11] Swiss entrepreneurs were increasingly adept at managing new and specially built larger hotels – a downside being increased demand that raised hotel prices.[12] Their skills were well-recognised ultimately spreading a service culture across Europe's tourist centres and with the emergence of high-end establishments making the country the first nation where prosperity was driven by increasing numbers of visitors.[13] On their home patch by the late nineteenth century, winter Alpine resorts took on new dimensions as they were promoted as attractive to the unwell for their recuperative qualities. They quickly assimilated Nice and Monte Carlo's structures by becoming more luxurious, increasingly cosmopolitan in nature, but nonetheless more exclusive.[14] Historian Dr Neil Matthews noted how in 1900 the Tourist Association of Thun suggested, 'Ways must be found to compensate people of quality for having to suffer the presence of the disgusting masses.'[15]

Like the Riviera, Swiss mountains resorts were an English refuge for well-known personalities. Sir Arthur Conan Doyle in 1893 did his winter's work a mile high taking up residence in Davos Platz in response to the 'delicate health' of his wife suffering from tuberculosis who was ordered to take high-altitude care.[16] Luxury trains criss-crossing Europe transported passengers to smart Swiss retreats as a complete service industry evolved around winter sports. In the summer months before the First World War, Britons arrived in great numbers – rail travelling time had been reduced to around twenty hours.[17] Wagon-Lits attracted the British traveller de-luxe to Switzerland with daily operations for three separate services connecting with London departures and Calais steamer crossings – *The Engadine*, *The Oberland* and *The Simplon Expresses*.[18] The Great War ruptured European passenger services (some permanently) across countries where great expresses ran. Ward Muir, *The Sphere's* true traveller 'deluxe', reviewed 'Cook's 1924 Continental Time Table'. He referred to how disappointed he was 'to see how many of those luxury trains are still marked "suspended" – although, absurdly enough, their times of departure and arrival are in most cases detailed with tantalising minuteness. Did the Great War wear out so desperate a proportion of the Sleeping Car Company's rolling stock? Or did it empty the purses of the Sleeping Car Company's patrons? If so, are there no gadabout New Rich?'[19]

Events were changing as Europe's prosperous classes rediscovered the delights of luxury train travel. Biarritz, in the south-west of France, was one of those visitor haunts of the wealthy made fashionable by the spring visits of Edward VII. The Basque resort's comfortable ambience, ameliorating temperature aided by fresh Atlantic breezes, and the much-patronized Biarritz Palace Hotel became stylish icons amongst an aspirational nouveau riche in late-Victorian times. Considered less ostentatious (and cooler) than the flashy Riviera, it became a focus of British society when Wagon-Lits introduced a trains deluxe service running from Paris (with direct London connections) to Madrid and Lisbon.

The *Sud Express* really was a boat train since it not only joined with Calais cross-channel steamers, its various route arrangements into Spain and Portugal connected with liners heading to Central and South America. By the mid-1920s stepping off new steel-sided carriages at sophisticated Biarritz was undoubtedly part of Europe's deluxe train travel traditions for the smart set. Adding to the regional dimension was a new through sleeping car service called

Whilst not part of a regular annual Riviera review, *The Bystander* produced a series of short verses providing a wonderful reflection of the state of new modern Continental luxury boat trains. This included the *Golden Arrow*, *Blue Train* and the *Sud Express*. Entitled 'Oh when I was a tiny boy, A train, it was my fav'rite toy.' (Illustrated London News Ltd/Mary Evans)

the *Pyrénées-Côte d'Argent Express* of the Orléans and Midi railway companies introduced in November 1925 and targeted particularly at the winter-sports enthusiast.[20] The Pyrenees were well-liked, but the Principality of Andorra, wedged between France and Spain, was not so popular with travel writers suggesting the destination had acquired a reputation for poor quality and dirty inns.[21] Some places, it appears, were still caught in the time-warp travel deprivations of the previous century – primitive Spanish inns had been lambasted since mid-Victorian times.[22] Up until later times, hardly anyone visited Spain or Portugal, yet by the mid-1930s Spain was home to significant pockets of Englanders, particularly those colonial members keeping a close-eye on living-costs, attracted by warm and dry winters where 'Spanish servants' could still be hired for a modest cost.[23]

Another factor impacting on boat train volumes in the inter-war years was the motor car which had assumed a man's fashion statement. Its increasing utilisation altered leisure travelling and holiday patterns but the state of 'A' class roads radiating from London meant that cross-country travelling of more than 150 miles per day could be gruelling and normally required an overnight stay somewhere. From the early years of the twentieth century, the motor car had been a trapping of wealth. For the rich, cars went with their owners; since the times of the floating ocean palaces, they were winched aboard as personal cargo on ocean going ships, or indeed, cross-channel ships, as France (without speed limits and a plentiful supply of workshops and refuelling points even in the smallest of towns), had become a favoured destination for motorists.[24] The establishment of motoring organisations like the AA and RAC, as well as Baedeker's guides, did much to facilitate Continental motoring adventure. From the 1920s, cars began to feature conspicuously in Continental travel plans. Bucknall observed wryly:

> The motor car had by then become a power to be reckoned with. Like the 'English milords' of the later Georgian and Regency eras who often took their private conveyances across the Channel with them, the modern motorists who took their cars abroad required reasonable sea transport only, for themselves and their vehicles. They were not concerned with boat trains.[25]

A new cross-channel motor ferry service taking four hours was launched in August 1936 linking Dover and Ostend relieving

Kenneth Denton Shoesmith's famous 1934 Southern Railway Dover poster included an illustration of the car ferry *Autocarrier* featuring its 'Motorists' service alongside the *Golden Arrow's Canterbury*. The Southern developed the first ferries allowing cars to be driven on and off by special side-loading spans as travellers started to take regular extended Continental holidays. Independent travel was in vogue.

much of the congestion of the peak summer months. A September 1936 edition *The Sphere Travel Bureau* highlighted the popularity of the new way to see Europe:

> More people than ever seem to have been taking their cars abroad this summer, and drive where you will on the Continent, it is never very long, even in the most out of the way places, before you see a car with a 'GB' plate standing outside the hotel where you thought you were going to be the only English visitor.[26]

By the end of the year, *Night Ferry* was operational introducing capacity for some twenty-five cars per trip. Fewer people were travelling first-class on the railways but at the same time at the top end of the market, they were looking for travel alternatives such as taking an increasingly reliable car abroad. Pimlott observed driving on the Continent was no longer the adventure it had been liking the experience to 'humdrum'; by 1937 there were some 17,000 British motorists in France.[27] After the Second World War, the trend for Continental motoring continued. *Night Ferry's* three specialist train ferries became a single-class specification regularly carrying up to 100 motor cars with their passengers and also running an additional supplementary car ferry service to cope with demand.[28]

The motor car is placed centre of attraction in this 1937 train ferry boat poster illustrated by Leslie Carr. The Wagon-Lits Type F sleeper carriages on the twice daily services are clearly evident, but the nature of taking, by now, much more reliable cars on Continental trips, increasingly became self-evident especially for those who could afford such travel luxuries. The Southern Railway clearly responded to market opportunities.

Newhaven Services

In summertime, the Newhaven-Dieppe route came into its own offering international travellers a cheaper alternative, and a more picturesque route to Paris than the Dover Straits ports, although the overall journey might be longer. Post-war, LBSCR sang the praises of Dieppe in promotional literature describing the town as the 'Finest

Whilst considerable emphasis was placed on the Nord railway links via Calais and Boulogne, Southern Railway was keen to attract French speaking visitors to its western-channel Dieppe-Newhaven and Le Havre-Southampton routes. This unsigned poster produced in 1924 was clearly positioned to elevate London's international status as a tourism destination.

resort on the Normandy coast. Superb Casino, excellent Hotels, Golf Links, Tennis Courts, etc. The Steamers plying between Newhaven and Dieppe are some of the finest and most comfortable boats in the Channel Services.'[29] In August 1928, *Worthing* became Southern Railway's first new steamer operating out of the port. A near sister, a fifth manifestation of *Brighton*, was completed in March 1933. At the same time with main line Brighton electrification, former LBSCR H1 and H2 Atlantic Class locomotives previously long-associated with the *Southern Belle* Pullman train, transferred to Newhaven's shed and assigned heavy-laden Continental boat train duties. This they repeatedly achieved and with some degree of panache as in pre-war days they regularly loaded up to 480-ton mark made of a twelve-coach formation first, second and third-class carriages plus van cars.[30] Although pitched as value for money travelling, the Newhaven-Dieppe boat train still commanded typical 1930s style running with a Pullman car with first-class coaches attached to one side and second-class on the other. Light meals and refreshments were served by Pullman attendants throughout the length of the vestibuled boat train. Imaginably as a throwback to society and its *Blue Train* party shenanigans, former *Southern Belle* Pullman kitchen car *Grosvenor* was converted for use as a bar car in 1936 running on the Newhaven-Dieppe boat train.[31] Whilst the boat trains managed to maintain some tradition, the state of the route's main steamers *Newhaven* and *Rouen* came under closer inspection. In 1939 Société Nationale des Chemins de Fer Français (SNCF) ordered two replacement vessels for the worn-out pair but their route adoption was delayed by the war.

Southampton Services

Whilst the Southern adapted to the needs of a changing marketplace, it did also consistently invest in its core boat train products with heavy marketing and promotion of cross-channel railway operations, particularly across the western channel and its south coast routes. In its final days LSWR introduced its new high-specification Ironclad carriage stock for Southampton boat trains. Southern Railway trains together with their new cross-channel twin-screw turbine steamers *Dinard* and *St. Briac*, introduced in the summer of 1924, still provided the quickest access to the region.

Aside the Channel Islands, the company invested in promoting Continental ferry services to western French ports. As a result, with year-round service provision, Normandy and Brittany lingered

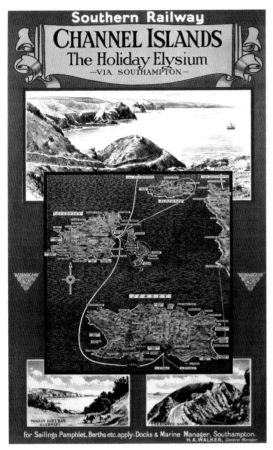

In its early years of formation, Southern Railway placed considerable efforts behind promoting Southampton as home to western-channel crossings for the Channel Islands. In this 1924 unsigned poster, the four isles with convenient departures, were portrayed as a place of ideal happiness. Likewise, by 1930 in the second piece of Southern literature, the Channel Islands and the Continent were again being targeted for daytime and short-break passenger business. (*Above right*: Southern Railway Publicity)

long in British affections. *The Sphere* magazine writing about the region suggested Brittany 'possesses all the characteristics dear to the English heart – antiquity, pageantry, quiet, beauty, sporting facilities, a respectful and picturesque peasantry and comfortable villas, hotels and clubs.' The publication also noted Brittany was a cost-effective place to live long-term, 'a man may live on £300 a year in a state of quiet luxury and dignity which, in our islands, has not been thought of these many years.'[32] Aside the railway company's push of France's western regions, Dean and Dawson were a long-established and innovative upscale travel agent who by 1924 had taken to organise summertime luxury touring of Normandy and Brittany with departures from Southampton involving one of the large liners in port.[33] Southern Railway also used Shep to produce artwork poster and postcard designs utilising a ship's image at the heart of eight Continental routes. The vessel's magnitude seemed to indicate it was a giant ocean liner as opposed to a cross-channel steamer.[34] Similarly, Canadian Pacific a few years later joined the action with an advertising headline 'Go Abroad by REAL Ocean Liners!' with 'delightful short return trip' services to Cherbourg. This was later expanded with itineraries to include Antwerp and Hamburg.[35]

From the 1930s the latest corridor stock together with Pullman cars would be included on 'special supper-car express' boat trains connecting with several new steamers brought in by Southern Railway.[36] On the busy Southampton and Channel Islands routes, the company introduced *Isle of Jersey* and *Isle of Guernsey* in the first half of 1930 to meet increased demand on day and

An inter-war shot of a Southern Railway boat train headed by no. 474 on the Town Quay – also known as Tram Quay – which by the 1930s was mainly used for passenger traffic due to significant commercial expansion taking place elsewhere on the docks at the time. The building in the background was the home of Parsons Oil Engine Co. of Town Quay Works, who were producers of marine and automotive engines. Over the years the company became one of the best-known names in specialist marine engineering. (J&C McCutcheon Collection)

night-time services. *Normannia* and *Hantonia* alongside *Lorina* covered the winter-time Jersey-St. Malo service during the 1930s. France (and the Low Countries) were prime territory for the company for what is termed today as the short-break. In the late 1930s *Isle of Thanet* aided capacity running summertime on the Southampton-St. Malo route.

ADD A DAY TO YOUR
HOLIDAYS IN FRANCE
by using the
COMFORTABLE NIGHT ROUTE
SOUTHAMPTON - HAVRE
Full particulars from Continental Enquiry Office,
Victoria Station or principal Travel Agents.
SOUTHERN RAILWAY

A Change of Scene

Why not try France this Autumn? Something off the beaten track, for preference. Brittany, Normandy, Picardy, with their quiet towns and villages and their quaint customs.

Or, maybe, the Western Seaboard, the "Wine Country," or the Sunny Riviera — those smaller places, which are just as picturesque as the more fashionable centres, and near enough to them for an occasional visit.

France is so near, by the ceaseless day and night services of the S.R. Short Sea Routes.

Write or call at the CONTINENTAL ENQUIRY OFFICE, Victoria Station, S.W.1., or any Travel Agent, for free copies of the S.R. "Off the Beaten Track" booklets, also full details of services, Cheap Fares, special rail concessions in France, etc.

SOUTHERN RAILWAY

This 1937 Southern Railway poster illustrated by Chas Pears extolled the virtues of taking the company's night-time crossing from Southampton to Havre with the delight of waking up next morning in France. The dusky maritime setting is beautifully depicted by the well-known marine artist. Whilst taking the car to the Continent progressively became a key component of cross-channel and short-sea ferry operations, so did the idea of touring and hiring a vehicle once abroad. The inter-war railway companies were adept travel packagers; Southern's Victoria Continental offices were busy places dealing with summertime holiday enquiries. What could be easier? The Waterloo boat train to the awaiting Havre bound ferry and next day, a car ready at the port for collection. In the second image France most certainly would be a scene of change with this Southern Railway *Bystander*, advertisement of 30 August 1939. The timing was unfortunate with war approaching, but the sentiments of the many-sided railway business of maximising the holiday season are evident. Southern, using a consistent promotional image in upscale popular titles was in the perfect position to mop up Continental leisure business as it presented itself. (*Above left*: NRM/SSPL; *Above right*: Illustrated London News Ltd/Mary Evans)

The Southern Railway also had Switzerland in its sights. Victoria departures and the short cross-channel routes offered travellers an alternative to the longer established Harwich and Hook of Holland route. Much of this was down to the rising value of the pound opening up more expensive destinations with cheaper pricing. Typical of this approach was a series of Southern Railway Swiss destination advertising appearing in the spring of 1939. Switzerland by the Short Sea Routes was 'as lovely in summer as in winter, with its quiet mountains, glorious patches of flower-colour and the cool grandeur of its lakes'.[37] The old traditional upscale *Engadine* and *Oberland* expresses connecting with Victoria services were again once again promoted as alternative routes assembled through Southern's Dover-Ostend and the new unique Dover-Dunkerque train ferry.

Weymouth Services

During the inter-war years, GWR placed considerable efforts developing its Channel Islands business. The company decided to replenish its fleet serving the islands with its first turbine steamers

GWR choose to take a different approach to Channel Islands destination promotion. Charles Pears illustrated this 1925 GWR cross-channel ferry poster to support their new fast steamers providing an accelerated summer service. Pears, like LMS's Wilkinson, was also a notable maritime artist and seemed to be a natural fit to capture a modern travel vista with the company's red and black trimmed funnels. From the mid-1930s, collaborative efforts to Channel Islands destination marketing was clearly evident. A more coordinated approach was taken by tourism authorities to promote the delights of island holidays in conjunction with railway company partners, and in Jersey's case, an embryonic air service. Sophisticated images were created enticing travellers on to Great Western's Weymouth and Southern Railway's Southampton routes. Top rank artists were utilised. The 1935 Jersey poster was illustrated by Leonard Richmond whilst Guernsey's 1938 poster was produced by Edmond Vaughan.

St. Julien and *St. Helier* in the summer of 1925. With new ships in place *Reindeer* was kept in reserve for the next three years, but also used for coastal, island and French day-trips as the Great Western leveraged considerable tourist interest. Much of this was done in tandem with the promotion of Weymouth as an ideal tourist destination – the resort benefiting from consistent GWR, Southern Railway and local authority advertising investment in the 1920s and 1930s. Some of this was promotion work was undertaken by all three parties combined as there were two facets to Weymouth as both shipping and tourism drove the local economy. In 1930 the town had an additional ferry placed at its resource – a new vessel *St. Patrick* – which was designed to operate on both the Weymouth and Fishguard stations providing additional capacity.[38]

Weymouth was positioned as the quickest gateway to the Channel Islands as continual improvements were made to the Paddington train service. In 1934 boat trains no longer ran via Swindon but were re-routed over the Berkshire and Hampshire line. Further improvements were made in 1936 speeding up and expanding services. By the late 1930s cross-channel traffic to the Islands was at an all-time high aided by refits to *St. Helier* and *St. Julien* which improved accommodation standards. B.L. Jackson picks up the story again as the '1938 season again broke records, when over 133,000 passengers used the service and 22,370 took the advantage of the excursion programme.'[39] And this also spilled over into perishable traffic with 4,624,612 tomato chips and 307,604 boxes of flowers carried during the year. All in all, a highly satisfactory position to be in before the clouds of war loomed.

Chapter 3

Post-war: International Travel Resumes

Dover Straights Services

Post-war the Southern Railway made strenuous efforts to resume luxury train services again. This convention continued well into nationalisation and the creation of British Railways Southern Region. In 1949 *Maid of Orleans* was the fourteenth and final turbine packet ferry designed as a day boat on the Folkestone-Boulogne service. Built as a scaled-up version of *Canterbury*, the 3,700-ton vessel fitted with radar and stabiliser and capable of prolonged twenty-two knot operation. The ship lasted until 1975 serving out her days as a one-class vessel between Dover and Calais. Post-war passenger demand was high as SNCF ordered their largest channel steamer yet. In August 1950, *Côte d'Azur* entered service mainly on day ferry operations between Calais and Folkestone.

In the mid-1950s British Railways promoted the Dover Straights as the short sea routes to France, and in making the cross-channel ferries and the sea trip as part of the holiday experience. Advertising netted the potential of an exotic realm. *The Sketch* suggested readers:

> Enjoy the tang of the sea and then that first thrill, reborn with every trip – as you walk down the gangway into France – the catch of the breath as you enter a new world. The gendarmes on the quay, peak-capped and cloaked – porters, blue-bloused and volubly French – even the engines seem to whistle in a foreign language. Then on to the train … Paris, Basle and beyond. All combine to welcome you to something new – something exciting – the perfect start to your Continental holiday![1]

SNCF's extensive efforts cultivating the independent travel trade emphasised how £25 could be stretched to encompass a fortnight's holiday in France quite comfortably, whilst pushing the benefits of mid-week travel and special family ticketing arrangements on return journeys of at least 186 miles.

DOVER FOR THE **CONTINENT**

←**THEN**
ONE SAILING A WEEK

NOW
↓ SEVEN SAILINGS A DAY

1850

FROM DOVER

dep.			
10.00	for Boulogne	—	Motorists and Cars.
12.20	„ Dunkerque	—	„ „ „
12.20	„ Ostend	—	from Victoria 10.00
13.00	„ Calais	—	„ { 10.30 / 11.00 "Golden Arrow"
13.30	„ Ostend	—	Motorists and Cars.
16.50	„ Ostend	—	from Victoria 14.30
0.40	„ Dunkerque	—	„ „ 22.00 "Night Ferry".

Summer Service — until October 7th, 1950

BRITISH RAILWAYS

1950

100 YEARS OF SERVICE BY THE SHORT SEA ROUTE

What a difference a century of boat train and cross-channel ferry operations makes. Once SER and LCDR had gained parliamentary approval to run their own vessels from the early 1860s, regular paddle ship services between Dover-Calais and Folkestone-Boulogne became the norm. But ninety years later, a new era under railway nationalisation marked a period when the motorist and their cars were increasingly identified as an important niche in the leisure and holiday travel market. Yet rail connections remained vitally important including the provision of the *Golden Arrow* and *Night Ferry* premier trains. This poster with artwork produced by Leslie Carr, demonstrates the progress made in 100 years of operations with the vast increase in the frequency of cross-channel sailings from one sailing per week to seven sailings per day.

The Dover Straights, since late-Victorian times, had always been a fulcrum for Continental travel to the Alpine regions of France, Switzerland and Austria. In the inter-way years, the emergence of northern Italy and the Dolomites was a new and invigorating winter-time destination. Even Norway offered rivalry for the visitor pound, as at the time it was marketed as a low-cost, high-quality destination. Winter sports by the mid-1950s were definitely back on the travel agenda with boat trains providing ideal access with

Dover Marine was an enormously busy station where frequent boat trains arrived and departed the port's quaysides all day long. Many post-war photographers chose to take colour photographs of international boat trains at Victoria or en route to the coast but these two selections showcase Dover. In the May 1959 shot of Bulleid Pacific Battle of Britain class locomotive no. 34085 501 Squadron, in un-rebuilt form, the train is seen departing Dover Marine heading a *Golden Arrow* service. The 501 Squadron was re-built the following year in June 1960. In the modern traction image, the scene at Dover shows Class 71 Bo-Bo electric locomotive no. 5010 heading a *Golden Arrow* train in 1963. A total of twenty-four of this class were built by British Railway's Doncaster workshops for the Kent Coast mainlines. The same batch of locomotives were used for the *Night Ferry* service. (*Above and below*: Colour Rail)

Off to the Continent?

Then choose the *always* reliable way and relax en route, knowing the exact time of your departure, eating and drinking in spacious comfort, booking right through to your destination. Whether it is a business trip or a holiday, you owe it to yourself to be free of travel-worry.

BRITISH RAILWAYS

CROSS-CHANNEL SERVICES

Dependable daily services are maintained all the year round with choice of several routes.

Services and fares from principal Travel Agencies, or the
CONTINENTAL ENQUIRY OFFICE, VICTORIA STATION, LONDON SWI
or BRITISH RAILWAYS TRAVEL CENTRE, LOWER REGENT STREET, SWI

A more generic approach was used by British Railways in this quarter page 'Off to the Continent?' advertisement from 1956 promoting cross-channel services. A busy platform alongside the new livery of blood and custard carriages with their *Continental Express* coach boards emphasised the dependability of services operating over the Dover routes. When *Golden Arrow* ran, a separate *Continental Express* train ran, a title first coined in the *White Pullman* era of the late 1920s, for those first and second-class passengers not wishing to pay additional Pullman supplement. The notion of a general Continental express was eventually applied to other day-time boat trains emphasising the swiftness and dependability of short cross-channel operations. (Illustrated London News Ltd/Mary Evans)

VIVE LE SPORT! GO BY RAIL...

Travel in the height of comfort at fares that are down to earth! Your dream of a holiday becomes a reality the moment you step aboard French Railways. For there you will find comfort, fine cuisine and courteous service as you speed towards the thrills and spills of Winter Sports.

THROUGH SERVICES. Winter sports through services from Calais to the Alps with wagon-lit sleepers which now cost considerably less, couchettes or ordinary seats.

TOURIST OR PARTY TICKETS offer big reductions on ordinary fares on certain conditions.

SPEED AND PUNCTUALITY. French Railways have the fastest trains (steam, diesel, electric) in Europe—in some cases, the fastest in the World—and they still maintain their already high punctuality record with 85% of their express trains arriving absolutely on or ahead of time.

COMFORT. The modern all-metal air-conditioned express carriages of French Railways with improved suspension and running on first-class track are a pleasure to travel in.

...GO BY

FRENCH RAILWAYS

Information, tickets and reservations from any good Travel Agent or French Railways Ltd., 179 Piccadilly, London, W.1

CVS-106

WINTER SPORTS

TRAVEL BY THE 12·30 pm TRAIN
from London (Victoria)

and arrive the next day...

...FRANCE		...AUSTRIA	
CHAMONIX	10. 1 am	KITZBUHEL	2.37 pm
LA CLUSAZ	9. 5 am	LECH	12.25 pm
MEGEVE	9.20 am	ST. ANTON	11.33 am
MORZINE	9.50 am		
VAL D'ISERE	10.30 am	ZELL AM SEE	3.33 pm

...SWITZERLAND			
ANDERMATT	11. 5 am	KLOSTERS	10. 0 am
DAVOS	10.35 am	MURREN	11.10 am
ENGELBERG	10.42 am	PONTRESINA	11.57 am
GRINDELWALD	10.48 am	ST. MORITZ	11.45 am
GSTAAD	10.14 am	WENGEN	10.49 am
KANDERSTEG	10.19 am	ZERMATT	11.17 am

Via Folkestone-Calais (Short Sea Route)

THROUGH CARRIAGES, SLEEPING CARS AND COUCHETTES FROM CALAIS

Register your baggage through to destination and have no worries en route.

If you are breaking your journey in Paris travel by the
"GOLDEN ARROW" (Pullman) or
"NIGHT FERRY" (Through Sleeping Cars) from London (Victoria)

BRITISH RAILWAYS

For tickets, reservations, apply principal Travel Agencies or the Continental Enquiry Office, VICTORIA STATION, London, S.W.1, or British Railways Travel Centre, Lower Regent Street, London, S.W.1

SNCF were intent on capturing British winter sports visitors before they stepped ashore in France, making available a wide assortment of free travel literature and practical information on journeys to and from France. The company ran a series of advertisements in upscale publications promoting themes of 'where the sun is hot, where the snow is firm and where the living is good'. In this creative French railway interpretation, speed provided by powerful Mountain Class locomotives is synonymous with skiing. The best part of twenty-four hours aboard Alpine connecting boat trains allowed chefs to offer excellent cuisine in restaurant cars with meals produced in true French traditions. British Railways on the other hand decided on a multi-destination approach, using the Dover Straights routes for the basis of their winter sports advertising. Through boat train combinations allowed international travellers to arrive at French and Swiss resorts next morning and chief Austrian centres by early afternoon. It also offered would be passengers a combination of securing a short break in Paris as part of Continental travel arrangements. As ever, *Golden Arrow* and *Night Ferry* were never far from copywriter thoughts. (Illustrated London News Ltd/Mary Evans) through carriages, sleeping cars and couchettes operating from Calais. One ace the railways held over the airlines was no restriction on luggage allowances and specially adapted vans for the transport of skis. It was a competitive environment with national and regional tourism organisations, railway companies, individual destinations, travel agencies and specialist companies promoting their respective wares. In addition, the railway companies went out of their way to be flexible, providing special concessions for special group travel which would include the booking of hotel accommodation. Noticeably reduced terms were offered for parties of ten or more.

Whilst airlines were providing speedier access, most Alpine routes went through France benefiting from heavy government investment in mainline electrification, resulting in an increase in punctual train arrivals. SNCF advertising promoted customer benefits that electrification and new air-conditioned coaches brought. 'The ever-increasing electric network throughout France offers the passenger even swifter and more satisfying travel.'[2] In 1953 British Railways began operating a *Winter Sports Express* departing London Victoria station at 12.30 pm daily.

Newhaven Services

The Newhaven-Dieppe service received two new ferries that had been ordered by SNCF in 1939. One, provisionally given the name *Londres*, was launched by the Nazis in December 1941 and sent to German waters but was returned to her French builders after the war. Her sister, *Arromanches*, was completed in April 1946. Both ferries had a passenger capacity of 1,450 divided between first and third-classes. Some degree of stylish travel was maintained with fourteen private cabins and 402 berths.[3] In May 1950, Newhaven-Dieppe received the largest British-built ship specifically for the crossing when *Brighton* was introduced. A couple of years later in 1952, SNCF's new ferry *Lisieux* joined operations on the jointly managed route which throughout the decade remained busy with cross-channel business.[4] Whilst port freight and goods business had always been supplemental to passenger traffic, Newhaven Harbour's railway station was busy with combined traffic until overall traditional boat train passenger numbers began to decline at the beginning of the 1960s.

As a sign of imminent changes in the way consumers would start to plan Continental holiday travel, William Hartley wrote a motoring feature on I January 1958 in *The Sketch* newspaper under

The first Newhaven boat train shot was taken at taken at Earlswood on the fringes of London on 23 July 1955, whilst the second was recorded at Lewes on 6 August 1956. Blood and custard liveried coaches with their Southern Railway heritage define the era. Despite wartime deprivations of materials and resources, Southern managed to build the two mainline electric locomotives at Ashford works in 1941 and 1942, numbered CC1 and CC2 with bodies and bogies designed by Oliver Bulleid and electrical equipment designed by Alfred Raworth. These were later renumbered as no. 20001 and no. 20002 after nationalisation. A third of the three rail Co-Co electric locomotive class no. 20003 was built by British Railways at Brighton works in 1948 and were largely designed as a proof-of-concept for three-rail electric hauled locomotives. When no. 20003 joined the boat train set in 1949, it was branded as the *Newhaven Continental Express* using up to the minute new British Railways livieried stock as well as the inclusion of the odd Pullman car. In the mid-1950s for two short periods nos. 20002 and 20003 were also used to haul *Golden Arrow* both ways. (*Above and below*: Colour Rail)

Taken at Wandsworth Common on 20 September 1964 no. 20002 is again featured, route code 76, and sporting an all green British Rail Southern Region livery. Lewes was a popular location to record Newhaven boat trains over the years. Nos. 20001 – 20003 after largely uneventful but productive careers, were eventually withdrawn in 1968 and scrapped in the 1969. Undated, the second shot includes the cross-channel service headed by D5010. Livery style suggests the setting was probably a mid-1960s photograph. The locomotive class was used to heavy boat train work with 5010 recorded as heading a *Golden Arrow* train from Dover Marine the previous year. (Colour Rail)

the heading of 'Taking Your Car Abroad'. He advised readers 'The Continent is near at hand, and each year it is becoming simpler to take a car across the Channel. For those who like to travel where and when they please, a touring holiday is ideal.'[5] By the early 1960s travel companies and individual destinations would engage in eagerly awaited holiday marketing binges which provided bumper advertising led editions for the weekly television listings guides. In June 1964 *Falaise* which had done sterling service on the St. Malo route since 1947, was converted as a stern-loading car ferry for operation on the Newhaven-Dieppe route. To coincide with this initiative, British Rail used the new facility to promote Newhaven-Dieppe as the perfect short-cut car ferry route to the Riviera and Spain.

Southampton Services

British Railways Southern Region ran two types of boat trains to and from Southampton; for regular cross-channel services, but also for increased numbers of ocean liners, reaping considerable media and public attention once the citadel of the port's new Ocean Terminal was opened.

Originally constructed by Southern Railway between 1926 and 1929, 'Lord Nelsons' were designed for heavier cross-channel passenger trains between Victoria, Dover and Folkestone. Little wonder then not to find them on Southampton boat train duties as large numbers of passengers and luggage created heavy formations for ocean specials. Taken here in June 1960, no. 30855 Robert Blake operates an untitled boat train within the dockyard estate. Headboards, as can be seen, were not always carried on special services hampering identification of the liners and shipping lines they served. (Colour Rail)

Less glamorous than their ocean liner brethren, special boat trains operated for cross-channel routes involving Le Havre, the Channel Islands, and further west to St. Malo and the gateway to Brittany. Southern Railway's previous marketing investment in cross-channel business yielded considerable benefits in the immediate post-way years. Yet competition for upscale travellers was already widespread and not just to confined to France, but also for Channel Islands traffic. In 1947 Channel Islands Airways was subsumed in to the newly created British European Airways Corporation (BEA). During that year, BEA's Channel

Islands operation (including a Southampton airfield) carried 72,931 passengers.[6] With the introduction of new, bigger and more efficient aircraft, and with a consolidation of permanent routes, the volume of passengers increased, especially those who might have been prepared to pay a Pullman supplement or for first-class accommodation on overnight ferry crossings. This undoubtedly had an impact on cross-channel operations in the longer run not just at Southampton but further west at Weymouth, as Channel Island flights were introduced to Bournemouth which had emerged from its war-time duties to become a fully-fledged airport. Despite the prospect of aviation competition, sleek modern vessels were added to Southampton's cross-channel schedules in the post-war years.

THE NEW T.S. "FALAISE"
SOUTHAMPTON, St. MALO AND CHANNEL ISLANDS SERVICES
SOUTHERN RAILWAY

Although Wilkinson's poster emphasises both the Channel Islands and St. Malo as destinations, *Falaise* in a sixteen-year career principally operated on the overnight St. Malo service. The vessel also provided relief on Le Havre and Channel Islands services, and also as the *Golden Arrow's* Dover Straights ferry for the winter of 1947–48. Later in the year, British Railways promoted a series of mid-week and week-end mini-cruises to a number of Western-channel destinations including Le Havre, along the Seine to Rouen, the Channel Islands, Cherbourg and Dinard.

Southern Railway's *Falaise* was part of a new generation of twin-screw turbine cross-channel ferries with distinctive single funnel profiles operating out of Southampton Docks.

Looking rather similar to *Falaise's* outline, *Normannia* was also delivered in January 1952 with her maiden voyage to Le Havre on 3 March; she replaced the ageing *Hantonia*. The new ferry with passenger compartments for 325 persons mostly operated on the French route, an all-year round service with three sailings per week in each direction. As a vessel she was ideal for night-time runs and remained on station, apart from occasional relief sailings elsewhere,

Throughout the 1950s, British Railways continued to heavily promote holiday trips across the English Channel. Whilst the Southampton and Weymouth routes connected with both islands, a degree of destination rivalry existed between Guernsey and Jersey with their different tourism profiles to attract visitors. In the 1958 Guernsey poster produced by Adelman, a more sedate and upscale image was created whilst Lander's work a year later portrayed Jersey as a fun location for families and young couples. Interestingly, the islands Continental style culinary offer began to gain more attention in poster imagery as did its status as a favoured honeymoon location.

The leisurely way to France . . .

via SOUTHAMPTON —LE HAVRE

A modicum of relaxation in the midst of business is always pleasant. And that's just what the night service from Southampton to Havre gives you between a flurry of business appointments in London on one day and the prospect of a repetition in Paris the next.

Whether you live in London or conveniently near to Southampton, there is no happier start than a crossing by the s.s. *Normannia.*

The boat-train leaves Waterloo at seven-thirty in the evening. Dinner is served on the train which gets to Southampton in ample time for some light refreshment on board before you go to sleep. By joining the ship earlier in the evening at the docks you can have dinner on board, a restful evening in the lounge — and then to bed. s.s. *Normannia*, one of our modern cross-Channel ships, has no less than three hundred and twenty-five sleeping berths, generous smoke rooms, lounges and bars, and a spacious dining room.

With good food and drink at reasonable prices, a really comfortable berth and the knowledge that s.s. *Normannia* has stabilisers to smooth out the roughest sea, you travel overnight across the Channel to arrive early next morning in France.

Then, if you are a first-class passenger in a hurry to get to Paris for an appointment, a connecting train leaves Havre at 7.00 to get you to Paris at 9.23 a.m. If you are not so rushed, then it is a leisurely breakfast-on-board and the 8.45 first and second class, arriving Paris at 11.41 a.m.

The next time you are visiting France book via Southampton-Havre — the leisurely way to cross the Channel.

Full information, Tickets and Reservations from Principal Travel Agents or Continental Enquiry Office, British Railways (Southern Region) Victoria Station, London, S.W.1.

SOUTHERN

BRITISH RAILWAYS

If you wish to take your car by s.s. Normannia, apply well in advance to the Central Motor Car Booking Office, British Railways (Southern Region) Victoria Station, London, S.W.1, or through the A.A. or R.A.C.

Overnight
TO THE CONTINENT
VIA SOUTHAMPTON-HAVRE

***Normannia* featured** in *Illustrated London News* advertisement from November 1957 suggests the boat train and plush ferry accommodation were still much in evidence for business travellers on both sides of the English Channel. In an effort by British Railways Southern Region to promote an alternative to *Night Ferry* on the Southampton to Le Havre route, connecting boat trains provided businessmen with an alternative London-Paris option timed for mid-morning appointments. Express trains still held an advantage over air travel in delivering passengers quickly to the heart of European capitals as demonstrated in the second modern 1960 cross-channel poster illustration. (*Above left*: Illustrated London News Ltd/Mary Evans) until December 1963 when she was converted for use as a car ferry. Pullman cars were added to the boat train's rake for *Normannia's* first outing with the service gaining the title of *Normandy Express* ready for the summer season on 30 June. Traditional cross-channel business was brisk. Weekend newspapers were reporting the August 1952 Bank Holiday rush had begun in earnest at Waterloo with long queues for the Southampton boat trains taking people to the Channel Islands.[7]

On 8 June 1954, a summer-only service to St. Malo acquired the title of the *Brittany Express*. It too included Pullman stock for a Continental ferry service running non-stop from London to the docks. The port now had two named ferry boat trains to accompany its prestigious ocean liner specials. But like the age of the liners that was rapidly coming to a conclusion, the same was for Southampton's ferry boat train business. By the early 1960s, many traditional rail/sea/rail travel routes, particularly those over longer distances, had run a natural course as passengers, especially those from the business community, sought the time saving convenience of short-haul aviation. Coupled to this was a hastening in private car ownership; increased accessibility brought about by new road networks around major conurbations, and the ease of airport car parking, was a strong inducement for business travel during this period.

Weymouth Services

With the Channel Islands boat train transferred from Southampton to run to Weymouth Quay, the nature of the Channel Islands services started to change.[8] Turbine steamers *St. Julien* and *St. Helier* lasted on route until the end of the 1959 summer season when the direct Paddington-Weymouth boat train service was withdrawn. From now on quay side boat trains operated from Waterloo with a no. 90 head code on non-steam services. This became a very familiar sight on diesel locomotives until the end of ferry operations in 1985. For steam haulage fans this was no great ordeal since the Waterloo-Weymouth line held out with steam traction until July 1967 when the line was electrified as far as Bournemouth and Poole and the rest of the line to Weymouth in 1988 replacing a push and pull diesel service.

In 1960–61 Weymouth received its last traditional passenger ferries for the Channel Islands services when *Caesarea* and *Sarnia* were delivered. Any notion of stylish travel disappeared as the modern stabilised vessels were single-class equipped to carry

When this illustration was produced by Claude Buckle in 1958, Weymouth's quay had been extended some twenty-five years earlier to accommodate full-length boat trains or approximately fifty freight vans. The poster also shows perhaps as an intentional throwback to GWR days, the ferry's funnel painted in red and black colours. Refreshment car expresses continued from both Paddington and Waterloo although this combined operation from two London termini was to change at the end of the following season. The Paddington boat train servicing the Channel Islands, which had run for over seventy years, ceased on 26 September 1959 when the connections were transferred to Waterloo.

There were three examples of the Collett-built 1366 class, introduced in 1934. Pictured here in the first photograph hauling a passenger boat train from Weymouth Quay on 4 July 1959 is 0-6-0T no. 1369. On another beautiful day in July 1959, tank locomotive no. 1368 in the second shot is in charge of a boat-train operating a service from cross-channel steamer *St. Julien*. This would have been *St. Julien's* final summer season on the Weymouth-Channel Islands route. (Colour Rail)

1,400 passengers. The down-to-earth nature of a new transport age was clearly evident as both *Caesarea* and *Sarnia* carried just 110 overnight berth and in addition aircraft style seats.[9] Railway passenger ships which conveyed fruit, vegetables and flowers in specialist vans played an important part of Weymouth's economy until the mid-1960s when British Rail raised transport costs considerably. By the time of car ferry introduction at Weymouth, perishable freight dwindled dramatically with Guernsey tomato business moving to a new sailing at Shoreham and increasing levels of Jersey's flower trade was moved by air signifying a gradual decline in both Channel Islands passenger and freight business over the coming decades.

CHAPTER 4

The Boat Train Has Had its Day

In November 1969 British Rail shipping services were re-branded as 'Sealink' in a move seen as moving with the times – or at least the national railway operator's corporate interpretation. Blue hulls, white upper superstructures and red funnels on ferries became familiar liveries clearly shown in railway poster advertising and other marketing material. Yet events were changing rapidly on the south coast. In spring 1973, *Falaise* was moved from Southampton to Weymouth inaugurating the resort's first Jersey ro-ro service, but by November 1977, a new competitive ro-ro route appeared between Portsmouth and the Channel Islands. When the Sealink operation was sold to Sea Containers in April 1985 – industrial strife paralysing Weymouth's operations – it was apparent the writing was on the wall for the port's cross-channel passenger business. Nonetheless, around 1981–82 a *Channel Islands Boat Train* headboard was still carried on the front of Class 33 diesels operating between Bournemouth and Weymouth Quay with the last titled boat train running recorded in 1988 as the line was eventually electrified. The time-honoured procedure of locomotives heading boat trains along the resort's backstreets to and from the quayside had ended; the last railway-connected vessel left Weymouth on 30 March 1990.[1]

Dover and Folkestone gained further momentum as cross-channel ports. Newhaven was relegated to secondary league status despite having ferry services in both directions seven days per week. Consequently, boat train operations were justified to provide services to and from London. Newhaven's endurance was in part due to the three-rail electrification network ensuring its survival, together with a London route that took in stops at Gatwick Airport. Sealink continued to sail regularly from the port with two pairs of dedicated train pairs operating in either direction. But with most customers choosing the car, Newhaven Marine gradually fell out of favour with a reduction in the number of ferry passengers arriving by train. From 2006 the station was still technically open but closed to the public following safety concerns over the condition of the roof canopy served only by a ghost train service. Station buildings were demolished in 2017 but it is still possible to access modern

Newhaven ferries by train. Regular services run from London arriving at Newhaven Town railway station which is only a short distance from the foot passenger terminal.

The opening of the Channel Tunnel effectively signed the death warrant for cross-channel boat trains between Britain and France. Eurostar's direct passenger services linking London Waterloo's international railway station and Paris opened for business on 14 November 1994 signalling the end of the boat train as a faster, more convenient rail transport solution was now available. On the British side through trains were restricted to slower progress until the High Speed 1 link was opened between St. Pancras International and the tunnel entrance on 6 November 2007.

On the leisure front, the modern-day equivalent of the *Orient Express* is the *Venice Simplon-Orient-Express (VSOE)* luxury dining train. *VSOE* owned by Belmond, a luxury travel company operating specialist hotel and train operations across the globe, re-fashioned the iconic express. In 1982 the company commissioned and painstakingly restored a fleet of period carriages. The original Wagon-Lits sheen of the dining and sleeping cars, mostly dating from the 1926 to 1931 period, was brilliantly recaptured running on European main line railway networks. This was a premier division boat train in the true sense with exquisitely restored Wagon-Lits dining and sleeping cars running from Boulogne to Venice again. In the coming years the *VSOE* concept was expanded to include an increasing number of other Continental destinations which in many ways mirrored operations of a bygone era many had thought had been lost for ever. *VSOE* branded luxury dining trains now ran across Europe with a frequent Boulogne, Paris to Venice train providing the company's flagship service, together with a much sought-after yearly re-running of the 1883 route to Istanbul. The Wagon-Lits dining and sleeping cars also ran to an increasing number of other European destinations. On the British side Belmond's British Pullman were utilised for boat train duties providing a high-end rail/sea/rail experience for first-class passengers until the Channel Tunnel was opened. The VSOE was repositioned to operate from Paris with London links via Eurostar.

Haulage of *Ocean Special* boat trains to the south coast had to wait some time until they were resurrected by Belmond's British Pullman operation bringing a modern fresh reawakening to the landside of glamorous travel. Although named boat trains had disappeared from scheduled on demand services, dock landscapes could still be enhanced by mainline locomotive services from time to time. On one such occasion, rebuilt Merchant Navy Class no. 35028 Clan Line, a stalwart of mainline running, appeared in 1999 with a *Union Castle Express* nameplate hauling period Pullman carriages with passengers joining *Victoria* on her commemorative millennium cruise in Union Castle colours. *The Cunarder* was refashioned bringing passengers from London for QE2 trans-Atlantic runs, but also for the occasion of the maiden voyage of RMS *Queen Mary 2 (QM2)*. Pullman boat trains were assembled on 1 May 2004 to meet the *QE2* and the *QM2* for the historic eastbound crossing as both ships arrived in tandem at Southampton. Surprisingly, however, demand for these trains was poor with the last running of the London-Southampton *Belmond British Pullman boat train* meeting the *QM2* on 25 October 2007. Over the years, the port has undergone a maritime transformation as it once again has become Europe's premier passenger port; home to some of the world's largest cruise ships, and headquarters to a number of corporate organisations that run them. But the boat train has no place in this modern world context as transport to and from the port has been replaced by the car, taxi and for many passengers, the bucket-list indulgence of the private chauffeured limousine.

Elsewhere in Europe, there are lamentably few places where regular boat train services still exist. By the time this book appears the Hamburg to Copenhagen boat train will have been rerouted via Odense, leaving just the summer-time *Berlin Night Express* to Malmö and the comparatively narrow cross-channel service separating Calabria, the last stop on the Italian mainland and the country's most southerly point connecting the toe in the boot region of the island of Sicily. The Straits of Messina rail/sea/rail boat train still makes the crossing as it has done since 1899 providing two day-time InterCity trains with at least one overnight sleeper service between Rome and Naples with Catania, Syracuse and Palermo. The twenty-five-minute crossing provides a glimpse of the previous seamless *Night Ferry* operation where dedicated Type F sleeper carriages ran effortlessly between England and France's capital cities for around forty years. Despite Italian operator Trenitia's constant pruning, the Rome-Polermo sleeper and its reverse service from Sicily, still provides the connection to the mainland on the specially adapted train ferry with its innard aligned track for parking the train's carriages. For railway enthusiasts the excitement of the short sea-crossing is a highly memorable experience; for travellers looking for something different the spectacular coastal scenery provides the train romance, irrespective of the luxury travel component, can get.

Whilst there has always been a deluxe leisure element allied to boat trains, for many it symbolised part of their working lives. Like the *Irish Mail* running between Euston and Holyhead, the Palermo to Rome night train was long favoured by Sicilian rank and file off to work in Italy's northern industrial heartlands. Periodically, the daytime and sleeper services come under threat from Trenitalia with the media immediately recounting tales of post-war southern migrants heading for Milan and Turin's factories, and new lives in the north of Italy. Notwithstanding, the boat-train ferry service has a long pedigree with a succession of steamers and ferries replacing older stock over the years – one in fact was raised from the seabed and brought back into service having been sunk by a Second World War mine. Whilst its hospitality element has been shorn of any culinary experience – guards complain the cappuccino machine is starved of coffee supplies with guests having to make do with fruit juice – it does at least appear to have a secure future as Italian national finances and lack of capital for major infra-structure projects, make the possibility of the building of a road and rail bridge across the Straits of Messina, a long-term possibility.

The time-honoured boat train constantly evolves especially so in the leisure rail sector where new itineraries deliver combined rail/sea/rail experiences. Golden Eagle Luxury Trains' *Caspian Odyssey* expedition is one such notable example where the train on arrival in Baku is loaded onto a cargo ferry for a twelve-fourteen-hour voyage across the Caspian Sea to the town of Turkmenbashi. Guests have the option of either taking the ferry crossing or flying.

For the most part, boat trains in their traditional sense, connecting with ocean-going ships, no longer exists in the same way. Progress, perhaps, at the motor vehicle reigns supreme as the primary mode of sea ferry transport for sea ferries, yet there are still pockets where it is still possible to indulge in traditional boat train travel experience between Britain and Ireland. But on the mainland, Thurso, the most northern railway station in Scotland (and Britain) no longer connects directly with NorthLink's Orkney and Shetland services; Scrabster the ferry port is a mile and half from the station. Similarly, at the other end of the country in Cornwall, the boat train does not take you alongside the Isles of Scilly ferry, but at least the new ferry terminal is only a short taxi distance away. How times change?

Chapter 5

Great Cross-Channel Boat Train Expresses

Belle Époque Europe: The Calais-Méditerranée Express, Côte d'Azur Rapide and the Rome Express

On the French side everything revolved around Paris whose entry to the railway age was somewhat later than in Britain. Like points in a compass, grand railway stations were built in the mid-nineteenth century as part of Napoleon III's vision of consolidating France with a national railway system. Gare de l'Est, Gare du Nord, Gare Saint-Lazare to the north-west and Gare de Lyon to the south were visible displays of the city's enthusiasm for rail and reconstruction. Gare Montparnasse originally built in 1840 was part of the initial station building boom, although nothing now remains of the station famous for the 1895 incident where a locomotive crashed through the station façade ending up nose-down in the street below. Gare d'Austerlitz, the start of the Paris to Bordeaux railway line and Gare d'Orsay connecting Paris with Orléans were later examples of station construction. To cement the importance of the London and Paris link, the cross-channel ports of the Dover Straights ensured the capitals had direct railway links for most of the Victorian period. With Nord affording fast and frequent services, Paris became the nodal point of the French national railway system. As an established regional railway, Nord's geographical operations may not have been as extensive as others, but importantly, it ran premier boat trains from Paris Gare du Nord to the French Channel ports of Calais, Boulogne and Dunkerque representing the cream of business and tourist traffic.

Originally opened in 1846 Paris Gare du Nord was rebuilt opening in 1864 and quickly becoming Europe's busiest rail terminal.[1] The station was the preferred gateway for many discerning travellers with Hotel Terminus Nord, for many years, the ideal location for visitors awaiting onward destinations across France and Europe. Wagon-Lits, the luxury train company, operated a range of services from mainline Paris stations building close operational links with Nord and Chemins de fer de Paris à Lyon et à la Méditerranée

(PLM). When Wagon-Lits was created on 4 December 1876, the next few decades would see a form of love/hate relationship existing between the company and the US (and initially the British) Pullman Company operations. The crux was the running of competing services across France and Italy and especially with the operation of Italian bound trains from Calais to Rome. Despite activity, an initial foray by Pullman in February 1883, who had developed relationships with Italian railway companies (and ably supported by Thomas Cook) was held in breach of prior contracts signed by Wagon-Lits with Nord and PLM.

Rome, since Grand Tour times, had always attracted significant numbers of travellers, especially Britons who increasingly made the country a long-lasting love affair and regarded as being the world's schoolroom.[2] It is said the English *owned* Rome during the mid-part of the nineteenth century, when the colony numbered over 4,000 individuals – many living as permanent residents – despite the travails of summer-time smells and poor sanitation. Upscale visitors poured into the city throughout the 1800s. Little wonder Wagon-Lits on 8 December 1883 should launch its second train-de-luxe service known as the *Rome Express* linking London, Paris and Rome via the French and Italian Riviera, effectively providing the bedrock for the next twenty years of quality day and night-time trains departing and arriving from Calais Gare Maritime.

In 1894 the *Manchester Evening News* reported on large numbers of English and US visitors arriving in Rome for the season. 'There will be the usual procession of the English colony to the grave of John Keats on the 23rd inst., the anniversary of the poet's death seventy-three years ago. Most of the British and trans-Atlantic visitors are foregathering at the Grand Hotel, which was opened last month.'[3] Mullen and Munson got to the nub of Rome's draw. They ventured 'a trip to Italy in the winter months, when Britain was freezing and smog covered, was now no more difficult than going to Paris. The snows of the Alps could be glimpsed from the warmth of a train.'[4] By the turn of the new century, Wagon-Lits' European ambitions were expanding rapidly, propelling the company's reputation into the stratosphere on both sides of the Atlantic. With indulgent experiences and luxuries built into the train's fabric, Wagon-Lits was now a high-profile luxury service provider in an internationalist expansion mode; its increasing business interests included moving into static hospitality operations with the acquisition, building and running of some the Continent's most prestigious and high-class hotels.

By 1897 Wagon-Lits made further moves on a burgeoning luxury travel market introducing an assortment of through train services from London, and across the water to Calais where travellers were met with awaiting trains with connections to a large number of European destinations. Wagon-Lits launched the teak clad *Calais-Méditerranée Express* – operating daily in the winter high season and three times per week in the off season – alongside a new Calais to Rome service with ocean going liner connections to Genoa in November of that year.[5] The frequency of the *Calais-Méditerranée Express* service would shortly be extended to three days per week, whilst a succession of other luxury trains such as the *Sud Express* with South African and South American mails and passenger traffic via Madrid and Lisbon on four days per week, the *Gibraltar Express* was launched in 1896 which could be reached in fifty-seven hours, a daily *Ostend to Vienna Express* dovetailing with London traffic, and the *Nord Express* linking London, Paris and St. Petersburg. In addition, the company provided daily services from its Paris hub to the Riviera, and from the east, the *Vienna Riviera Express* ran daily. Unsurprisingly, Wagon-Lits advertised extensively in the British press. The company's offices in Cockspur Street, London was a busy place dealing with customer enquiries in person and sending out official guides on request. In the summer of 1894, the company produced its own English-language travel literature *The Continental Traveller* under the editorship of Mr H.M. Snow. According to *The Sketch*, the indispensable guide was written in a very simple and entertaining way. The newspaper went on:

> The apotheosis of luxury in travelling has been accomplished by this company, whose sleeping-cars are a model throughout Europe. With the aid of this handbook, which includes a list of fares to the principal cities in Southern Europe, the most timid of old ladies may safely venture from her native land, and the average man who is seeking to reach Rome will be in no danger of awaking on the top of the Righi. The various routes to the Riviera, to Constantinople, to Italy, to Germany, and even to remoter Russia, are laid down with the greatest clearness, and the whole book is so good that it may properly become the traveller's *Vade Mecum*.[6]

Wagon-Lits' London operations were managed by Mr Snow, a man according to *The Railway Magazine* who was 'an expert in travel, who studies the would-be tourist, and immediately determines what scenery and surroundings are necessary to the patient's well-being'.[7] Snow (and Sir Davidson Dalziel) regularly courted travel correspondents and journalists; many were happy to recount the hospitality offered by the company in later years.[8] Wagon-Lits had worked closely with SER prior to its amalgamation to smooth as much as possible, long journeys to the winter sun ably supported by extensive advertising across upmarket titles. *The Globe* newspaper reported on 'through trains deluxe to the Riviera' with important arrangements being made for the convenience of those desiring to travel.[9] Whilst European travel was a still a novelty for many people, particularly for the lower middle-classes, for wealthy elites it was an almost obligatory part of the winter season. Notwithstanding, Italian and Iberian delights Wagon-Lits so adequately provided luxury trains for, it was the French Riviera and its association with London society that was set to make it *the* fashionable destination favoured by upscale English tourists. Suffice to say British railway companies, PLM and Wagon-Lits did not act in isolation always preferring to ensure customer needs were met in-house and loathe to admit even other railway companies existed.

In Autumn 1904 there were further improvements and frequency of services. Wagon-Lits made important improvements to its winter schedule for the *Calais-Méditerranée Express* connecting with the 11.00 am Victoria departure. The service became a luxury night only train composed entirely of restaurant and sleeping cars designed to take Britain and America's elites to the Azur coast's warmer climes. The chance for London's smart-set to avoid winter chills was a must do for many of the leisured classes keen to escape coal fired-air pollution of industrialised urban life. From 4 November, the *Calais-Méditerranée Express* departed later in the day allowing London passengers the opportunity to take a more leisurely breakfast in the capital. Previously passengers bound for the Riviera had to make-do with the 9.00 am departure slot. The new arrangements were well received in both the British and French press helping to position the sleeping train as a highly respectable winter train-de-luxe service.[10] On the French side of the channel, the *Calais-Méditerranée Express* was a joint operation between the Nord and PLM railways. On Tuesdays and Thursdays in the season the train would leave for Paris arriving on the Petite Ceinture without stopping and then on to the blue Azur. Passengers on the 9.00 am crossing from London could elect to take a train to Paris and leave later in the day from Gare de Lyon aboard the evening *Riviera Express*. New ticketing arrangements between English and French railway companies meant journeys could now be broken in Paris, providing the capital with an unprecedented tourist boom. Despite all these advances French railway locomotives did not always have their supporters. One anonymous travel correspondent suggested to readers that one has only to look at a Continental locomotive, with its rows of domes along the top of the boiler, like pots on a farmhouse range, to realise that French engineering has its lapses!

A steady stream of well-heeled British travellers was brought to Paris by railway companies and shipping lines, often operating in complete unison; they also brought wealthy Americans 'hungry for French fashion, cuisine and culture'.[11] As Mullen and Munson spotted 'the rivulet of American travellers in the nineteenth century became a mighty stream in the twentieth'.[12] Paris was defined by the *Belle Époque*, an ideal location to spend a culturally infused day or so surrounded by great buildings of decadence and opulence the world wanted to see. The period was marked by a tremendous fusion of art and technology showcased in many forms; Picasso and his new styles of Impressionism were accepted by intellectuals, the early days of manned flight provided great aerial spectacles using Eiffel's tower as a backdrop; crowds in their thousands witnessed communal experiences and a home-grown cinematic industry prompted by the work of the Lumiére Brothers and others was in its infancy but nonetheless the talk of the capital. All inspired public imagination providing Paris with a kind of vibrancy few other city destinations could match and with its magic routes to the south of the country.

Aside railway splendid hotels with their impressive high-end eateries, there was the birth of a new eating and drinking culture courtesy of the Parisian café with its unique culinary and social settings establishing a melting pot of French society flavoured by a new educated elite and intelligencia all eating together. The bistro, and the more upscale brasserie, was home to French regional cuisine. Comfortable, slow-cooked foods produced in convivial atmospheres were the perfect alternative location to wile a few hours prior to boarding the very different conventions and prescriptions of the evening aboard the train-de-luxe services. Many Paris mainline stations were destinations in themselves. Ina Caro, presenting an American perspective, says the:

Stations were built for the middle-class traveller – not what we call the middle class in America, the upper middle class, the nouveau riche of the late nineteenth century, whose main desire was to live and be treated as the aristocracy once had been, as aspiring, bourgeois French middle class who built their new mansions along the boulevards that replaced the slums.[13]

Baron von Haussmann's endeavours had changed the city into Europe's premier urban destination. And Paris railway stations were part and parcel of this transformation possessing restaurants noted for their opulence. The Gare d'Orsay built at the turn of the twentieth century was converted into museum in 1978 and protected as an historical monument. Musée d'Orsay – and the second-floored frescoed dining room now provides a glorious culinary experience. Ina Caro goes on to note, 'In fact, this restaurant is not even the most sumptuous remnant of the age – that honor goes to Le Train Bleu at the Gare de Lyon. To really feel as though you were back in the nineteenth century, you should have Sunday dinner there. Its opulent turn-of-the-century decorations are simply breath-taking.'[14]

In 1904 the *Calais-Méditerranée Express* was relaunched. In addition, PLM introduced an extra fast day-time service to the French coast – the *Côte d'Azur Express* – or known in France simply as the *Rapide*, with Wagon-Lits providing restaurant and saloon cars and the catering. The new *Côte d'Azur Express* day train-de-luxe connected with the previous night's 9.00 pm London Charing Cross service.[15] The luxury train incorporated the latest modern railway amenities of flushed lavatories, hot and cold running water, electric lighting, but also featuring specially adapted carriages for the needs of invalids drawn to the therapeutic powers of the Riviera's waters.[16] PLM had a strong interest in promoting railway tourist traffic as the Azur coast as new, more comfortable hotels sprung up.

The *Côte d'Azur Express* was designed for a Parisian elite drawn by its year-round hospitable climate, and its growing reputation as a haven for glamour, creativity and culture. Paris's cosmopolitan and international privileged required the quickest possible route to the south-east of France and its Riviera dream factory. The line from Paris via Dijon, Lyon and Marseilles was PLM's primary trunk route with the first half of the route to Marseilles particularly fast, even at the turn of the twentieth century. From Marseilles the route along the Azur coast was slower since it was constructed in several stages between 1858 and 1872. The route was designed as a multi-purpose

SUPPLEMENT TO THE BYSTANDER, NOVEMBER 30, 1904   569

The Riviera for the Christmas Holidays

By EUSTACE REYNOLDS-BALL, F.R.G.S.

ALL THE PHOTOGRAPHS OF RIVIERA RESORTS IN THIS SUPPLEMENT WERE TAKEN SPECIALLY FOR, AND ARE THE COPYRIGHT OF, "THE BYSTANDER"

Off to the Riviera: A typical scene on the Continental departure platform at Charing Cross

The Sunniest Region in Europe

At the present juncture, when London seems shrouded in funereal gloom, and the fog fiend looms in the murky atmosphere, it is only natural that one's thoughts should turn with longing to the Land of Sunshine—the ideal place for a winter holiday.

Perhaps no more delightful winter quarters exist, within little more than a day's dry of London, than the popular Riviera.

A Comparison with our own South Coast

It is curious that the popularity of the Riviera does not seem much affected by the fluctuation in the tide of fashion, which draw its votaries to Rome, Naples, or Sicily, or across the tideless sea to Algeria or Egypt. It is beside the mark to say, with that occasionally exasperating individual, the "intelligent tourist," that Nice, Cannes, and Monte Carlo are hackneyed and banal; one might, with equal reason, find the same fault with Bournemouth or Torquay. Besides, those mainly anxious to spend a pleasant holiday in a genial climate do not pine for distant or experimental winter resorts, and are quite content to find at Cannes or Monte Carlo a kind of aftermath of the London season.

No doubt the advocates of our own South Coast winter resorts will be up in arms at the suggestion that it is necessary to go ahead to find pleasant winter quarters, and I may be bombarded with climatological records and statistics proving incontestably that the actual winter temperature of Ventnor or Bournemouth is only a few degrees lower than that of the Riviera resorts. Granted; but the point is, the South of France can show an immeasurable superiority in the matter of continuous sunshine, and, after all, that is the chief thing the average holiday-maker cares about. Of course, in the matter of sanitation, English resorts stand first.

Interior of Drawing-room car of the new Côte d'Azur Express, which runs from Paris to Mentone daily

---

570   SUPPLEMENT TO THE BYSTANDER, NOVEMBER 30, 1904

But I have neither space nor inclination to embark here on the controversial question of the relative merit of home and foreign resorts.

The Cost of the Journey Considerably Cheapened

Hitherto, no doubt, the great expense of the journey has placed the Riviera out of court for a short holiday, except for those of ample means, travelling expenses taking up a disproportionate amount of the total cost of the holiday.

Many visitors, in consequence, whose thoughts have turned towards the delights of the Sunny South, have to put up with the English counterparts of Nice and Cannes—Brighton and Bournemouth.

Now, thanks to the enterprise of the South Eastern and Chatham Railway, all this is changed, and a special through service at reduced rates has been arranged for those wishing to spend Christmas on the Riviera, for which the return ticket to any of the Riviera resorts from Hyères to Cannes costs only £9 12s. and £6 12s. respectively. The train, too, being composed of lavatory corridor carriages and a restaurant car, is, to all intents and purposes, a *train de luxe at popular prices*.

One of the most attractive features in this new service is the second-class bookings, for, as is well-known, on the ordinary P.L.M. expresses no second-class passengers are carried. This concession seems more liberal when it is remembered that the ordinary express to Nice costs nearly double the £6 12s. charged for the special Christmas Service. The service, which leaves London on December 23, at the convenient hour of 2.20 p.m., will arrive at the various Riviera resorts the next evening (Christmas Eve).

Railway Travelling de Luxe : A berth on the Côte d'Azur Express

The French "Flying Scotchman"

Tickets are available for the return journey from January 5th to 30th, and the journey can be broken in Paris. Any of the *rapide* and express services to the Riviera can be used, including the famous Côte d'Azur Express—the French counterpart of the

A Smoking Car on the Côte d'Azur Express

SUPPLEMENT TO THE BYSTANDER, NOVEMBER 30, 1904   571

The "Côte d'Azur" in Monte Carlo Station

Dining-car in the new Calais-Mediterranean Express

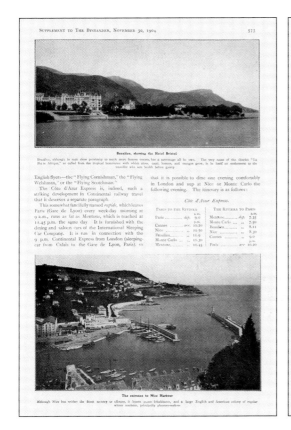

The Azur coast's development was shaped by PLM's railway operations as international express trains provided the life blood to one of Europe's busiest lines. Little wonder the company (Wagon-Lits and British partners) would turn to extensive promotional activity aimed at maximising wealthy visitor traffic around the turn of the twentieth century. In addition, poster advertising (in many languages) became a permanent marketing feature helping to maintain a tradition both companies would adhere to across the years fashioning the latest styles in exquisite art forms. (*Opposite left*: Illustrated London News Ltd/Mary Evans; *Opposite right*: Wagon-Lits Diffusion)

twin line for express, regional and suburban trains as well as freight traffic so essential to transport fresh produce for the Riviera and its rapidly expanding hospitality industries. Little surprise, French railway companies engaged in a degree of joined up thinking with British and other national railway operators, and this was clearly in evidence as the 9.00 pm London boat train left Charing Cross with sufficient time to meet up with the next day's train-de-luxe service. In time, PLM's luxury trains would be inextricably linked to Wagon-Lits. In January and February, the French Riviera geared up for the winter holiday season as international trains brought their diverse audiences all eager to participate in the indulgences of the 'Land of Sunshine' as described in a well-known travel handbook of the time and the constant rounds of social etiquette to be observed in the destination's numerous resorts. Glamorous nightlife had been opened by the PLM's extension to the towns and suburbs of Cannes, Antibes, Nice, Monaco, the luxurious hotels of Monte-Carlo's hill-top, Menton and Ventimiglia on the Italian border.

But it was the destination's association with the great named expresses that cemented its long-term reputation. In 1896 Wagon-Lits was influential in establishing the *Nord-Sud Brenner Express* linking Berlin, Munich and Verona and an extension to the Riviera via Milan to Cannes. Two years later the company extended its interests eastwards to cater for a lucrative market launching a St. Petersburg-French Riviera service designed to attract Russian and Habsburg aristocracy from the harsh cold of the winter months. The Russian train running from Warsaw linked with the *Vienna-Nice Express* service running speedily to the Azur coast. Such operations were a magnet for the international travel trade before the Great War with trains arriving from all directions affording travellers a fascinating snapshot of fin de siècle Europe. Food historian Jeri Quinzio captures a flavour of the time describing first-class passengers as totally wrapped in a cocooned environment where 'they enjoyed exquisite service, fine-dining, and the company of friends, or at least people with whom they felt comfortable'.[17] Such conviviality was a must as the fastest journey to the Riviera from Britain's shores was still some thirteen hours.

The French and its Italian cousin by the last third of the nineteenth century was the place to be seen coinciding with a period of spectacular growth. In short, it was regarded by its upscale clientele as the most fashionable and romantic destination on the globe central to the life of the upper-classes much in the same way a visit to Bath would have been in the previous century.[18] The Riviera's appeal and popularity as a great pleasure resort attracted increasing numbers of Americans drawn by travel writings, amongst others, of Henry James. When *Saratoga* was penned in 1870, the Riviera railway network was in its infancy with through trains to Paris only recently established.[19] Indeed, James's first visit to Italy at the time was completed by foot – but his short and crisp prose painted a picture of the Azur appealing to his American readership: 'privately I thought of the blue Mediterranean, and the little white promontory of Monaco, and the silver-grey verdure of olives, and the view across the outer sea toward the bosky cliffs of Italy', he pealed.[20] Yet until the arrival of Monte Carlo's gambling phenomenon, Monaco was perceived as an impoverished principality.[21] To accommodate visitor demand considerable emphasis was placed on developing the shoreline's facilities, and in particular the new construction that favoured exclusivity and luxuries the bourgeoisie preferred.

The building of infrastructure, quays, promenades, terraces and new expensive restaurants and hotels intermingled with the region's natural beauty, and its assortment of honey-coloured medieval hilltop and fishing villages created a raft of sophisticated resorts. Predominantly driven by a British middle-class who turned the Azur and nearby Switzerland 'into English playgrounds complete with English churches, English-speaking hotel staffs and statues of Queen Victoria'.[22] White-washed villas and large, sophisticated Mediterranean hotels were developed incorporating tastefully decorated suites accompanied by individual rooms fit for a king, together with monumental public spaces reflecting the most decadent fashions of the day. With new hotels every aspect of the guest experience was recalibrated to individual desires. Of these developments' writer Jim Ring remarks 'there were huge sweeping staircases to showcase Parisian gowns, vast ballrooms and dining rooms that would not have disgraced the courts of Nebuchadnezzar'.[23]

Personal attention to detail was never compromised. Coupled to this was the building of attractions catering for a wealthy clientele with a mix of casinos, golf links, yacht clubs and marinas and the Riviera equivalent of exclusive London gentlemen's clubs. Establishments on the littoral – a delightful nineteenth-century shoreline description rapidly gone out of common usage – all commanded panoramic positions, transforming the coastal region in little more than a generation as the English played their foremost part.[24] The French Riviera by late-Victorian times had its deliciously raffish establishments partly driven by the notoriety of the Prince of Wales's association with Azur coast life. His love of good living and extravagance – he had a twelve-wheeled royal carriage ready for his use in a Calais shed – had made him a focus of British society. Yet the Riviera based on its casino culture was not just a pleasure palace for the rich but was also developing as a string of resorts with a portfolio of hotels, restaurants and things to do appealing to an appreciative and erudite traveller – perhaps the forerunner of the modern-day 'culture vulture'. And whilst some of these were independent visitors there were others pressing the needs for travel agent's specialist services.[25]

The principality of Monaco with its Monte Carlo gaming halls was transformed by railway access in 1870. A veritable winter-time industry was created pandering to the whims of the Riviera's well-heeled who had both time and money on their hands. By the late 1800s, PLM was running trains to meet the specific needs of its gambling passengers.[26] One thing the Riviera could not quite compete on at the time, was the swish new English resorts of Bournemouth and Brighton, and the quality of hygiene and sanitation mattering greatly to upscale British visitors. As Mullen and Munson observed, 'For almost a hundred years the most important thing for writers of travel-guides, railway companies and travel agencies was to bring European inns and hotels up to British middle-class standards of domestic comfort and cleanliness.'[27] It was this passion for spotlessness that divided the British from their Continental neighbours far more than the Channel.[28] And there was international competition, too, as by the 1890s Swiss, German and Italian hotels were advertising for middle-class patrons with promises of sanitary arrangements regarded as faultless. Advertising was specifically directed towards British audiences highlighting hotel accommodation possessing English-speaking staff, comforts that appealed to English tourists, and even the enticement of on-site churches and resident English ministers.[29] But the pace of Riviera expansion was noteworthy attracting new money, investment and redevelopment of residential property and a resultant influx of new incomers. London was home to several weekly tabloid magazines or the 'illustrated weeklies' as Graves and Hodge preferred to describe them.[30] Publications such as *The Bystander*, *The Globe* and *The Pall Mall Gazette* (both titles merged in 1921 and then subsumed by the *Evening Standard* two years later), *The Graphic*, *St. James's Gazette*, *The Illustrated London News* and *The Illustrated Sporting*, and *Dramatic News* spoke in an increasingly enthusiastic and poetic manner about the Riviera's way of life. What these publications had in common, sharing similar upmarket readers, was the ability to report on society events in its widest context that also appealed to middle-class readerships keen to adopt grander leanings. Articles on travel and accompanying holidaymaker interests became the publication's mainstay.[31] As Dr Ross McKibbin reports in his book *Classes and Cultures: England 1918–1951*, published by Oxford University Press in 2000, 'Britain had a powerful and technically sophisticated mass press which gave immense publicity to society and which was in turn exploited by it.'[32] Travel arrangements for the coming Riviera season always provided suitable editorial opportunities. Fleet-footed railway companies and hoteliers responded enthusiastically maximising the value of promotional space invariably including a degree of tactical advertising support to garner favourable correspondent reporting. In a special *Bystander* travel supplement, the Perambulator column pointed to the veracity of a coastal strip between Cannes and Mentone being so studded with English villas and hotels that a modern-day Rip Van Winkle awakening from a deep sleep might have imagined that 'a great European war had broken out, with the result that the department of the Alpes Maritimes had been annexed by Great Britain!'[33] Nice, still semi-rural in the 1850s, came to be favoured by an Anglo-American community: British railway companies used the term 'watering hole' to describe a place that was not necessarily a spa town, but a phrase used frequently in their promotional literature. Nice's fine water reputation fuelled growth; the town grew rapidly boasting some 90,000 inhabitants with a large gathering of regular English and American winter residents masquerading as a 'who's who' of the British establishment. Such was the infusion. In time Nice would become almost totally dependent on the tourism economy. Similarly, Cannes, which developed a standing as the most fashionable of the Riviera's resorts, would see its population doubling by the early 1890s.[34] As Mullen and Munson distinguished 'one hotel in Cannes boasted that it had "three Lawn Tennis Courts considered the finest and largest in Europe" as well as a billiard room'. A rival establishment boasted a gymnasium.[35] Further east San Remo was described as the 'social capital' of the Italian Riviera with its old town, residents and coastal heritage finding favour with many lotus-eaters. Here, Perambulator, goes on: 'During the "gay season", from Christmas to Lent, there are frequent balls, re-unions, and concerts, at which the permanent English colony turn out in force.'[36]

The British had had a love affair with the French Riviera since the days of the days of the eighteenth-century Grand Tour, even though today's legacy is studiously downplayed or even ignored by tourist authorities.[37] A hundred years later their enclaves were customary having set up camp on the shores in the 1830s, when the first members of the English aristocracy arrived in numbers sampling the warm winter airs. Cannes was nothing more than a small fishing village before Lord Brougham arrived. In the years before the railway's arrival British presence was notable as in time a series of coastal resorts developed as a result of British interest. Nice inaugurated its 'Promenade des Anglais', a seafront walkway paid for by English residents as a means to assist local people who lost their jobs when winter frosts destroyed orange orchards.[38] English tourist interest over the next fifty years would help to guarantee the transformation of the Riviera from a rural backwater into one of the world's plushest destinations. The Harmsworth publishing dynasty were close to the landslide majority Liberal government of 1906. Future Prime Minister David Lloyd George spent his holidays at Harold Harmsworth's coastal villa retreat. Professor David Cannadine suggests leading members of the Liberal administration lived in 'riotous luxury' and were 'in thrall to big business and the plutocracy'.[39] The French Riviera provided the perfect location away from the capital to conduct clandestine liaisons and discreet meetings in private away from London's prying eyes. Over the post-war years, Lloyd George would be seen on the Riviera coast on many occasions along with other senior politicians of the day.[40] Lloyd George exploited his connections chartering the 500-ton yacht *Argosy* from Thomas Cook for the auspices of a 'Mediterranean health cruise'.[41]

With the railways the full effect of tourism development was felt from 1860 onwards.[42] Significant numbers of new British tourists arrived together with a few rich Russians. European aristocracy was always well represented on the Riviera's shores. A constant procession of crowned heads of state (and their families) in the winter season kept railway companies busy providing much local interest and intrigue: European monarchies possessed a semi-magical character.[43] Even British royalty was to be seen on the

Riviera setting a seal of approval for the wealthy pleasure resort as the centre of the fashionable world. The Prince of Wales made the first of his many regular Riviera appearances in 1872 setting a trend ten years later for his mother (Queen Victoria) to make regular visits all contributing immensely to the Azur coast's fame.[44] The Riviera, portrayed as the sunniest region in Europe, incorporated some of the world's finest, stylish and up-to-date hotels permanently altered the regional economy from an artisan base to one where locals were lured to work in newly established hospitality businesses. The servicing of prosperous tourists became big business especially as railway upgrading brought ease of access and new facilities. Wagon-Lits opened two Riviera Palace Hotels at Cimiez, Nice and Monte Carlo following a business model developed by British and French railway companies who built grand hotels at their city centre terminuses. Nagelmackers, who had founded Compagnie Internationale des Grand Hotels in 1894, operated a string of luxury hotels across the Mediterranean including Cairo, Nice, Constantinople, Lisbon, Therapia, Brindis, Ismailia, Maloja, Bordeaux as well as the Belgian coastal town of Ostend to where he had run one of his earliest upscale train services a decade before.[45]

In the south of France, Riviera hotels were busy promoting themselves in the British press having put together a 'Syndicate of Hoteliers' designed to attract British visitors.[46] The Hotel Bristol in Beaulieu, regarded as one of a dozen best hotels on the Riviera strip with a patronage all its own, placed its accommodation as 'the rendezvous of the elite' and the most convenient hotel for all points of the littoral. Similarly, Strand based Gordon Hotels group promoted their Monte Carlo and Cannes hotels with full page advertisements in selected publications targeting London's elite.[47] The dazzling light of the Azur Sea and its rocky shores ensured the Riviera was well-positioned to maximise the pre-war splendour of the *Belle Époque* years. Winter sunshine on the Riviera was very much a continual celebration of life for the privileged in late-Victorian and Edwardian times.

Britain's Empire interests were self-evident. In 1872 the *Globe* newspaper reported on Wagon-Lits installing an *Indian Mail Train* to the Italian port of Brindisi via Ostend, Cologne, Munich and the Brenner in the early 1870s.[48] Passengers for Brindisi changed at Bologna on to a Wagon-Lits Pullman Express as both mail and passengers dovetailed with British merchant ships heading east.

50 Les Chemins de Fer français (P. L. M.)

Le L. 22 " Calais-Méditerranée " machine Nᵒ 6113 Pacifique. Train de luxe de la Compagnie Internationale des Wagons-Lits entre Calais, Paris, Nice, Vintimille, arrive à Paris à 8 h. 50 du matin

F. F. Paris

PLM and Wagon-Lits between November and April provided its best-known trains for its pleasure-seeking customers heading south. Around 1913 PLM commissioned a series of photographs to record their express trains – their composition and length varied according to season. F. Fleury, Ave de la Republique, Paris published these as postcards. In the first two images, the crack day-time Calais-Méditerranée express with Wagon-Lits stock is shown headed up by Pacific Class locomotives PLM 6113 – serie 6101/6171 built in 1911, and in the second by PLM 6114 – serie 6101/6171 also built in 1911. The fast night-time service highlighted in the third postcard is headed by PLM 2494 – serie 2430/2599 engine which entered service in 1913. (*Above and below*: French Railways Society)

54 Les Chemins de Fer français (P. L. M.)

Le L. 22 " Calais Méditerranée ", Train de luxe de la Compagnie Internationale des Wagons-Lits, machine Pacifique Nᵒ 6114 entre Calais, Paris, Marseille, Nice, Vintimille

F. F. Paris

55 Les Chemins de Fer français (P.-L.-M.)

Le 18 " La Côte d'Azur " de nuit. Machine Nᵒ 2494 Train extra-rapide entre Paris, Marseille, Toulon, Monte-Carlo, Menton et Vintimille

By 1881 the South Italian Railway and Adriatic Lines operated the *India Mail* between London, Brindisi and Bombay. The Italian port could be reached from London in forty-five hours aboard a weekly boat train service via Calais known as the *Peninsular Express* formed part of joint facility between several railway companies and shipping lines. By late-Victorian times, P&O used its own dedicated company boat trains (courtesy of Wagon-Lits) timed to meet with its own steamers. In 1898 P&O introduced two fast steamers to its Italian port operations. Ambrose Greenway, a maritime writer describes how the company took delivery of two rather unusual vessels. 'Akin to cross-channel steamers, 1,728-grt twin screw *Isis* and *Osiris* were specially designed to convey the overland mail and seventy-eight first-class passengers, who had arrived by train from London, from Brindisi to Port Said where they caught up the mail steamer that had left the UK some two weeks before.'[49] The combined rail/sea/rail/sea/sea operation worked like clockwork.

Although further west, Marseilles established itself as a major Mediterranean Sea port as many upscale passengers were tempted by shipping services avoiding longer sea journeys from Britain, and the unpredictability of the Bay of Biscay with its potential for rough sea passage. The PLM route to the south-east of France extended into Switzerland, and along the Riviera corridor to Italy which for most part of the second half of the1800s, had been an important destination for British and American travellers due to its close geographical proximity to the antiquities of the eastern Mediterranean. A downside though of the Italian Riviera route was no direct through service. Notwithstanding, Switzerland had been much favoured by returning tourists from Italy looking to break their journeys.[50] The *Clifton Society* reported:

> The increase of travel by the St. Gotthard during the last two seasons has been quite remarkable. People are going more and more to Bellagio, Lugano, Como, Locarno, and all the other charming spots which dot the shores of the Italio-Swiss lakes; and the through travel from India and the Orient, *via* the Suez Canal, is now largely finding its way over this attractive and picturesque route, delivering its passengers in London in the surprisingly short time of sixty-one hours after their landing in Brindisi.[51]

A new Italian express, launched on 15 November 1897, was an innovative direct service 'composed exclusively of sleeping

The Brindisi *Peninsular Express* route established itself as the important mail boat train anchor providing weekly passenger shipping access via P&O to India and beyond knocking off several days of sea transit. It was also an important axis point for tourist traffic.

The second image shows the M71 mail train from Calais to Brindisi. This particular weekly service did not carry passengers but was dedicated to carrying dispatches from the UK to India. (*Right*: Wagon-Lits Diffusion; *Below*: French Railways Society)

There were other Italian route connections linking Europe's principal cities. The Mont Cenis Tunnel and the Turin route was Europe's first great Alpine tunnel construction; a second mountain route conquest arrived with the St. Gotthard Tunnel and Milan line in June 1882, and from 1906 the opening of the Simplon Tunnel. (French Railways Society)

Completion of the Simplon Tunnel allowed a further round of railway company and shipping line collaboration. Apart from their substantial British operations, Canadian Pacific had an European toe hold running steamers in and out of the then Austrian port of Trieste. The *PLM L34 Simplon Express* boat train, in this shot hauled by PLM 2982 - serie 2971/2990 built in 1907, linked Calais, Paris, Milan with Trieste at the head of the Adriatic. Wagon-Lits dining and saloon cars provided stylish travel arrangements to awaiting Canadian Pacific steamers or for onward journeys to Vienna and other parts of the Austro-Hungarian Empire. The Trieste-Vienna route had been completed as long ago as 1857. At the other end of the journey, passengers could cross from Calais on steamers, boarding an SECR Pullman boat train to London for awaiting Canadian Pacific ships at Tilbury or alternatively take a LNWR or Midland Railway Liverpool express. (French Railways Society)

and restaurant cars' that did not involve passengers with train changes.[52] It brought fast and convenient access via Mont Cenis supported by French, Swiss and Italian railway company's crack locomotives. The *Rome Express* was a luxury train with a stylish service designed to bring the city's splendours and its superior grand hotels in quick fashion; Italy could now be reached in around thirty-six hours. Rome, throughout the later period of unification, graciously accepted Europe's many aristocratic visitors building with it a reputation for affluent tourists attracted by the Grand Tour idyll. The *Rome Express* had a certain degree presence and panache that the first generation of pan-European named train expresses delivered for business travellers and tourists alike. On the first run, an anonymous but well-connected passenger, known simply by his initials T.E.L.G., said of the new Wagon-Lits service:

> Standing spick-and-span, ready to receive us into its warm corridors. We were ahead of time, and after depositing our impediments in our compartments and enjoying a wash in warm water preparatory to sitting down to lunch, we found that were not timed to start for another five minutes, so we took a stroll on the platform to look at our new train. The season for the rush to Italy of Britishers not yet commenced, the train was not a heavy one. It was composed of two sleeping cars, one restaurant car, and two mail and baggage cars, all on the bogie principle. The three passenger cars were about 55 feet long and weighed about 27 tons each. The sleeping cars had berths for twenty passengers in each, divided into compartments, some for four and the others for two persons.

Home luxuries could now be found on the *Rome Express*: 'Not the least of the many advantages of a *train de luxe* is that one can make one's self as comfortable as in one's own home, the temperature of the train being kept at about 68 degrees Fahrenheit.' Our distinguished traveller spoke about his next morning's experience of being awakened by a tap on the shoulder by the waiter requesting details for breakfast before the train's Turin arrival:

> In less than five minutes a nice white serviette was spread on the little table in my compartment alongside my bed, and I was served with a delicious cup of *café au lait*, some toast, and a *brioche*. He went on to finally describe the final destination of the train

at Rome's Stazione Centrale where he arrived 'in the greatest comfort and without a sign of fatigue or the stain of travel!'[53]

The value to the company of such unsolicited but positive exposure must have been immense. On introduction, the train initially ran once per week every Monday for the winter season. The British side of the service was run in conjunction with the then SER leaving Charing Cross and Canon Street stations at 9.00 am to meet the *Rome Express* in Calais. British and French railway partners exercised a great deal of planning as the train-de-luxe made up exclusively of sleeping, restaurant and saloon cars would follow the same outer Paris route as the *Calais-Méditerranée Express*. Italy could be reached from London through the French Riviera arriving at Ventimiglia by a daily coupé-lits-toilette and first-class carriage leaving Boulogne at 2.13 pm in the afternoon. Connecting with the Rome-Cannes train from the south, it brought Italians and many British and American visitors returning from exploring the cultural citadels of the eastern Mediterranean. The fusion of individual states into the modern Italian nation ensured passengers toured the country by rail at ease and with a degree of safety – although not necessarily the case on the other side of the Adriatic coast in the Balkans. The Balkans were bandit country with peripatetic groups running rural and remote mountainous regions as personal fiefdoms. All this conjured destination intrigue with the troubles brewing between various eastern European states and the constant political posturing and manoeuvring of the big powers who did their best to ensure no one gained an upper hand.

At the turn of the century travelling to the French and Italian Riviera from Britain did not present too many practical difficulties apart from journey length and cost. A journalist penned as Cosmopolitan, wrote an article for *The Railway Magazine* entitled 'to the sunny south by railway' where he certainly did not mince his words informing readers PLM's aim was 'to fleece the unfortunate traveller to the greatest possible extent, and to give him the smallest imaginable return for his money'. He goes on with acidic condemnation to describe the PLM as being 'in the possession of an absolute monopoly, and the Sleeping Car Company of a virtual one' where 'Riviera traffic is derived almost exclusively from two classes of the community – *i.e.*, from rich people, to whom money is no object, and from invalids who *must* go the South, and are therefore forced to pay any fare, however exorbitant.'[54] Certainly a train deluxe first-class return with sleeping accommodation from London to Nice in 1899 was expensive, almost two and a half times the cost of a comparable journey in length from London to Wick in the north of Scotland. 'Comment is superfluous,' Cosmopolitan added wryly.[55] The winter seasons of the new century presented some difficulty for the Riviera's prime resorts but were countered by SECR issuing Italian circular tickets proving attractive to travellers who were able to combine visits to both Italy and Riviera. By the January 1903 railway companies felt the new season's prospects were on the up again withdrawing the combined facility.[56]

Despite high costs of travelling to the Continent rapid railway infrastructure development on both sides of the English Channel brought about continual service improvements with resultant competition between various groups of British and French railway operators, presenting passengers with a choice of alternative routes and itineraries. At the eastern end of the English Channel SER and LCDR, and from 1899 the SECR as the merged successor organisation, had the pick of the short packet-mail crossings. Apart from Wagon-Lits upscale sleeping car offerings, the new SECR company experimented with other services. For the 1905 Christmas holiday it offered a Riviera bound train from Boulogne described as 'a special train, composed of first and second class lavatory-carriages and a restaurant-car'.[57] However, they could not rest on their laurels as alternative first-class train services with through routes to Paris (and other connecting destinations) were offered by competitor railway companies operating out of western channel ports.

The prospect of the Riviera for the 1904 Christmas holidays prompted considerable competition amongst railway companies. SECR and PLM tapped into the newly discovered middle-class affluence creating a special second-class through train 'composed of lavatory corridor carriages and a restaurant car' dubbed in the British press as a train-de-luxe at popular prices. International interest was not just confined to Britain's southern based railway companies. The LNWR placed an office on the Boulevard des Italians in Paris from 1899 and later an agent was based in Cannes to tap into the rich vein of American travellers visiting France, but who would undoubtedly arrive and depart Britain from the company's Liverpool (and Glasgow – their Caledonian Railway partner) port gateways.[58] Glasgow did not possess a dedicated port railway station within the city with Caledonian Railway regularly providing boat trains for trans-Atlantic liners and Irish Sea steamers from Central Station to Greenock.[59] By the eve of the Great War specialist corridor coaches were attached to a boat train connection on a speeded up LBSCR and ETAT London to Paris route that left Dieppe for Milan, and the Italian tourist centres via Lausanne and the Simplon tunnel. Visitors for Switzerland, the Tyrol and Italy welcomed the convenience of this facility.[60]

The French capital, with a string of radiating routes was home to Parisian society, which like their British counterparts, decamped to warmer climes at the height of the winter months. Paris in the autumn of 1910 suffered a great railway strike bringing the city to a standstill. *The Sketch* reported, 'For some while, the great railway strike in Paris paralysed practically all the traffic and cut Paris off from the world so far as train communication was concerned.' The newspaper went on 'Travellers in a hurry to leave Paris had in many cases to get to their destinations by motor-cars, and the drivers of taxi-cabs, in particular, did a roaring trade at very high fares.'[61]

On the return to a degree of normality the south beckoned. In the years leading up to Europe's conflagration, PLM's Riviera bound expresses – 'constructed so as to give the maximum of reliability' – were the way to travel. Paris's elite customers could rely on year-round connections to the firm Riviera favourites.[62] And for the 1914 winter season, Italy was back in vogue. Southern Italy's mild winter climate ensured Rome and Naples, prone to falling in and out of fashion, attracted many international arrivals in the months before the lights went out. In 1913 Naples decided to promote its wares to the British press extolling itself as the 'Home of the Picturesque'; Italian's had learnt the trick of taking tourism in its stride.[63] The Eternal City was home to a considerable level of entertaining with English society arriving in force mingling with the resident colony. The illustrated weeklies reported on the Riviera season as per norm emphasising the highly integrated travel facilities that could be relied on. SECR and LBSCR on the English side and Wagon-Lits and PLM on the Continent provided upscale travellers with a seamless service.

But as a potential hint in the way society and the middle-classes would spend their holiday recreation time in the future, *The Bystander* reported on PLM's year-round access to destinations suggesting the railway was 'both for health and pleasure in summer and in winter the paradise of the tourist. It covers a tract of ground where any climate is found. Snow in summer – sun in winter – the site of innumerable natural beauties and of many splendid monuments of the Roman and Mediaeval Ages'.[64]

French Magic: The Blue Train and the Côte d'Azur Pullman Express

The First World War proved difficult for Europe's railway companies, and in particular Wagon-Lits, since much of its stock outside of France simply disappeared or returned in a derelict state. Aside the *Orient Express*, the company by 1914 had a time-honoured thirty-or-so-year track record of successfully running high-class deluxe train operations with its French and other international railway partners to the Riviera, the Swiss Alps and to Italy. But it was France that quickly assumed a degree of importance once the Armistice had been signed with the *P&O Express* becoming one of the first international boat trains reinstated. Brindisi was abandoned in favour of a Calais and Marseilles route cementing the city's position as a major Mediterranean passenger liner port. British interests were paramount: P&O liners sailed from Marseilles providing a mail service to maintain written communication with the Empire. Not that luxury was much in evidence at the time. European travel was nothing short of an adventure as many carriages were left in a deplorable condition. Much deluxe coaching stock was literally a shell, stripped of their velvet and tapestry coverings, metal fittings broken off and sold as scrap metal and wooden superstructure carried away as firewood.

Yet for international travellers this was about to change for the better as in 1922 Wagon-Lits' all-steel sleepers were introduced to form a newly named *Bombay-Express*. The *Indian Mail* later became known as *Overland P&O Express* with the introduction of new luxurious 'LX' type sleepers in 1928. For European travellers (and those serving in colonial posts) used to extravagant rail and ocean travel, on reaching India's vast interior railway system, the sub-continent represented good value for money. It was a huge sprawling network of some 40,000 miles which helped keep Empire interests intact by keeping the lid on the cauldron of Indian nationalism. Given the country's mystical and spectacular hinterland, reaching particular destinations could take days of travel. First-class dining and sleeping accommodation aboard long-distance trains, even if progress was often conducted at a snail's pace, was on a grand scale comparable with some of the best found in European rail travel.

In the meantime, the French Riviera assumed a new persona. Not content with its position as a leading winter haven, it aspired to a new chic year-round visitor role for the rich and famous.

Some destination rebuilding was evidently required as Europe distanced itself from the miseries of war. George Behrend summed up the position precisely as by the early 1920s 'a whole generation had grown up ignorant of the delights of the Côte d'Azur'.[65] Luxury train travel did return with typical Gallic flair as the *Calais-Méditerranée Express*, with lineage dating to 1880s, became a prestigious new service later colloquially known as the *Blue Train*. From 1922 PLM/Wagon-Lit's premier first-class only night-train sped to the Riviera with more luxury, panache and unrivalled sophistication than any preceding service; it proved to be a magnet for America's plutocrats and family-legions of rich industrialists. For a new generation of pleasure-seekers, from both sides of the pond, the new sleeper train with its designated 'S' type carriages offered an opportunity to party to the dazzling coast, and a chance to escape the horrors of recent history. The Riviera set included some of the English-speaking world's leading authors; for them a night aboard the legendary train had to be pressed into prose and railway travel folklore. Like Britain's new premier and glamorous expresses, the *Blue Train* was synonymous with a unique and sophisticated experience combining hope, anticipation and reward conjured in Robert Louis Stevenson's memorable exhortation of travelling hopefully is a better thing than to arrive. It set the seal of approval as one of *the* preferred trains of the well-heeled.

Affluent travel was to some extent restored in August 1919 as London society decamped en masse to the Scottish Highlands for resumption of the grouse season. The following year, the sky-blue coast was open for business as a few intrepid devotees found their way ahead of regular rail connections. Some stayed for the summer, with exploits covered in gossip columns on both sides of the Atlantic, and perhaps, registering as the forerunner to the summer-time destination attraction which would take such a hold in a few short years. Favourite winter-time haunts much admired by the English were back on track. The Gordon Hotels group announced their Cannes and Monte Carlo Hotel Metropole establishments would open on 1 November providing guests with a continuous motor service to and from main railway stations. The *Riviera Season* kicked off officially on 16 November 1920 as PLM/Wagon-Lits express trains once again sped between Paris and Menton on the Italian border. Sleeping berths on trains to Cannes and Nice were booked up months in advance. By the following year the Riviera was packed as thousands of people made their way south as the tradition of affluent British families renting villas on the Azur rapidly returned.[66] So, too, were wealthy Americans who started arriving almost as soon as the ink was dry on the Armistice documents, spending a greater part of their European tour in France although visiting Britain was invariably on itineraries.[67] By May 1922, the *Western Daily Press* reported on the degree of the American invasion steadily increasing 'as the season advances, developed to the extent of another two thousand visitors to Europe from New York by the White Star liner *Olympic*, which arrived at Southampton on Saturday'.[68]

Sport played a bigger role. Interest in golf and tennis had spread from social elites to the more populous middle-classes as well as an increasing American fondness. Always a crowd-puller for larger than life members of high society, the sky-blue coast attracted international characters, but its nature was changing quickly prompting 'cries of social and intellectual snobbery' from literary notaries like Beverley Nichols and Scott Fitzgerald.[69] Society in the post-war period progressively became a British and US affair where many hostesses saw their roles as 'social entrepreneurs' integrating Anglo-American elites. Ross McKibbin noted the drive came from both sides flavouring many an upscale social gathering.[70] This all formed part of a reconfiguring of roles and responsibilities towards the organisation of foreign travel. The boat train played its key role as increased numbers of women had the time, money and the wherewithal to plan the year's social calendar. The Riviera was still perceived as an exotic destination with half of English society reckoned to spend some part of the winter in the south of France.[71] It also attracted Americans in their scores for Christmas festivities. *The Scotsman* newspaper noted:

> Many American visitors are arriving on the Riviera, and quantities of British golf clubs are in evidence at the Gare de Lyon. A tribute to British prowess at the game stands on the Nice course at Cagnes, where a tablet proclaims that Mr Lloyd George made a certain hole in one, constituting a record. The ex-Premier will, it is stated, endeavour to equal this record on the Valescure links, where he is now bound by sea.[72]

Despite the problems of getting to France in the immediate post-war years – coal shortages and what coal was available was often of poor steaming quality – prevailed across Europe, but by the early 1920s, the full night-time first-class only international expresses returned.[73] The *Calais-Méditerranée Express* was trumpeted as a brand-new service – the *Blue Train* – incorporating bespoke British carriage stock as the 'most luxurious express ran from Calais Maritime to Marseille and thence along the Riviera into Italy'.[74] *The Blue Train* commenced operations on 9 December 1922 with the great and good present for the launch event including Sir Herbert Walker, the Southern grouping's forthcoming general manager. Europe needed colour to brighten up drabness and a rank of high-quality famous named expresses heralded a new age of European luxury train travel. And the new train did not disappoint. Author Jim Ring captures the moment of culinary canonization aboard the 'Voiture Restaurant' of the luxury steam-hauled boat train: 'The dining car, with its movable scenery, upstaged Maxim's, the Café Royal, Simpsons and the Savoy. Standards of craftsmanship and joinery made the carriages seem a creation of the cabinet-make rather than the railway works.'[75]

The Bystander did its bit assisting the Azur coast on its feet again by attracting the old guard. Despite a wealthy American cohort, inflation and the war had taken its toll on personal finances for numerous Britons. They declared 'even the Riviera is returning to normal prices'.[76] Press interest in the *Blue Train* was immense as the company ran two separate trains catering for the fifty or so invited journalists on its Nice inauguration, representing a galvanising point for trans-Continental luxury express travel. It also coincided with Southern Railway's birth, but more importantly, here was a new railway organisation committed to becoming a major advocate in the sector's expansion. Southern was able to lay down a blueprint with Continental partners for future development ultimately revealing itself in the launch of two of the world's most glamorous luxury trains: *Golden Arrow* in 1929 and *Night Ferry* in 1936.

Walker, previously LSWR's general manager, discussed preliminary ideas with Lord Dalziel of Wooler, President du Conseil and chairman of the Wagon-Lits management committee as Dalziel's British Pullman company had had close working relationships with Southern's two other former constituent companies; LBSCR and SECR. Dalziel was intricately involved with both luxury train organisations as his daughter had married Wagon-Lits' founder Georges Nagelmackers' son Rene. Through these connections, Dalziel had orchestrated US investment in the company (through financier John Pierpont Morgan and steel magnet Charles Schwab)

A LITERARY LETTER : On "the Blue Train."

LONDON, December 20, 1922.

I am supposed in this letter to write about books, although there are frank readers who tell me they would always prefer that I write about places. But after all, I write this letter to please myself mainly, and so take things as they come.

Since I last wrote I have spent forty-eight hours on the Riviera, and have taken about the same length of time in reaching that beautiful land and returning from it. One solicitous friend, whose good opinion I value, suggested that once on the Riviera I should stay there for a few days, that the journey involved in travelling 2,000 miles in a four days' holiday would do me more harm than good. But to me the exhilaration of a long railway journey is what horse-riding or a sea voyage is to another man. To me that journey from London to Monte Carlo and back, with only one night in an hotel, was a crowded hour of glorious life. Then I am entirely dependent on companionship in travel, and the prospect of seeing once again that gifted and kindly Frenchman, M. Margot, the president of the P.L.M. Railway, was itself an inducement.

Moreover, I am a creature of sentiment, and thirty years ago Mr. Henry Snow, the London Chairman of the International Sleeping Car Company, came to me and invited me to go to Bosnia and Herzegovina with him. The Austrian Government of that day were anxious to show French and English journalists what they were doing with these Balkan provinces they had just taken over from the Turks. I recall that M. de Blowitz was of the party, and I have very interesting impressions of Sarajevo and Mostar. I had scarcely seen Mr. Snow in the interval, and here he was, still full of enthusiasm for this famous Sleeping Car Company. And so, when I was told that Sir Davidson Dalziel had invited a party of railway magnates and a few journalists to the inauguration of a new method of travelling, I gladly accepted an invitation to accompany the party.

For the first time in the history of railway enterprise the continent of Europe has adopted the system in vogue in England—one sleeper for each person. Hitherto, I understand, sleeping cars have been constructed on a framework of wood. In these new cars of the Sleeping Car Company, wood has only been used for the interior decoration of compartments and corridors, and the framework and all other parts of the car are made entirely of steel. Vibration has, moreover, been reduced to a minimum. Hence this journey was not as formidable as it might appear, and, indeed, I feel all the better for it. It is ever the cross-Channel passage that perturbs me. I am not a good sailor. But at the cost of three pounds sterling I secured deck cabins from Dover to Calais and return, and this, with the prospect of being a guest for the rest of the journey, even a poor journalist could afford.

That journey to Nice was a delightfully comfortable experience. It is pleasant to get into a train at Calais and to pass in the night into the glorious sunshine of the Riviera. It is true that to me the pleasure is chastened by the knowledge that I am missing in the hours of sleep some of the most entrancing spots in France, the varied picturesqueness of Provence—Avignon, Tarascon, Arles, and Nîmes. But the memories of these towns must always be cherished. Then there were the fragrant hours of lunch and dinner, meals which one may be sure were the more perfectly served in that we carried so many railway potentates among the guests. My companion at dinner was Sir Henry Lunn, whom I have known for long years, and with whom it was pleasant to talk over old times.

Then I was glad to meet again Mr. James Greig, the art critic of *The Morning Post*, the biographer of Gainsborough and Raeburn, whose name appears on the title-page of the first volume of *The Farington Diary*, just published by Hutchinson. Mr. Greig's romantic discovery of this diary, which has occupied so many vivid columns of *The Morning Post*, is set forth in his introduction to the first volume. I was glad also to meet again Mr. Sutherland, the editor of *The Pall Mall Gazette*. He is young and gifted, and I hope will outlast in time of office very many of his predecessors, for I think in my journalistic career I have dined with a full dozen of *Pall Mall* editors, including Greenwood, Stead, Morley, Straight—names upon which I could write columns of reminiscences. But I must not talk about the journalists I met in "the Blue Train," for these were completely overshadowed by the magnates of the great English railways, some of whose names, like that of Sir Sam Fay of the Great Central, have been household words with me for many years.

To give a logical completeness to the scheme of things, a thick fog had settled over London when we embarked at Victoria. A popular and vivacious M.P. enlivened my journey across the Channel, and there at Calais was the brand new train of deeper blue awaiting us, and the compartments, with our names on each, duly in evidence. I was disposed at first to criticise the narrowness of these compartments, for I am a portly person, if not Falstaffian. But it was explained to me that the railway companies—the combined North of France and Paris-Lyons—

demand that there shall be sixteen compartments in one carriage, whereas the L. and N.W. Railway and the Great Western in England are content with but nine compartments to a carriage. Be that as it may, the new order of things is an entire success. Most of my readers have travelled in the *wagon-lits* ; have, if with a friend, " tossed up " as to who should sleep in the upper berth, or have hated the stranger whom fate has ordained should have captured the lower berth before they arrived. Now there is but one berth in each compartment, a neat wash-hand basin, and a variety of deft conveniences, including a light for reading. One could easily devour half-a-dozen novels on this journey across France, but I had so many friends with whom to compare notes, and was content with one wonderful story, *Futility*, which Mr. Cobden Sanderson sent me just before I started.

I am not going to attempt to describe Nice, which we found that morning bathed in perfect sunshine—the majority of my readers are familiar with it. Nor will I dwell upon the pleasure with which I looked out upon the Mediterranean from the windows of my room at the beautiful Hotel Ruhl, nor the motor drives to Monte Carlo and Mentone, the wonders of the Corniche Road, nor the drives on the Monday to Saint Raphaël, whence we took train back to Paris and London. The Riviera is a veritable paradise, and I marvel that the people who can afford it do not spend the winter there in much greater numbers.

*   *   *

By a curious coincidence, two books have just appeared in which Dr. Johnson is skilfully parodied. The first is *The New Boswell*, by R. M. Freeman (John Lane), the second, *Dr. Johnson in Cambridge*, by S. C. Roberts. Of Mr. Freeman's book I have already had many pleasant foretastes in the pages of the old *Westminster Gazette* when

Cultivating Literature
In the luxurious surroundings of the International Car Company's carriages from Calais to Nice and Monte Carlo

it was an evening paper and beguiled the hours of the railway traveller by its many brilliant excursions in literature. One was enchanted by the picture of Boswell and Johnson in Elysium discussing a hundred and one modern topics, Johnson showing all his capacity for verbal dialectic. The picture on the wrapper of Dr. Johnson on the telephone is a key to the attempt to present the great Cham in the modern world.

This is truly a delightful book for every Johnsonian, and if I might offer one remonstrance, it would be that although Boswell had a prejudice against Goldsmith, based upon the fact that he was really jealous of Goldsmith's influence with Johnson, and was able to distort the character and mentality of the author of *The Vicar of Wakefield* to a degree which has lasted to our own day, that when Boswell and Johnson had reached another world I venture to think that both would have taken a more enlightened view of Goldsmith's character, and would have seen through superficial traits what a really great man he was. This is a small matter. On the whole, the Johnson of Mr. Freeman is a delightful personality. The spirit of Boswell has been captured by this book.

Mr. S. C. Roberts has attempted the same thing in what he calls essays in Boswellian Imitation in *Dr. Johnson in Cambridge* (G. P. Putnams Sons). Mr. Roberts is the new secretary of the Cambridge Press in succession to my old friend, Mr. A. R. Waller. His little book is quite in the spirit of Boswell's narrative. One is surprised to think that it should be possible for two men at almost the same moment to capture so cleverly the spirit of Boswell. But Mr. Roberts's is a very small volume. It is published at 2s. 6d., whereas the *New Boswell* is published at 6s. 6d. This does not indicate the relative value of the books but their relative sizes. Both will become the property of every good Johnsonian.

C. K. S.

I have received the following books:—

THE BEAUTIFUL AND DAMNED. By F. Scott-Fitzgerald. 7s. 6d. net. (*Collins.*) DANDELION DAYS. By Henry Williamson. 7s. 6d net. (*Collins.*) AS OTHERS SEE US. By Marmaduke Pickthall. 7s. 6d. net. (*Collins.*) AUCTION BRIDGE STANDARDS. By Wilbur C. Whitehead. 2s. 6d. net. (*Heinemann.*) ROSSETTI AND HIS CIRCLE. By Max Beerbohm. 25s. net. (*Heinemann.*) HIS DOG. By Albert Payson Terhune. 4s. 6d. net. (*J. M. Dent.*) ELIZABETH ANN'S DELIGHT. By Maud Dowson. Pictures by Ethel F. Everett. 6s. net. (*J. M. Dent.*) GARDEN COLOUR. By Mrs. C. W. Earle, E.V. B., Rose Kingsley, and the Hon. Vicary Gibbs. Coloured Sketches and Notes by Margaret Waterfield. 18s. net. (*J. M. Dent.*) TRIAL OF GEORGE JOSEPH SMITH. Edited by Eric R. Watson, LL.B. Illustrated. 10s. 6d. net. (*William Hodge.*) MISS MAPP. By E. F. Benson. 7s. 6d. net. (*Hutchinson.*) THE OPTIMIST. By E. M. Delafield. 7s. 6d. net. (*Hutchinson.*) THE BOX OF SPIKENARD. By Ethel Boileau. 7s. 6d. net. (*Hutchinson.*) TO TELL YOU THE TRUTH. By Leonard Merrick. 7s. 6d. net. (*Hodder & Stoughton.*) THE HIDDEN RICHES. By David Lyall. 7s. 6d. net. (*Hodder & Stoughton.*) EL DIABLO. By Brayton Norton. 7s. 6d. net. (*Hodder & Stoughton.*) THE UNSPEAKABLE GENTLEMAN. By J. P. Marquand. 7s. 6d. net. (*Hodder & Stoughton.*) ALAS, THAT SPRING! By Elinor Mordaunt 7s. 6d. net. (*Hutchinson.*) PUPPETS OF FATE. By Selwyn Jepson. 7s. 6d. net. (*Hutchinson.*) THE RIDER OF GOLDEN BAR. By William Patterson White. 7s. 6d. net. (*Hodder & Stoughton.*) A CHRISTMAS CAROL IN PROSE: Being a Ghost Story of Christmas. By Charles Dickens. With Four Illustrations in Colour and Four Woodcuts by John Leech. A facsimile of the Original Edition. With an Introduction by G. K. Chesterton and a Preface by B. W. Matz. 6s. net. (*Cecil Palmer.*) BILLY BARNSCOAT: A Fairy Romance for Young and Old. Written by Greville MacDonald. Illustrated by Francis D. Bedford. 8s. 6d. net. (*George Allen & Unwin.*) THE VELVETEEN RABBIT. By Margery Williams. With Illustrations by William Nicholson. 7s. 6d. net. (*Heinemann.*) CERTAIN PEOPLE OF IMPORTANCE. By Kathleen Norris. 7s. 6d. net. (*Heinemann.*) THE ORDEAL OF MARK TWAIN. By Van Wyck Brooks. 12s. 6d. net. (*Heinemann.*) PLAYS FOR CHILDREN: "Goldilocks and the Three Bears," etc. "St. George and the Dragon," etc. "Bluebeard," etc. By S. Lyle Cummins. 1s. 6d. net. (*Methuen.*) A KIPLING ANTHOLOGY: "Prose." 6s. net. (*Macmillan.*) THE LAND OF THE LIVING. By Calcott Reading. 7s. 6d. net. (*Leonard Parsons.*) THE LITERATURE OF ECSTASY. By Albert Mordell. 7s. 6d. net. (*Melrose.*)

In Albert Brenet's record sleeve image, the *Blue Train* sported a new livery capturing the Azur coast's reflection of a shade of metallic blue whose colours evoked a mixture of gooseberry, blackcurrant and rhubarb pastels. Its look and feel an essential component of Wagon-Lits' future brand and integral to defining its future reputation as Europe's premier luxury train operator. In the second poster illustrated by Charles Hallo in 1925, the company's acquisition of Thomas Cook several years later provided the opportunity to promote Riviera summers to a wider accessible British market. For the top end of society, the Riviera was an extension of London life developing in to one of those special places offering ladies of a certain class all the fun that comes the way of the modern young woman. Last minute return travel arrangements for the *Blue Train* could be concluded swiftly by a call to Cook's offices in Monte Carlo. (*Opposite*: Illustrated London News Ltd/ Mary Evans; *Above*: Wagon-Lits Diffusion)

when the business slumped into financial difficulties as the result of rapid hotel over-expansion in the late in 1890s. Some forty steel-sided Type 'S' sleeping carriages were required for the new luxury train and Wagon-Lits' other notable European services. The carriages were built by the Leeds Forge Company, so the seeds were sown for classic Anglo-French commercial cooperation on a grand scale. Each sleeping car contained just ten sleeping compartments with each carriage managed by an attendant.

The Bystander's masterstroke was the production of a regular French Riviera season feature. With the train's launch, they remarked on how impressed they were with the new boat train. 'Old travellers are charmed with the new through train *de luxe* – the last note in comfort – with its royal blue and gold carriages meeting you at Calais composed of nothing but *wagon-lits* and a restaurant car.'[77] Boarding the British section at London Victoria, sun-worshiping passengers were reminded to 'Sleep your way from the City's fogs to the Riviera sunshine.'[78] In the Roaring Twenties, the glamorous, *Blue Train* was labelled as the train to paradise and the millionaires' train, gaining an immeasurable level of international popularity frequented by Europe and America's leading celebrities who joined the journey south to escape the winter cold.[79] From 1926 there was a change as the nightly south-bound sleeper train started its journey from Paris Gare de Lyon – the usual Parisian staging coast for the Azur coast. From London, first-class passengers boarded the *White Pullman* from Victoria, crossed the channel on a steamer, and continuing with the *Flèche d'Or* Pullman to Gare du Nord – the traditional arrival point for countless Britons over the years. None of these really inconvenienced travellers since the journey south was regarded as a great adventure; guests never quite knowing who might be aboard the 'nouveau-riche blue' express. According to Andrew Martin Gare de Lyon 'had a rush hour of the blue trains. Between seven and nine-thirty, the *Simplon Orient Express*, the *Rome Express* and the *Blue Train* itself would take their leave, in theatrical style'.[80]

Wagon-Lits cars were labelled as cosy little self-contained flats furnished with personal belongings and occupied with the pleasant knowledge that the miniature home was a castle until journey's end.[81] Monte Carlo was promoted as a destination in its own right reached by the combined efforts of Southern Railway, PLM and Wagon-Lits but importantly no longer regarded as a demanding journey. Copy writers' advertising copy promoted its superb scenery, unrivalled attractions, its excellence as a centre of sports and an auto-Riviera garage providing fine cars for hire and a host of daily excursions to all parts of the sky-blue coast.[82] In their November 1929 review, *The Bystander* produced a detailed reflection to escape London's worst winter conditions pursuing the sun with the train's meticulous journey south.[83]

During the inter-war years, the English colony's winter invasion was still much in evidence as the Riviera proved to be an attractive location for society weddings. Much of the destination infrastructure – casino, golf clubs and leading hotels such as Hôtel de Paris and Café de Paris were now open all year round with prices reported to have returned to a degree of normality with resident members of the golf club and *habitués* of the villas

In a special November Riviera review, *The Bystander* produced a similar appraisal of the *Blue Train* which by this stage had acquired an almost legendary reputation. The *Blue Train* and the winter Riviera season were almost identical components; travellers simply could not make do without the other. One of the key contributors was E.P. Leigh-Bennett who wrote for Southern Railway's growing list of highly informed travel literature publications. (Illustrated London News Ltd/ Mary Evans)

back in abundance. At the height of the season, such celebrity endorsement led the train on many occasions to being simply oversubscribed. Royalty weaved a magic spell with the inclusion of Prince of Wales and resident Prince Louis of Monaco. Early celebrities included stars of the silent screen such as Charlie Chaplin, 40-year-old designer Coco Chanel, an acute observer of fashion and a successful businesswoman, who was said to have invented sunbathing and made suntan fashionable, a literary circle of F. Scott Fitzgerald, Evelyn Waugh and Somerset Maugham, bohemians, intellectuals and music composers such as Cole Porter anxious to escape the numbing and claustrophobic environment of post-war America, together with the usual clutch of well-known British politicians. Porter on one occasion was said to have hired a complete carriage for his entourage. The presence of the Prince of Wales did much for the *Blue Train's* image and status, instilling an aroma of brand exclusiveness and privilege as everyone made their way aboard the winter season Riviera pilgrimage. McKibbin observed the Prince of Wales was a man that became *Americanised* developing a liking for 'smart company' and 'the Ritz bar'. Above all, he was an example of charm par excellence inhabiting a desirable world where other glamorous upper-class figures like Lord and Lady Louis Mountbatten, film stars, and, increasingly, sportsmen and women and popular entertainers, had much in common.

All of them became fodder, not unwillingly, for the gossip columnists.[84] Evelyn Waugh connected to a bright young set acquired a taste for Riviera life when he stepped off the train in Monaco in February 1929.[85] He joined novelist Scott Fitzgerald and his wife Zelda, who had first taken the train south in 1924, establishing literary connections cementing the Riviera's arts reputation for writers and performers. The destination's extraordinary light also installed a great artist affiliation in the same way Monet and Renoir had done in the early 1880s; Picasso would do so again in the inter-war years. Some literary residents such as D.H. Lawrence preferred a quieter life set in reliable and unspoiled coastal villages and small seaside towns free from the visitor hoard. Some sky-blue resorts still contained a tinge of authentic Provence attracting a discrete clientele looking for genuine France. Interest in rural areas and desire to see 'real France' had only begun in earnest at the start of the twentieth century.[86] The impact of the depression years dented international traveller numbers, with second and even third-class sleeping cars added to the *Blue Train*.[87] Numbers recovered by mid-decade, but not before many Riviera hotel and villa properties had gone under the auctioneer's hammer. Yet the *Blue Train's* guest list during the 1930s included eminent members of the political class. Winston Churchill gained a considerable liking for Wagon-Lits/PLM trains where, such was the frequency of his first-class travels to the Azur, had a rail equivalent of Air Miles existed, he could have flown around the globe several times.[88]

The high-octane motor car was also an essential transport prerequisite, but despite well-publicised speed stunts, they had their limitations on time-consuming journeys favouring the long-distance luxury train. Cars by and large were used for short journeys as Continental road networks were far from developed; Boulogne to Monte Carlo would take five days minimum.[89] Besides, an array of the latest French and Italian super-car was always on disposal at the choicest of resorts, and a far cry from the early days of motoring when the Riviera's dust tracks and unmetalled roads were little equipped to handle the demands of the horseless carriage. As food historian Jerry Quinzo recounts: 'Sensible people did not want to drive all the way across Europe (or America) in an unreliable automobile when they could enjoy the elegant surroundings and excellent service of a first-class railway carriage.'[90] Yearly motoring festivities such as the Monte Carlo Rally and the Monaco Grand Prix became key anchor events, but they had yet to make a serious impression.

Social conventions were to be observed especially for prosperous and even middle-class Americans visiting Europe for the first time. Fiona McDonald quotes an extract from a 1920s publication, *Perfect Behaviour: A Guide to Ladies and Gentlemen in all Social Crises*, advising Americans how to travel on Continental trains:

> Europeans usually prefer to ride backwards, and as an American prefers to face the engine, it works out beautifully. It is not etiquette to talk with fellow passengers, in fact it is very middle-class. If you are in a smoking carriage (all European carriages are smoking unless marked 'Ladies alone' or 'No smoking') and ladies are present, it is polite if you ask if you may smoke. Language is not necessary, as you need merely to look at your cigar and bow with an interrogatory expression, whereupon your fellow passengers bow assent and you smoke.

Whether such advice was ever heeded on *Blue Train* journeys by young ladies lacking the appropriate self-confidence is not known as the luxury train quickly acquired a reputation for celebration. The guide, however, went on to describe the 'Spoiled American Girl' syndrome, where reprehensible behaviour should not be tolerated 'in public places generally - but most particularly in the large and expensive hotels of Continental resorts.'[91]

From 1929, a brand-new first-class luxury service linking the two capitals arrived in the form of the *Golden Arrow/ Flèche d'Or* Pullman, coming with its own dedicated steamer ensuring a total journey time of around six and a half hours. The *Blue Train* had another batch of new LX10 Class sleeper stock. Post-recession, London passengers, or those boarding in Calais heading to the French Riviera, were allocated Wagon-Lits sleeping cars added to the rear of the *Flèche d'Or* Pullman. The train would begin its fast run to Paris Gare du Nord, and then follow a short shuttle on one of the two orbital railways around Paris between main-line stations, as the Wagon-Lits sleepers were attached to the main part of the *Blue Train* express at Gare de Lyon. Despite new arrangements, the complexities of moving heavy luggage between main Paris stations was avoided; the train lost none of its panache with passenger capacity remaining high for the main November-April season.

Post-recession, the Riviera attracted a broader customer base with Wagon-Lits and Thomas Cook launching a new generation of third-class sleepers meeting the approval of the travel press. *The Sphere* noted:

> Third-class railway travel on the Continent usually strikes a chill to the hearts of most people, but these new sleepers are third only in name and price. The accommodation is all that could be desired by the most fastidious traveller and includes well-equipped and comfortable sleeping-berths.[92]

Passenger numbers recovered post-recession, aided by a party tag designation as several Wagon-Lits Pullman coaches were converted and repainted in blue to create bar cars attached to dining cars. Innovation was the key to attracting loyal clientele. George Behrend points out the first diner car fitted with a gramophone was in 1929 but 'people have been dancing their way across Europe in Trains de Luxe for almost a century'.[93] The modern dance craze was imported from the United States with arrival in 1917 of American troops. In the immediate post-war years, jazz became mainstream, highly popular and permeating all strands of life. Historians Graves and Hodge echoed slight misgivings arguing 'it did seem a little odd that a negro jazz-band could earn more in a season than the Prime Minister did in the course of a whole year'.[94] Jazz or the 'Jazz Age' – coined by Fitzgerald – brought a degree of dynamism to the inter-war years, and together with the 'flapper look' changing the course and style of women's fashion. The trend towards hemline reductions and shorter skirts on both sides of the Atlantic had been around since 1912, but, as Perkin argues, in Britain 'it took the war, with its self-confident and self-assertive women workers, to impose this unprecedented change in women's dress and feminine psyche'.[95]

In tandem with these developments, the number of women involved in professional work and white-blouse occupations increased.[96]

For Perfect Holidays

THE RIVIERA!

Sunshine, sport, gaiety and brilliance all converge on the Riviera at this time of the year. Reduced Summer Hotel Tariffs. Through trains from Calais every day including the Calais—Nice Express, also "Le Train Bleu" (Mondays, Wednesdays, Fridays). Send for a copy of "The Peerless Riviera" (price 1/-) and folder giving fares and services, to the Continental Enquiry Office, Victoria Station, London, S.W.1.

"*Short Sea Routes*," says *Sunny South Sam*

SOUTHERN RAILWAY

SOUTH FOR SUN—BATHING

Southern Railway began promoting the Riviera using Sunny South Sam as a spokesman in the summer of 1930. This particular insertion appearing in *The Bystander* from June 1931, began to establish a destination for all feel, accessible by daily Calais boat trains, albeit with advertising skewed to upmarket British titles. The quickest way to sunshine offered a variety of marketing brochures from 1926, including *The Peerless Riviera* and *Summer Time Riviera* – targeting the smaller Riviera resorts – which all helped build the sky-blue coast's reputation. The 1929 edition of *Summer Time Riviera*, and from the early 1930s, the eighth and ninth editions of *The Peerless Riviera* clearly indicates how the railway supported the many travellers who migrated annually to the sun. (*Previous page*: Illustrated London News Ltd/Mary Evans; *Above and left*: Southern Railway Publicity)

By the early 1920s this amounted to the perfect recipe for women to assert themselves in a way not understood before. No small measure as the worlds of fashion and the dancing mixture of jazz and ragtime music, symbolised the Roaring Twenties era and beyond. Dance and fashion fusion spread across all social classes, but for wealthy elites it was a breath of fresh air and one they would immediately latch on to. Dances like the 'Charleston' had prescribed formats bringing patronage amongst the fashionable and wealthy including the likes of Edwina and Dickie Mountbatten and the Duke of Kent.[97] And there was dance etiquette too as McDonald advises us: 'It is not enough to know the steps, or even to have a good sense of rhythm. Dance in the 1920s was taken seriously, even if it was as fast and as fun as the Charleston.'[98] By the 1930s the swing kids were on the blocks; British and American society took to it with gusto beginning a process where fashion, music and style tribes meshed together in a way that was set to become a dominant feature of later twentieth and twenty-first century life; the noughties marking the ascendency of the UK as the second largest creative industries economy in the world.

The party atmosphere on the Riviera train in the 1930s was said by some to be a little more restrained, less risqué than perhaps a decade before, yet a certain aura still pervaded the *Blue Train's* first-class. Mary Penman (one of Winston Churchill's secretaries) boarded the Paris to Antibes train in January 1939 recording her experience of the trip. This proved to be her only trip abroad as she never left Britain again, but as a young secretary in her mid-twenties, the journey to the Riviera was intoxicating. She recalls:

The attendant to our coach was a very nice old fellow, spoke good English. I was shown into a compartment next to Mr Churchill's. Along one side was a wide seat with a comfortable back, with head rests covered in white linen. The walls were panelled in light coloured wood, with mahogany strips between the panels. In the centre of the panels there was a pattern of flowers in inlay, rather sweet in pinkish shades and black. There were, I counted, nine different kinds of wood in each panel. Unlike English trains, all was spotlessly clean. In the corner of the compartment two doors curved outwards. I opened these. Inside each door was a full-length mirror and, in the enclosure, a decent wash basin, brackets holding glasses and water bottle etc, and at the back a further mirror. There was a special electric light for this little cubby hole. Over the basin were, of course, hot and cold taps, but the kind little old man attendant explained to me apolitically that owing to the snow and ice the pipes had frozen and the taps did not work, so would it be all right if he brought me some water in the morning. Naturally, I said it would be quite alright.

Miss Penman goes on to describe the ambience and good food and wine aboard the *Blue Train* dining car:

About ten minutes after we had left the station we went to dinner. Mr Churchill and I had a little table for two to ourselves, and as might be expected, all eyes were turned upon us. Mr Churchill is well known and loved by the French, and the English passengers were interested and a little curious also. On our table was a lamp and a vase with some mimosa and two bright salmon carnations. Mr Churchill asked me what I would drink, and I said I would like something light, so he ordered Graves. He had champagne in a bucket of ice. I refused the aperitif because I was not quite sure what it was and Mr Churchill, the lazy thing, had not done the *Daily Telegraph* article and proposed doing it after dinner so I had to be awake and sober too.[99]

Prior to the Great War winter occupation of the French and Italian Riviera was time limited; it was considered far too warm for civilised life during the summer months. As Jim Ring reported 'no Englishman dreamed of staying on the Riviera after Easter'.[100] But things were to change as the Azur coastline slowly developed into a string of year-round resorts, so marking a change to destination seasonality where the then exclusive winter resort transformed itself into a popular summertime holiday location as more and more members of English society spent their solstice months there.[101] Pugh nonchalantly explains old winter habits 'increasingly gave way to summers spent soaking up the sun'.[102] Dr Juliet Gardiner's assessment is of a similar manner:

Whereas before the First World War it was the moneyed who had fled abroad in the winter months, by the 1930s it was mainly the elderly who sought the winter sun's warming rays abroad: the young wanted full-on sun in the hottest months, and sought it in Antibes, Menton, Juan-les-Pins, Nice and Cannes.[103]

There was in addition the old guard – Britain's aristocracy – who withdrew from county and London society finding solace on the Riviera or buying villas elsewhere on the Mediterranean.[104] It is said the Antibes and Cannes locations were only really discovered as summer holiday destinations in the early 1920s by New York

This half page *Tatler* editorial from January 1930 portrays the effortless ease of luxury boat train travel to the Riviera either aboard the cross-channel *Blue Train* service or from the Paris based *Côte d'Azur Pullman Express*. The summertime setting of F Whatley's earlier 1928 Southern Railway French Riviera travel poster demonstrated the company's sprightly response to changing market conditions. A broader customer base attracted to the destination's inexpensive, amusing and gloriously warm attributes, filled boat trains to the Azur coast all year round. (*Above*: NRM/SSPL; *Overleaf*: Illustrated London News Ltd/Mary Evans)

THE TATLER

The Luxury of Modern Travel

[No. 1492, January 29, 1930]

Glorious Sunshine and Cloudless Skies.

IT was the climate that in the first instance made the Riviera what it is, then came the luxurious hotels, the train facilities. Even during the early months of the year sunshine may be enjoyed for weeks together; the sun often rises in a cloudless sky, shines for several hours with a brightness and warmth surpassing that of a British summer, and then sinks without a cloud behind the secondary ranges of the Maritime Alps, displaying in setting the beautiful and varied succession of tints which characterise that glorious phenomenon of the refraction of light—a southern sunset. Bathing prevails all through the season and at all times, there being little rise and fall of the tide.

En Route for the Riviera.

IT was generally considered that the height of luxury in railway travel had been achieved when the Golden Arrow and the Blue Train, with a brief sea passage, conveyed visitors to the South of France. The journey, to those who can sleep when travelling, seemed so short, and of course to the greatest possible extent all difficulties connected with Customs and passports were eliminated. The only thing that one was unable to see the country through which one passed; of course those who were sufficiently energetic always got up to see the sun rise over the glorious snow-capped mountains, a scene which never fails to excite even the most seasoned traveller. The Blue Train still continues, but it has encountered a rival in the Côte d'Azur Pullman Express.

The Côte d'Azur Pullman Express.

THIS train leaves Paris rather before nine, and with only a few stops, reaches Marseilles rather before eight o'clock in the evening. Cannes at 10.30, and Nice at 11. Among the many advantages of the Côte d'Azur Pullman Express is that a night may be spent in Paris, as the Golden Arrow arrives in the afternoon. The train is composed of the very latest type of all-metal Pullman coaches, which have been variously and beautifully decorated by the artistic genius of M. René Prou and M. René Lalique. There is a separate kitchen for each pair of Pullman cars, and most excellent meals are served throughout the day. As a matter of fact the requirements of the most exacting gourmet have been carefully studied, and the standard of catering is probably higher than that on any other train in the world.

The Drawing-room Car.

A new feature is a drawing-room car corresponding in a way to the American observation car. In it are comfortable adjustable arm-chairs and a selection of all the latest illustrated papers, including THE TATLER. It is also equipped with a specially-designed electric gramophone. Passengers will therefore be able to spend an odd hour at any time listening to the music, and will even be able to dance if they wish—and what could be a more delightful way of passing the time on a long journey? The floral decorations are wonderfully artistic, the sweetly-scented mimosa being well represented. Messrs. Thos. Cook and Sons, who are associated with the Wagon-Lits Company, can give all further information regarding this train and can arrange reservations either at their head office in Berkeley Street or at any of their branches.

A bird's-eye view of Monte Carlo, and a car on the Côte d'Azur Pullman Express decorated with panels of Lalique glass

socialites Gerald and Sara Murphy who first visited at the invitation of Cole Porter.[105] They were renowned for holding a season of 'off season' parties which in the years before a second bout of world conflict, the summer-time Azur coast was transformed into the world's most glamorous playground; something not lost on Southern Railway. The company grabbed every opportunity to maximise French traffic and to the Riviera with a host of travel-related marketing material not normally associated with Southern. In the autumn of 1931, it produced a new railway guidebook under the title of 'Southern Ways and Means' written by E.P. Leigh-Bennett, a magazine journalist and novelist, with illustrations by Fougasse. This was effectively a reworking of Leigh-Bennett and Leonard Richmond's earlier 1929 Southern *Come Abroad With Us* work designed to tempt Britons abroad. *The Bystander* described the effort as:

> A delicious book; no guidebook this, nor advertisement; on ordinary travel book; but a most 'individual' and unconventional 'temptation to travel,' dealing with just those items that you personally have always considered more important than the usual information that is given.

And this caught national media off-guard since it was produced by the 'Southern of fog-services, rush hours and Monday morning gloom at London Bridge' dealing not only with the Riviera but a variety of Continental destinations – the most delightful corners of Europe – including Normandy, Brittany, Belgium, Italy, Germany and the contested area of the Dolomites.[106]

Leigh-Bennett's candidature to write Southern's new travel publication, aimed at an expanding middle-class market, came as a result of John Elliot's eagle-eyed press relations function. In addition, Leigh-Bennett was also the author of *The Errant Golfer* and a regular contributor to society musings and Riviera life.[107] *The Sketch* in reviewing Southern Ways and Means enlightened its readers. It was 'full of useful information to travellers, conveyed in an unconventional and amusing manner' enlightening 'passengers as to passports, luggage abroad, routes to the Continent, combined rail and air routes, circular tours, and special visits to liners'.[108]

For travellers wishing to access France's Mediterranean shores quickly, in style and without involving a trip aboard an overnight sleeper train, the *Côte d'Azur Pullman Express* provided a new solution. There had always been day-time Paris trains to the Riviera, but this train was something special. On 10 December 1929 Wagon-Lits and PLM introduced the *Côte d'Azur Express* – also known as the *Côte d'Azur Pullman* Express – making rapid daytime runs for the winter season departing Gare de Lyon at 10.06 am and arriving at Cannes at 10.06 pm. In 1935 *The Sphere* commented in its weekly travel notes that the service, which by now had been running for five years, represented the last word in comfort.[109] When the new Riviera day-time luxury train commenced operation, its all-Pullman train consisted of two sets of steel-sided couplages and two baggage cars making an exclusive and almost private club six-car express built for speed.

Wagon-Lits' service ran from Paris along the precious sea view landscapes of the Riviera to Menton and Ventimiglia on the French/Italian border, mirroring earlier luxury trains dating from the 1880s. Like the *Blue Train* bar cars, Wagon-Lits piloted a dancing car, but it was disliked by its upscale domestic clientele. Initially the *Côte d'Azur Pullman Express* was limited to wintertime running suffering a drop-in passenger number in the depression years with its destination limited to Menton. However, by 1931 the Riviera destination and the *Côte d'Azur Pullman Express* were being marketed to British audiences by Thomas Cook which by now had become a Wagon-Lits operation. 'Spring on the Riviera by Côte d'Azur Pullman car trains' was promoted as complete packages in selected British regional newspapers.[110] Like many other luxury trains around Europe, passenger volume suffered with the depression but progressively recovered throughout the rest of the 1930s. By mid-decade day-time travel was far easier and a little quicker. *The Sphere* reported:

> Intending visitors to the Riviera will learn with interest that the famous 'Côte d'Azur Pullman Express' has started running for the winter season. This train makes the journey from Paris to the Riviera by day, leaving Gare de Lyon daily at 10.15 a.m., arriving at Cannes at 10.06 p.m. The average speed for the distance of 660 miles is 55 m.p.h., including stops. The train is composed entirely of 1st and 2nd class modern Pullman cars, which represent the last word in comfort.[111]

Horizons were modified from 1938 as the French railway system was nationalised. The days of the *Blue Train* and the *Côte d'Azur*

Pullman Express as symbols of truly luxury express trains were coming to an end. The *Blue Train* was relegated in status to an ordinary night express train. With war clouds looming, day and night services ran for the last time within weeks of Britain declaring war on Germany. For many of the Riviera's expat community, the penny soon dropped how difficult life may become with a German ally parked just over the Franco-Italian border.[112] Powerful PLM Mountain Class and rebuilt class 231K and 231G PLM locomotives provided the necessary steam-hauled traction for overloaded expresses heading north and west in what was loosely a mass evacuation of the Riviera and Provence's English colony.[113]

The Golden Arrow

The early 1920s were ideal times for two of the newly formed Big Four railway companies to create plans for truly luxury international boat trains. LNER was quick off the mark using enhanced Great Eastern Pullman stock for its Harwich services, but it was left to Southern Railway to envision the future. To some extent this came about as a result of customer exasperation. Writer Andrew Martin sums up the position commendably:

> There were complaints from users of luxury boat trains that the trains weren't quite luxurious enough. The delays in the customs sheds at Dover were too long; the Channel boats were overcrowded. There was a desire for a smoother, more coherent journey.[114]

Southern Railway's general manager Sir Herbert Walker must have glimpsed the future of deluxe train travel in private discussions with Sir Davison Dalziel, chairman of the Wagon-Lits management committee in Calais on 9 December 1922 as they officiated over the inauguration of the glamorous *Calais-Méditerranée Express*, better known as the *Blue Train*. Doyen C. Hamilton Ellis considered that the moment the new modern era in luxury train travel really commenced was in November 1908 when Dalziel acquired the Pullman business, initiating the *Southern* Belle, and thereby transforming the company. In a later review, *The Railway Magazine* commented 'in his blood was that of the good old Border Rievers; he was to complete his life as Lord Dalziel of Wooler'.[115] Whilst Dalziel's company created bespoke British Pullman services, Sir John Elliot considers he was the brains behind international rail travel development as Wagon-Lits' French operation threw down the gauntlet. On the English side it was up to Southern and the Pullman Company (both companies enjoying close working relationships with Wagon-Lits) to create a similar first-class offer catering for an increasingly discriminating market, particularly high-spending American tourists keen to rediscover their European roots. According to Elliot, the glamour of an international service was likely to work as Walker had already persuaded Dalziel the service should be first-class only built for an elite clientele in mind. As Elliot wittily noted: 'Before the war the *Golden Arrow* departure platform at Victoria was like a page from *Who's Who.*'[116]

These three mid-1920s images typified the *White Pullman* cross-channel boat train traffic found on the London Victoria, Folkstone and Dover routes. In the first shot, the Maunsell 4-4-0 headed *White Pullman* is likely to be a D1 or E1 and taken around 1925, probably near Sevenoaks. The King Arthur, without smoke deflectors, is in almost new condition, as delivered from the North British Locomotive shop in Glasgow around 1925/26. Seen in mid-Kent hauling a nine car *White Pullman* boat train, the last carriage in the formation appears to be a bird cage brake van providing one of the signature images of the period characterising these specialist trains. Not all cross-channel boat trains though were celebrity-imbued workings since wealthy clientele in the immediate post-war years represented quite a small passenger market that was being picked off by an embryonic airline sector operating between London, Paris and other European capitals. The ex-LSWR T9 4-4-0 at Dover, is one of a batch transferred to the south-eastern division of the Southern Railway in the mid-1920s and paired with a six wheeled tender, for use on boat trains and for general passenger business. (*Below and opposite*: John Scott-Morgan Collection)

Prior to *Golden Arrow's* launch, Southern's interim measure in 1924 was the naming of the *Continental Pullman Express* boat train, also known as the *White Pullman*, running from Victoria to Dover. The new Pullman service included a facility for sending

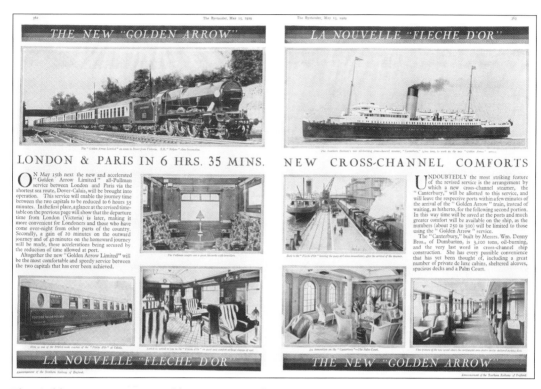

The **Golden** Arrow service would see an array of new marketing material introduced by Southern Railway's advertising department. Part of the initiative involved warmer advertising which included this arresting poster advising consumers of the improved travelling times with details of departure and arrival times and of the new dedicated ferry.

Very little needs to be said about this double-page advertising spread which appeared in *The Bystander* except to say it was typical of the efforts Southern went to position their new '*Golden Arrow Limited*', as it was officially known at its launch, to an upmarket audience used to subtle touches. The *Canterbury's* Palm Court relaxation area received considerable plaudits in the press. (*Opposite*: NRM/SSPL; *Above*: Illustrated London News Ltd/Mary Evans)

luggage or goods freight in customs-sealed boxes on flat wagons that went in advance, with the train or as a separate operation. The problems of crossing borders and dealing with customs on both sides of the English Channel had been thorny issues in travellers' lives since the inception of the Wagon-Lits' *Orient Express*. The *Continental Pullman Express* had a new external appearance with what was to become the standard umber and pale cream livery originally introduced on the London-Brighton *Southern Belle* and was the precursor for Wagon-Lits' Calais-Paris Pullman *La Flèche d'Or* boat train. The *White Pullman's* pale cream upper panels were very distinctive and known amongst the company's top link drivers as 'the white elephant'.[117] With a 10.45 Victoria departure it was extremely well-supported by passengers becoming one of the best-paying Continental trains. The Pullman first-class supplement of 3s 6d per head did not appear to deter customers since not only were most seats taken but booked well in advance. Despite its undoubted success, Southern refrained from adopting the *Golden Arrow* title until plans were finalised. Whilst Pullmans once again graced Dover Marine Continental passenger terminal, Southern's astute management team was devising an integrated luxury train product and offer that would be sufficiently distinctive and set the world talking. This finally came on 15 May 1929 with the full launch of the London-Paris *Golden Arrow*. With its inauguration, one of the world's most celebrated and legendary luxury trains was born.

In a few short months, aided by smart integrated marketing, promotional and public relations, the combined *Golden Arrow/ Flèche d'Or* service (in reality the product of both the Southern and Nord railway companies was recognised as the world's best-known interconnecting boat train. David St. John Thomas and Patrick Whitehouse viewed the launch from a wider historical and social narrative announcing it was 'Britain's front door, at least three quarters of all visiting royalty and political and other famous people first glimpsing our countryside through its windows. In the days that Gatwick airport was a grass field and London's airport was at Croydon all the world of politics and fashion was to be seen at Victoria before the departure of the *Golden Arrow*.'[118]

The train/boat/train service had its own dedicated first-class only steamer crossing the channel between Dover and Calais – *TSS Canterbury* the pride of Southern Railway's fleet. In July 1930, the *Golden Arrow* was appointed with eight renovated umber and cream art deco Pullman cars: *Adrian, Diamond, Ibis, Lady Dalziel, Lydia, Onyx, Pearl* and *Princess Elizabeth*.

An exotic *Golden Arrow* became famous for its personalised service and haute cuisine menus frequented by society's well-heeled classes. *The Bystander*, in its 29 May 1929 edition, with the help of its illustrator Helen McKie, captured the spirit of super de-luxe Paris travel. McKie produced a set of three impressions of the combined rail and sea journey establishing a seal for stylish travel. Themes surrounding the celebration of glamour, the sophistication of international travel and the charm of Paris as a destination hung around for a long-time and still being utilised by British Railways for *Golden Arrow* advertising some thirty years later. The grandiose start unfortunately was not to last as darkening economic clouds downgraded the train from its exclusive first-class Pullman status. The train then having to accommodate first and second-class passengers as well as Pullman's clientele. Conditions on the Continent were no better forcing the French to make a similar response to their Wagon-Lits Pullman operation. At the height of the depression cross-channel passenger traffic plummeted with total journeys taken nearly halving in 1932 against a long-trend average of 1.5m over the years 1925 to 1930. In the period 1933–35 recovery resumed with an average 1.125m passengers per annum crossing the channel by train/boat/train. By the summer of 1937, the number of Continental passengers had recovered to its long-term trend with Saturday, 31 July experiencing an all-time high of 22,828 passengers for the day – requiring a huge number of additional boat train workings. Until revival, the look and composition of the multi-class *Golden Arrow* changed, typically made up of three to four (or more) Pullman coaches located in the middle of the train with one or more luggage trucks and general utility vans at one end with a mix of ordinary coaches at the other end. In 1938 the Maunsell first-class rake was upgraded and renovated with new upholstery sporting a new Southern Railway green livery. Four of the Lord Nelson Class locomotives regularly used on the service were similarly repainted in malachite green providing the international train with a much-needed facelift. The new-look luxury train's carriage stock according to Bucknall had 'been completely refurbished, redecorated and refinished in the new style which, with the complement of contrasting Pullman Cars, looked very well'.[119]

The inter-war life of the *Golden Arrow* was not only disrupted by economic pressures, but also by competitive pressures as fledgling airlines began to contest a share of upscale Continental travel trade. British airline Imperial Airways were part of an expanding market for European commercial air services made up mostly of at the time of a wealthy clientele. They 'expected exemplary on-board service'; by 1927 Imperial Airways had evolved its offer into an 'high-end dining experience' leading the way 'in European on-board catering' extolling the experience of 'comfort in the air'.[120] These changes were important since consumer choice and new travel options started to nibble away at the edges of the luxury train service.

In 1923 the newly formed Southern concentrated its cross-channel boat train operations at London Victoria; the terminus provided up

The new-look *Golden Arrow* is shown to its full glory as the train headed by no. 861 Lord Anson leaves London Victoria bang on time having been taken by well-known railway photographer Bishop Eric Treacy. This 1939 11.00 am departure timing is visibly shown on the clock of Imperial Airways new London Victoria headquarters. Treacy's distinguished reputation as a railway snapper allowed him special access to the permanent way often denied to other photographers. As a man of the cloth, he had the characteristic ability to befriend many of the crews on footplates, occasionally persuading them to create special smoke effects for the camera. (NRM/SSPL)

to seven weekday services linking Britain, Belgium and France. The Southern's Docks and Maritime Committee were first briefed with the *Golden Arrow* proposal by the general manager at a meeting on 25 January 1928 where he gave intention for the company to introduce an additional steamer to supplement the new service. The *Golden Arrow* became the jewel in the crown of day-time international trains when it commenced operations coinciding with the delivery of Southern's new luxury steamship *Canterbury* which had a total capacity for some 1,700 passengers but for the first part of its operational life carried just a small number of passengers in its sumptuous accommodation, mirroring the number of seats automatically reserved on the train. In July 1930, the train was appointed with eight renovated Pullman cars: The French had their *La Flèche d'Or* counterpart since September 1926, but Southern's management held back until they could provide a distinctive and memorable English offering. For de-luxe first-class travellers aboard the boat train, the steamer *Canterbury* provided exceptionally spacious surroundings.[121] When Southern Railway announced the new train's development, the company did not hang around with the vessel's commissioning process. New oil-burning quality cross-channel steamers were an important aspect of the company's plans. Throughout the luxury boat train's operation, the service was provided by just two cross-channel steamships – *Canterbury* and its replacement *Invicta* in 1940. *Invicta*, launched a year earlier, was not fully fitted out and quickly requisitioned by the Admiralty and pressed immediately into war-time duties. She did not commence life as the dedicated *Golden Arrow* ship until mid-October 1946 when she took over sea crossing duties from *Canterbury*.[122] Maritime author Richard Danielson says that over the years, British and Continental shipping companies owned by their railway masters produced reliable, fast and for holders of first-class tickets, luxurious vessels.[123] The new 4,178-ton vessel, the largest traditional packet ship operating on the English Channel, indubitably did not disappoint and clearly built upon the legacy created by *Canterbury*. Built by Wm. Denny & Bros. Ltd at Dumbarton, *Canterbury* was launched on 13 December 1928 at a contract price of £220,225. She had a larger capacity but was always planned as a special steamer, starting life catering for typically up to 300 de-luxe first-class *Golden Arrow* travellers who paid a special £5 inclusive fare covering fare, reserved Pullman seats and supplements. As a single-class ferry, up-scale facilities included a 100-cover dining saloon on the main deck, private deck cabins and a garden lounge as well as screened alcoves all finished in a warm cream décor. Jeremy Hartill presents a similar picture. He says:

> Those who remembered the pre-war era probably seen through rose tinted glasses had memories of polished engines, first class service and luxury. This was not entirely untrue. The *Canterbury* was the epitome of this, built as an all first-class ship carrying 400 passengers complete with a Palm Court between their express Pullman trains en-route from London to Paris.

Commenting on service levels provided by Southern, Hartill ventures further:

> The ship had one crew and made a single trip a day between Dover and Calais. The low level of utilisation and single crew meant the ships were always in excellent condition with staff who took pride in the job. There are parallels here with the flagship trains and railway engines having specific drivers allocated to them.[124]

With the economic downturn *Canterbury* was converted to a two-class vessel in 1932, but despite the change the ship still maintained her own distinctive atmosphere as a turbine steamer. With a broader customer base, the revised on-board facilities provided meals, drinks and gifts in the ship's restaurants, bars and duty-free shops; these were highly valued by Southern as a source to generate additional gainful revenue streams. As the vessel was always dedicated to the *Golden Arrow*, she was always immaculately maintained by the ship's single crew, and for a while in the mid-1930s the ship was only covering one leg of the Pullman cross-channel service any one day due to routing changes via Folkestone. Several iconic locomotive classes hauled the international train. In the early years, the service was normally hauled by Stewarts Lane based 4-6-0 Lord Nelson Class locomotives but similarly as with the slightly less powerful King Arthurs. Both locomotive classes were used for increasing traffic to and out of Southampton Docks on ocean liner boat train duties. In the ten years before the Second World War, Lord Nelson and King Arthur Classes were the backbone of the *Arrow*.

Canterbury reintroduced the *Golden Arrow* service on 16 April 1946. The following May, train was made a first-class Pullman service only having to make do with a temporary travel ban on overseas holidays required to shore up the nation's currency. However, the train's composition changed again in October 1949 when second-class Pullman travel was reintroduced. The train's specialist insignia continued to be carried on carriage sides whilst a distinctive headboard was devised with Anglo-French flags positioned at the front of British locomotives.

Canterbury provided many years of service and was used principally on the Folkestone-Boulogne service until laid-up in September 1964. The following July she was towed away for

T.S. "INVICTA" LEAVING DOVER IN THE
"GOLDEN ARROW" SHORT SEA ROUTE
SOUTHERN RAILWAY

Two promotional posters feature the new tailor-made cross-channel ferry *Invicta*. The first is a 1946 poster promoting the resumption of daily rail and sea services to the Continent from London Victoria. By the time the poster appeared, the new vessel was now the *Golden Arrow's* established maritime partner having displaced *Canterbury*. The second poster is an oil on canvass portrayal of *Invicta* at Calais by Terence Cuneo designed as artwork for a 1952 British Railways Southern Region poster entitled 'Bon Voyage'. In this illustration, the ferry is positioned alongside a powerful bank of awaiting SNCF Chapeleon Pacific locomotives providing international travellers with an evocative setting, capturing all the excitement of spending a summertime holiday in France again. (*Left*: NRM/SSPL)

breaking-up. Her successor *Invicta*, like *Canterbury*, was built by Wm. Denny & Bros. Ltd and launched on 14 December 1939. *Invicta* had a passenger capacity of 1,400 passengers but was only converted to full operational service after the Second World War. However, the vessel together with the *Golden Arrow* train immediately became a key marketing tool used both by Southern and British Railways for travel inspired promotional films, posters and advertising for the in the late 1940s and 1950s. Price ticketing structures started to match those of airlines whose aircraft were filled with a travelling public on short-haul routes attracted by new style tourist fares. *Invicta* had a long-service life accompanying the *Golden Arrow*. She made her final trip on 8 August 1972 (the month before the final journey of the train) and was then laid-up at Newhaven until towed away for scrapping in the Netherlands in September of that year.

The 1949 all-Pullman luxury train was made up of ten coaches with three second-class Pullmans – two parlours cars and a brake parlour – being converted and renumbered together with three first-class kitchen cars, two parlour cars, a brake parlour and a new product innovation – the *Trianon Bar* car. Ideas for a dedicated bar car stemmed from Wagon-Lits' luxury *Blue Train*

Locomotive no. 35027 Belgian Marine painted in British Railways dark blue with black and white lining livery looks rather suave in this 1952 Victoria station setting. An earlier experimental light blue colour with red lining was rejected by officials at 222 Marylebone Road. Several of the Merchant Navy Class were painted in dark blue working Dover boat trains. The Victoria March 1954 picture captures a perfect moment when an impeccably dressed mother and son observe no. 35027 Port Line getting ready for a *Golden Arrow* departure. Port Line was one of the ten last batches of 'Merchant Navies' introduced by British Railways going into service in December 1948. The locomotive was re-built in May 1957 and was one of eleven class members that have made it into preservation. (*Above and opposite*: Colour Rail)

French Riviera service which also led to British Railways Southern Region experimenting creating a Tavern Coach set made up of new Bulleid stock used on many longer-distance non-Pullman services. Post-war *Golden Arrow* was hauled by powerful air-smoothed 4-6-2 Merchant Navy Pacific Class locomotives - each one named after shipping lines. The Merchant Navies in their resplendent new malachite green liveries were soon to become regulars – the post-war inaugural run headed by the appropriately named no. 21C1 Channel Packet. In a few weeks, the *Golden Arrow* would be joined by Stewarts Lane based, but at the time unnamed, 4-6-2 light Pacifics which were later classified as the combined West Country and Battle of Britain classes; they and Merchant Navies were set to become familiar sights.

The combined *Golden Arrow/Flèche d'Or* was always deemed a luxury boat train service, and for most of its operational life it was well supported by its railway masters on both sides of the water. On 11 June 1951 coinciding with the Festival of Britain celebrations, the international train received another significant make-over with the introduction of seven newly built first-class Pullman cars (being part of a suspended pre-war order), and three rebuilt second-class cars making it a truly luxurious train again headed by new Britannia Class locomotives. In October 1952 the most famous of all international trains, which for the previous twenty-five years had an 11.00 am Victoria departure, now changed to 2.00 pm (and 1.00 pm from 25 October when summertime ended). On the outward journey the *Golden Arrow* embarked her passengers at Folkestone instead replacing that of Dover. The reason given was to prevent congestion at Dover, and to maintain something of an equilibrium between the two ports during the winter months. Passengers in the revised timing now reached Paris at 9.34 pm whilst the timing of trains and boats from Paris to London were unaffected.[125] There were also some minor changes to the Pullman composition, but the overall ten-car provision continued throughout the 1950s. To commemorate the Festival of Britain, the train was hauled by a new generation of British Railways brunswick green painted 4-6-2 Britannia Class Pacifics. No. 70004 William Shakespeare and no. 70014 Iron Duke undertook duties, as well for sister service *Night Ferry*. The combination of the newly introduced ten-car Pullman stock hauled by Britannias conjured powerful images of the modern post-war Britain; *Golden Arrow* was extensively used for all-round promotional purposes.

Golden Arrow could always be relied upon for news stories. The Duke and Duchess of Windsor, acclimatised to a certain living style, continued their annual London Christmas shopping trips aboard the international boat train.[126] Two famous Polish musicians were reunited after eighteen years apart (Poland had become a Communist satellite state after the Second World War), as the *Golden Arrow* boat train steamed into Victoria Station. The *Western Mail* oozed: 'On to the platform jumped 39-year-old Witold Malcuzynski. He ran into the arms of Andreze Panufnik and, speechless with delight, they hugged and shook hands for some seconds. To-day they are to fulfil an eighteen-year-old pledge when they take part with the London Symphony Orchestra in a special concert at the Royal Albert Hall in aid of the welfare of orphaned Polish children in Britain.'[127]

Bromley was the setting for this April 1957 photograph of a down *Golden Arrow* service. Headed by no. 70004 William Shakespeare, one of the 4-6-2 Britannia Class Pacifics assigned to premier cross-channel boat train operations, the mix of blood and custard coaches and Pullman stock provide a textbook impression of mid-1950s railway life. Likewise, many of the carriage prints found in the compartments of British Railways era coaches of the same time were illustrated by Richard Ward. The painting of the Britannia Class locomotive heading the *Golden Arrow* Continental express was a very iconic image featuring the world-famous Dover Cliffs. (*Above*: Colour Rail; *Below*: Courtesy of Greg Norden Collection & www.travellingartgallery.com)

"GOLDEN ARROW" CONTINENTAL EXPRESS

From a Water Colour by RICHARD WARD

Going to FRANCE?

WHERE SUMMER LINGERS LONGER

When it's autumn in the Highlands it's still summer ''over there''. Think of Paris, bathed in late summer sunshine, with its shows and exhibitions just beginning . . . the sun-drenched plages of Brittany, Côte d'Emeraude, Côte d'Argent . . . the Basque Country, the Riviera, the vineyards of Burgundy, Provence, Champagne.

Or, maybe, a shopping trip appeals to you. Remember — there is more room on the ''Golden Arrow'' and Night Ferry at mid-week than at week-ends.

In any case, most of the summer services by the Short Sea routes will be maintained until the end of September, with their variety of route, their regularity, excellent service and good meals.

For tickets, reservations, etc., apply Continental Enquiry Office, VICTORIA STATION, S.W.I, or principal Travel Agencies.

* Leave ON THE DOT . . arrive ON THE SPOT if you

travel by

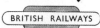

| SHORT SEA ROUTES | BRITISH RAILWAYS | DAY & NIGHT SERVICES |

Crossing to FRANCE?

Whether you are going for business or to seek sunshine, British Railways' *day and night services* offer you comfortable, regular and reliable travel by rail and sea . . . with a choice of routes

Day Services via	*Night Services via*
● **Dover — Calais**	● **Dover — Dunkerque**
● **Folkestone — Calais**	● **Southampton — Havre**
● **Newhaven — Dieppe**	● **Southampton—St. Malo**
● **Folkestone — Boulogne**	● **Newhaven — Dieppe**
	(from July)

Including direct services London—Paris every day in the year
"**GOLDEN ARROW**" (All-Pullman) "**NIGHT FERRY**" (Sleeping cars)

SPECIAL CAR-CARRIER SERVICE BETWEEN DOVER AND BOULOGNE IF TRAVELLING WITH YOUR CAR

DAY AND NIGHT TO THE CONTINENT

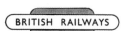
BRITISH RAILWAYS

For tickets, reservations, etc., apply principal Travel Agencies or the Continental Enquiry Office, VICTORIA STATION, London, S.W.I

British Railways always sought to showcase the modernity of both its ferries and locomotives as the centrepiece of its premier cross-channel services. From 1949 France was back on the agenda for many travellers with the Southern Region providing day and night trains from several departure points to the Continent. Mid-week travel a few years later was promoted on the *Golden Arrow* as well as *Night Ferry* as both services were deemed to be less crowded than weekend traffic. (Illustrated London News Ltd/Mary Evans)

Due to extensive electrification work taking place in south-east England British Railways Southern Region experimented with differing combinations of steam motive power. With electrification came frequent route disruption, and also on both sides of the Channel, repeated industrial troubles. The worst perhaps occurring in late October 1957 when rail strikers in protest against the rising cost of living tried to block the train *Golden Arrow* in Calais – still regarded in the media as Europe's most luxurious train – by putting railway sleepers across the tracks. Under a hail of stones, police eventually removed the sleepers with the train eventually leaving for Paris.[128]

Notwithstanding, the train remained tremendously popular with heavy train load formations resulting in haulage by larger rebuilt Merchant Navy Pacifics and 6,000-gallon tenders. Just before the

British Railways was also experimenting with new traction to replace mainline steam which would include heavyweight prestige boat trains. In a distinctive black livery, an impressive looking diesel-electric locomotive no. 10203, of Southern Railway antecedence, is seen here at the Petts Wood Junction with a down *Golden Arrow* train during its allocation to the service in March 1955. No. 10203, the third locomotive of this particular design incorporating various improvements with power capacity uprated to 2,000hp, was completed in 1954. The mid-decade also saw the service promoted in first-class carriage advertising providing an appropriate environment to target the right customer profile. (*Above*: Colour Rail; *Below*: Courtesy of Greg Norden Collection & www.travellingartgallery.com)

1960 summer season, *The Sphere* noted a return to the old schedule of the boat train service. They gushed:

> Everyone will be delighted to hear that the *Golden Arrow*, the all-Pullman express train between London and Paris, will once again leave Victoria at 11 am each day instead of 1 pm, arriving at the Gare du Nord at ten past six in the evening. This journey, which in many ways is preferable to travelling by air to Paris, has never been the same since the time of departure was put back (1952). The seven-hour journey in the old days never seemed so long, due perhaps to that excellent lunch served on the other side of the Channel, which always resulted in the last three hours

From the end of the 1950s British Railways did much to maintain the *Golden Arrow's* promotional aura as the best and only way to reach Paris during the day. The portrayal of a chic, sophisticated couple wallowing in Paris's evening atmosphere, helped reinvigorate the international train's reputation based on its luxury nature and impeccable service. Likewise, a similar styled illustration used in poster advertising captured the elegance of stepping on to the international train at Victoria whether it be steam or electric traction. (*Above left*: Illustrated London News Ltd/Mary Evans; *Above right*: NRM/SSPL)

being spent sleeping or dozing in a comfortable armchair. You arrived in Paris refreshed, in good time to settle down in your hotel and consider where it would be best to dine. The one o'clock departure made the journey tedious in comparison. The return service leaves Paris at 12.45 pm, arriving in London at ten minutes to eight in the evening. Once again, the timing enables you to lunch in state.[129]

For the most part steam haulage was always part of the *Golden Arrow's* magic and special charisma, it ultimately had to bend to a new world of railway modernisation. Electrification provided a speedier service, but in so doing the train had lost part of its unique personality. On 11 June 1961 on its last steam hauled outing, *Golden Arrow* was conveyed by no. 34100 *Appledore* thus ending an iconic period of steam traction that had been such an instrumental feature of the special boat train's image. Class 71 electric locomotives were built for non-multiple unit heavy-weight international services with no. E5000 taking over the following day.

Perhaps another sign of the imminent utilitarian nature of cross-channel travel to come, was the transfer of single-class Channel Islands vessel *Sarnia* replacing *Invicta* for the 1962–63 winter season. Similarly, *Caesarea* did likewise in 1966/67. All *Golden Arrow's* little extras were slowly eroding. With electrification locomotive failures were not unheard of undermining the service's proposition. On 2 January 1966, some 400 seasonal holidaymakers were held up at Selling, Kent when the cross-channel boat train failed.[130] Second-class Pullmans were withdrawn with the train made up of first-class Pullman stock and ordinary second-class coaches, but Pullman management did their best to ensure the boat train was as smart as ever. Cars were refurbished by dedicated and long-service craftsmen at the company's own workshop at Brighton. It was only in the final years that British Rail and SNCF began to view the service as a relic of another age. The railway unions on the other hand had become much more militant since nationalisation doing their best to displace the luxury train service. They took great exception to Pullman as they perceived it to be a privately-owned operation. In 1968 British Rail decided to give the train one final throw of the die with a livery change when Pullman cars were repainted in corporate blue and grey just like the *Brighton Belle* service. The *Golden Arrow* name on the lower blue panel replaced the coach name and class designation, and car numbers appeared

In this 1960 photograph of a departing *Golden Arrow* service, the train is still headed by steam. Re-built West Country Class no. 34101 Hartland provides a typical period location with a combination of both British Railways maroon and green stock and a recognition that the international boat train had lost just a tad of its former Pullman desirability.

Electrification in the twilight years of the *Golden Arrow* service changed the nature of the train somewhat, steam hauled glamour gave way to the modern but grey efficiency of electric traction. Notwithstanding Victoria's changing face, railway authorities were still resolved to turn out the premier boat train in the most splendid way possible. Taken in March 1963, no. E5015, which seems to have been a regular performer, looks totally resplendent in malachite green with red and lined white stripe, leaves Victoria with the Anglo-French boat train. (*Above and below*: Colour Rail)

at coach ends. With this make-over the Pullman had lost its unique branding, but customers (formally known in British Rail speak as passengers) found it difficult to differentiate the vehicles. A total of six Pullmans – two kitchen cars, three parlours and a parlour brake – formed part of the train which was hauled in its final

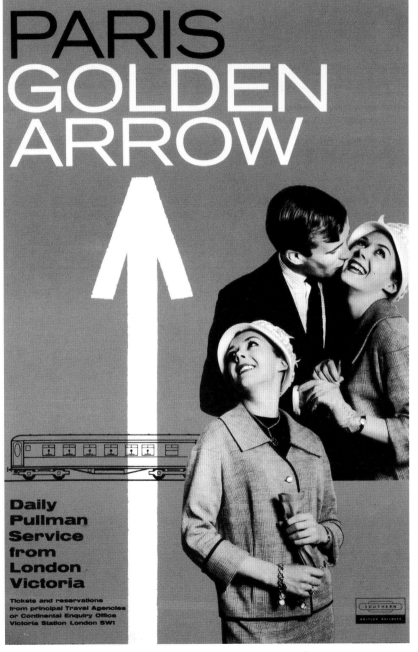

PARIS
GOLDEN
ARROW

**Daily
Pullman
Service
from
London
Victoria**

Tickets and reservations
from principal Travel Agencies
or Continental Enquiry Office
Victoria Station London SW1

SOUTHERN
BRITISH RAILWAYS

Into the swinging 1960s, British Railways began to adopt a thoroughly modern image to its marketing communication. Southern Region portrayed Paris as the 'City of Love' in this 1961 *Golden Arrow* poster produced by an unknown creative team. The attire worn by the models in this promotional piece is sharp but stylish, but perfectly complementary for a return trip on the Pullman boat train. The copy also alludes to 'principal travel agencies' suggesting the importance of packaging leisure and holiday trips to ensure hotel bookings and to the competitive nature of managing travel at the time. (NRM/ SSPL) years by blue liveried with full yellow ended E class locomotives. In France, the *Flèche d'Or* suffered a similar humiliation losing its Pullman cars in 1969.

This period was really the pinnacle of international boat trains between Britain and France, but it was not to last because of regular and reliable air services and the increasing fashion to taking the car on a new generation of ro-ro ferries – many ironically operated by British Rail. International boat trains ultimately succumbed to railway modernisation on 30 September 1972 *Golden Arrow* ended. The international Pullman boat train's passing was really a response to changing travelling habits, and a prevailing British Rail policy which effectively decreed the Pullman brand as outmoded and no-longer required.

Continental travel became less glamorous with its passing, but the memory of the *Golden Arrow* and the *Flèche d'Or* as arguably Britain and France's most famous luxury and easily recalled named-trains lives on. The scheduled boat train did live on for some years before

The last week of steam on the *Golden Arrow* is caught in this June 1961 photograph. Looking resplendent no. 34100 Appledore is ready to depart Victoria. Perhaps the schoolboy train spotter is another relic of the steam railway age as with its demise, the loss of steam traction on mainline services, the recording individual locomotives was never quite the same. (Colour Rail)

superseded by cars, vans and lorries rolling on and off shuttle ferries in vast numbers. Yet author Andrew Martin says there are echoes of the past if you look carefully, 'The pink-shaded table lamps that were a feature of Pullman cars appear in *Eurostar* Business Premier Coaches, and *Eurostar* like the *Flèche/Arrow* is a joint Anglo-French operation. But the *Arrow* was a boat train, and it was the advent of *Eurostar* in 1994 that finally killed off the boat trains.'[131]

On the other side of the Channel French railway officials probably looked back at the inter-war years with a degree of professional elation. Wartime occupation and substantial network damage had its impact as the former regional railway companies morphed into SNCF's nationalised structure. The various companies had run many of the Continent's long-distance luxury expresses with distinction making Paris the hub of a radial network with its many integrated service connections to the Riviera and Europe through non-German territories. When *La Flèche d'Or* was established in September 1926, the Calais-Paris Pullman express became an integral component in many south bound railway journeys. *La Fleche d'Or* in its early days was formed up of ten Wagon-Lits chocolate and cream Pullman cars (Voiture Salon Pullman) displaying the arrows of gold painted on the coach sides. The Pullman coach liveries later changed to more familiar blue and cream in the early 1930s as used on the *Côte d'Azur Pullman Express* for the day-time Riviera service. *Flèche d'Or* Pullman carriages bore British coach manufacturer nameplate – the Leeds Forge Company – who had built the glamorous 1922 stock for the direct link *Calais-Méditerranée Express* and the *Blue Train* several years earlier. Carriage stock as utilised for the night-time sleeper service from Paris.

The *Flèche d'Or* had a capacity of 300 first-class passengers who were transported to Gare du Nord in the most luxurious fashion possible at the additional cost of approximately 13s. 6d (£0.68p). The steel-sided French Pullman coaches – assembled in pairs or couplages – were longer in length, 77 feet buffer to buffer, with a maximum width of 9 feet 7 inches. A feature of the pairs, seating sixty guests, was the incorporation of kitchens, so passengers were served with meals in their seats without having to make their way to a separate dining car. The train would wait alongside the Calais quayside facilitating rapid passenger transfer from ferry to train. Another unusual feature of the train in earlier years was the luggage brake. The French brake had a middle section which looked like a bird-caged van but had two detachable containers or sealed luggage boxes on either side. Depending on passenger volumes, train formations would include two luggage vans, or fourgons as they were known in France, containing passenger luggage loaded at London Victoria, together with any other important freight items and documents requiring sealed transit. This might also include a registered baggage car clearing frontiers without customs examination until it reached its final destination where officials would examine everything. This formed part of plans to accelerate the *Flèche d'Or* which by 1929 the Paris train arrived twenty minutes quicker than its predecessor, and up to forty minutes earlier on the return journey. On top of this there were deliberate efforts to enhance the customer experience.

The Sketch wrote of 'special arrangements with the Customs authorities are being made to ensure little waiting, and that the hand luggage is examined on the train between Calais and Paris'.[132] Predictably, there were press comments of how much time and trouble was being saved en route – if one had the money, then they could pay for such conveniences. Prior to this arrangement on the English side things were slightly different as a low loading truck carried a row of the containers fastened securely with chains and hauled at the rear of the train. At Dover Harbour containers would be unchained, taken off and loaded on to the steamer; once at Calais they would be winched off again and rapidly loaded on to the special French luggage van without passengers having to deal with French customs at the port. This process enabled a quick get-away of the heavy Paris train which, if full, could weigh more than 500 tons.

The *Flèche d'Or* like its British side of the operation lost its exclusive first-class Pullman preserve during the 1930s depression with the train's make-up changing to a multi-portioned luxury express more in common in concept to the British Southern Railway Atlantic Coast Express (ACE) service. Different onward destinations needed to be accommodated as several sleeping cars were attached to the rear of the *Flèche d'Or* with its new rake of Pullman cars. Some sleeping cars formed part of the celebrated evening *Blue Train* and *Rome Express* departures where on arrival at Paris du Nord, the sleepers would be worked around to Gare du Lyon attaching to the rest of the Riviera bound *Blue Train*. The *Rome Express*, comprising both first and second-class sleepers, would leave France passing through the Mont Cenis Tunnel en route to Turin, Genoa, Pisa and Rome. In busy summer periods at Calais,

Paris-bound Pullman sleepers might form a complete second train together with a third Nord train for ordinary passengers – all three trains leaving one after another and making a non-stop run to the French capital and access to the greater European railway network. In October 1935, there were again some changes in France as the Calais-Dover service was re-routed via Boulogne and Folkestone so that the Wagon-Lits Pullman cars could be used both ways. The Paris departure time was changed to allow more time for the empty Pullman cars to be worked from Boulogne to Calais. With the introduction of *Ferry Boat de Nuit*, the *Flèche d'Or* services were increasingly talked about in the same breath. On 24 January 1939, Winston Churchill and Mary Penman were heading to London from Paris. She writes:

> We had to take a taxi at 9.20 pm to the Gare du Nord to board the Golden Arrow at 9.50 pm (the night ferry) … Mr Churchill was preparing to leave his suite at the Ritz, as usual we had not too much time to spare and I could not think why he was delaying our departure and fussing around.'

Scheduled departures wait for no man; even budding Prime Ministers have suffered the ignominy of running to catch a train:

> We made a rapid taxi journey to the Gare du Nord, grabbed a porter and made undignified haste towards the departure platform. I was carrying among other articles the old black leather hat box (housing Churchill's used undergarments!), the lid became unfastened and the mouth of the box tilted downwards revealing some underwear, only prompt action on my part avoided spillage, 'We must not wash our dirty linen in public,' Mr Churchill said as we ran the last stretch to the barrier.[133]

Post-war SNCF, like their British counterparts, prioritised track damage and maintenance work allowing some degree of normality to resume with prestige services. The *Flèche d'Or* recommenced on 15 April 1946 made up of first-class Pullmans and SNCF first and second-class ordinary coaches. Journey times between Calais-Paris were rather long because of the state of the line but French authorities put considerable efforts to improve the position so by the late 1940s mainline operations began to resemble pre-war running for *Flèche d'Or*. In the 1950s SNCF commenced its northern France railway electrification plans but steam traction was continued by the company with their 4-6-2 (231E) Chapelon Super-Pacific Class locomotives for many years remaining in full service until total electrification of the line. During the 1960s the *Flèche d'Or* would be headed by both steam and diesel-electric traction which necessitated a stop to change locomotives – the route between Amiens and Paris being turned over to electric traction. Throughout this period the powerful Chapelon steam locomotives similarly handled the Paris-Calais section of the *Ferry Boat de Nuit*. Steam was to last longer in France on both the *Flèche d'Or* and *Ferry Boat de Nuit* services. The last steam hauled *Flèche d'Or* run was on 11 January 1969 with Wagon-Lits Pullman cars being taken out of service at the end of May that year. On both sides of the channel direct train connections in the 1960s and 1970s became far more utilitarian.

Night Ferry

The mid-1930s heralded the start of the direct *Ferry Boat de Nuit/ Night Ferry* train/boat/train era. Its impact was profound since few luxury trains evoke such passions as *Night Ferry* – a train service linking London and Paris, and in time, several other European destinations – making it Britain's only truly international train. The night train conjured many different images; it was exceptionally comfortable, elegant and simply the most convenient and civilised way of travelling between Europe's pre-eminent cities without the need to travel by day. National Railway Museum (NRM) carriage custodian David Jenkinson was involved with the decision to preserve one of the sleeping cars. He described travelling on *Night Ferry* as 'a most fascinating and unique experience' with carriages that possessed 'distinctive character'.[134] The trend-setting *Night Ferry* over the years was the haunt of well-to-do businessmen, tourists from both sides of the Atlantic, in modern parlance media celebrities, aristocracy and royalty, civil servants, diplomats and the dark arts professional espionage. Wagon-Lits provided the hospitality and sleeper service; an organisation who by this time had experience of running similar European services for half a century.

The *Night Ferry/Ferry Boat de Nuit* and *Golden Arrow/La Flèche d'Or* were natural extensions to the Dalziel British Pullman concept forming part of broader inter-war super train market found across Britain, Europe and North America.[135] Certainly, the early years of the night train was a unique travelling experience and well supported. Within the leisure sector the sleeper service attracted repeat guests, and as David St. John Thomas and Patrick Whitehouse commented: 'Most passengers swore by the train, especially enjoying the comfort of lying out in privacy if the sea were rough. More usually it was a gentle motion of the waves that induced sleep.'[136]

There was something about *Night Ferry* that was enthralling and very special as the sound of the ship's turbine soothed most passengers to sleep. The new international train was the jewel in the crown for Southern Railway and developed on the back of the *Golden Arrow*, and their first night-time sleeper operation for many years, when first commercial journeys were made in October 1936. The launch timing was considered coincidental to a decision to stimulate trade between Britain and France resulting from a currency realignment.[137] This side of the water's inauguration comprised the cream of Anglo-French society including political luminaries such as the British home secretary, the French Ambassador, and many important railway representatives.[138] Home Secretary Sir John Simon was on the maiden VIP trip completing a whirlwind trip to Paris whilst commenting 'the new service would remove the average Englishman's fear of rough Channel crossings'.[139] By mid-December, the new operation was two months old; used heavily and commercially 'judged to be a legitimate success'.[140]

Prior to *Night Ferry's* launch there had been a long story of several aborted attempts over the years to establish an English Channel train ferry service. In 1872 a bill went before parliament but was defeated; a subsequent proposal in 1911 was scuppered because of concerns on the horizon over events gradually taking place in Europe.[141] The First World War's and military supply demands did, however, provide the technological capability and experience of regularly moving locomotives, carriages for ambulance trains, armoured wagons and low-loaders carrying tanks and freight and goods wagons moving supplies to and from the Continent. Military train ferry services were developed from Southampton to Dieppe in December 1917, from Richborough, a few miles north of Dover to Calais and Dunkerque, and in February 1918 from Newhaven to Dieppe supporting a final push on the war front. Quite naturally, a cross-channel train service was closely entwined with continually delayed plans for a Channel Tunnel. Sir Edward Watkin, Chairman of the Great Central Railway (GCR) had promoted a parliamentary

John Elliot's skilful media cultivation was clearly evident in the run up to *Night Ferry's* launch, judged by the column inches secured in national, regional and local newspaper, as well as, in overseas press coverage. The promotional aspect was more low-key as this quarter page *Bystander* advert reveals in the run up to the launch of the service. The accompanying poster produced the following year with artwork by illustrator G Massiot, demonstrates through imagery, the intricate partnership needed to run the international through train involving Wagons-Lits, Southern Railway and Nord. True international cooperation across waters and conceivably represents the culmination of collaboration between British and French partners first begun some eighty years before. (*Above left*: Illustrated London News Ltd/Mary Evans; *Above right*: NRM/SSPL)

bill to construct a tunnel in the late 1800s never getting beyond pilot drilling. There had been other efforts in the intervening years, but in 1929 a British Royal Commission was set-up to examine the feasibility of a Channel Tunnel. After wide-spread consultation, the idea was eventually rejected by the Defence Committee in the following year. This provided Southern Railway with a chance to resurrect plans for a suitable train ferry service. Yet the idea of linking the crossing between England and France took several more years to firmly take root precipitated by the financial crisis of the Depression gripping the western world in the early 1930s.

Notwithstanding, the combined *Golden Arrow/Flèche d'Or* service was an outstanding success becoming one of the world's best known luxury trains. Could a comparable night-time service achieve similar success? Certainly, there were parts of the travelling public who were not exactly happy with elements of cross-channel activity. As noted, British and French railway companies received complaints from luxury boat train users that services did not meet expectations especially with regards to the quality of night-time crossings. This prompted serious consideration by both British and French authorities but in truth the idea was never far from the mind of Southern Railway's Walker; he considered prospects for a Channel Tunnel were still distant dreams. Expensive commercial flights with limited luggage space was still in its infancy and only available to a lucky few who could afford it, so the only effective way for greater numbers of prosperous passengers to reach the Continent was by train/boat/train.

Following the British rejection of a Channel Tunnel Sir Herbert was keen to resurrect plans to promote a through London-Paris train and ferry. At a board meeting on 27 November 1930 he proposed such a service involving a sea crossing between Dover and Boulogne. The following month Southern's board was informed of Nord's investigation of a freight ferry operation. Board members were told in no uncertain terms they must not let such potentially lucrative opportunities fall into competitor hands. The French were considering an LNER sponsored alternative between Harwich and Calais – a Harwich-Zeebrugge freight train ferry had been successfully established in 1924 – and further proposals to develop the port at Tilbury with its close links to London which from 1927 had seen an LMS Dunkerque mail boat service operating. A new French company the Angleterre-Lorraine-Alsace Société Anonyme de Navigation of Dunkerque (ALA) was created in October 1926 to run the new operation and in April the following year they purchased three cross-channel ships from the LMS – *Rathmore*, *Londonderry* and the *Duke of Argyll* and renaming them *Lorrain*, *Flemish* and *Alsation*.

Southern made their first overtures to operate a night-time through train passenger service. Consideration of a variety of routes and ports followed with Southern Railway in June 1931 announcing they would supply specialist ferries and a new terminal at Dover. A Dover-Boulogne route was considered as the best route option, but the company prevaricated about a final decision until the

TILBURY FOR THE CONTINENT

LMS

S.S. "Picard" leaving Tilbury Marine for Dunkerque

By NORMAN WILKINSON, R.I.

The nightly Tilbury-Dunkerque Service affords connections with all parts of the Continent and is the most convenient Route from the Midlands and North of England to Paris, Basle, Italy, and Central Europe.

Norman Wilkinson was one of the finest marine painters of the twentieth century having cut his teeth with a variety of shipping lines including Geo. Thompson & Co's Aberdeen Line, Alfred Holt & Co's Blue Funnel Line, Blue Star Line, Booth Line, Cunard, Dominion Line, P&O and White Star, many of whom operated from Liverpool. His Royal Academy initiative together with his long-term association with LMS and the many Anglo-Irish boat train services made him a natural for the Tilbury for the Continent poster designed to promote a night-time operation which turned out to be the forerunner to *Night Ferry*. SS *Picard* shown above was the former *Duke of Cumberland* and one of a batch of old LMS ferries from Anglo-Irish services recycled for new duties by ALA and given the French name. Despite LMS's best endeavours to promote an inexpensive service, passengers did not flock to Tilbury; they were put off by vessel unreliability, fog delays, and worse still, the worn out and dirty state of the ships. The service lasted until April 1932.

French threatened to support a rival offer. The Southern Railway Board finally sanctioned the introduction of train ferry for a night service between London and Paris on 19 October 1932 – this decision taken at the height of the slump but a strong business case and a commercial logic that better days would return underpinned the company's approval. A month later Dunkerque was announced as the preferred Continental location since it was enclosed and unaffected by tidal rise and fall. ALA agreed to provide the French terminal facilities and a formal announcement and application for tenders duly took place. ALA was in an ideal position to develop French operations as they were already operating several former LMS ferries to run the Tilbury-Dunkerque mail boat train. ALA developed with Nord onward train connections to Paris-Nord and with Chemin de Fer de l'Est to the major cities of eastern France and the Swiss border which according to Behrend and Buchanan, authors of the definitive *Night Ferry* work, 'could be reached for as little as £4.00 return from London'.[142] This service was later transferred to Folkestone on 1 May 1932 with a new and well and truly time-honoured business relationship under Southern's nimble management team.

On the English side, Dover Harbour was selected as the terminal since Southern had already concentrated most of their boat train/ferry operations there. The port was well-developed for cross channel purposes enjoying comparatively close London access which could be reached within two hours. But the choice of Dover did not come without complications. There were enormous engineering problems to overcome because of the harbour's 25-foot tidal rise and fall. Rough seas compounded the construction process which suffered from leaking from fissures in the porous chalk beneath the dock floor. These difficulties were eventually overcome, and a train ferry berth was built within Dover Harbour. Work began in 1933 requiring the construction of an enclosed dock more than 400 feet long and 70 feet wide sealed with a pair of gates together with a long-length loading ramp or link span to meet the specially designed train ferries. Once the ferries were inside the sealed dock the level of the water was then either raised or lowered depending on the state of the tide – the pump house capable of moving nearly 750,000 gallons of sea water per hour. Dover Ferry was probably the only timetabled passenger station on the British railway network without platforms.

In 1933 Wagon-Lits Type F (for Ferry) British loading gauge sleeping cars were designed. Between November 1935 and May 1936 twelve were built by Ateliers de Construction du Nord de la France Blanc-Misseron carrying no. 3788 to 3799. Between 1937 and 1947 a further six Type F sleepers were built no. 3800 to 3805, but completion was delayed until hostilities had ended. Following Wagon-Lits instructions delivery took place before the war commenced, but they were incomplete as their bogies were removed to prevent the Germans using them. In 1952 a further seven Type F sleepers no. 3983 to 3989 were constructed to replace five original coaches lost to the war. All the original sleeper cars had been requisitioned by MITROPA under Nazi instructions. Nos: 3788 and 3795 simply disappeared in the six-year conflict whilst 3793, 3796 and 3799 were rebuilt as MITROPA dining cars and never returned. A feature of the F Class vehicles was that there were doors at one end of the coach only with the vestibule space at the non-door end converted for use by the attendant and for storage of equipment. The gangway to the next coach was retained for access to dining cars. Another car feature was the sides above the waistline were tapered in a few degrees to clear obstructions such as tunnel walls. The carriages had nine two-berth cabins (some adjoining each other) which meant the total number passengers per carriage could vary between nine and eighteen – effectively a very selective club as even in the busiest of times the ferries rarely transported more than ten sleeping carriages. To the casual observer the London Victoria *Night Ferry* was certainly an unusual looking train. Wagon-Lits sleeping cars and the accompanying four-wheeled baggage vans (fourgons) were painted metallic blue. Pre-war, there were umber and cream liveried twelve-wheeled Pullman coaches providing a full catering service, standard olive green painted Southern Railway Maunsell coaching stock together with the motive power – invariable locomotives were out of sight beyond the platforms as the train was too long.

On the French side, powerful steam locomotives handled the Paris-Dunkerque section of *Ferry Boat de Nuit*. They were headed in both Nord and SNCF days by 231E Chapelon Pacific locomotives until eventual electrification of the line. A range of larger Continental coaches accompanied the train in France including a Wagon-Lits dining car sandwiched between the Type F sleeping cars and the seating coaches. In the early years, this would have included a 1926 luxury dining car originally forming part of the French president's train but in 1952 this was replaced by a larger Wagon-Lits WR fifty-six-seater restaurant dining car. In the Nord period ending in 1938 seating coaches would comprise two first-class and five second-class coaches both in green livery with oval windows. In the first SNCF epoch, this was changed to two Rapide Nord first-class and four Rapide Nord second-class coaches. In the 1960s, they were replaced by six DEV INOX coaches whilst

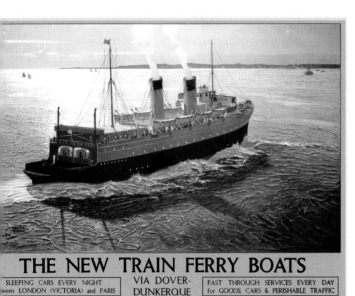

THE NEW TRAIN FERRY BOATS

| SLEEPING CARS EVERY NIGHT veen LONDON (VICTORIA) and PARIS | VIA DOVER-DUNKERQUE | FAST THROUGH SERVICES EVERY DAY for GOODS CARS & PERISHABLE TRAFFIC |

Full details of Services, Fares, Rates, etc. from
SOUTHERN RAILWAY CONTINENTAL DEPARTMENT. VICTORIA STATION. S.W.I.

The specially designed train and boat ferries for *Night Ferry* attracted considerable media attention when services began, as did the ship's versatile capabilities to provide through perishable freight traffic. Walter Thomas's 1936 majestic illustration in an evening setting of the near identical vessels helped establish the luxury train's image. Likewise, this painting of the train on the British side of the water reinforced the image of civilised international train travel. (*Below*: Malcolm Root)

by the 1970s *Ferry Boat de Nuit* was updated with up to six UIC stock – 1,237 were built between 1963 and 1976. Whilst the all-metal construction of the *Night Ferry* F Class sleepers – designed to minimise fire risk especially at sea – and the fact they were smaller than standard Continental carriages, interestingly, they were not prohibited from working elsewhere in Europe. Two Type Fs were allocated to Gare du Nord stock and included on the Paris-Hanover *Nord Express* train ensuring the carriages could effectively appear anywhere on the European network as indeed British Pullman cars did in the past as special or supplementary vehicles.

The last part of the *Night Ferry* equation was the three dedicated vessels built specifically for the service. The ferry ships were designed to carry a maximum of twelve British loading gauge sleeping cars and attendant baggage vans. The ferry's train deck had four tracks which converged to two at the stern accessed via the loading ramp or link span. Swan Hunter and Wigham Richardson of Wallsend-on-Tyne built the vessels. In July 1934 *Twickenham Ferry* was delivered followed by *Hampton Ferry* in November, and in March 1935 *Shepperton Ferry* became the third ship for the unique service. The ferries were owned by Southern but as the new service would displace an existing French Folkestone Harbour to Dunkerque run operated by ALA, the French authorities demanded that one of the ferries be placed under the French flag. *Twickenham Ferry* was transferred to ALA on 22 September 1936 and manned thereafter by French nationals. Initially, the three ferries were coal-fired but post-war they were converted to oil burning. They could carry some 500 passengers for the overnight sea voyage. When the ferry was heavily booked, a second relief boat train for foot passengers would run ahead of the *Night Ferry* from Victoria. For those not travelling in Wagon-Lits sleeping cars some sleeping accommodation was provided in separate ladies and gentlemen saloons as well as separate first and second-class designated restaurants. During the Second World War *Hampton* and *Twickenham* were adapted to ship the 932 WD Class Austerity 2-8-0 locomotives destined to Europe once the D-Day landing bridgeheads had been secured. On each trip some sixteen fully loaded locomotives and twenty loaded coal wagons were accommodated.[143] Post-war the ferries became single-class vessels. On 28 July 1951, a new diesel-powered train ferry was added to the roster by SNCF. The Danish built *Saint-Germain* was of the latest design and would last operationally for a further thirty-seven years. Both *Shepperton Ferry* and *Hampton Ferry*

I always go the PERMANENT WAY *to Paris*

When I have to be in Paris by breakfast-time I always go by rail. How? I spend a comfortable night on the Ferry without moving from the through "sleeper" from Victoria and arrive just before ten in the morning, well-rested, well-fed. *Right in the heart of Paris, too.* No customs delays and no hotel bill ; I can leave Paris again on the "Golden Arrow" at 12.15 and be back in London in time for dinner ! How's that for speed and comfort ?

FOR BUSINESS

For tickets, reservations, etc., apply CONTINENTAL ENQUIRY OFFICE, Victoria Station, London, S.W.I, or principal Travel Agencies.

TRAVEL

London-Paris by

NIGHT FERRY   BRITISH RAILWAYS   GOLDEN ARROW

Paris by morning

URGENT appointments in Paris can be most easily and restfully kept by sleeping your way over on the Night Ferry (Victoria depart 10 p.m.). There is no changing. Breakfast on the train and, just after, you are in the heart of the French capital. If necessary you can return by the Golden Arrow leaving Paris at 12.30 p.m., and be back in London by early evening. Alternatively, you can leave London by Golden Arrow, at 11 a.m. arriving in Paris in time for dinner. Either way means excellent meals, courteous personal service and pleasant, *punctual* and *dependable* travelling.

★ *PARIS CELEBRATES! This year Paris celebrates her 2,000th anniversary. Will you be there?*

Travel LONDON-PARIS *by*

BRITISH RAILWAYS

NIGHT FERRY · GOLDEN ARROW

For tickets, reservations, etc., apply Continental Enquiry Office, VICTORIA STATION, London, S.W.I, or principal Travel Agencies.

business or *pleasure*

PARIS, with her gay scene, her wonderful shops and restaurants, Montparnasse, the Bois in Spring, is within a few hours of you. The "Golden Arrow", the modern-day 'magic carpet', the train of the elegant, of the diplomat, transports you quickly and luxuriously to the very heart of the capital. The "Night Ferry" sleeping car train, which goes straight there without changing, saves precious daylight hours !

London—Paris by

"GOLDEN ARROW"
All-Pullman
*10 a.m. daily
London, (Victoria)
arrives Paris 5.52 p.m*

BRITISH RAILWAYS

"NIGHT FERRY"
Sleeping Cars
*9 p.m. nightly
London, (Victoria)
arrives Paris 9 a.m*

*For tickets, reservations, etc., apply Continental Enquiry Office,
VICTORIA STATION, London, S.W.I, or principal Travel Agencies*

These three advertisements taken from *The Sketch* and *The Illustrated London News* demonstrates post-war deluxe rail travel services were quickly back on the agenda as first-class travel was increasingly adapted for the needs of the business community. Not surprisingly, British Railways advertising should target business travellers using the London and Paris axis by promoting the combined benefits of using *Night Ferry* on outbound journeys and returning on *Golden Arrow* or vice versa. Another feature of business tourism was extending a visit by a day or two, often over a weekend, and by taking a partner along on the trip. The business or pleasure headline appears to be part of a developing travel theme. (*Above and left*: Illustrated London News Ltd/Mary Evans) provided Stranraer relief capacity following the *Princess Victoria* disaster in the northern Irish Sea on 31 January 1953; *Hampton Ferry* continued support every summer until 1961.

One of the most intriguing aspects of the three original *Night Ferry* vessels was their additional capability to carry up to twenty-five private cars in a garage facility on the upper deck. Access was side loading via a concrete ramp alongside the ship which began in June 1937. Such initiatives led to other cross-channel services being developed including a new motor ferry operation between Britain and Belgium.[144] Post Second World War, the ferry capacity was extended to up to 100 cars and their passengers providing a significant contribution to what was to become British Railway's drive-on car ferry business. When not on passenger duty, the ships provided a valuable additional resource for moving vast quantities of perishable foodstuffs from the Continent and return outward cargoes consisting of British manufactured cars, tractors and machinery destined for European export markets. The vessels could each accommodate up to forty special loaded goods wagons as well as motorised heavy goods vehicles. The scale of importing European produce – fruit, vegetables, fresh flowers, foodstuffs and other perishable goods – was so significant that by 1960 a large new depot was built by British Railways at Hither Green in south London for onward distribution of food produce that had been hauled by rail from Dover.[145]

For passengers, *Night Ferry* provided a very distinctive experience. Respective journeys would begin at either London Victoria or Paris Gare du Nord; for many travelling on the *Night Ferry* was simply a thrill. At Victoria passengers wishing to travel incognito could simply leave the Grosvenor Hotel via a back-entrance door opening on to the station concourse, but everyone had to negotiate passport control and customs. Once through the tiny passport control room sleeping and foot passengers were separated. Sleeping passengers on platform two were directed towards one of the glamorous blue and gold sleeping car berths; T.S. Elliot referred to the cosy compartments as little dens. Foot passengers would stroll down platform one to the point where they were beyond the sleeping cars to the awaiting restaurant and buffet cars and ordinary boat train coaches.

Night Ferry was something special with sleeping passengers met by brown uniformed Wagon-Lits conductors and shown to their berths. When the service resumed again in 1947, the Continental

THE
NIGHT FERRY
THROUGH SLEEPING CARS

NIGHTLY IN EACH DIRECTION
(EXCEPT CHRISTMAS DAY)

dep 9 0*pm	↑LONDON↑	arr 9 10 am
	(VICTORIA)	
arr 9 0 am	↓PARIS↓	dep 9 45 pm
	(NORD)	

FOR INFORMATION, RESERVATIONS, ETC., APPLY TO:
CONTINENTAL ENQUIRY OFFICE, VICTORIA STATION, LONDON, S.W.I;
BRITISH RAILWAYS' TRAVEL CENTRE, LOWER REGENT STREET, LONDON, S.W.I;
OR TO PRINCIPAL TRAVEL AGENCIES

BRITISH RAILWAYS

This *Night Ferry* execution was the first produced by British Railways in 1953 to promote the company's night sleeper service operation between London Victoria and Paris Nord. The poster with artwork by Barber created a fascinating period image of the train as it was loaded on to the ferry. The previous year, *Night Ferry* had received another makeover as seven new Type F sleepers were introduced to combat war-time losses making a total fleet of twenty sleepers to meet increasing service demands. Quite naturally British Railways was keen to ensure cabin bunks were filled with passengers. Tactical advertising continued to support *Night Ferry*. Much was done in tandem with *Golden Arrow* promoting combined high-quality day and night travel solutions for both prosperous business and leisure passengers. The second image shows un-rebuilt Merchant Navy Class locomotive no. 35017 Belgian Marine, still in blue livery at Bromley South and taken in 1953. Belgian Marine was a particular powerful Pacific used on the *Golden Arrow* boat train, but also for the transportation of affluent passengers taking their motor cars on holiday aboard the *West Country Car Tourist Service* express. A father and son watch the heavy-weight *Night Ferry* train pass, providing a fascinating glimpse of 1950s social life. (*Left*: NRM/SSPL; *Below*: Colour Rail)

This poster was produced by John A. Greene who specialised in oil and watercolour to promote the Paris *Night Ferry* through sleeping car train service. Greene, like Barber, was part of a new generation of artists producing work for the British Transport Commission. His attention to detail is seen in this 1957 work with the French portion of the train service hauled by steam locomotive providing a very distinctive impression of the capital. Business levels were brisk leading to a succession of British Railways Southern Region marketing material over the coming years including the second Night Ferry image which appeared as carriage advertising. (*Right*: NRM/ SSPL; *Below*: Courtesy of Greg Norden Collection & www.travellingartgallery.com)

train's operators could again focus on exclusivity. As author Michael Williams notes. 'Among the little luxuries of the post-war era were the small wrapped parcels of Palmolive soap, complete with the train's monogram.'[146] From the moment, the guest stepped on to the train a very distinctive atmosphere was guaranteed. The compartment interior walls were of 1930s design with metal painted brown to look like wood, and steel blue. The only real differences in the sleeper compartments were the luggage racks which contained life jackets and netting to stop luggage falling when sea conditions were rough. The made-up bunk beds (which could be converted into brown velvet sofas for day-time travel) had crisp white cotton sheets and traditional monogrammed brown wool blankets which were later to be replaced by blue blankets of Scottish woven tartan. If a customer did not want to adjourn to the dining car, drinks and snacks could be brought to the individual sleeping compartments which also contained a few extra luxuries as mementoes of the trip. Given the train was a late departure many passengers choose not to eat in the dining car having eaten earlier in the evening, but they might have been missing out on a gourmet treat since post-war rationing did not apply to respective national showcases. The dining car came into its own the following morning for *le petit déjeuner* – Wagon-Lits describing it as Le Meat Breakfast – a French dining car train ritual that stayed unchanged for seventy years.

During the 1950s when regular short-haul air flights presented a viable alternative, *Night Ferry* enjoyed patronage and occupancy rates many luxury hotels would have jumped at. Similar to *Golden Arrow*, the train carried its fair share of VIPs. HRH Princess Elizabeth travelled in February 1948, the Duke of Windsor on occasions visited the country in a private capacity as well as prime ministers. Winston Churchill had a particular liking for luxury trains and a frequent user of both Pullman and Wagon-Lits services. Former Pullman executive Julian Morel summarised perfectly: 'When Churchill travelled there was always a sensation, so great was his prestige. He was a legend. He also liked the good things in life.'[147] And there was always a 'fund of Churchillian anecdotes'. Morel reported on one particular occasion of an early morning war-time departure, Churchill 'requested a bottle of port, a large glass and some cracked ice' at breakfast. There was work to be done!'[148] Over the years Churchill routinely travelled on *Night Ferry*.[149] He visited Paris several times in the early 1950s, both before and after becoming peace-time prime minister. On one occasion Sunday, 16 December 1951, it seemed almost half of the British Cabinet was on the luxury train as Churchill was joined by Foreign Secretary Anthony Eden, Sir Norman Brook, Secretary to the Cabinet and Sir Roger Makins, Deputy Under-Secretary of State in the Foreign Office.[150]

Churchill used all his state powers announcing he would join the train at Sevenoaks Tubs Hill Station, close to his Chartwell home, to avoid going to London. This was a unique and historic occasion as the train made its one and only special stop. Customs and immigration authorities were appalled, insisting the entire station was closed by the police when the train stopped to pick up the premier's party. Whenever Churchill travelled on *Night Ferry*, the *chef du train* (chief conductor) would go out of his way providing in his travelling berth a bottle of his favourite whisky. On one occasion Julian Morel noted, 'Conductor Bew was in charge and his instructions were for a bottle of Dewar's White Label, soda and cracked ice to be placed in Churchill's sleeping compartment.'[151]

The train's motive power altered with the introduction of the powerful nautically themed 4-6-2 Merchant Navy Pacific Class locomotives (each one named after shipping lines) that could accommodate the normal *Night Ferry* make-up. The Merchant Navies in their resplendent new malachite green liveries soon became regulars. The train would also be hauled by the similar but lighter 4-6-2 West Country and Battle of Britain classes, but these would require additional piloting with 4-4-0 D1 or L1 locomotives when pulling the heaviest loads. Eventually lighter class engines were withdrawn as they were no longer able to cope with popular night-time operation loads. Like *Golden Arrow*, *Night Ferry* from 1951 was hauled by a new generation of British Railways designed 4-6-2 Britannia Class 7P locomotives. Bucknall commented of these commanding beasts: 'They were massive, powerful and quite orthodox 'Pacifics' whose keynote, apart from that of an ability to do the required job, was accessibility and simplicity.'[152] No. 70004 William Shakespeare and no. 70014 Iron Duke (who worked the *Golden Arrow*) were assigned *Night Ferry* duties. For a six-week period, no. 70034 Thomas Hardy was borrowed from Eastern Region and added to the Stewarts Lane roster. Brunswick green liveried locomotives remained unaltered until electrification took over on the English side of the Channel.

Generally acknowledged amongst many railway writers, the Southern possessed the smartest and best cared for carriage stock

St. Mary Cray Junction is the location for this photograph of the up *Night Ferry* service in June 1959. By this time, many Merchant Navy Class locomotives were allotted duties elsewhere on Southern Region metals, so before electric traction double-headed locomotives were still required for the heavyweight international boat train. No. 31789 pilots no. 34027 Battle of Britain 46 Squadron. (Colour Rail)

in the aftermath of the war-years when railway maintenance and cleanliness were at their lowest ebb. During this period the *Night Ferry* complement could have been restricted to only three or four sleeper coaches for each journey as several cars were destroyed during the Second World War – the rest of the train being made up of a rake of extra Maunsell and new Bulleid coaching stock which began to come through production. Typically, the Southern Railway coaches attached at Dover Ferry terminal could comprise a restaurant and kitchen car, buffet car, corridor first, two corridor seconds, another restaurant and kitchen car, and a first-class brake. Over a ten-year period, carriage stock would go through three sets of livery changes from malachite green, to British Railways blood and custard, and latterly Southern Region green. Catering cars were important since the train breakfast was always an essential part of the service. Post-war *Night Ferry's* British portion did not carry Pullman cars but catering was still provided by the Pullman Company.

This 1959 Paris and Brussels *Night Ferry* poster, with artwork by P Dullous, was created in tandem with SNCF producing an identical Paris-London French-language version. A Brussels extension was relatively low key in the copy with Southern Region preferring to place emphasis on the main Paris train. The distinctive Continental advertising flavour echoed similar styles adopted for the *Golden Arrow* promotion targeted at the UK market. *Night Ferry* business volumes at this stage were probably at their height warranting continued investment in marketing. Another up *Night Ferry* shot taken in June 1959 but this time at Weald Box. No. 31789 is the lead locomotive but this time piloting no. 34093 West Country Class Saunton shortly before the locomotive was taken in for re-building. *Night Ferry* evidently a popular service in this early summer recording of a ten-car train. (*Right*: NRM/SSPL; *Below*: Colour Rail)

The late 1950s and early 1960s were *Night Ferry's* heyday as the service never lost its popularity even with foot or walking passengers. Whilst passengers on Wagon-Lits sleeper coaches came over with the ferry, foot passengers had to board awaiting coaches that alter on a frequent basis according to season, and the total number of combined sleeper and foot passengers. Whilst the civilised travelling nature of *Night Ferry* was clear, less consideration was given to foot passengers – reclining seats on sleeper trains was not on the agenda until the late 1960s – crossing the channel at night may have been a less memorable event although they would have had the same access to quality dining facilities. *Night Ferry* still possessed an aura of selectness, and in June 1956 the train became first-class only again continuing to attract many VIPs as a matter of course.

The following summer *Night Ferry* added a new destination with a through sleeping car service to Brussels normally made up of one or two cars. The Brussels sleeping cars together with first and second-class foot passenger coaches had to leave Dunkerque before the first-class only sleeper service left for Paris. Line electrification in time would guarantee a rapid transit from port to the capital – ideal for important early morning meetings - but steam remained the standard motive power. By 1959 extensive electrification work was taking place in south-east England. With weekend disruption, *Night Ferry* haulage remained in steam with Merchant Navy 4-6-2s with 6,000-gallon tenders for several years yet.

In this 1961 *Night Ferry* poster execution by Bromfield, the Brussels extension was far more prominent. A lighter approach was taken in the creative style with an illustration using a cartoon character of a man wearing pyjamas and sleeping in a hammock representing the shape of the moon. (NRM/SSPL)

As has previously noted, the winter sports sector with its steady stream of enthusiastic upscale travellers had been a key component of both British Railways and SNCF marketing activity.

SLEEP YOUR WAY TO EUROPE
LONDON-PARIS-BRUSSELS
NIGHT FERRY

THROUGH SLEEPING CARS EVERY NIGHT.
PICK UP A LEAFLET AT PRINCIPAL
STATIONS OR AGENTS.
Inter-City ⇌ Sealink

Even in 1978 *Night Ferry* could still rely on dedicated marketing support for a service to Paris and Brussels that operated every night. The British Railways Southern Region logo had been replaced by a combination of new Inter-city and Sealink branding. The poster was illustrated by an unknown artist highlighting an illuminated train hauled by an electric traction locomotive travelling along under a night sky. Perhaps a fitting creative accomplishment for a service that only had a few years left to operate? (NRM/SSPL)

At the end of 1967 a new winter ski service to Strasbourg and Basle commenced, but unfortunately only lasted two seasons due to increased competition from more dependable and quicker air services. *Night Ferry's* twilight years were the 1970s precipitating a downward spiral in passenger demand. To borrow a carriage interior upholstery metaphor, the service quite literally became a little frayed around the edges. Although work on the proposed Channel Tunnel stopped in 1975 it was still downhill as the Wagon-Lits staffing contract ended in 1976 replaced by British Rail and SNCF catering staff. As the train was purported to be losing £120,000 a year, both organisations claimed they could not warrant the outlay for long overdue replacement stock: life-expired sleeping cars had had their day and proposals to rebuild British Rail Mk I sleeping cars for *Night Ferry* came to nothing.[153]

So, on Friday, 31 October 1980 – the same day as the closure of the *London Evening News* – with seated passengers already carted off to a separate EMU, the end came of perhaps of the most celebrated luxury railway service with its imbued romance and nostalgia the continent of Europe had ever seen. There was a considerable degree of excitement at Victoria particularly with media droves in attendance. At 21.25 pm headed by a somewhat sombre-looking mixed-traffic diesel-electric locomotive no. 33043, *Night Ferry* made up of just seven sleeping cars, two luggage vans (the first fourgon having 'Goodbye' written on it) and one ordinary Mk I BSO coach made its final outward journey from Victoria. A replica style headboard made by staff from Stewarts Lane was placed on the front of the locomotive, but it did not return on no. 73142 *Broadlands* which brought in the inward leg to Victoria the following morning. As railway author Derek Winkworth ruefully commented: 'BR had finished with their sole international through train and could devote its energy to the commuter traffic – it was all over!'[154]

But the memory of Britain's first truly international train still stays alive.

The Blue Train's Swansong and the Mistral

The post-war years are the third and final stage of our French Riviera luxury train trilogy. Times were certainly changing as the rail journey to the Azur coast now had to compete with Paris domestic flights shortening travelling time to around two hours. The French Riviera night-time service became a named train again as the *Blue Train* was resurrected. As *The Railway Magazine* reported in their February 1950 edition on European travel that Paris Lyon was a hive of activity as 'the Riviera sleeping cars are attached to the '"Blue Train," composed, as its name implies, entirely of Wagon-Lit Company's dark blue stock, and due out 20.00 hr'.[155] Yet despite media coverage the night-time train was not the pre-war success it had once been, as a scheduled Paris-Nice airline service took away wealthy customers attracted by speed and the glamour of flying. And the run from London via Paris by rail to the south was somewhat different now. Yet French national railway operator SNCF responded to a competitive new world where prosperous business travellers became the primary focus of commercial activity introducing a fast-new day-time service known as *Le Mistral/The Mistral*. French recovery from war-time ravages to its railway network, which like most of its transport infrastructure had virtually collapsed, with a massive programme of reconstruction and the electrification of large parts of the railway system. By the late 1940s the route south to the Côte d'Azur had become a major plank of SNCF's planned development. The resorts of the French Riviera gradually returned to star quality status reinventing themselves in the 1950s as a series glamour style destination but having to be achieved without the assistance of the British upper classes initially who had made the Riviera their second home. Mary Lovell captures the mood splendidly: 'In the post-war years a new set took over – Americans and Europeans mostly, and then it was fame and glamour that counted.'[156] She goes on to recount the views of journalist Charles J.V. Murphy who, writing for *Life* magazine in 1947, noticed the absence of the former English colony: 'The most striking thing was the virtual extinction on this coast of the once-swarming British peer – a phenomenon so startling in scope as to recall the famous disappearance of the passenger pigeon.'[157]

McKibbin also took a parallel view:

Paper rationing reduced the amount of space newspapers were prepared to devote to society news; government action, particularly during the war itself, suspended many of the occasions on which society was made manifest; foreign currency restrictions largely emptied the Continental resorts of the English who had been so conspicuous there before 1939 – dollars or Swiss francs, legally or illegally acquired, were highly coveted by the former travelling classes.[158]

Demand to escape the harsh British winter was great; 1947 was particularly savage, as well as the Attlee Labour government imposing a ban on overseas holidays outside the Sterling Area caused by an acute shortage of foreign exchange. The travel ban was eventually lifted by early 1948 when some degree of normality resumed.[159] The look and feel of the Riviera started to change in the late 1940s attracted by a new visitor class, greater in numbers but with more modest expectations. Not only, the French started to reclaim their local patch. Like the London's west end in the inter-war years, where large family houses were torn down and replaced with smart apartment blocks, a comparable situation developed on the littoral as great hotels and estates were demolished and rebuilt as eight-storey blocks.[160] Those top-end hotels that survived reinvented themselves by still managing to appeal to a much smaller number of socialites that had made the Riviera's character unique. If the early years of the cinematic industry helped to define the *Belle Époque* at the turn of the twentieth century, then the silver screen played a similar pivotal role in promoting Cannes and the Riviera some fifty years later with creation of an annual film festival showcasing new films and documentaries from around the world to especially invited audiences. Planned as a great international event before the Second World War, the Cannes Film Festival resumed properly in 1946 with a unique blend of French cinematic heritage providing the film fan with a yearly immersion in culture, establishing specialist genres, and a destination draw based on glamour as Hollywood's studios started to weave their spell. Movie stars like Rita Hayworth and would-be starlets congregated in the south of France attracted by the exotic atmosphere and congenial climate.[161]

It was into this grove that railway recovery would see the establishment of a new crack train to replace the *Côte d'Azur Pullman Express*. The new inter-regional train, initially steam-hauled for the entire journey, commenced service in 1946. Known as *Trains Rapide 33* and *Rapide 34* the train combination of SNCF stock together with a Wagon-Lits dining car and Pullman car from the former Côte d'Azur service. In addition, a *new Blue Train* sleeper sevice made a welcome return and a sure sign that a resumption of normality was on the cards.[162] Charles Graves was a chronicler of Riviera life: 'The Blue Train is waiting,' he wrote in the *Riviera Revisited*, 'with a six-course dinner of clear soup, red mullet, pâté with truffles, *chouxfleur aux gratin*, cheese, fruit and coffee.'[163]

Despite the vagaries of international travel in the post-war years, British Railways attempted to garner winter-time Riviera trade with this example of a 1949 special fare leaflet that was used in conjunction with destination guides. (Southern Railway Publicity)

In 1950 Rapide 1 and Rapide 2 were renumbered and as SNCF's flagship train was given the title of *Le Mistral/The Mistral* named after a strong, cold, dry wind running down the Rhone Valley corridor. In 1952 a modernised *Mistral* service was extended to Gare de Nice-Ville recreating the exclusiveness of the pre-war *Côte d'Azur Pullmans* – and a train service heritage dating from the turn of the twentieth century. The Riviera by this time was gearing up for the jet-set age; travellers waiting in airport lounges, instead of main train stations, was just around the corner. Whilst swift air travel to the Azur coast was the desired method for many, SNCF's efforts in providing fast train access was openly encouraged, and widely reported on in Britain. Express it most certainly was as the electrification of the Paris-Dijon section shortened the time-consuming journey south. Riviera bound trains were now hauled by electrified Class 2D2-9100, the CC7100 and then BB9200 series locomotives making it the fastest train in the world at the time. The notion of *Mistral* as one of the quickest long-distant services in the world brought back a degree of exclusiveness to the Riviera train. By the spring of 1954, aided by a new clutch of films stars such as Cary Grant and Grace Kelly installing the destination with true celebrity status.[164]

In the south, *Mistral* retained some of its character by remaining steam-hauled until the first half of the 1960s powered by formidable four-cylinder compound 241P Class locomotives. Series d 241P1/P35 were built between 1948 and 1952 at Messrs Schneider. Beyond Marseille, the 141R glided effortlessly through Provence at 62 miles per hour. The service similarly had a new streamliner look with American-looking stainless-steel styled carriage stock built under licence from the Budd Corporation together with traditional Wagon-Lits dining and Pullman cars. In 1962 the *Blue Train's* luxury environment was further eroded as second-class carriages were added. The nature of the Riviera was changing fast as the French retrieved access to their own lush garden view. Author Jim Ring notes: 'While the *Blue Train* continued to run, the French were planning a high-speed rail network that would bring visitors to the coast even faster, and in greater numbers.'[165] Change was inevitable with life-expired carriage stocks and nine years later the original Wagon-Lits stock was sold signifying the end of the luxury night train era to the French Riviera replaced by modern, but characterless high-speed services.

FRENCH RAILWAYS NEWS

ADVICE AND INFORMATION REGARDING TRAVEL IN FRANCE

PARIS-DIJON SPEED-UP
Electrification shortens the journey

The electrification of the Paris-Dijon line has knocked an hour off the old timetable. Travelling at an average speed of 77 m.p.h., the Paris-Lyons high speed rapide, hauled by its 4,880 h.p. electric locomotive, covers the 196 miles between Paris and Dijon in 2 hrs. 32 mins. and arrives with stopwatch precision.

More couchettes put into service

...and so to bed. These 1st class couchette passengers can look forward to a night's travel in comfort.

Night travel on French Railways has been improved considerably during the past two years by the introduction of more couchettes and sleeping cars. During 1949 for example 124 First class and 61 Second class couchette services were run every night. In 1950 this figure was increased to 230 First class and 124 Second class—very nearly double the number! It is hoped in 1951 to increase the figures still more. First class couchettes (4 berths per compartment) or Second class (6 berths) may be reserved, through your Travel Agent, or | French Railways Ltd., at 16s. 6d. per berth for any destination in France.

ROAD-RAIL TRAVEL SAVES YOUR £'s

Holiday makers who are planning a French tour should get to know about the reduced-fare Road-Rail Tickets. These offer a choice of thirty-six composite tours—part by rail, part by motor coach—through some of France's most lovely scenery. Fares from London range from | as little as £13.8 : 2 for a 1,865 miles tour! Full details and reservations may be obtained from any Travel Agent or from French Railways, 179 Piccadilly, London W.1.

ACCENT ON COMFORT

New lightweight all-metal coaches, now in service on the French Railways, are a pleasure to travel in. They give more space per passenger and ride with a gentler motion. Ventilation is excellent; the air is renewed every four minutes. | **GOURMETS' DELIGHT**

In France the word Buffet stands for "good food". Many of the railway buffets provide delightful meals featuring the specialities of the province. These special meals comprise four full courses and the price per meal at most buffets is 600 francs, including local wine and tips.

WRITE FOR FREE BOOKLET

You will enjoy the fascinating new booklet "France", packed with pictures in full colour and monochrome. Write for your copy now.

Information, reservations and tickets from your Travel Agent or

SNCF **FRENCH RAILWAYS** LTD
179 Piccadilly, London W.1

FRENCH RAILWAYS NEWS

ADVICE AND INFORMATION REGARDING TRAVEL IN FRANCE

MORE COUCHETTES PUT INTO SERVICE

Night travel on French Railways has been improved considerably during the past two years by the introduction of more couchettes and sleeping cars.

During 1949 for example 124 First class and 61 Second class couchette services were run every night. In 1950 this figure was increased to 230 First class and 124 Second class — very nearly double the number! It is hoped in 1951 to increase the figures still more. First class couchettes (4 berths per compartment) or Second class (6 berths) may be reserved, through your Travel Agent, or French Railways Ltd., at 16s. 6d. per berth for destinations in France.

...and so to bed. These 1st class couchette passengers can look forward to a night's travel in comfort.

ROAD-RAIL TRAVEL SAVES YOUR £'s

Holiday makers who are planning a French tour should get to know about the reduced-fare Road-Rail Tickets. These offer | a choice of thirty-six composite tours—part by rail, part by motor coach—through some of France's most lovely scenery. Fares from London range from as little as £13.8.2 for a 1,865 miles tour! Full details and reservations may be obtained from any Travel Agent or from French Railways, 179 Piccadilly, London W.1.

ACCENT ON COMFORT

Besides the increase in the number of couchettes and sleeping cars, French Railways have made other important contributions to passenger comfort. More restaurant cars have been introduced, also streamlined all-metal coaches with controlled ventilation. Track improvements have led to greater speeds and more comfortable riding, while the extension of electrification has brought speedier and more efficient services. | **See lovely France by Luxury Coach** 🚌

French Railways also run other Motor Coach tours so that visitors may see France's beauty spots at close quarters. Services include the Alps, Jura, Vosges, Pyrenees, Auvergne, Riviera, Provence, Côte d'Argent, Normandy and Brittany.

WRITE FOR FREE BOOKLET

You will enjoy the fascinating new booklet "France", packed with pictures in full colour and monochrome. Write for your copy now.

Information, reservations and tickets from your Travel Agent or

SNCF **FRENCH RAILWAYS** LTD
179 Piccadilly, London W.1

FRENCH RAILWAYS NEWS

SERVICE STREAMLINED SINCE WAR

Comfort-Study aided by popular vote

Faced with a virtually demolished rail system in 1946, French National Railways took a poll of passengers' preferences before ordering new rolling stock, and carefully examined suggestions of the public before planning the trains and time tables that today serve 5,700 stations and 25,000 miles of track. The result is the most efficient rail service in Europe.

Light-weight metal coaches with controlled heating and ventilation, give increased comfort to passengers and more coaches per train. Compartments built since the war are very comfortably upholstered and all have head and arm rests and incorporate, as far as possible, the results of a study of the ideal degree of inclination of the back. Development and improvement still continue.

On the principal services between the Channel Ports and Paris, and on most of the international trains crossing the French frontier, time and trouble are saved by Customs examination of hand luggage on the train.

Reservations and tickets for both outward and homeward journeys can be booked in advance through good travel agents anywhere in | Britain, and paid for in sterling, leaving the passenger's continental holiday allowance intact.

REDUCED FARES FOR TOURISTS

Tourist tickets at reduced fares will be maintained during 1952. These offer reductions of 20%, and 30%, on ordinary fares for return and circular journeys of at least 1,500 and 2,000 km. on the French Railways. A holiday bargain worth investigating.

BOUILLABAISSE AT STATION BUFFET

Fish Soup, many varieties of omelette and deliciously "different" Continental dishes are normal station fare in France. Of course there are straightforward egg, meat and vegetable dishes too for the more conservative traveller. Buffets provide five-course meals, local wine and tips included. Prices from 650frs.

AIM FOR MID-WEEK TRAVEL

Note for those who can pick their dates, French Railways remind intending passengers that mid-week journeys are less crowded than week-end, and that holidays taken outside the peak period from July 15 to August 31 can cost less and are no great hardship in a country where summer starts early, stays late.

FREE BOOKLET—a Feast of Colour

The touch of a Parisian artist breathes glamour and romance into "France" a new, exquisitely colour-printed booklet available free on application to French Railways Ltd. Write today, a postcard will do.

STOP PRESS

Even £25 can ensure a good holiday in France. Ask for details of holidays off the beaten track. Remember, your railway fare does not reduce your currency allowance.

Information, tickets and reservations from the principal Travel Agents and—

SNCF **FRENCH RAILWAYS LIMITED**
179 Piccadilly, London, W.1

In the early 1950s SNCF turned on a destination marketing offensive in the British press with regular advertising and a campaign running under the banner of 'French Railway News' providing advice and information on French train travel. Advertising, naturally, appeared in upscale titles encouraging travellers to use their new comfortable streamlined services with particular emphasis on routes from Paris to the south of the country. Interestingly, the advertising theme headlines used illustrations combining both state of the art electric and traditional steam-hauled locomotive traction on the routes to Provence and the Riviera. Recent period set films like 'Chocolat' starring Juliette Binoche, and the writings of Peter Mayle turned into screenplay, have helped popularize British tourist interest of an alternative lifestyle based on the tranquillity of rural French life, a creative theme SNCF appeared to capture at the time. (Illustrated London News Ltd/Mary Evans)

In the mid-1970s *Mistral* was added to the TEE international railway network, established in 1957 by the six state railway companies of the then Common Market and the Swiss, to run international day trains with a standardized red and cream livery. The *Mistral TEE* Paris-Nice section became electric traction. First-class only, the express train was equipped with facilities targeting the business traveller being one of the few French trains to provide secretarial support, although the idea of telephone access would have to wait until the late 1980s. The remainder of the Côte d'Azur Riviera service had a locomotive change at Marseilles. Prior to these developments, all of the older Wagon-Lits stock was retired in 1969 replaced with new purpose-built SNCF carriages all designed to attract the business community who were happy to make the additional Pullman style supplement to travel in style. In order to combat increasing numbers of travellers using domestic air flights, SNCF re-badged *Mistral* as a luxury train marque running two restaurant cars with catering supplied by Wagon-Lits together with other carriage amenities including a bar, bookstall, and hairdressing salon to make the journey more of an experience as in days of old. However, before the service could really establish itself, the *Blue Train* was abandoned, and with it the once grandeur outmoded boat train concept, severing for many the Rivera's links with the country's defining *Belle Époque* times.[166] On *Mistral* the carriages were discontinued as the first high-speed French Train à Grande Vitesse (TGV) was introduced on the route south to the Mediterranean in September 1981.

CHAPTER 6

Ocean Liner Special Boat Trains

Liverpool Riverside and Gladstone Docks: LNWR American Specials, LMS and British Railways London Midland Region boat trains

By late-Victorian times, Atlantic liners sailing to and from America, as well as many other international destinations, used the port of Liverpool with a level of regularity previously unheard of. The two main trans-Atlantic shipping lines – Cunard and White Star Line – provided New York steamer crossings from the late 1890s on a weekly basis and even more frequently at the height of the summer season. Luxury liners started to sell their own stories as regular seafarers identified preferred shipping lines and their ships to cross the Atlantic. From the 1890s White Star's *Teutonic* and *Majestic* sisters became firm passenger favourites. Their selection, in modern parlance known as brand loyalty started a trend where customers deliberately choose particular vessels to make sea crossings. And it was not unheard of for passengers to book journeys only when they were aware that a certain steward was known to be in attendance. First-class passage would become even more pleasurable as White Star moved away from the outright pursuit of speed and holding the Blue Riband, by challenging Cunard (who were still the dominant line) for the North Atlantic's best customers with vessels with enhanced facilities. With vastly increased levels of trans-Atlantic freight and passenger traffic, Liverpool's burghers, anxious to protect their interests, deemed direct railway access to a dedicated rail and port terminal an absolute business necessity. Liverpool's position by the turn of the twentieth century appeared unassailable based on the dominance of Cunard and White Star as the principal lines operating from Great Britain and Ireland. Nevertheless, it was a moving seascape as Southampton had demonstrated by working closely with American Lines. In addition, the average number of saloon passengers carried by the two main German shippers increased as LSWR's Solent based port resource slowly tightened its grip.

Yet it was not to be one-way traffic as with much invention and astuteness, Victorian enterprise ensured passengers had a unified

Produced around 1913 by an unknown artist, this SECR poster embodies the competitive nature of combined trans-Atlantic travel business at the time. It was probably prompted by the loss of cross-channel traffic at Dover as Red Star Line moved its British port of call liner operations to Southampton, and again a reflection of IMM consolidation. Would be American Line passengers in the south-east could reach Southampton via a combination of LSWR and SECR services.

boat train travelling experience from Euston to a new station at Liverpool Riverside, and its adjacent Prince's landing stage. From a business perspective it was a highly collaborative arrangement putting LNWR at the centre of events, and certainly prompted by the Great Western's efforts to secure American travellers via their Birkenhead terminus. LNWR dealt directly with both the port authorities and the main shipping lines with all three parties working hard to service the needs of a first-class passenger market dominated by America's new financial nouveaux riche, the British aristocracy and upper-classes, a multitude of foreign monarchs, princes and nobility, business chieftains and from the live entertainment sector, actors, opera and music hall stars.

This added to international travel but for some the impact of technology created a loss, especially for those who remembered the heritage of older vessels. By the turn of the twentieth century rapid progress in mercantile marine advancement, had already consigned many ships to another age. In 1920 William Forwood reflected about the ships that had so defined Liverpool's commercial atmosphere with their spirit of sport and adventure, their romance, their daily happenings, and their hardships by contrasting them 'with the luxury on such a ship as the "*Aquitania*" or "*Olympic*" with all their attractions of a first-class hotel, bridge parties, dancing, and entertainment of every kind, regardless of weather – with everything, in fact, but that spirit of adventure which appeals so strongly to the imagination of the Britisher, and which, after all, has built up his character and made him the doughty man he is either on land or at sea'[1]

As late as November 1906, White Star was still reporting large numbers of passengers aboard *Oceanic* and *Teutonic* returning to and from Liverpool with special rail travelling arrangements put on from Riverside for North Sea destinations.[2] Despite the city losing White Star's premier business, the port was still able to retain considerable volumes of New York and Boston traffic including American Line's route to Philadelphia and Canadian Trade business. This was all facilitated by the opening of the first stage of the new Gladstone Dock in 1913 designed to accommodate ever larger vessels including Cunard's new *Aquitania* leviathan; the biggest vessel to be regularly berthed in Liverpool. The war years interrupted completion of the dock system, but by the early 1920s new liner facilities were operating at a high level of capacity despite a significant loss of vessels to enemy action. But Liverpool

RIVERSIDE STATION, AND LANDING STAGE, LIVERPOOL.

This Tuck postcard was part of a set introduced in April 1904 showing one of the new Atlantic liners and Liverpool's new ocean terminal. They were displayed as part of seventy years of progress demonstrating the latest integrated transport efforts of securing affluent international travellers. Riverside Railway Station was clearly marked on the new building's roof indicating LNWR's close working relationship with Liverpool's port authorities and individual shipping lines. (Tuck DB) was Cunard and Cunard was Liverpool which was all based on the American Ferry business model that had stimulated a great impetus to the city's ship-owning heritage. By 1917 the company's new headquarters was completed at the port's pier head. The iconic building is still an indelible feature of Liverpool's skyline, and acted as Cunard's home until the 1960s. By the end of the Great War the company commenced a replacement programme for intermediate ships lost in the conflagration ordering some thirteen new vessels which is still considered to be the largest single order placed with British shipyards by an individual organisation.

For prosperous America-bound passengers wanting a more leisurely approach prior to embarking on an ocean liner, unhurried but prestigious train services were also available to the city. By this time Liverpool was home to several classy grand-hotel establishments serviced by both the LNWR and Midland Railway. Yet this was not always the case. In the mid-1880s the city was not exactly a salubrious place. Oliver Wendell Holmes on arriving at the port aboard a steamer from the United States recorded his first impressions. 'When I landed in Liverpool, everything looked very dark, very dingy, very massive, in the streets I drove through.'[3] Nearby Chester was regarded as a much more amenable first or last-stop solution. Holmes went on. 'Americans know Chester better than most other old towns in England, because they so frequently stop there awhile on their way from Liverpool to London.'[4] In 1894, *The Sketch* reported the Great Western had 'issued an attractive illustrated pamphlet containing information for American passengers travelling by their system between Liverpool and London. The railway passes through Chester, Shrewsbury, Stratford-on-Avon, Leamington, Oxford and Windsor, and many other places specially interesting to Americans'.[5] Aside international travellers, competition for hospitality business was widespread. In 1871, the LNWR built the much-admired London & North Western Hotel in Liverpool and continued to invest in its infrastructure. Progressively over the years, the railway fitted out the hotel with all the latest modern trappings to entice wealthy guests. Featured strongly in railway publicity material from September 1896, the hotel situated at Lime Street station provided a quick transit to and from London and as part of the 'American special train arrangements'. Liverpool's North Western Hotel was a renowned establishment 'lighted by electricity' and containing upwards of 250 bedrooms.

New amenities such as a ladies and gentlemen coffee room, ladies' drawing room, and its close connection to the most important railway station in Liverpool.[6] For trans-Atlantic passengers, the hotel provided refuge before and after ocean crossings, but its location involved a certain degree of hassle and 'the inconvenience of the transit in cabs and omnibuses from Lime Street Station across the city'.[7]

Liverpool's other grand hotel was Midland's Adelphi Hotel acquired by the company in 1892 and rebuilt between 1911 and 1914. Once completed it was pronounced as one of the most luxurious hotels outside of the capital. Described as the 'most modern hotel in Europe', the Adelphi was equipped with luxurious early-Art Deco furnishings with public rooms and restaurants resembling the style of Atlantic liner staterooms.[8] The hotel was large by regional standards and certainly complemented the company's position as a luxury travel provider, but falling levels of trans-Atlantic customers due to Southampton's increasingly dominant position as the country's leading passenger port in the post-war years, ensured the Adelphi was never ever destined to achieve its full potential before being absorbed as part of the new LMS railway hotel portfolio.

Getting prosperous passengers to Liverpool was paramount. LNWR advertised their fastest journey times between the two cities at around four hours and twenty minutes but by 1898, the *American Special* non-stop journey time between Euston and Liverpool Edge Hill was just three hours forty-five minutes with around fifteen minutes allowed for locomotive change and the short tank locomotive shunt to the landing stage. Since LNWR was the sole railway company to use Riverside, the company was always anxious to maintain efficient, fast and regular train services. Whilst the boat train was a direct service, it was nonetheless, subject to delays at times with some journeys taking more than five hours. Docking and departing liners allowed around half an hour for train arrival and turnarounds, however, this could be subject to interruption because of continuous silting and the Mersey's tidal flows. From the shipping lines' perspective, first-class passenger requirements were always paramount. Liverpool Riverside was effectively a branch line, but like most port links constructed at the time to facilitate Britain's growing merchant marine (and increasing numbers of profitable foreign shipping lines too), the country's harbour and port main line termini were fast-transit venues. Passengers, unless they stayed in the city, never had much of a chance to visit the Empire's second city (as Liverpool liked to refer to itself at the time), since liner and railway transfer arrangements were always speedily conducted. Whether arriving or departing, travellers were simply whisked away; lost opportunities rankled the city's commercial business owners as large numbers of passengers just passed through. But for the first-time, prosperous overseas travellers could gauge how well port authorities and shipping lines managed the liner transit, how self-important customs officials in the examination hall behaved, and the overall helpfulness of railway companies in organising onward journeys and accommodation plans. From Liverpool's perspective the combined travel experience was under serious scrutiny prompted by Southampton's rapid development. When Riverside was opened *The Liverpool Mercury* reported on the official opening ceremony where the board chairman of the Mersey Docks and Harbour observed that he was sure that 'it was due to some extent to American enterprise in connection with the port of Southampton that they in Liverpool had been stimulated to take their recent important action'. A state of 'friendly rivalry' existed between the two ports in their cultivation of Anglo-American relations.[9]

LNWR had provided Liverpool with dedicated boat trains since May 1884. By the end of the Victorian period, the company was increasingly mindful of the numbers of American travellers arriving on eastbound liners and then returning home. The opening of the Riverside terminal coincided with significant increases in ocean liner passenger traffic across all social classes. By October 1895, LNWR's *American Special* train was making experimental runs of 299 miles to Liverpool Riverside station 'without a bait'. On one steamer departure that month, the press reported Cunard's *Campania* left with 750 passengers with the 'proportion travelling direct from London being larger than any similar occasion'.[10] To meet demand LNWR introduced a new set of dedicated 50-foot carriages especially designed for international liner traffic.[11] Four sets of *American Special* corridor stock, whilst not ground-breaking, were a considerable improvement incorporating steam heated eight-wheel bogie carriages when introduced at the tail end of the 1890s. Four sets provided LNWR with flexibility, since at peak times Cunard and White Star's largest liners required two separate train movements to handle passenger numbers. Boat trains arrived and left in quick succession with passenger manifests chiefly made up of discerning first-class travellers. Railway writer V.L. Whitechurch, who made the Euston to Riverside journey aboard the new stock, observed 'the number of passengers carried by an "*American Special*" average from sixty to one hundred first-class, twenty second-class, and twenty third'. However, the key operational requirement was coach capacity and a certain degree of flexibility in operations. Whitechurch further noted: 'as far as possible, the train is made up with about one-third more seats than passengers in order to avoid overcrowding'.[12] The bulk of traffic were first-class travellers, and at times in the busy summer season between March and September, over 200 first-class passengers might be carried with LNWR running two specials for one steamer in quick succession. The company employed sophisticated techniques (at the time) to monitor passenger numbers such as canvassing hotels where travellers might be staying and checking with various London booking offices to ensure it always knew roughly how many passengers might be carried. In winter, the number of first-class passengers making trans-Atlantic crossings would be far fewer, especially with the main shipping companies' smaller intermediate vessels. Single dining and saloon carriages were employed leaving Liverpool and then running down to Crewe before attachment to another express train for onward transmission to London.

Dining standards too, were enhanced with twelve-wheeled dining cars and combined dining and kitchen cars. On *American Specials* dining access was exclusive restricted to first-class; other passengers having to make do with dinner baskets if meals were required. On busy trains, dining would be split between two sittings. Speaking in September 1897, Frederick Harrison, LNWR general manager spoke enthusiastically about their service, which from 29 February 1896 ran without a stop:

> Yes, we have undoubtedly laid ourselves out for the American traffic, and it is an open secret that we have been successful in securing the cream of it. Every time one of the Cunard or White Star steamers sails from Liverpool, we run a special timed to connect with it at the Riverside Station at Liverpool, performing the journey from London to Liverpool in four hours, and sometimes even less, practically without a stoppage. The trains are thoroughly up to date, with corridors throughout, and containing dining saloons, in which luncheon or dinner is served, as the case maybe, *en route*.

He goes on:

> I think a journey at the present time from London to Liverpool exemplifies in a very high degree the extent to which luxury and convenience have been carried in modern travel. A family staying in London and wishing to go to America have really nothing to do but pack their trunks and send for one of the Company's omnibuses, and from the moment they step on to it they are relieved of all trouble and anxiety as to themselves or their luggage.[13] Travel on the *American Special* was indeed 'special'. As *The Railway Magazine* observed 'a trip on one of the very 'crackest' of crack trains in the country.'[14]

The Edwardian period represented a golden era for railway company and shipping line managements as trains and liners were the fast

In 1904 the prestige Liverpool boat train was promoted as the *American Vestibule Express* forming part of a series of LNWR inspired Tuck postcards. This tied the express railway service to the city's new Riverside station and landing stage and was undoubtedly part of concerted efforts to promote the Old World to new international audiences. John Alsop in his 'The Official Railway Postcard Book' links these postcards to the St. Louis Exposition 1904 which was more likely the Louisiana Purchase Exposition better known as the St. Louis World's Fair held in St. Louis, Missouri from 30 April to 1 December 1904. More than sixty different countries were represented at the fair. (Tuck DB)

and fashionable means to see the world. The wealthy certainly travelled and dined in unparalleled sophistication as LNWR targeted high spending first-class passengers destined for Liverpool's ocean liners. Quality dining, as noted, had been introduced with their first generation of *American* luxurious carriages in 1898. Further enhancements came in 1907–08 when new stock set the latest standards of opulence, and in the absence of the private carriage, became the quintessence of plutocratic excess for those contemplating international travel. K. Longbottom writing in *The Railway Magazine's* June 1950 edition suggested they 'were claimed as the best-appointed trains in the world'.[15] The name suggests these coaches were designed to be totally at home with America's flamboyant Gilded Age travellers; there appeared to be no disagreement with this in New York's press columns. But at the same time their style met the approval of old moneyed classes bound by traditional Victorian conventions and strictly orderly affairs. For Britons, pampered by a decade or so of increased travelling comfort and refinement, the new *American* stock might have been considered the slightest nouveau.

To some extent this was a response by the company to White Star Line's decision to move its premier Atlantic services to Southampton the year before, but the LNWR also had a track record in first-class traveller courtship over longer distances with high-class boat trains and Anglo-Scottish expresses providing the high-standards of excellence demanded by an intercontinental clientele during the closing years of the Edwardian period. LNWR was a pioneer in quality luxury trains establishing standards that perhaps for several decades was not really comparable, and a perfect example of a trend for unrivalled elegance. Floating palace ocean steamers and luxury trains in the early 1900s were special places for the social, artistic and financial elite of two continents. For the first time, first-class facilities aboard liners and trains could be considered as individual pleasure citadels espousing a level of untold affluence for a privileged few. What was never disputed was the level of research LNWR conducted. When launched with a media fanfare, first-class passengers were eager to inspect the pleasures of the company's newest equipage and clearly directed towards the prosperous American visitor market. Railway writer Robert Hendry captures the character perfectly by telling us 'it was luxury and convenience far excelling anything that today's international traveller might dream of'. The carriages were built with 'intricately carved woodwork' and a 'degree of elegance' that craftsman presently is unlikely to deliver.[16]

Railway companies were by now paying real attention to the needs of their most prosperous customers particularly as the Midland continued to set the luxury travel stall domestically. But it was the prospect of the company accessing lucrative boat train passengers in Liverpool that set alarm bells ringing at Euston. In 1898 LNWR had introduced the first batch of specially commissioned carriage stock to service this aspiring market, but it was also prompted by LSWR who had one eye on wealthy passengers travelling to or returning from the south-west on express steamers stopping off at Plymouth Sound or at Southampton. The term 'American boat train' had come into common usage from the early 1900s. Whilst US passengers were not quite so keen on LSWR's early morning sleeping cars; a more relaxing experience was available from LNWR with their new *American Special* stock. Dedicated to this discrete market, one of the train's features was the provision of carriage armchairs and sofas which on the face of it might have appeared a perfect example of Edwardian decadence, but in fact they were designed for passengers who had suffered with the ship's crossing to provide highly comfortable rail transit to London.[17] Crossing the North Atlantic in mid-winter could be notorious with literally days of seasickness endured by many passengers.

As noted in late 1906, White Star made its decision to move its premier Atlantic operations from Riverside to the quite remarkable developments taking place at Southampton Docks. Fletcher taking a contemporary view said White Star Line's decision caused 'no little surprise' and 'to the general amazement the Cunard line remained at Liverpool'.[18] What was probably missed by period commentators was the likely small print embedded in Cunard's mail contracts which insisted on the Queenstown call. Government pressure to ensure continued support of Irish members of parliament was probably behind the decision to stay at Liverpool. Yet the company's motive to move was probably the commercial pressures of German steamships calling at southern English ports, as well as the imminent prospect of competitive and equally luxurious German super-liners joining the throng; something even the Morgan combine had little direct influence over. NDL had a quartet of liners whilst HAPAG's well-appointed SS *Amerika* with its high-end culinary offering provided a steady drift of American international travellers.

Notwithstanding, railway writer Michael Baker described the move as 'a blow to Liverpool's pride, and its prosperity, and a tremendous boost for the Hampshire port'.[19] So for the time being

Cunard stayed put with its new generation of super-liners being the only major trans-Atlantic company wholly committed to the Liverpool and New York crossing. The *Lusitania* and *Mauretania* were the largest ships in the world to use the port providing berths for 2,200 first, second and steerage-class passengers. Despite the port's big liner attraction, there was a degree of consternation amongst some Liverpudlians that Cunard's new Fishguard drop might damage the city's business interests:

> At a meeting of the Mersey Docks and Harbour Board at Liverpool, Mr. R. Gladstone, the chairman, said it was not true that the calling of American liners at Holyhead and Fishguard was injuring Liverpool. One-third of the passengers from America formerly went direct from the Liverpool Riverside station to London. Those were the passengers that would be landed at the Welsh ports, and there was absolutely no loss to Liverpool, the steamers came on to Liverpool. The Board's revenue was unaffected, and the more attractive Welsh ports were made, the more would they draw into them vessels which would otherwise go Channel ports.[20]

For those international travellers happy to use Liverpool, LNWR's impressive boat trains commanded considerable support despite journey's length. And there were many too; *Lusitania's* record breaking trans-Atlantic runs from New York in the first decade of the twentieth century was packed to the rafters with first and second-class passengers. On occasions this required LNWR to put on as many as three special boat trains to handle all disembarking passenger needs.[21] Fletcher also noted improvements made to Riverside's combined railway and landing stage facilities:

> These have recently been added to and extended, with increased seating accommodation and other comforts; and the period of waiting, though inevitably tedious, has not to be passed in the physical discomfort of sitting on one's luggage or on the floor, or standing.[22]

When the biggest liners moored alongside the landing stage, they were major events in Liverpool's daily life. By 1914 Cunard added the impressive *Aquitania*, a twentieth-century speed merchant of a comparable luxury and size to White Star's Olympic class liners. Whilst Riverside performed a certain role, the Port of Liverpool, in response to developments at Southampton planned for change. What the city required was a dock system capable of handling the world's largest liners. Certainly, at the time Cunard remained committed to the port. Its four funnelled express leviathans were still a feature of the city skyline whereas its main competitor had given notice to move its premier services south. Yet there was still a strong business case to invest in new passenger port infrastructure. Not only was there regular New York traveller and cargo traffic, Riverside's existing facilities served other US destinations such as Boston and Philadelphia and blossoming Canadian Trade. Both Cunard and White Star were busy on these routes as well as the acquisitive Canadian Pacific shipping line quickly cementing its relationship with Liverpool in the early 1900s.

The new Gladstone Docks were designed around this time and built to fulfil the demands of shipping lines for larger accommodation of their trans-Atlantic liners. Part of the developments included a graving dock, completed in 1913, capable of taking Cunard's *Aquitania* which came on stream joining a first generation of super-liners which included *Olympic* and HAPAG's new goliaths. The rest of the new dock complex was not completed until 1927 whereby Cunard, like White Star, in 1919 had now moved their largest liners to Southampton. The new Gladstone Dock system was built around a railway system originally pioneered by Lancashire and Yorkshire Railway who opened a dock station on 7 September 1914 preparing to handle many thousands of trans-Atlantic passengers. Whilst the graving dock was operational, the rest of the harbour development's construction was held by the war, and the uncertain economic climate of the immediate post-war years. By the time Gladstone Docks were up and running with its quays and extensive warehousing, Liverpool had become home to a new generation of intermediate liner class as well as a multitude of combination vessels. Some of the more enduring photographs surrounding Liverpool and the Great War period were of the subdued preparations for *Aquitania's* maiden voyage.

Unfortunately, there was no special send-off because of the tragic loss of Canadian Pacific's *Empress of Ireland* the previous day, where after a collision in fog in the St. Lawrence River, tragically some 1,024 lost their lives, as well as the news, from the same neck of the woods, a few days earlier of Canadian Northern's *Royal Edward* liner hitting an iceberg in fog off the eastern seaboard. Fortunately, despite bow damage – the vessel was travelling at just a few knots –

the ship did not take on water and was able to continue with her voyage. Another picture involving *Aquitania*, was of a deserted station platform with the liner's superstructure and funnels appearing in the background as she was converted for war-time duties. Promotional literature was also created for the new docks complex featuring Cunard's flagship vessel as well as a host of other smaller two funnelled liners. With Gladstone Dock's focus on liner replenishment (and the graving dock's use for liner repairs), the passenger dock station was something of a white elephant closing as long as 7 July 1924 although the rail links remained open to freight traffic for many years up until 1971. During the 1930s White Star's *Britannic* (the largest motor and single cabin-class ship in the world) and *Georgic* and Canadian Pacific's *Empress of Scotland*, *Empress of Japan*, *Empress of France*, *Empress of Canada* (previously *Duchess of Bedford* and *Duchess of Richmond* respectively) and *Duchess of Atholl* when in Liverpool were home-berthed in Gladstone Docks moving up to Riverside landing stage to receive passengers. Another long-term resident at the time was the Pacific Steam Navigation company's liner *Reina del Mar* which operated between Liverpool and South America up until the 1950s.

One shipping line that specialised in the operation of intermediate sized ships and symbolised the relationship with Liverpool was Canadian Pacific Railway. The company, its origins from 1884, crystalized into one of the foremost transport systems anywhere on the globe as well as becoming a North Atlantic shipping dynasty. The Canadian Pacific or its full title of the Canadian Pacific Steamships Ocean Services Ltd became one of the world's major shipping lines carrying vast amounts of cargo as well as passengers. Its principal routes were across the North Atlantic from Britain to Canadian waters but also for straddling the Pacific Ocean from Vancouver. As well as operating passenger services across the North Atlantic and Pacific, the Canadian Pacific was a significant player in the cargo carrying business especially with operations between Liverpool and Montreal. In time, Canadian Pacific gained a reputation for both speed and luxury facilities offered by its *Empress* named vessels. But not only could the company take you to the Americas in comfort, but its trans-continental railroad provided an enticing prospect of a journey across the prairies and the Rockies to Vancouver and continuing to Canadian Pacific's waiting liners with their trans-Pacific services to the Orient. The company's first trans-continental east to west train service began on 4 July 1886 to

Port Moody, British Columbia. After the Great War, Canadian Pacific developed into a totally integrated travel company – its company advertising would carry the strapline the 'World's Greatest Travel System' in later years. Not only did it operate shipping services across two oceans, but it had its own railway system and for passengers a supporting hotel network, a traveller cheque payment system and set to become a stalwart in the blossoming world of twentieth-century cruising.

When White Star departed to Southampton, LNWR quickly realised it had to do more to preserve Liverpool's top liner traffic; hence the long-term plans for Gladstone Dock. However, affluent passengers expected the highest standards of comfort and care between London and Liverpool resulting in radical approaches to carriage design, facilities offered, and generally an improvement in the speed of boat trains. When the company introduced its new *American Special* – a series of superior designed twelve-wheeled luxury carriages measuring some 65 ½ feet in length – they were of a quality and standard of excellence not witnessed in Britain before. Jenkinson sets the stall for the new stock: 'As vehicles, they were probably no better, technologically, then those of maybe half a dozen other lines, but conceptually they were real pioneers, setting standards which were never approached, let alone exceeded, for decades.'[23] In adopting a progressive carriage design suiting the needs of first-class passengers, LNWR followed in the footsteps of its arch rival the Midland by clearly signposting an intention to compete in the luxury train market by providing services that met the travelling needs of Britain's well-off and those of America's Gilded Age. Other commentators suggested the design style and quality of the *American Specials* was found in the heritage of the company's 1902–03 Royal Train. Here was a British luxury train service possessing a certain degree of mystique fully meeting the high expectations of global passengers who increasingly grew to demand and expect the best. Britain's private railway companies savoured the Edwardian era relishing in a phase of railway development where they outflanked Pullman (until the company was acquired by Dalziel) in terms of 'lavish decor and luxurious accommodation' particularly in dining provisioning.[24]

From July 1907 onwards LNWR placed considerable efforts marketing the *American Specials* through a series of press announcements. In November, the LNWR ran a three-page special in *The Railway Magazine* advising enthusiasts the company had 'recently put into service, between London and Liverpool, three

The LNWR *American Special* international boat train illustration was created as a special commemorative plate appearing in the 1 January 1908 edition of *The Railway Magazine*. Produced as a folded supplement, printed by Bull, Austin & Co and stitched into the publication, it showed the complete formation of the luxurious appointed corridor saloon train. It comprised three sets of six-coach trains (known as Riverside Sets nos. 1, 2 and 3) incorporating a three-coach dining set made up of a second and third-class diner, kitchen car and separate first-class dining saloon and a centre of focus for top travellers. The out-and-out boat train correspondingly had two first-class corridor coaches linked to the first-class dining car, so all premier-class passengers were self-contained. Each train had a capacity for around 100 passengers with first-class carriages positioned at one end in the formation and second and third-class at the other. Second-class travel arrangements were dropped a few years later. Passenger luggage would be accommodated in two separate specially adapted brake vans attached to the front and rear making it an eight-vehicle train. In the second image carriages could be swapped around so that first-class passengers were presented with minimal inconvenience walking to or from the landing stage and its trans-Atlantic steamers. (*Above*: The Railway Magazine Archive; *Below*: Ian Collard Collection)

RIVERSIDE STATION, LIVERPOOL.

luxurious corridor trains for the use of ocean passengers via the Mersey port. The idea of the management, which Wolverton has admirably carried out, is to provide a train that shall be a fitting introduction (or complement, as the case may be) to the palatial accommodation now found on ocean liners.'[25] In December, the company turned on the integrated promotion tap by a joint announcement with *The Railway Magazine* of a special presentation picture to readers of the new American boat train. With the January 1908 edition of *The Railway Magazine* came a commemorative high-quality water colour drawing of the American boat train together with the Precursor Class locomotive presented on a twenty by nine and a quarter plate on engraved art paper.[26]

The brand new *American Special* salon-de-luxe vehicles built for the Riverside boat expresses ran in fixed formation; its carriages ranked alongside the best Europe (Wagon-Lits) could offer. The American boat train operated in both directions to meet the express needs of shipping lines. White Star Line's decision to move its premier services to the south of England meant capacity LNWR might have planned for from the larger Olympic class liners was simply not there. However, the new stock serviced elite travellers from Cunard's new super-liners and other intermediate vessels, White Star's popular medium-sized ships as well as Canadian Pacific and Dominion Line steamers – the latter had become the fourth largest Atlantic operator in 1901.[27] The first outing of the new *American Special* carriages was on 25 July meeting the White Star's *Baltic*. Passengers according to the *Morning Post* newspaper were 'emphatic in their praise of the comfort and luxury of the journey'.[28] English rigours of afternoon tea were now firmly engrained in Edwardian service culture, and indeed formed the focus of one of LNWR's special boat train postcards. American travel storyteller Blanche McManus quipped in her book *Our Little English Cousin*, 'You must know that everybody in England takes what is called "five o'clock tea," and would no more think of going without their tea in the afternoon than their Dinner.' Britain's magnetic pull of decadence was much in evidence.

LNWR's best stock was used for the much-publicised departure of *Lusitania* from Liverpool in September of that year. *The Standard's* correspondent was present for the giant ship's departure:

As she lay against the Prince's landing stage her funnels towered high above any of the buildings in the vicinity, and specially constructed gangways had to be used in order to permit

The cosiness of LNWR's stylistic *American Specials* was recorded later in the year in a set of seven picture postcards featuring the luxury boat train. The four images illustrated here display the standards of laid-back leisure afforded by the train's compartment and dining interiors. Upscale Edwardian railway travellers tended to take such facilities for granted. Notwithstanding, the colour printed issue was exceedingly popular with two separate print runs as 8,000,000 and then 9,250,000 cards were sold respectively. Other promotional opportunities presented themselves for the transnational boat train. G.A. Sekon, a former *Railway Magazine* editor, left the organisation to set up a rival publication *Railway & Travel Monthly*. The new publication spotted a gap in the travel enthusiast market, drawing together a fusion of railway and maritime (ocean liner) features thus attracting many interested readers. (*Above, below and overleaf*: J&C McCutcheon Collection)

passengers to go on board. Luggage was transferred to the vessel by a continuously moving platform, of the kind which, on a smaller scale, has been at various exhibitions in recent years. By the time the special trains from Euston arrived alongside night had fallen, and the vessel presented a magnificent sight with her thousands of electric lights gleaming from the decks and through the portholes.[29]

Whilst the Atlantic Ferry concentrated on New York traffic to the other east coast ports of Boston and Philadelphia and Canadian Trade also occupied considerable attention. Aside the country's position as a western bound short-cut to the Far East, Canada's eastern provinces and Prairies, by this period, entered the serious tourist gaze. *The Sketch* waxed lyrical about the prospects of a trip across the country aboard the Canadian Pacific Railway. They ventured with a certain turn-of-the-century-style, the idea of visitor exploration:

> Across Canada! What a glorious vision of sun-steeped prairie-lands and glittering, snow-capped mountain-peaks is conjured up by these words, for the charm of contrast chains the senses of the traveller captive as he is carried along the transcontinental line of the Canadian Pacific Railway, from the eastern city of Montreal to the western port of Vancouver, where out through the Lion-guarded gateway of the "Narrows" tall-masted ships sail away to the Orient over the sunny summer sea.[30]

Canada's Royal Route even had a named train known as the *Imperial Limited* and forever captured in photography of the train cutting through the Fraser Canon. Across the Atlantic, Liverpool and Canadian Pacific were interlocked as the gateway to the St. Lawrence, Montreal, Quebec and to the vast open Canadian interiors. At the height of Edwardian affluence, the celebration of the Quebec Tercentenary and its 300th founding year was a great opportunity for Canada's integrated railway and shipping line organizations to merge national festivities and royal visits attracting better-off visitors who had the time to take long-distance international travel. Key statements such as the largest and fastest steamers to the Dominion, only four days in open sea and direct connections by Canadian Pacific trains to all parts of Canada punctuated half-page press advertising.

For in-bound Canadian passengers wishing to reach London as soon as possible, direct boat train expresses were accelerated, but as always, an engine change at Edge Hill slowed down proceedings. Few passengers noticed or complained when the luxurious and palatial *American Special* carriages – built with a level of comfort and convenience that has rarely been surpassed – were used. As the stock was not time-tabled they were not excessively used before the Great War. Less intensive usage did, however, have its advantages as the carriage stock retained its smartness lasting well into the LMS era. For first-class travellers, the attendant's personal service was flawless, and something few other British railway companies could match at the time – even the Pullman Company itself was undergoing a complete transformation with new ownership. Some observers argue the excellence of the LNWR rail based 'travelling palace' even a hundred years later could not be bettered. The diners did not have a match anywhere else in Britain with a build quality described simply as excellent. Compartment doors were never draughty and as Jenkinson observed 'To be candid, they were ahead of their time' and 'undoubtedly designed to impress the trans-Atlantic clientele.'[31]

Before the Great War Liverpool Riverside's landing stage was extremely busy with liners almost queuing to arrive and depart requiring many special trains handling passenger volumes. In their early life, the *American Specials* would have been used around twice a week on regular Cunard sailings, and for White Star's intermediate liner traffic. By 1910 boat train business was brisk with two extra first-class corridor carriages added to the standard boat train formations which now included special trains for Canadian Pacific sailings. This added considerable weight coming in around 370 tons excluding passengers and luggage.[32] Accommodation on the *American Special* was three-class tier up until January 1912, but then reverted to the standard first and third-class carrying specification. The period before the First World War really represented a career high spot for the *American Special* as post-war demand was somewhat on the slide.

Post-war many of the new replacement vessels were already on the drawing boards as Cunard and other lines began to replace wartime loses which were substantial. By 1921, all of Cunard's big liners had transferred to Southampton operations leaving only secondary United States and Canadian port services especially the Liverpool-Halifax and the Liverpool-Quebec-Montreal itineraries.

Cunard's replacement liners for war-time losses took time to materialise, but by the mid-1920s Liverpool was synonymous with the company's new single funnel intermediate 'A' and 'S' class vessel fleet. With the new ships the port became home to Cunard's secondary services. Prior to the Great War, Cunard had taken the opportunity to supplement its Canadian operations with additional facilities from London and Southampton following an agreement between the Canadian and French governments whereby goods shipped through British ports received a rebate. Apart from Cunard, there were several other shipping lines active on the Canadian routes. In the first quarter of the twentieth century a degree of consolidation took place largely driven by emigrant traffic which saw some 2 million people seek new lives in the Dominion.

By the early 1920s a succession of new Cunard vessels had entered service predominantly based at Liverpool. The first A class ship delivered in 1921 was the *Albania* but she was not successful, withdrawn from service and sold some four years later as new single funnel identical looking sister ships entered the Canadian and US trade. Two batches of ships were built *Antonia, Ausonia* and *Andania* in 1922 and *Aurania, Ascania* and *Alaunia* in 1925. The vessels averaging around 14,000 tons had large refrigerated storage areas and were constructed essentially as emigrant ships for the Canadian market. A class liners were designed as two class ships; around 400 to 500 'cabin class' passengers and circa 1,000 third-class to cater for the west-bound travellers making new lives in the Dominion. Built to the same specification, they were never considered to be in the luxurious mode of the bigger S class vessels, and the large trans-Atlantic liners on the New York run, but the reworked designs of first-class public rooms of were termed comfortable and spacious incorporating facilities such as a garden lounge, drawing room, smoking room, gymnasium and children's crèche. The second trio of ships had continuous superstructures which gave them sleek, modern looks.

Cunard's new S class fleet, built principally for Liverpool's North Atlantic Boston and New York routes, were intended as twin-purpose capacity ships incorporating new efficient oil-burning technologies facilitating rapid ocean transit but also for cruising, a slower and less expensive operating format. Sea travel was changing as emergent middle-classes on both sides of the pond looked for new opportunities and experiences and quite naturally shipping lines reacted acknowledging the growing importance of the lower priced market sector. Passengers now became 'hotel guests' as shipping firms recognized the importance of a new revenue stream whereby middle-class wealth created demand for holidays and new destinations previously beyond access. In effect, the S class vessels were part of an ambitious rebuilding programme designed with cruising in mind. They followed the A class construction route with a trio of 20,000 tonners *Scythia*, *Samaria* and *Laconia* all commencing operations between 1921 and 1922. Sandwiched in between was the new 16,000-ton Anchor Line vessel *Tyrrhenia*. The ship did not commence operations until 1922, initially operating on the Liverpool, Quebec and Montreal route, but she was not popular; so, in 1924, Cunard took the opportunity to convert her to a two-class cruise ship renaming her *Lancastria* also serving on the Liverpool-New York run. The S class ships were slightly larger vessels with a three-class passenger specification. Cunard, like its key shipping line competitors, were actively involved in the fast-developing cruise market with many cruises originating out of eastern seaboard ports; ideal locations to operate luxurious, warm-weather cruises in the lean winter months. Ships could be rapidly turnaround for cruise operations with a single first-class designation facilitating a much more favourable travelling environment and cruise experience. *Laconia, Franconia* and *Carinthia* were the second batch of S class ships delivered several years later.

A developing feature was the increasing involvement of international travel companies in running cruises. Firms such as Thomas Cook, and the Frank Tourist Company of New York were particularly industrious. In 1922 American Express chartered Cunard's *Laconia* which completed its first 'Around the World Cruise'. This forced shipping lines to take more proactive roles in sea-based holiday planning especially around ideas of shore-based excursions providing valuable sources of secondary income. For the first-time cruising took the form of managing experiences where ideas surrounding how one travelled was just as important as the itinerary itself. For passengers, it was more about like-minded guests; congenial parties comprised of educated and interesting people, guided visits ashore in motor coaches, and everyone indulging in the wealth of uncovering something new. Whilst organizations like Thomas Cook argued this was something they had been practicing for many years, the 1920s marked a period when the modern guided travel industry was effectively born.

This all came to the boil with Cunard's *Samaria* undertaking a world cruise from New York in January 1923. Single-class cruises allowed the planet's oceans to be opened with a vast awry of new global destinations and especially those in the southern hemisphere.

Cruises to the Mediterranean remained a keen favourite for American visitors as well as shipping lines maintaining their summertime southern line voyage routes particularly to Italy. Around the world cruises typically lasted three to four months call at over twenty ports. *Scythia* made its maiden cruise from New York to the Mediterranean in February 1924 – a cruise so successful that a second was repeated the following year and thereafter on a further three cruises up into January 1927. One feature was the general reduction in the numbers of passengers on deluxe products typically restricted to around 400 guests. *Scythia* was one of the first vessels in the class to introduce a tourist class designation from its second-class capacity recognizing upper-middle-class families could now find overseas travel affordable with many well-educated customers from Britain's new red brick universities that came on stream at the turn of the last century. S class vessels *Laconia, Franconia* and *Carinthia* were the first Cunard ships to be designed specifically for cruising although as deep-hulled vessels they could be involved in Liverpool-New York runs.

The frequency of these vessels appearing in Liverpool led LMS to reappraise its boat train operations. The company ran attractively priced day excursions from Birmingham and other Midland stops to Liverpool Docks and other attractions in the area that included expert guided ship tours.[33] All three vessels were placed on regular cruising duties undergoing periodic refits to upgrade on-board facilities. *Franconia* and *Carinthia* had a mix of high-standard accommodation. Although not on the same scale as the large trans-Atlantic liners whose facilities would include a daily newspaper prepared on ship, shopping malls made up of local stores, hairdresser, theatres and cinemas and swimming pool and gymnasium, *Franconia's* first-class facilities were still described as a floating palace of rest and recreation akin to the top hotels and country houses of the day where the wealthy and influential took their holidays. S class intermediate liners did not disappoint variously described in Cunard marketing literature as 'complete in every respect'.

This involved first-class smoking rooms in the style of an English inn, El Greco styled smoking lounges, twin garden lounges decorated with ferns and potted palms, individual retail outlets, and indoor swimming pool together with other facilities for physical exercise and recreation that had not been seen before on smaller vessels. *Carinthia* was noted as the finest cruise ship in the world, and particularly popular with travellers many of whom would book again for the following year. She and her sister ship *Franconia* were both employed in long-distance winter cruising from 1925–26. *Scythia* in 1929 was the last of the S class group to have her passenger accommodation re-designated cabin, tourist and third-class brought about by a changing customer base. By the late 1930s Cunard's S ships were part of a cruising boom where cruise lengths were extended by as much as 144 days with itineraries made up of many remote and less visited destinations attracting discerning travellers all supported by a raft of new and perceptive travel literature pitching many new authors to the lime light. *Carinthia* and *Franconia* were the first modern Cunarders to sport new-look heat-resistant white hulled liveries which became a must for tropical operations. Even the ageing *Mauretania* was repainted in white for warm-water operations.

Although there was a rapid consumer demand for this new type of holiday, competition during this period was rife with White Star's northern based ships and even Canadian Pacific's new white hulled *Empress* passenger liner fleet suffering to some extent. Liverpool's Riverside simply did not attract the same volume of first-class travellers as Southampton. From a railway management perspective, and as the providers of boat trains to Liverpool's quayside, Cunard's S class liners were often on longer winter cruise duties (a purpose they had been specifically designed for) and away from the port for many months at a time. A further downside to the *American Special* stock was its bulk with a poor tare weight/ seating capacity requiring a full load of first-class passengers to safeguard profitability. Whilst there were other liners and shipping line vessels, particularly involved with South American traffic, utilisation of the *American Specials* at best was intermittent.

By mid-decade under LMS ownership a rapid spiral followed as the *American Special* ended its days over Riverside metals. By the early 1930s they were withdrawn from boat train operations as LMS deployed its new steel-sided Period II and III stock. These coaches were of a very high-standard and comfortable, but LMS's first-class designation was never considered luxurious. The once-great North Western hotel in Liverpool closed and a sure sign that perhaps the

Another shipping line LMS teamed up with was Ellerman Line, one of the UK's foremost shipping dynasties. This poster by Odin Rosenvinge characterised their post First World War fleet with its distinctive single buff and black top funnelled and grey hulled ships. War time losses were substantial but by 1939 their passenger fleet, largely made up of combination liners and cargo ships with limited accommodation, had been successfully rebuilt. There were not many parts of the world that Ellerman did not sail to. The inter-war routes to the Far East operating out of Glasgow and Liverpool were typified by the Indian island palace imagery used in the poster's creative treatment. A strong relationship with the British government ensured colonial service business was a mainstay of their operation. Most of its fleet were requisitioned during the Second World War, and like a generation before, suffered significant losses. Their replacement fleet, largely built by the mid-1950s and consisting in the main of fast cargo-liners carrying no more than a dozen passengers in considerable comfort, was a mainstay of their operations before the advent of containerisation. (NRM/SSPL)

long-luxury travel trek to Merseyside's liners was over. At Euston, dedicated Riverside boat trains were clearly evident on operating schedules, but by mid-decade, the flamboyance of luxury boat trains had been transferred to Southern Railway with their London-Southampton Pullman services.[34] On Southern's metals, Pullman *Ocean Liner Specials* also doubled up as royal trains. In July 1930, King Alfonso of Spain left Waterloo aboard a 9.30 am boat train departure involving heavy security measures which disrupted inbound suburban commuter traffic. Herbert Walker was one of the main station guests as the company made special arrangements for the royal event.[35]

Yet inter-war boat train traffic was not completely centred on Southampton and, to a lesser extent, on GWR's Plymouth operations. LMS had access to ports at London Tilbury, Glasgow, and of course, Liverpool which still remained a hub of a good many ocean liner workings. The port was home to a large proportion of Canadian Pacific, Cunard and White Star's vessels line voyage and cruise business. Cunard, by this time, had taken over their struggling former competitor, but smaller and more intimate liners had a particular following especially amongst northern traveller elites. Similarly, from a North American perspective, many passengers were loath to make long and arduous train journeys to and from New York, despite the preponderance of luxurious facilities provided on many famous named trains operating in and out of the eastern seaboard. Facilities encountered on board intermediate liners served the bill for countless travellers. Boston and Philadelphia as well as Canadian ports at Quebec City and Montreal retained extensive liner business using northern British ports like Liverpool. Also, Canadian Pacific, went on to develop significant cruise operations in the inter-war years with around the world cruises and especially itineraries to Norwegian and Baltic destinations. Warmer climes were also on shipping line itineraries. In August 1938 the *Liverpool Echo* reported on the success of the port in attracting cruise business:

> Ocean holiday cruises are keeping Liverpool liners well employed. To-day the Cunard liner *Lancastria* returned from the Mediterranean with 700 passengers; whilst berthed with her at the Prince's Landing Stage was the Lamport and Holt liner *Vandyck*, back from a similar trip with nearly 500 passengers. Both vessels leave the Mersey to-morrow for another Mediterranean cruise.[36]

To cater for an expanding Canadian destination and cruise market, LMS launched their dedicated Liverpool Canadian Pacific boat trains with fast services from Euston hauled by their latest locomotives and carriage stock. To transport first-class passengers, LMS made serious investment in quality carriage stock throughout the 1920s and 30s and new coaches. Specialist kitchen and dining cars would be a key feature and attached to Euston boat trains catering for Liverpool's liners. Whilst LMS did not apply locomotive headboards, carriage roof boards were a feature of the inter-war travel scene. LMS equally serviced Cunard's extensive Liverpool operations, similar carriage roof boards were applied to boat trains. Just out of shot in this photograph a Cunard roof board might be scene in this left-hand trolley. (NRM/SSPL)

As a result, boat trains would run with Cunard and Canadian Pacific coach boards serving smaller and intimate vessels particularly on old colonial routes. Liverpool was home to many other passenger shipping lines bound in the city's maritime history requiring specialist LMS boat train support. Yet for first-class passengers, Canadian Pacific's *Empress* liners whether on long distance voyages or shorter cruises were particularly well appointed and always attracted a certain glamourous clientele. The most celebrated

SEE THE NEW WORLD IN A NEW WAY

Silver rivers run between the banked-up fires of maples burning in autumn glory of crimson and gold. Frosted mountains trace a delicate outline upon the enamelled blue of the sky. Lakes lie so blue and vast that old explorers mistook them for new seas. Shadowy forest gloom where Indians once lurked in paint and feathers. These are only a few of the pictures that lie before you when you leave the White Star Liner *Laurentic* at Quebec—fresh from seven days of sunshine and cool Atlantic breezes. From then on your tour traces history clear across a continent right from its rise with the sun in old French cities of the East, to its setting in the harvest gold of the Western prairies. Here is a new way of seeing a new world—a perspective that brings untold wonders within the scope of seven weeks' luxurious travel.—A cabin cruise to Quebec aboard the palatial liner *Laurentic* begins this glorious seven weeks' holiday. Thence to the Pacific coast over the Canadian National Railways; every hour of this specially escorted tour is planned for pleasure. The fare, including return voyage from New York by White Star s.s. *Albertic*, £185. Let us send you complete descriptive literature.

SAILING DATES: FROM LIVERPOOL, JULY 19; FROM BELFAST JULY 20; FROM GLASGOW, JULY 20. RETURN VOYAGE, SAILING FROM NEW YORK AUGUST 31. SUPERIOR CABIN ACCOMMODATION IS A SPECIAL FEATURE ON EACH STEAMER

WHITE STAR ☆ CANADIAN NATIONAL RAILWAYS

Seven Weeks Tour to Pacific Coast

WHITE STAR LINE; Head Office, 30 James Street, Liverpool. *London* : 1 Cockspur Street, S.W. and Leadenhall Street, E.C.3. *Belfast* : 31/37 Victoria St. *Glasgow* : 153 St. Vincent St., or Local Agent. CANADIAN NATIONAL RAILWAYS : 17-19 Cockspur St., London, S.W.1. *Liverpool* : 19 James St. *Southampton* : 134 High St. *Cardiff* : 82 Queen St., or Local Agents.

Service Advertising

of Canadian Pacific's fleet, the *Empress of Britain* had a relatively short life as she was sunk by German submarines in the Second World War. Before its takeover by Cunard, White Star had been a long-term dweller at Liverpool Riverside's landing stage. The company, basing its intermediate liners at the port, had always competed for Canadian travel and Atlantic cruise business. White Star also placed advertisements in the national and regional press with an additional stop in Belfast targeting approved settlers with special low fares with guaranteed work and no repayments.

Little wonder, Canadian Pacific unveiled similar competitor travel products. Under the mantra of the 'World's Greatest Travel System', the company was able to market the serenity of the Canadian Rockies accessible by combined ocean and boat train services

White Star was also involved in the cruise business and in 1928 introduced a savings club scheme for ocean travel encouraging people on moderate means to spend their holidays on luxury liners which normally plied the Atlantic. The following year the company teamed up with Canadian National Railways to organize longer-length travel packages to explore Canada and returning by sea to Liverpool from New York. The boat train concept now had a further product extension as it moved into the escorted luxury rail cruise market. Upscale rail/land cruises with restricted numbers of travellers would become a prominent feature of the late-1920s and early-30s selective holiday. By 1932 White Star expected to handle upwards of 16,000 English holiday makers secured through a variety of marketing channels. Canadian National had mounted a serious promotional campaign to attract British visitors as early as April 1927 with headlines of 'Canada calls you to an ideal holiday' and 'Canada – the Playground of the Empire'. (Illustrated London News Ltd/Mary Evans) in just twelve days as well as exclusive personally conducted tours of Canada's Pacific Coast. Lake Louise in the Rockies was portrayed as one of the most beautiful sights in the world.[37] Canadian Pacific liners on integrated ocean and rail holiday packages also collected passengers at Glasgow and Belfast.

Canadian Pacific and Cunard's post-war relationship continued with Liverpool. British Railways London Midland Region enhanced Riverside boat train services introducing special express named boat trains. First-class was not stylish but modern, representing a new age of utilitarianism. Whereas in the past the best carriage stock was always made available for Liverpool boat trains, *The Railway Magazine*, reported in a June 1950 article that it was now a case of make do, though it was said better fare was provided on dining cars for the benefit of foreign visitors. Glamorous boat trains, however, were reserved for Southampton whilst management still retained stiff resistance to the Pullman product on the Riverside run; their defiance ultimately ended when British Railways Midland Region introduced the *Blue Pullmans* at the end of the 1950s as the new diesel trains became a regular feature of north-west life.

Riverside's roof had been replaced after bomb damage with the station looking rather splendid in these two post-war photographs of royal trains taken on 31 May 1951. As was normal practice with royal visits, the station, locomotives and carriages were extremely well turned out looking spick and span. Two sets of trains were required to co-ordinate the royal party heading for *HMS Sheffield*, moored outside the landing stage and on their way for a tour of Northern Ireland. Rebuilt Royal Scot no. 46168 *The Girl Guide* had brought Queen Elizabeth (the queen mother) from Manchester whilst Class 5 Black Five no. 44911 arrived earlier bringing Princess Margaret. A police presence is noted as well as railwaymen keen to record the event. (Ian Collard Collection)

The *Empress Voyager* connected with Canadian Pacific sailings from May 1953 whilst the house coloured *Cunard Special* began in 1956 servicing the company's intermediate liners. Locomotives were given red background headboards whilst new blood and custard liveried Mk1 stock were clearly signposted with coach boards. Almost as a final flourish Riverside's boat train business was not to last as trans-Atlantic passengers opted for far quicker air links.

Anchor Line's *Circassia* on her final voyage from India arrived at the landing stage on 16 March 1966; the awaiting boat train was waved away with the Anchor flag. Canadian Pacific and Elder Dempster continued to off-load their Liverpool ships. Cunard special boat trains ended as *Sylvania* made its final departure to New York from Liverpool on 24 November that year.[38] Boat train specials continued for a few more years, but the final departure from the terminus was a special train for troops returning from Northern Ireland on 25 February 1971. Liverpool Riverside station finally closed on 1 March. Canadian Pacific struggled on with its

Again, another view of the rebuilt station roof at Riverside with a G2 Class locomotive bringing out a boat train on the slow trek around the Mersey Docks & Harbour Estate out to Edge Hill and mainline locomotive change. Whilst the G2's number is partially obliterated, standing passengers admiring the locomotive, suggest a post-war timing. (Ian Collard Collection)

Liverpool operations, but this ended on 23 November 1971 when *Empress of Canada* made its final voyage up the Mersey from Montreal. After the best part of a century of dedicated operations the days of the Liverpool boat trains were finally over.

Scotland as noted had been a focus for trans-Atlantic travel which was fuelled to some extent by large waves of emigrant traffic. The net result was Glasgow became a well-known passenger port aided by the home-city's resident shipping line. Anchor line with its distinctive sleek and luxurious black-funnelled liners was one of the Clyde's best-known shipping lines and a significant player in the first half of the twentieth century providing regular passenger services between Glasgow, Derry, Co. Donegal and New York and regular operations. From Glasgow and Liverpool to Bombay. Since Anchor's promotional stance positioned the shipping line as 'Scotland's Atlantic Ferries', the Glasgow and New York route were extensively advertised becoming an important conduit characterized by frequent crossings of a distinctively Scottish flavour. Advertising extolled 'Scotland's very own line for the past 70 odd years' and in saving time and money by avoiding 'tiresome and unnecessary railway journeys. Sail from Glasgow by Anchor Line and have the satisfaction of being with Scottish passengers and Scottish crews'.[39] Clan Line operated out of Glasgow with a variety of South African destinations whilst Canadian Pacific developed routes operating between the city, Quebec and Montreal. Likewise, Anchor-Donaldson, a joint venture shipping line operated services from Glasgow to Canada up until 1935. Between the port and important Scottish cities, LMS instigated special boat train connections targeting first and second-class passengers who wanted to arrive at liners on the morning of departure.

Anchor Lines new 1920s fleet of vessels were also built with the cruise market in mind. Their Caledonia branded cruises were popular. Operating out of Glasgow, their fourteen-day itineraries were based around Portugal and North Africa, the Mediterranean and Scandinavia. Anchor's inter-war ships such as *Circassia* and *Caledonia* also operated out of Liverpool; the company's squat black funnelled cargo-liners a familiar sighting at Riverside. Similarly, Canadian Pacific used Glasgow and Belfast for its St. Lawrence routes to Quebec and Montreal. Anchor Lines involvement with trans-Atlantic passenger traffic ended in 1956. Yet Glasgow like many other port fortunes suffered as shipbuilding collapsed with the arrival of the jet. In the 1960s some liner traffic continued further down the Clyde Estuary at Greenock but this was all to end with the jetliner's march. Pullman stock was never used on West Coast boat trains. Glasgow Ocean Special boat trains operated into the 1960s. Destination coach boards were attached to special Cunard and Canadian Pacific boat trains running through to Glasgow and Greenock Princes Pier.

Southampton Docks: LSWR, Southern Railway and British Railways Southern Region boat trains

Southampton's relationship with the boat train is said to have dated from the mid-1850s with Union Line Cape Town departures. Within a short period of LSWR acquiring the port, the company's dock interests expanded fast. In September 1893 the LSWR as previously noted, devoted resources for special new boat trains to service prosperous American passengers on trans-Atlantic liners using Southampton and Plymouth. The order for the *'Eagle'* stock, known by a variety of names - *American Eagle Express*, *American Eagle* or simply, the *American Boat Trains*, had been placed by W. Panter, LSWR's Carriage Superintendent. The prestigious first-class accommodation was designed to attract the cream of passengers from American shipping firms using the port.[40] Following financial difficulties, in 1886 British shipping company Inman Line was bought by the US International Navigation Company (INC). In February 1893, the company's US owners decided to relocate from Liverpool to Southampton where its shipping operations were rebranded as American Line.[41] The existing Liverpool-Philadelphia US mails contract was re-awarded following the shipping line's decision to move its business operation as the new contract specified a series of Antwerp-Southampton-New York crossings including eastbound Plymouth mail and passenger drops.

A precondition of the mails contract required INC to commission new liners from American yards. In the same year, Inman Lines *City of New York* and *City of Paris* liners had their names shortened to *New York* and *Paris*. Relaunched under the American flag, these well-known Atlantic greyhounds put in consistent high-speed crossings attracting a strong customer following. American Lines parent company INC duly complied with the US government request by investing in two new state of the art steamers. SS *St. Paul* and SS *St. Louis* provided a premium weekly service by the mid-1890s. The company had grown expeditiously since their Philadelphia-Liverpool service commenced in 1873. This at the time

This oil painting by J. Longden is based on an 1899 setting of an LSWR boat train special heading to Southampton characterising travel proceedings at the tail end of the Victorian era. Headed by a powerful 4-4-0 locomotive, no. 294, the train is made up of a mix of corridor-connected carriage stock including a six-wheeled brake van for passenger luggage and a single *American Eagle* coach with its open settings for first-class passengers. Over the coming decade, much would change including the naming of dedicated shipping line boat trains as the company's Waterloo based services dashed prestige international passengers to awaiting liners. (NRM/SSPL)

was achieved without the assistance of government mail contracts. By the late 1800s, the company was in the enviable position of operating a quartet of quality liners working the North Atlantic. In a few short years of the Southampton move, American Line was third busiest shipping line (after Cunard and White Star) on the North Atlantic carrying high numbers of first-class passengers. In 1901 the company carried some 52,172 passengers on the Atlantic Ferry between Britain and the United States of which 25,006 were designated first and second-class. The company's steamers were renowned for the superiority of their first-class staterooms incorporating both combined bathrooms and toilets and based on the same return had average occupancy of 310 cabin passengers per vessel greatly aiding the shipping line's profitability. Such was their popularity; their departures and arrivals were the subject of

New York society gossip columns. Certainly, American Line's fleet met the exacting standards of New York's *Four Hundred* grouping. The company's move to Southampton presented LSWR with the business case to introduce the *American Eagle* carriage stock made up of eight wheeled, forty-six feet six-inch length coaches and dining saloon and in 1901 further investment in the prestige *American Line Express* boat train unit. Despite the company's upscale leanings, it created some consternation amongst its best clientele by deciding to compete for steerage-class customers. *The Daily Telegraph* reported in May 1904:

> Following the lead of German companies, the American Line yesterday announced that, commencing on Saturday next, they will carry emigrants by their steamers to the United States at £2 per head. This sum will cover the railway fare from London to Southampton, the voyage from that port to New York, and maintenance while on board. The service will be initiated by the *Philadelphia*, which leaves Southampton this week-end.[42]

Whether this decision was prompted by LSWR remains unclear but the railway company clearly saw business opportunities as it later built three sets of slimmed down dual-fitted third-class coaches between 1905 and 1908 designed for emigrant traffic, as well as renting the sets out to other pre-grouping railway companies to go to Liverpool or any other British port. Ringfenced emigrant boat trains, which arrived at ports several hours before those of first and second-class departures, were good sources of supplementary revenue. But American Line's entry into emigrant business on the south coast raised the question of excessive competition and capacity on the Atlantic Ferry for the first time. An issue *The Daily Telegraph* sought to comment on:

> Our Liverpool Correspondent wires: The drop in the third-class fare from Southampton to New York by the American Line to £2 is thought to be the prelude to the cutting of rates by all the companies of the Morgan combination. Already there have been inquiries from Englishmen with regard to the cheap fares via Continental ports, and the opportunity of getting a cheap rate from an English port by the steamers of the American Line will be readily seized, and the effect will almost certainly soon be felt by the vessels sailing from Liverpool. If the companies of the

Shipping Trust lower their fares the Cunard will, it is believed, be compelled to follow suit, and the Canadian Lines will be drawn into the struggle. The reduced fare to New York, plus £1 15s 10d railway fare from New York to Toronto, makes a total of £5 15s, compared with £7 10s. The Allan, Canadian Pacific and Dominion Lines will be prejudicially affected. No change in the rates of those companies has yet been announced.[43]

American Line did not hold back in promoting its emigrant package in the British press. It frequently advertised in Cornish and Irish newspapers – productive sources of emigrant business – and by the summer of 1907, made announcements of a special winter rate reduction that led to a general Atlantic rate war for steerage-class passengers. However, their *St. Paul* returned after a refit prompting speculation of impending mergers amongst Morgan's shipping brands. The *Shipping Gazette and Lloyds List* speculated:

A good deal of nonsense is being talked by pessimists as to the White Star Line swallowing the American Line for good and all. If there are any surprises in store it will not be in that direction. If some of the ships are removed from Southampton at any time, it will only be that they may be replaced by more modern craft, and developments in this direction may come sooner than is anticipated. The *Adriatic* (White Star Lines newest trans-Atlantic vessel) had a big boom, but the American liner which preceded her, and the one that followed yesterday (*St. Paul*), had nothing to complain of. The American Line is the American Line, and those who know the trend of things are looking forward to an expansion rather than a curtailment of activities in this connection.[44]

The kinds of luxury developments propagated by the likes of Cunard and the White Star Line were just a few years down the road starkly contrasting with the steerage travellers' lot. *The Daily Telegraph* reported on one series of departures:

The liners (from New York) for Europe sailing yesterday were well filled, but some of the most expensive suites were unoccupied. The reason probably is that the average first-class accommodation is now so excellent that even rich people, some of them caught by what your Financial Correspondent called the rich man's panic in

America recently, do not see the necessity of paying big sums for millionaires' apartments.[45]

Yet the excesses continued. Elaborate suites of private apartments (parlours, bedrooms and bathrooms) and private outdoor promenades could be found on *Titanic* for the princely sum of £830 for the ship's singular and uncompleted crossing. Notwithstanding White Star's occupation of the media agenda, and as could be expected, American Line just carried on churning its own furrow, but expanded its interests by working closely with US railroad companies to encourage first, second and emigrant traffic on to their services. On the Liverpool-Philadelphia route special ticketing arrangements were set up for settlers (mainly Irish and Scottish) heading to California; advertising headlines proclaimed the Pennsylvania Railroad had the shortest and most direct route to all places in the Western States. Similar arrangements were made on the Southampton-New York route for Canadian Trade passengers heading to Toronto. US and Canadian cross-border tourist traffic became big business as special hospitality inducements, tied to railroad travel, were put in play targeting visitors and encouraging them to spend a few extra days in the Big Apple - yet to be popularised as the city's nickname in the 1920s.

Everyone, it seemed, wanted a piece of the action. In 1907, Thomas Cook produced an ocean sailing list containing all that resolute travellers needed to know about steamship passages, providing information on all classes and types of steamers, location of berths, and on longer passages, hints of seasonal change and necessary clothing. Crossing the Atlantic and the prospects of travelling across the Continent on the US and Canadian railroad systems must have appeared daunting for the first-time Atlantic Ferry passenger. Allaying fears was down to the roles of the many travel and shipping agents found on prosperous city and market town high streets. Would be presentations by managers, widely reported on by local press, were a feature of the time. Slideshow talks on destinations linked by international railway and steamship travel, and on the range of Empire emigration packages available to those seeking a new life away from these shores always attracted large audiences. Whilst the servicing of boat trains for ocean-going steamships was a highly reputable affair in Britain, Ireland and Europe, it was somewhat different on the other side of the Atlantic. In the US and Canada, the main ocean ports liner ports were centred on large metropolitan cities of New York, Boston, Philadelphia, Quebec and Montreal and a local proximity to major railroad systems on which travel was organised. Personal recollections of such visits were also very popular during Edwardian times. One such person was the Rev. W.A. Wilson, a Presbyterian Church pastor from Coleraine in Northern Ireland who according to the *Northern Whig* newspaper 'gave a graphic, witty and informative description of his experiences on board the White Star liner *Baltic*, the landing in New York, characteristics of the country and people' and the 'contrasts and affinities of railway travelling experiences in America'.[46] Whereas ports at Bristol, Glasgow, Liverpool and London were key departure points, it was the convenience of Southampton that much attention was focused upon. LSWR working in conjunction with shipping lines did much to foster the convenience of its Waterloo boat trains over that of competitor services.

By 1908 the White Star Dock had still to be constructed, but the land immediately to the east was now occupied by the Empress Dock extension, passenger and cargo sheds, a network of railways bringing boat trains alongside liners, and home to many Union Castle liners. Shown here is RMS *Briton III*, built in 1897, and the first Union steamer to exceed 10,000 tons incorporating extensive and comfortable facilities for the fifteen-day journey to the Cape. Only trans-Atlantic liners were larger. The *Briton* was the largest vessel of her day to operate between Southampton and South Africa. (J&C McCutcheon Collection)

Notwithstanding American Line and White Star's planned activities hogging much limelight, Southampton also had a raft of other shipping lines using the port. Union Castle (through its previous constituent businesses) had been a long-term resident since the 1870s developed on the back of a flourishing South African trade. Special LSWR boat trains were put on for regular Saturday timetabled mail services transporting passengers and mail to Union Castle's ever-increasing fleet of steamers. Superior boat trains were also put on at the other end of the voyage too. In time, the *Union Express*, a luxury first-class only train for the 1,000 mile or so run to Johannesburg was established. They were sent down to the docks in Cape Town by the South African Railway authorities meeting passengers and mail spilling off the steamers. Many of the shipping lines' vessels were put on loan to the Admiralty (short of requisitioned) from October 1899 to conduct the Boer War resulting in an enormous increase in business for both the port and the shipping line. Troop and supplies traffic were particularly heavy for the next couple of years, although on cessation of hostilities as railway writer Michael Baker reports 'no less than fifteen Union-Castle ships were laid up in Southampton Water' for a while.[47] Yet the port remained the focal point of Britain's involvement in sending resources for the South African skirmish. Lord Kitchener's return to England aboard the steamship *Orotavia* in July 1902, and its procession up the Solent to the port received widespread national newspaper attention. Indeed, LSWR's involvement was considerable putting on a highly decorated special train which conveyed Kitchener and his party to London from the city's western station.[48]

Another shipping line to regularly use Southampton was the Royal Mail Steam Packet Company (RMSP) which provided a variety of operations to South America, Australia, the West Indies and Norwegian cruises to the North Cape. Under the dynamic leadership of Owen Philipps (later to become Lord Kylsant), the RMSP group from 1903 grew to become one of the country's major shipping combines. By 1906 the company had acquired a new contract for West Indian Mails having previous moved its Falmouth based West Indian operations to Southampton some years before in 1902. In less than three years of the revised contract, it reported considerable success in the growing connection with New York, by means of their Caribbean mail steamers providing routes for general passenger and tourist traffic between

New York, Jamaica, the Isthmus of Panama, Colombian and West Indian ports.[49] RMSP with a consolidated position at Southampton extended its operations significantly in Edwardian times acquiring a modernised fleet of intermediate liners for its River Plate route whose itineraries included en route stops at Lisbon and the Canary Islands. Each of its new vessels began with the letter "A" establishing a trend which continued to the 1930s of referring to RMSP ships as "A-liners". Lamport and Holt Line was also a shipping line with South American interests who started to use the port regularly requiring boat train formations for their Brazil and River Plate routes.

Great Western had running rights into Southampton operating a boat train known as the *Southampton Express* to the docks from Paddington in the first decade of the twentieth century. Although designed for GWR London suburban services, shown here is no. 2228 County Class tank engine hauling the up boat train express. A batch of Atlantic tank locomotives – running numbers 2221–2230 – were built between 1905 and 1906. To what extent the Great Western held individual relationships with shipping lines at the docks to harness its share of international liner traffic is not known. Previously the company provided RMSP with boat trains for Falmouth mails and passengers, but GWR's circuitous route and restricted running rights in to Southampton made London journeys far slower and less popular with passengers than LSWR's direct Waterloo trains. Whilst RMSP held regular routes to the Caribbean, another GWR boat train known as the *West Indian Mails Boat Train* ran predominantly into Bristol Avonmouth. (J&C McCutcheon Collection)

Despite the level of activity in the first years of the twentieth century, the real jewel in the crown for LSWR's planned operations was undoubtedly the move of White Star Line to Southampton future-proofing the movement towards larger and grander vessels. In 1907 the port was chosen to operate the company's premier North Atlantic services marking a long-term association between the port owners and White Star Line. Dedicated boat trains known as the *White Star Express* formed part of a broad panoply of specialist services LSWR providing for the shipping line. The *White Star Express* was a late breakfast departure for first-class passengers that included new corridor compartment carriages for British passengers as well as utilising part of the *American Eagle* stock with its open style coaches much preferred by US travellers.[50] When plans for the Olympic Class liners were first conceived, the nature of liner traffic across the Atlantic was changing fast. Railway historian Dr David Turner describes the rapport between the two companies as an 'intimate relationship' where from the commencement of work on the Olympic Class liners '*Titanic* had been destined to sail from Southampton.'[51]

With White Star Line moving its premier liners to Southampton, LSWR focused its interests on developing opportunities at the port it owned with the company and progressively with other shipping firms. This was something as port owners they could subtly influence. Whilst Victorian times saw the first examples of integrated approaches between business owners (particularly railway companies and shipping lines), the arrival of the Edwardian era really marked an age of sustained business collaboration, especially where it involved the infusion of modern design and hospitality approaches witnessed across many service-based firms. Pullman's influence on Dover, Folkstone and Newhaven cross-channel boat trains was clearly evident by 1910 with a heady mixture of New York and Paris in the cocktail. White Star's long-term ship builder was Harland & Wolff. It's Chairman Lord Pirrie, one of the best-known industrialists of the period, joined the LSWR board simultaneously holding directorships of White Star Line and running his substantial shipbuilding interests in Belfast. Ports quite naturally worked closely with the shipping lines and railway companies to create the necessary on-site supporting infrastructure for the smooth running of operations and the facilities to provide for a rapid turnaround of liners and their passengers. The Port

LSWR's Southampton Docks Station building formed part of an adjoining complex that included the company's high-class South Western Hotel shown here. By 1915 promotional literature proclaimed the hotel's key benefits including 'Entrance from station platform and facing the docks' whilst 'hotel porters meet all principal trains and boats'. LSWR carriages can be seen to the right of the image and all designed to minimize passenger inconvenience ensuring prosperous travellers did not have far to go to awaiting ships. For passengers not staying at the company's hotel, the station provided a unified travelling experience from boat train to liner. Travellers arriving from other parts of the country, and not on dedicated boat trains, a special hotel motor bus was put on to meet 'all expresses at Southampton West station'. In 1920 LSWR celebrated resumption of Atlantic crossings again, as shown in the second image portraying Anglo-American ties in a modern Mayflower context, in a deliberate ploy to attract prosperous US passengers. (*Above*: J&C McCutcheon Collection; *Below*: Southern Railway Publicity)

of Bristol Authority (PBA) was another notable example at the time of where their substantial investments at Avonmouth were systematically planned with the aid and recommendations of other rail and sea transport partners.

LSWR was required to develop a completely new dock system to service White Star's massive new Olympic class liners erecting a terminal, cargo sheds and dedicated warehousing for luggage, new laundry facilities and first-class hotel accommodation. Luxury travel had well and truly arrived but despite the quality of luxury boat train stock, LNWR could not quite match LSWR's star offer with its Liverpool Riverside station and landing stage facilities.

White Star's decision to operate its premier service vessels from Southampton was a straightforward business decision given the company was part of the IMM shipping businesses portfolio that included the Antwerp based Red Star Line, and American Line. This undoubtedly provided IMM with the chance to rationalise its premier brand activities in one port, thus allowing time for its partner LSWR to develop superior port side services and the necessary rapid London transfers. Such opportunities allowed LSWR to far exceed Liverpool Riverside's amenities and matching anything LNWR could provide on its much longer route to Liverpool. In addition, there appears to be evidence of an *Ocean Boat Express* running from the Midlands and the north of the country over the Midland & South Western Joint Railway metals.[52] Clear evidence of the position Southampton would gain as an international port and the importance LSWR would give in 'making special arrangements to meet the additional traffic requirements occasioned by the transfer from Liverpool of the White Star Line Royal Mail steamers *Adriatic*, *Oceanic*, *Majestic*, and *Teutonic*, which are to be employed in the Southampton-Cherbourg-New York service, calling at Plymouth eastbound'.[53] On 5 June 1907, the new palatial twin-screwed *Adriatic*, the fastest ship in the then company's fleet and making only its second Atlantic crossing, inaugurated a weekly service to New York. That man John Pierpont Morgan kept on popping up being one of the passengers aboard *Oceanic* making the crossing from Southampton to New York in August 1907.[54] The move to the port almost never happened as when *Oceanic* made her final sailing from Liverpool Riverside on 22 May, almost 100 firemen and seamen were locked in dispute with White Star over additional payments to cover return railway journeys from Southampton to Liverpool.[55]

By early 1908 the logistics of establishing new facilities had largely been put in place including the branding of boat trains for the company's Southampton liners.[56] White Star's premier liners sailed for New York on Wednesdays with 8.30 am and 9.45 am boat train departures from Waterloo. The later departure, primarily for first-class passengers, was formed of new corridor stock. For many years, White Star had created class-leading industry standards for the quality of its passenger accommodation and facilities on board its liners. The company simply laid down the ground rules for which all other shipping lines followed, significantly improving all passenger classes over a twenty-five-year period. Southampton's Olympic Class based liners were designed to challenge existing conventions by unseating Cunard (and the port of Liverpool) as the dominant shipping power on the Atlantic Ferry. *Olympic* and *Titanic* were statements of shipbuilding progress, equipped with the latest refinements delivered by science and technology. Delivered in April 1912 *Titanic* was designed to be best of all time variously accoladed as a travelling palace, epitomising bewildering luxury, and promoted as the greatest ship on earth attracting the uber rich of the day.

The *White Star Express* or as some quarters referred to as the *Titanic Special* boat train employed a mix of open and compartment first-class stock considering a significant British accompaniment for the liner's maiden voyage. Some 427 first and second-class passengers boarded the vessel at Southampton; the vast majority making the short rail journey from Waterloo although a number of passengers were known to have stayed the night before at LSWR's opulent South Western Hotel. Part of the *American Boat Train* stock is likely to have been used in the train's formation although by this stage its open style carriages had probably seen better days.[57] Writer Richard Davenport-Hines points to their inclusion:

Passengers could lounge, if they wished, as if they were in a club. Americans were accustomed to undivided railway carriages, where they could gaze down long aisles studying their fellow passengers and found it odd of the privacy-conscious English to seclude themselves in separate compartments. The black and white photographs, with coloured-in details, of picturesque scenery like Bedruthan Steps or Boscastle harbour, which were framed above the seats, seemed quaint to travellers from the great republic.[58]

John Jacob Astor at 47 was one of the richest men on the globe. Davenport-Hines describes his pose in this photograph alongside the *Titanic Special* boat train as resembling a conventional ruling-class Englishman, with a trim moustache, erect bearing, bowler hat, rolled umbrella and overcoat with velvet collar; the perfect appearance for period first-class travel. Whilst Father Frank Browne had arrived early, having already stowed his luggage on the train, whether he deliberately sought out Astor to record the event is unknown, but he appears more than a willing participant amongst his travelling cohort. Maiden liner voyages were always serious affairs for LSWR as this photo demonstrates allowing the company to showcase premier boat train services. The inaugural (and only running of the *Titanic Special*) boat train was no different clearly demonstrating the efforts the company took to cater for prestigious events. From the long platform and looking towards Waterloo Station's canopy, a mix of the best carriage stock can be seen included in the first-class train formation headed by a crack locomotive. A London fog appears to haze the background, but the posse of well-dressed passengers appears totally unconcerned. (*Above left*: NRM/SSPL; *Above right*: Davison & Associates)

By time of the great ship's departure, LSWR had had twenty years' experience of prestige dedicated boat train operations to and from Southampton and providing bespoke travelling services for a finicky first-class international customer.

Two boat trains left Waterloo delivering a fast one hour forty-minute port-side transit. The first comprising second, and third-class passengers was characterised by loud singsongs, left platform twelve at 7.30 am with apparently no third-class stock included in the formation. The first-class train ticket was eleven shillings and with a 9.45 am departure a far more leisurely pursuit expected by premier class passengers on prestigious boat trains at the time. LSWR's preparations for Olympic Class liners was impressive mirroring a close-working partnership between the two organisations. Davenport-Hines paints a colourful picture:

'London & South Western carriages allotted a yard-wide seat to each first-class passenger: two seats (covered in blue cloth with gold lacing) faced one another in each compartment, and the luggage racks were gilded.'[59] The ornately furnished *American Boat Train* carriages would have provided the luxury open sections which for the past year or so would have been used exclusively for the Southampton service since the company's decision to relinquish its Ocean Quay, Plymouth operations.[60]

Following resumption of normal Atlantic traffic after the Great War, LSWR in 1921 provided its new flush steel-sheeted Ironclad carriage stock for international boat trains, but it would be several years until the company's successor, the Southern Railway, introduced glamorous Pullman stock at Southampton docks to meet the world's premier liners. As the port was owned by Southern, the company felt there was undoubted potential for upscale boat train business. Consequently, the company began to formalise plans to compete aggressively for liner passenger and cargo traffic. This was helped by Cunard deciding to move its larger vessels to the port in 1920. Dock expansion would gradually attract new international shipping customers. In 1925 P&O started using Southampton again for various combinations of long-haul voyages, whilst three years later the port attracted NDL as a tenant. New boat train services would be further enhanced by Southern romanticising and bestowing them with special names as the company now possessed a bank of new powerful locomotives; King Arthur and Nelson Classes described as the region's aristocrats.[61] Given an increase in premium liner traffic it was hardly surprising the Southern Railway should not respond to the activities of its arch competitor with their Plymouth based boat train operations. Southern enjoyed close working relationships with the Pullman Company fashioned over many years of co-operation with two of its previous constituent companies. When the Great Western went its own way with its own luxury stock, Southern Railway snapped up capacity and launched a series of short-distance Pullman hauled trains, thus beginning a process of making their blue water boat trains more glamorous.

Southampton was now home to the biggest of vessels - White Star Line's *Olympic* and *Majestic*, and from the early 1920s, Cunard's trio of express liners *Mauretania*, *Berengaria* and *Aquitania* providing the fastest ocean crossings in the world. During the

Four stackers from the early years of the twentieth century always provided photogenic subjects. A distant view of *Olympic* in the background together with departing boat train was taken on 10 August 1930 from a window of the South Western Hotel. Another view of *Olympic* in Ocean Dock was taken in August 1929 showing the extensive network of railway lines that brought boat trains alongside the quay. (J&C McCutcheon Collection)

inter-war years, this provided a mini-tourist industry in its own right as summertime paddle-steamer cruises of Southampton Water allowed visitors to survey the largest ocean ships at close quarters. Ocean-going vessels were also well supported by travellers, and perhaps a throwback to the pre-war days of luxury travel. The *Western Mail* reported on 'Gay Times On Ocean Liners' as *Aquitania* arrived back from New York, where passengers had enjoyed a foretaste of Christmas. The newspaper went on:

> The weather was fine, and many and varied were the Yuletide festivities organised. There were dances, concerts, Christmas tree for the children, and a grand dinner held in the true old English style. The hog's head was borne in on high by the chef followed by attendants in costume with barons of roast beef of old England. A choir of 100 voices sang in the gallery of the saloon, the chief rendering being a carol written and set to music by Mr. Sax Rohmer, the well-known author, who was on board. In all there were over 2,000 passengers.[62]

LSWR put on a succession of boat trains to whisk the Atlantic travellers off to London for the Christmas season.

Although Germany had lost most of its large liners for war reparations with a consequential loss of passenger demand from central mainland Europe, towards the end of the 1920s new iconic looking vessels began to arrive at the port again. Historically, Bremen and Hamburg based liners had frequently stopped en route at Southampton providing a steady stream of prosperous American passengers. In March 1930 NDL's super-liner *Bremen* was joined by her sister ship *Europa* whose trans-Atlantic entry had been curtailed by a serious fire whilst being fitted out. The German liners, described in some parts of the British press as 'ocean monsters', were modern in design and particularly noted for their low streamlined profiles. Quite simply, the pride of the German fleet of ocean liners were speed queens establishing new standards of premium sector travel. They were an ever-present duo in a decade always associated with excitement, glamour and out-and-out sophistication, but towards the end of the decade they became the subject of subtle Nazi propaganda. On *Europa's* final homeward trans-Atlantic sailing at the end of August 1939 days before war was declared, she missed out her Southampton call heading straight for Bremen and taking with her some forty American and British passengers who were due to disembark off Newport, Isle of Wight with awaiting tenders. The returning London boat train was cancelled leaving stranded in this country around forty odd German citizens wishing to return to Germany who were later advised to contact their embassy in London for further information. *Europa's* failure to call made many newspaper front pages.[63]

Southampton was operating at the premium end of the market servicing the world's most luxurious liners either as a home port

Express boat trains waited alongside Germany's prestige inter-war liners ready to shuttle international passengers to and from Berlin, as well as connecting with various routes in Germany. Locomotive no. 38.2221 is almost certainly taken in Bremerhaven as it was one of the Type P8 passenger locomotives of the Prussian Railways, built for express and general passenger services. This particular engine was built in 1918 by Berliner Maschinenbau AG (formerly Schwarzkopff) with works number 6550. After delivery, the engine was deployed first to Belgium in the spring of 1918, whilst in April of that year, the locomotive was transferred to Hanover where it worked all its life, first with fleet number 2569 and later as 38.2221. Many of these engines had a long life until the 1960s and were used on passenger services into Cuxhaven and Bremerhaven from Osnabrueck and Hanover. (Hapag-Lloyd/William Miller Collection)

Le Havre really developed as a port in the late nineteenth century as more modern facilities emerged, including provisions for a large tidal dock, a 1,000-metre quay and a dry dock for liners. All of this work was eventually completed in 1929 as ever-larger liners frequented the port. New infrastructure was built including up-to-the-minute berths for ocean liners aided by quick Paris rail access. During the inter-war years, Le Havre was home to more large ocean-going liners as well as regular cross-channel ferry traffic. By 1930 the French travel industry was performing well with over 500,000 passengers passing through the port. In 1935 the most luxurious of the inter-war liners – *Normandie* – was indelibly linked to Le Havre as its home port. As could be expected ETAT operated stylish boat trains in and out of the port. As long ago as 1882 the Pullman Company, working in conjunction with Ouest, gained a degree of momentum providing a saloon-dining car on the Le Havre-Paris route catering for wealthy American travellers traipsing off trans-Atlantic steamers. As can be seen in the second image, probably taken in 1908, ETAT deployed *Train Transatlantique* luxury cars for Le Havre liners. This service was hauled by Ouest locomotive 2518 – serie 2501/2570 and built in 1898.[64] (*Above and Below: French Railways Society*)

LES GRANDS TRAINS FRANÇAIS
6   *Chemins de fer de l'Etat. — Train transatlantique Paris-Le Havre. — ND Phot.*

or alternatively as a port of call for impressive vessels making their way to European locations. The port by the early 1930s had bypassed Liverpool as Britain's main liner port. Cherbourg and Le Havre in close proximity to Southampton offered the highest level of Continental traveller facilities during the inter-war years including the provision of crack boat trains servicing the ports to and from Paris.

Little wonder given this competitive international environment; Southern Railway saw comparable opportunities with *Ocean Liner* boat train business. From 1 January 1931 Pullman cars taken off the unsupported GWR *Torbay Pullman* experiment were immediately redirected to Southern metals for initial use mainly on the *Ocean Liner* services. Railway writer Kevin Robertson reports: 'Within two months passenger loadings were being reported, with 50%, 997, of the 1,932 passengers who has used the special Ocean Liner workings in the first month of operation electing to travel Pullman and in so doing paying the additional supplement.'[65]

Southampton *Ocean Liner* expresses were made up with combinations of Pullman cars fluctuating with individual liners, but invariably providing between two and four Pullman liveried cars in the rake with stock shared with the *Bournemouth Belle* whose inaugural running was in July 1931. Railway writer R.W. Kidner noted that on one busy day in 1932, twelve out of seventeen boat trains contained Pullman stock.

Increasingly Cunard's ships were known for their luxurious surroundings allowing the company to flex its muscles dominating the prosperous first-class market on the North Atlantic. In the inter-war period, its trans-Atlantic routes carried a third of all passengers with a customer base predominantly made up of well-off Americans. The policy of continually investing in port facilities and dock infrastructure at Southampton that begun with LSWR continued into grouping. Southern Railway countered as growth in passenger shipping traffic led to the further port investment. By the early 1930s the port was in the middle of an expansion programme establishing itself as the UK's leading passenger liner port. Whilst Southampton was owned by Southern Railway, other Big Four railway companies were keen to exploit opportunities and to ensure trains brought prosperous passengers to and from their heartlands to the port.

Such commercial activities quite naturally attracted other shipping lines. In 1936 Baltimore Mail Lines initiated a new North Atlantic trans-Atlantic Southampton-Baltimore and Norfolk, Virginia service. Likewise, Union Castle, a long-term port customer,

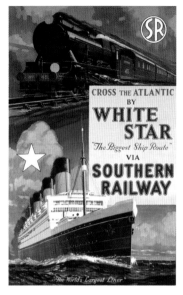

The 1926 Southern Railway poster by William McDowell featured White Star's flagship *Majestic*, then the largest ship in the world, promoting combined trans-Atlantic rail and liner services. Swiftness and modernity were key themes. Positioned alongside *Majestic* at Southampton Docks is an awaiting Southern Railway ocean liner boat express. By the mid-1930s the company's port had grown to become Britain's premier port for long-distance traffic with some 30,068 ft of quay length. The average boat train carried around 400 passengers. (*Left*: NRM/SSPL; *Below*: John Clarke/Railway Wonders of the World)

were developing services from Southampton with their weekly South African departures. Holidays in Madeira, first promoted by Booth Line in the early 1900s, were included as part of a cruise itinerary dovetailing with the shipping line's arriving and departing liners. Their quayside facilities at Southampton were widened

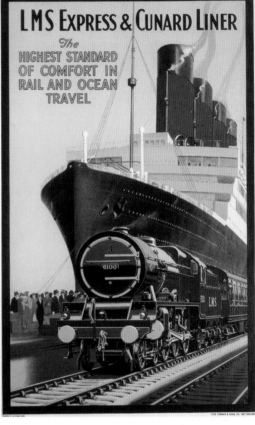

Norman Wilkinson was one of LMS's prestige Royal Academy illustrators charged with enhancing the railway company's image as the country's leading railway operator. Wilkinson was well versed with the maritime sector choosing to link the White Star liner *Olympic* with the new generation of Royal Scot locomotives. Whilst the poster was centred on Southampton, the LMS in addition ran a succession of boat trains from Euston to Liverpool Riverside for White Star Line's intermediate liner fleet. Using this as a backcloth, LMS from the late 1920s, working in conjunction with Midlands based newspapers such as the *Nottingham Journal*, ran special reader trips to visit liners in Southampton Docks. Not to be outdone, Cunard also undertook an inter-war joint marketing initiative to promote rail and sea services with LMS using *Aquitania* alongside an express train. LMS by this time had run a series of posters emphasising the quality of their train carriages. Using the line 'the highest standard of comfort in rail and ocean travel' fitted well with one of Cunard's trilogy of Southampton based luxury liners regularly crossing the Atlantic. Likewise, LMS ran their boat trains into Riverside for Cunard's Liverpool domiciled intermediary liners. (*Above left*: William Miller Collection; *Above right*: NRM/SSPL)

as *Stirling Castle* and her sister ship *Athlone Castle* were added as home ports. But it was the port's association with the new super-liners and its healthy pool of prosperous passengers that altered much in the 1930s upscale travel landscape. Pullman boat trains were extremely busy.

"THE EMPRESS OF BRITAIN READY TO LEAVE SOUTHAMPTON DOCKS FOR CANADA"

SOUTHAMPTON DOCKS
THE GATEWAY TO THE WORLD
Owned and Managed by the Southern Railway.

S.S. "EMPRESS OF BRITAIN," SOUTHAMPTON.

Leslie Carr produced this captivating illustration of Canadian Pacific's *Empress of Britain* which entered service in 1931 to emphasise ground-breaking developments taking place at Southampton Docks at the time. Shown moored in the eastern docks, she was an exceptionally lavish vessel carrying comparatively few passengers for her size but holding 465 in sumptuous first-class surroundings. The second image of the Canadian shipping line's flagship is taken around 1932. The vessel regularly returned to Southampton from line voyage and cruise duties where the *Empress* garnered a particularly favourable reputation. (*Below*: J&C McCutcheon Collection)

Luxury liner cruising was enormously popular in the 1930s. Shipping companies like Cunard, P&O, Canadian Pacific and new entrants such as Swan Hellenic, who employed well-informed lecturers, operated in up market holiday business targeting prosperous patrons. But cruising was becoming democratic, too, with customers from a growing middle-class. In 1931, 70,000 Britons were taking cruises each year; two years later the figure had risen to 175,000 whilst the figure had reached 550,000 in 1937.[66] And for every liner on cruise duty, leaving and returning to port there would be an accompanying boat train. Whilst the 1950s were depicted as the decade of the shipping line named boat trains, the 1930s saw similar developments with trains serving a succession of specially adapted vessels for cruising.[67] The port of Southampton and Southern Railway did well from the popularity of pre-war cruising.[68]

Whilst Canadian Pacific operated in the cruise market, they also had one eye on exploiting tourist demand for their home territory. For upscale visitors Canada had been on the horizon since the beginning of the twentieth century, but given the conglomerate's scale of sprawling business operations which included owning first-class hotels - many becoming famous landmarks - and a travellers' cheque operation, it was of little surprise their passenger shipping and railway businesses were positioned at the forefront of tourism development and in leveraging alternative routes to the United States, so holiday visits could combine American and Canadian dimensions. Ernest J. Chaloner writing about 'Britain's New Leviathans' in *The Illustrated London News* observed:

> The new Canadian Pacific 40,000-ton liner, the *Empress of Britain*, will be placed on the Southampton-Canada service. She will be double the size of the other famous ships on this route, and a *de luxe* liner without equal in her class. Her speed will be 24 knots, and this leads her owners to assert that it will be possible for passengers leaving Southampton to reach Quebec, and then go on to Chicago by a special train, just as quickly as if they had used the fastest liner on the New York service.[69]

The boat train really had achieved international dimensions. Similarly, *The Railway Magazine* was taken by jointly produced American Express Company and New York Central Railroad travel literature. It rang:

> American Tourists' Handbook: United States and Canada', distributed by the American Express's Liverpool office, was 'a well-produced booklet, with a number of interesting illustrations, scenic and railway (some in colour), with notes likely to appeal

BEST WISHES FOR A HAPPY & PROSPEROUS NEW YEAR . 1929

CUNARD

Christmas and new year cruises were a fresh spin off developed by shipping lines in the years between the wars. Largely as a result of long-distance 'Around the World' cruise formats, special itineraries provided a combination of winter sunshine, destination exploration, as well as time at sea with all the festive traditional celebrations and trimmings. A specially decorated Christmas cruise boat train in 1932 took Madeira-bound tourists to the *Arandora Star*, a recently converted Blue Star Line cargo-liner developed for cruise duties and based mainly in Southampton where it developed a strong following with travellers. The second image shows a special New Years' Day menu prepared for guests aboard the Cunard liner *Caronia* on 1 January 1929. A sumptuous pre-Christmas dinner ably attended by the chefs is highlighted in this December 1934 setting on board White Star liner *Homeric*. She was not a particularly fast vessel and more suited to cruising duties; in this shot she has left Southampton for a fourteen-day cruise. (*Left*: Illustrated London News; *Top right*: UIG History/SSPL; *Above right*: Planet News/SSPL)

to the prospective tourist. Information is also given as to arrangements for checking baggage, with a table of railway and sleeping car fares from New York to various centres in the United States. Included is a large folding map.[70]

Prior to the arrival of new *Empress* ships, Canada as a national tourist destination, like many other European countries, began appearing regularly in British press advertising. National railway systems became the focus of country destination marketing activity. Canada possessed two such systems; Canadian Pacific Railway and Canadian National Railways - both of which had become engrained in the country's landscape. Canadian National Railways was the younger of the organisations having been incorporated in June 1919 and growing rapidly as a network out of a mix of regional railway operations that had fallen on hard times, had financial problems or were in the hands or already owned by the federal government. Likewise, they had run their own shipping line, albeit of a temporary nature due to the Great War, but also built and operated their own resort hotels, initially constructed to provide overnight passenger accommodation. However, their profile increasingly adapted for upmarket visitors and added to travel itineraries in their own right as attractive holiday locations. Both companies targeted British travellers through advertising and editorial led travel stories supported by networks of individual offices or specially appointed travel agents.

Whilst Norway was hardly a new destination, shipping lines also experimented with mini-cruises from Southampton to Norway's wilderness, fjords and the North Cape. Cunard's *Carinthia* and *Franconia* were both involved in shortened cruise formats, but it was Canadian Pacific - known globally for conducting bespoke world tours - that established reputations for northern water exploration. Their cruise product was built an unparalleled level of luxury, comfort and white-hulled liveried ships. International travellers could bank on Canadian Pacific vessels as the company actively promoted its travellers' cheque service as 'Good the World Over' establishing a safe comfort zone for passengers. And with it came a flurry in personal financial service firms especially targeting the well-heeled American passenger who as they travelled expected ships and onshore establishments to accommodate them in the appropriate manner they expected; in other words, in glamorous and luxurious surroundings. Money followed money

This later LNER poster (by this time Cunard had acquired White Star), again used the well tried and tested approaches of combining railway company and shipping line connecting rail and sea services. The artwork by an unsigned illustrator complements Cunard's three-funnelled *Berengaria* – a ship described as a first-class hotel but a third-class ship – by her former German owners with that of LNER's eye-catching Flying Scotsman locomotive and train. Such creative treatments were designed to appeal to affluent free-moving American and Canadian tourists visiting London, the north of England, Scotland and the Continent. (NRM/SSPL)

in the entrepreneurial hot shops of inter-Continental travel.

Despite the depression, demand throughout the 1930s for Southampton non-stop luxury boat trains was exceptionally strong. The docks by mid-decade were used by over thirty separate shipping companies and hosted many new super-liners as trans-Atlantic traffic increased with new capacity. During the two days of 11 and 12 June 1937, seventeen large ocean liners arrived or departed representing some 430,00 gross tons of shipping handled by the port. Boat train schedules were indeed exceptionally heavy.[71] *Bremen* and *Europa* were often regarded as the spark that ignited the building of Europe's finest and most expensive inter-war express liners – many requiring some form of government intervention or subsidy. The German pair called regularly with *Bremen* in 1929 even using the floating dry dock to have her hull painted. *Normandie* on her maiden voyage from Le Havre on 29 May 1935 made a stop whilst the following year Cunard White Star's RMS *Queen Mary* began a thirty-year career on 27 May 1936 with regular crossings between Southampton and New York.

Juliet Gardiner observed (the *Queen Mary*) 'was a gamble that despite a world depression this luxury liner, this super ship, would enable Britain to recapture its prestige on the seas, would win the coveted Blue Riband for the fastest crossing of the Atlantic, and would rekindle a glamorous and moneyed lifestyle that seemed lost'.[72] Prior to her first voyage Cunard had to be persuaded to ensure the new *Queens* would make Southampton their home involving the construction of a new graving-dock for regular servicing requiring active intervention and direct supervision by Southern's general manager Herbert Walker who Simmons described as someone who 'grew to be the biggest man of all'.[73] The opening of the King George graving-dock on 26 July 1933, and the maiden voyage of the *Mary* marked the passing of the shipping crown from Liverpool to Southampton; a process Walker had always planned for.[74]

In April 1937 Cunard began a programme to look at other port capabilities for their new generation of super-liners, and in particular Plymouth's preparedness for managing the biggest of ships. *The Western Morning News* newspaper reported that the visits to Plymouth 'have clearly established the fact that the giant liner can be expeditiously handled in the port, and the travelling public have freely availed themselves of the opportunity of disembarking at Plymouth. By doing so they have gained many hours'.[75] The Great Western put on three distinct boat trains including the *Super Saloon* stock to accommodate passenger volumes. But it was New York's luxury liner row and Southampton the liner would be forever associated with.

By the end of the 1930s new super-liners just kept arriving. In 1938 the well-appointed 36,000-ton Holland America liner *Nieuw Amsterdam*, a vessel that lingered long in Dutch national affection and whose accommodation and public spaces were said to have created an atmosphere of refined comfort rather than ostentatious luxury, came into service followed the next year by Cunard's new 35,000-ton *Mauretania* joining the party.

The late decade also represented significant strides in luxury travel development across the panoply of trains, boats and planes. The early stirrings of long-distance commercial air travel came with the introduction of glamorous flying boats in a fast-developing international aviation industry. Pullman boat trains found a new niche. In March 1929 passenger and air mail services were launched to India using a combination of land planes, flying boats and rail facilities. As aviation enthusiast Mike Phipps observed it was all part of 'Imperial Airways' grand plan, with British Government backing' to provide air services to the Empire.[76] In July 1938 Imperial made Southampton a permanent home with

Cunard-White Star Line.

Maiden Voyage of R.M.S. "QUEEN MARY"

London-Southampton   May 27th, 1936.

Luncheon 4/-

MENU

Grape Fruit Cocktail
Tomato Juice Cocktail

Salmon Mayonnaise

Grilled Lamb Cutlets
Green Peas - New Potatoes
or
Roast Chicken - Ox Tongue
York Ham - Pressed Beef
Salads Various

Chartreuse of Fruits
Fresh Fruit Salad and Cream

Cheese - Cress - Biscuits

Southern Railway initiated a series of maiden voyage boat train specials with locomotives displaying commemorative headboards. The *Queen Mary* commercially was a highly successful liner carrying at times a full complement of passengers requiring a host of special service trains on arrival and departure days. Her maiden voyage required five separate boat train movements. The first of these was made entirely up of prestigious Pullman stock creating a lasting representation encapsulating a whole new era of exclusivity, luxurious settings and pampered, western lifestyles. The railway company's best-looking Lord Nelson Class locomotives were on duty to haul the boat train. No. 852 Sir Walter Raleigh leads the special RMS *Queen Mary* Pullman train on to the dock's estate bringing passengers to join the new Cunard-White Star liner. A special maiden voyage lunch was also prepared by Pullman chefs to commemorate the London-Southampton trip. In the third image Leslie Carr was once again called upon again to mark such an exceptional occasion in British life. (*Above left*: Getty Images; *Above right*: J&C McCutcheon Collection)

FIRST SAILING of R.M.S. "QUEEN MARY"
from SOUTHAMPTON
WEDNESDAY, 27th. MAY

COMBINED RAIL   Including Rail from WATERLOO   10/6 (Children)
& SEAT TICKETS   at 1.18 p.m. and reserved seat   5/3
                       at SOUTHAMPTON DOCKS

COMBINED RAIL   Including Rail from VICTORIA at   25/- (Children)
& STEAMER TICKETS   10.45a.m EAST CROYDON 11.1 a.m   12/6
                       to NEWHAVEN and CRUISE
                       the Channel to SOUTHAMPTON WATER

BOOKINGS ALSO FROM CERTAIN SUBURBAN STATIONS.

TICKETS STRICTLY LIMITED.
BOOK IN ADVANCE AT STATIONS.

Ask for handbill giving full details
at S.R. Stations.

SOUTHERN RAILWAY'S SOUTHAMPTON DOCKS

a mile-long 'runway' off Netley, plus the existing slipway and sheds at Hythe.[77] Imperial Airways *Empire Flying Boat Services* were first moored at a terminal at Hythe and then Berths 107 and 108 at Southampton Docks. The International Empire Air Mail Scheme began in stages; South Africa June 1937, India and Malaya the following February and the third and final stages to Australia and New Zealand between June and August 1938. A particular feature of the air mail service were cheap postal rates intended to encourage the volume of correspondence to and from the Empire. Hythe, as a result, was retained as a maintenance base as air mail volumes increased substantially.[78] And to service the Empire routes came newly designed aircraft - the Short 'C' Class Empire flying boats – to ferry accompanying passengers, many of whom were employed on government business, but also a group of prosperous customers making private journeys. Aviation writer Leslie Dawson reminds us there was clear demand: 'the Australian service took nine days instead of the thirty required by ocean liners'.[79]

From 6 June 1939, Southern Railway boat trains were adapted for a new audience. Part-Pullman trains hauled passengers into Southampton where relatively small numbers of privileged travellers were transported fast, conveniently and in luxury to new air routes served by Empire flying boats around the globe. Platform seventeen at Victoria station was nominated as the new Imperial Airways Terminus for International Empire Flying Boat services and close to Imperial's new London Victoria HQ 'Airways House' in Buckingham Palace Road where overseas passengers completed airline travel formalities including having their weight and that of their luggage recorded. Passengers embarking on European journeys by land plane were ferried to Croydon by motor coach. According to the *Birmingham Post's* 'Women's Interests' correspondent, the new building's designers were to be complemented for the way they took into account the comfort of women passengers whose numbers were significantly on the increase by the mid-1930s, accounting for some 30 per cent of all air travellers. They commented in a 'Travel Luxuries' column:

> In the basement of the building there is a spacious lounge, off which opens the women's rest-room. This is panelled with Empire woods, has upholstered armchairs and a carpet so soft that footsteps make no sound. The toilet room into which it leads is surrounded by separate cubicles hung with heavy and beautiful

curtains of old gold satin patterned with coral that matches the coral carpet and chair-seats. Each cubicle contains a washbasin, dressing-table and mirrors, and by drawing the curtains a passenger is quite private and can make a change of clothing. The company has thoughtfully provided daylight lamps over the dressing-table besides all manner of toilet necessities.[80]

Most Imperial train services were in the evening as flying boat departures were scheduled for the early hours of the following day. Everything was in keeping with a first-class travelling environment. The home route between London and Southampton Docks was only temporary as the prospect of war looming in Europe meant facilities were only fully utilised for two and a half years. The first outing of the *Imperial Airways Empire Special* was a high-status occasion. Just a short walk from the company's Victoria Terminus, passengers found a well-groomed Southern Railway T9 4-4-0 Class no. 338 locomotive for the journey to Southampton Docks. The T9s were ideal engines for what was not a heavy train – commanding and quick – and more than sufficient power in reserve to handle the relatively short carriage formation boat-train if it was held up en route. Passengers, nonetheless, travelled in some style. The part Pullman service carried commemorative headboards displaying *Imperial Airways - Special Train*. On arrival, travellers were met by uniformed officials and taken by coach to the South Western Hotel where they would be called at four o'clock before being taken by coach again to the dockside terminal building prior to boarding the awaiting aircraft.[81]

By November 1939 the airline merged to create British Overseas Airways Corporation (BOAC). As a result of war, operations in 1940 were moved along the coast to Poole Harbour where they remained until 1948; Southampton attracted too much attention from the German Luftwaffe. Special Pullman trains known as 'Ghost Trains' or 'Hush Hush' ran from London Victoria to Bournemouth West station carrying many high-ranking officials to all parts of the world on Poole Harbour flying boats or land-based aircraft operating from Hurn Airfield.[82] Pullman services, known as *Bournemouth Air Specials*, continued anonymously throughout the war years. Passengers on the evening departures were not able to see much from Pullman car windows as heavy curtains blacked out views. With the transition to peacetime, Poole's BOAC operations were kept busy; throughout 1945 VIP passengers, mainly British

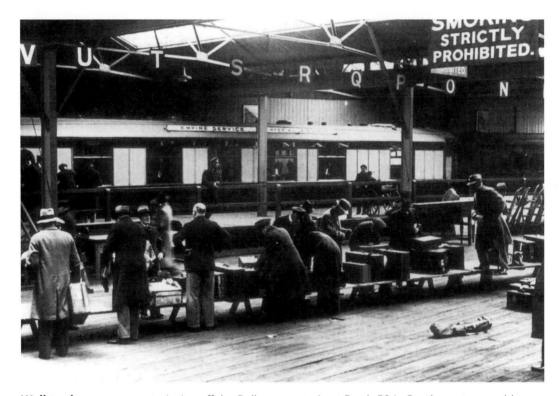

Well-to-do passengers traipsing off the Pullman car train at Berth 50 in Southampton would have made do with liquid refreshments or light snacks (similar to *Brighton Belle* Pullman fare) since many would have eaten at the Imperial Airways Terminus basement restaurant beforehand. When opened the restaurant was positioned as one of London's finest new air-conditioned eateries and described as an 'Oasis of Quiet' away from rush and bustle of the vast travel centre building. The 'Smoking Strictly Prohibited' notices at Southampton gave passengers, when they were collecting their luggage, a clear warning that they were close to the high-octane surroundings of awaiting flying-boats in the docks area. The limited number of passenger weight-restricted suitcases also provides a strong indication of their eventual flight destinations rather than the mountains of luggage that might normally be encountered with ocean liner voyages from the port. (Mike Phipp Collection)

and Allied military and government officials, continued to arrive by Pullman train with overnight stays at either the Harbour Heights or Sandacres hotels ready for early-morning departures. A sure sign that normal life would once again resume came with an announcement that from 1 January 1946, civil aviation was permitted.[83]

Alun Booth who edited *Brats*, a magazine for retired British Airways cabin crew, did several trips on the Bournemouth Pullman flying boat train in his early career later recalling his experiences:

I worked on the Pullman during the autumn of 1945 before flying on Lancastrians. I was based at Airways Terminal in Buckingham Palace Road. There were two Pullman carriages, about thirty seats with tables in each. The crew for each Pullman was a steward, a chef and a second steward (commis waiter - me). We left early evening and served dinner on the way to Bournemouth, and the journey took about two hours. The tables were ready laid with table clothes, cutlery, condiments etc.

We took soup plates out and then served soup with a ladle from a large tureen, not easy with the movement of the train, even if you had Cunard feet! The Pullman steward would sell and serve the wine. The main meal would have the meat served on the plate, and silver service for the vegetables; remember rationing was still enforced. Coffee was served from coffee pots, black or white. When the meal was finished the steward, chef and I would wash and pack all the dishes. After arriving in Bournemouth, I think the passengers were taken to Harbour Heights Hotel in Sand Banks. We two apprentices also went to Harbour Heights, where it is possible, we slept in the attic!

The next morning, after breakfast, the passengers would be taken by coach to Poole Harbour or Hurn for their flight. We would then, with the passengers who had just arrived from overseas, go to Bournemouth Station to return to London. The Pullman steward and chef would have restocked the train for the lunch, which we served, returning to Victoria Station.

The days of the *Bournemouth Air Specials* were limited though, as flying boat services were gradually replaced by new and faster land-based aircraft capable of transoceanic flight. As post-war Britain emerged from the ravages of war; Southampton regained its position as the country's foremost ocean liner port. The nation had been almost brought to its knees and bankrupted in the process, but despite war damage the port was relatively quick to recover its dominant position as the country's premier gateway to the world. Southern Railway (and later British Railways Southern Region) responded almost immediately not resting on laurels bringing new forms of profitable upscale traffic. Southampton boat train operations provided the railway operator (Pullman, was gradually assimilated in to new the nationalised ownership), with a captive customer base until the end of the 1950s. New first and third-class carriages provided a modern twist; Bulleid sets nos. 350-356 were

A rather unusual view of Southampton's glamorous brand-new Ocean Terminal taken from the rear of the bridge of one of Cunard's *Queens*. The quayside shows a network of rail lines which apart from bringing passengers to the terminal allowed freight to be delivered alongside to speedily replenish ocean liners. The Ocean Terminal, conceived by Southern Railway at the height of Art Deco design popularity, was eventually completed by British Railways. Its long-awaited construction was put on hold to avoid wartime bombing by enemy aircraft. When it finally arrived, its shore facilities, like those of New York's luxury liner row, set the seal for another rather shorter but equally golden age of gracious travel. As Britain entered a new decade, the unveiling of the modern styled building ushered in another era of combined rail and sea luxury travel captured by iconic pictures. Locomotives, hauling heavy loaded boat trains alongside the world's greatest liners, delivered and sped away from the port, London bound passengers in a highly efficient manner. (Associated British Ports Collection/Southampton City Museums)

often used for prestige Ocean Liner boat train formations. And the old adage of travelling in style aboard a boat train was not completely consigned to another age as some, especially for the *Mary*, as Pullman services continued with the opening of the city's new prestigious Ocean Terminal.

Southampton Dock's new Ocean Terminal was opened by the then Prime Minister Clement Attlee on 31 July 1950. New travel facilities introduced glamour, style and a certain degree of swagger at a time of austerity for the clear majority of British citizens. Despite post-war soberness, the building became synonymous with modernity and iconic images of the giant Cunarders - RMS *Queen Mary*, RMS *Queen Elizabeth* and the SS *United States* together with the many Pullman boat trains that connected directly alongside. By the early 1950s Southampton was entrenched as the country's leading passenger port and had never been busier. Aside Cunard's super-liners, the company (having quietly dropped the White Star brand) adapted to new trading conditions building smaller liners, primarily using the port, that were equally at home making line voyages and with the holiday cruise market.

To aid the travelling spectacle, the biggest of liners were back on duty although there were notable omissions. Canadian Pacific's pride of fleet, the *Empress of Britain* was a war-time casualty. France's flagship *Normandie* caught fire at Pier 88 in New York whilst converted for troop carrying duties, and later scrapped in October 1946; German super-liner *Bremen* suffered a similar fate gutted by fire at Bremerhaven in 1941. What was left of her superstructure was towed to Nordenham and sunk on 1 April 1946. But there were new faces too; the declaration of war in 1939 prevented the *Mary's* sister *Queen Elizabeth* and from making her commercial maiden voyage from Southampton until after the war. Likewise, the new United States Line flagship, the 33,500-ton liner *America* launched in August 1939 did not commence her commercial trans-Atlantic duties until November 1946.[84]

Royal Mail Line's *Andes*, a contemporary luxury ship plying South American routes, was a new addition to Southampton's shoreline from January 1948. The original plan was for *Andes* to make her maiden voyage on 26 September 1939 to celebrate the centenary of the original RMSP company, but war got in the way forcing her to serve time as a troop carrier before post-war conversion back to a luxury liner. As Bill Miller comments, 'She was intended and promoted always for the 'upmarket'

Two contrasting views of railhead ocean liner terminals; one at Southampton and the other at Plymouth. Southampton's new building was on a much grander scale than anything else previously offered to ocean going passengers in Britain. Passengers simply did not have to walk far. The look and feel of the building were rather different to traditional railway architecture better reflecting the new upscale facilities first coined at Imperial Airways/BOAC's Victoria terminus. Facilities for all passenger classes were considered luxurious by standards of their day with spacious waiting areas, dedicated baggage areas and spectator galleries as well as a host of other amenities to aid the international travelling experience. Whilst Southampton's Ocean Terminal had a far more grandeur appeal, post-war liner trade at Plymouth was no-nonsense as passengers trooped off both glamorous French Line ships as well as increasing numbers of combination liners. Millbay Pier's waiting rooms were refurbished in a mix of styles that included a new refreshments bar. (Associated British Ports Collection/Southampton City Museums)

trade'.[85] Royal Mail Lines' South American operations put the region's capitals, with their fabulous European infusions, very much on the international tourist view. Two innovative American vessels of the early 1950s – *Independence* and *Constitution* were the first fully air-conditioned luxury liners built. Many Americans were deeply fascinated with how their southern neighbours conducted their lives. Over the years Madison Avenue had created a strong regional image; Buenos Aires and Montevideo were perceived what we call today as 'cool destinations', whilst Rio de Janeiro was promoted as the most beautiful city in the world whose natural assets and lifestyle were uniquely cultivated by an infusion of Brazilian music genre and dance styles. By the late 1950s the Bossa Nova and the Samba became strong cultural icons driving visitor interest. In 1958 this fusion coincided with the commencement of regular operations of Moore-McCormack's new luxury liners, *Brasil* and *Argentina*, and their popular line voyages and cruises to South America. Both vessels were expressly designed for South American traffic, fully air-conditioned, spacious and comfortably attired carrying a little more than 550 passengers all in first-class. Life on board exuded a festival atmosphere where guests were actively encouraged to participate in entertainment and shows.

In many ways everything offered at the Ocean Terminal might be considered somewhat superfluous, since travellers boarding leading liners from the 1920s had incorporated sophisticated and substantial on-board shopping mall facilities. Gone were the bloated luxuries of the past, but on some British liners these were akin to the Edwardian idea of upscale shopping arcades, whilst Germany's inter-war super-liners were cultural icons of modernity. Professor Bernhard Rieger describes *Bremen's* shopping area as 'a temple of consumerism' reflecting standards expected by American travellers used to New York's built environment of fine new hotels and apartment buildings.[86] However, it must be remembered the port attracted huge numbers of visitors; the vista of arriving and departing oceans liners was a powerful tourist gaze. Waving goodbye to friends and relatives was slightly less frenzied; the vaguely hazardous pursuit of boarding a liner was made easier with the Ocean Terminal's power-operated gangways.

In the inter-way years, Southampton's consolidation as the leading liner port was already in play; Liverpool, London and Glasgow continued to provide secondary support with Plymouth still acting as a port of call. Post-war Southern Railway relaunched their boat trains as large vessels with scheduled worldwide sailings were returned to civilian use. Southampton's commercial passenger and cargo services resumed normal activities again, but the position at Plymouth was about to alter as the new nationalised railway saw no reason to provide competing boat trains to Millbay. In a few short years, many shipping lines - Cunard, P&O, Orient, United States Lines and other smaller firms - began withdrawing their Plymouth stops leaving Southampton as the premier port.[87] CGT French Line vessels were the only pre-war shipping line to continue using Plymouth as a port of call. By 1963 British Railways Western Region ceased all boat train operations from the port.

Southampton with its double daily tides had capacity with the Old (or Eastern) Docks serving a variety of shipping lines with predominantly smaller liners, whilst the New (or Western) Docks built in 1934 could accommodate large super-liners. P&O was also allocated a permanent berth. Steam hauled expresses standing alongside grand liners next to the cavernous structure of the Ocean Terminal set the tone for the period. Maritime author William Miller described the time in one of his many titles as 'Boom Times: Heyday of the 1950s'.[88] The port was an extremely busy place as boat trains serviced the most prestigious liners reaching the docks from Waterloo in just over an hour and a half. The Ocean Terminal's ground floor island-type platform was over 1,000 feet long and able to accommodate two full-length boat trains simultaneously.[89] By 1952 passenger liner traffic volumes had started to reach a pinnacle. Railway author Tim Bryan remarked 'By the 1950s over 6,500 boat trains were handled at Southampton annually.'[90] In one twenty-four-hour period ending 16 September 1955, thirteen liners entered or left the docks requiring nine special down trains and eighteen up specials including two trains that had to be diverted to London Victoria to avoid congestion. The standard coach roof board – *Ocean Liner Express Waterloo Southampton Docks* – was still applied to Pullman stock.

A new generation of streamlined cased Merchant Navy Class Pacific 8p locomotives were introduced by Southern Railway. Named after British shipping companies well-known to the public, these powerful engines hauled some of the heaviest express loads. Named trains created an exclusive club for passengers as many boat trains carried Pullman carriages for first-class passengers praising a luxurious feel for New York travellers, and for those sailing further afield to destinations in South Africa, Australia and New Zealand. The great post-war liners were supreme symbols of national prestige, culture, cuisine, and hardly surprising the newly nationalised railway company would not seek to capitalise on this heritage. In the years before the coming of the jetliner and the 1960s assault on class and privilege, each ship bestowed a unique character and personality of its own. Whilst notions of traditional luxury might have gone out of fashion, the Atlantic Ferry's key vessels were much loved by people travelling on them embellishing a period never to be replaced.

As previously mentioned, it was not completely one-way traffic as the United States Line *America* was joined in 1952 by the SS *United States* providing further competition for Britain's national maritime flag carrier. The vessel was the largest American passenger ship ever built and constructed with a dual purpose designed for military action if ever needed. She was equipped with impressive aircraft carrier type engines and rumoured to have achieved

The *Queen* *Mary* and *Queen Elizabeth* were the last of the large prestigious liners to have survived intact from the 1930s with their original owners. With these vessels Cunard had both the fastest and largest liners afloat helping to maintain an illusion, before the SS *United States* arrived, that Britain still ruled the waves practically having the North Atlantic luxury runs to themselves. The ships nearly always had a full guest complement as this busy *Queen Elizabeth* Southampton arrival from 1952 shows. First-class Pullman stock awaited their passengers. Yet not all boat trains carried named locomotive headboards as in the second image. A Cunarder leaving alongside the *Elizabeth* indicates a busy Atlantic crossing for the super-liner. Headed by no. 34094 West Country Class *Mortehoe*, the boat train's carriage mix suggests that a Pullman service has already departed. The Spam Can's early tender emblem and inclusion of blood and custard coach stock is likely to place the boat train in the undated photograph, probably made up of tourist class passengers, around the mid-1950s. (Associated British Ports Collection/Southampton City Museums)

some forty-five knots during her sea trials. The new US flagship's accommodation was designed to a modern style, but with fire resistant asbestos replacing the opulent wooden panelling found on the *Queens'* interiors, there was a rather unsmiling element to her due to a requirement for immediate conversion for use as a troopship within twenty hours' notice. Nevertheless, she was tastefully decorated maintaining a special American allure as on her maiden voyage, she smashed the Blue Riband, taking some ten hours off the *Queen Mary's* best time and setting a record for a passenger liner that still stands today. The SS *United States* was undoubtedly built for speed operating with good passenger loads throughout the mid-part of the decade. So much so, that a sister ship was even considered by US authorities for a while. Yet few passengers would be aware crossing the Atlantic was about to change forever in the coming years as regular jet engine air services were introduced.

Against this backcloth no small wonder why British Railways Southern Region in the early 1950s decided to name a series of boat trains for Southampton's ocean liner expresses. Boat expresses were bestowed with specialist titles connecting shipping lines to the port they used. Waterloo reverberated with high-status ocean liner workings as Cunard and United States Line were initially all-Pullman. *The Cunarder* and *Statesman* pulling away providing lasting images of the port's boat train era. Henry Miller's immortalised phrase of one's destination is never a place, but rather a new way of looking at things was rather appropriate since well-heeled and tourist-class American visitors headed to Britain and Europe in their droves. And it was important for British Railways to record these premier arrivals and departures with specially named stock. *Cunarder* was the first on 2 July 1952 followed by *Statesman* a week later on 8 July. Prior to July 1953 most boat trains using Southampton, apart from Cunard and United States Line traffic, did not possess the distinction of a named headboard. This was all about to change mirroring a general trend amongst British Railways to name many express trains.

The era of the Southern Region named ocean liner expresses had begun in earnest. These two expresses were certainly the most prestigious titled boat trains carrying distinctive locomotive headboards and Pullman carriage roof boards. Due to the comparatively short journey time from London, full catering was not provided on the Pullman boat trains. Buffet type services akin to those provided on the *Brighton Belle* were more in tune. Six former Hastings line Pullman cars together with the Hadrian Bar used on the east coast route were allocated for boat train duties in 1958, but they lost their distinctive liveries and were painted in Southern Region green. By 1963 the Pullman's had had their last run on British Railways Southampton boat trains.

This early shot of the *Cunarder* all Pullman boat train is recorded at Eastleigh in 1954. Headed by West Country Class no. 34102 Lapford, she was a relatively new locomotive having only entered service in March 1950 whilst retaining her un-rebuilt form until withdrawn in July 1967 as one of the last operational steam locomotives on British Rail Southern Region. In the second photograph is another *Cunarder* shot at the popular Eastleigh location with its nearby workshop sheds was taken a year later on 1 April 1955. Headed by West Country Class no. 34005 Barnstaple being a locomotive that had a direct Southern Railway pedigree from July 1945. Whilst *Cunarder* was portrayed as an all Pullman service, as this shot demonstrates, from time to time, additional standard blood and custard carriages were added to the train's formation especially where standard first and third-class passenger volumes did not warrant a second relief train. (*Above and below*: Colour Rail)

The Waterloo-Southampton route became home to a succession of specially appointed boat trains represented by a cross-section of shipping lines - some home-based, some foreign-owned - who regularly used the port providing a very valuable passenger stream. In 1953 three shipping lines were immediately bestowed with ocean liner boat trains. One of these was Holland-American Line, a long-established Dutch shipping line principally operating on the North Atlantic. With liners such as *Nieuw Amsterdam* and the smaller *Maasdam* they made regular trans-Atlantic sailings between Rotterdam, Southampton and New York. The official naming of Holland American boat train came on 15 July 1953 and with it a practice that continued for the best part of the next fifteen years as the company maintained regular trans-Atlantic and cruise sailings. Signposting more modern and luxurious vessels to come from Holland America, new liners were still made big news stories. In December 1956 *The Sphere* reported on the near competition of SS *Statendam*:

> A break has been made with tradition in that the customary two masts which no longer serve any purpose on a modern passenger liner have been replaced by this single radar tower. The maiden voyage of the new liner is from Rotterdam on February 6, 1957. She will call at Southampton on February 8 outward bound on her way to New York.[91]

Launched on 13 September 1958, the distinctive and sleek-looking SS *Rotterdam* became one of the North Atlantic's Grande Dames noted for its ability to transform itself from a two-class specification on trans-Atlantic crossings to a single-class luxury cruise ship. The ship's single mast became a feature of Holland-America Line, but the company's combination of line voyages and attractive cruise programmes became a regular feature of Southampton maritime life. In a throwback to earlier days of elegant ocean travel, the new and completely air-conditioned *Statendam* undertook two successive world cruises from the port. Operating as a single-class luxury ship with limited numbers of passengers, an itinerary involving 111 days of global cruising she visited twenty-three countries and twenty-seven ports capturing public imagination. The running of named boat trains to and from the port worked well for the company, and with the coming of a new decade, Holland America positioned itself in up-market press as the most elegant way to travel to the US and Canada. It also had

A Holland American boat terrain departs Southampton Ocean Terminal bound for London Waterloo with passengers from one of the company's ocean liners. The non-appearance of the Holland American vessel suggests a rapid turnaround as the ship continued its voyage to Rotterdam. The boat train in this photograph is hauled by no. 30773 King Arthur Class Sir Lavaine which was withdrawn in February 1962. The dating of road vehicles and the sparkling condition of the locomotive suggests a late 1950s setting. (Associated British Ports Collection/Southampton City Museums)

flagships that were contemporary, and despite being Dutch owned, priding itself with bilingual staff and crew. Typically, advertising copy spoke of 'Headed by the £13 million flagship, SS *Rotterdam*, the Holland-America Line possesses the most modern Atlantic fleet. Stabilisers. Completely air conditioned. The Food and Services are superb. Most rooms have private facilities. Yes, "it's good to be on a well-run ship."' From Southampton.[92] With the popularity of air travel, the *Rotterdam* was retired from Atlantic Ferry duties in 1969 continuing as a single-class cruise ship after a major refit. The ending of the named boat train operation eventually ceased the following year, the company being one of the last recognised European shipping lines to end their New York runs.

Union Castle Line was an old established Southampton regular. The shipping line had three named services for their regular

In this shot Battle of Britain Class no. 34062 17 Squadron with its Holland American named board is being prepared for departure from Southampton Docks. The date of the photograph is unrecorded but the rather dirty and dishevelled nature of the re-built locomotive would probably point towards a point in time at the end of her career when 17 Squadron was removed from service in June 1964. (Colour Rail)

4.00 pm Thursday afternoon sailings to South Africa; *Union-Castle Express* from 16 July 1953, *Springbok* from 1957 and *Union-Castle Safmarine* from 2 February 1966. Modern looking mail ships such as *Transvaal Castle* appeared in 1962.

Royal Mail Line's named train - the *South American* – was allocated on 9 October 1953 for their South Atlantic routes. The company's flagship *Andes* had established herself as main vessel in true luxury liner style on the River Plate trade and was considered as the way to travel to South America until she was replaced by new ships in 1959 before moving into the cruise sector. Typical itineraries involved an *Andes* winter cruise sailing from Southampton on 10 January 1961 and returning to the port on 28 February. The extensive itinerary included Las Palmas, Barbados, Jamaica, Vera Cruz in Mexico, Antigua, St. Lucia, Trinidad and Tangier. Fares were not cheap though with accommodation ranging from £495 to £1,220.[93]

The colourful Greek Line - its funnels sporting a North Atlantic livery of yellow, blue and black, with roots going back to 1939 - was traditionally linked with operating on the southern Mediterranean

Many of the carriage prints found in the compartments of British Railways era coaches were illustrated by Richard Ward. His mid-1950s depiction of an ocean liner express at Southampton features one of the lavender hulled Union Castle liners. Whilst not of the size and dimensions of Cunard's super-liners, they were still nonetheless commanding vessels, offering South and East African passengers enhanced travel facilities for the duration of their voyages. Little wonder, the shipping line was afforded named train status. The aerial view shows three vessels from the company's fleet in port. The facilities afforded at the New Docks scheme were extensive. In this shot Berths 101–108 were served by a wide-ranging rail system that brought boat trains alongside liners. A new carriage shed, adjacent to the Flour Mill constructed in 1934, provided a resource to house boat train coaching stock for a who's who of the shipping world including Cunard, P&O, Orient Line, Union Castle, French Line, NDL and United States Line. Union Castle was ultimately awarded its own dedicated liner berth in 1960. (*Above*: Courtesy of Greg Norden Collection & www.travellingartgallery.com; *Overleaf*: J&C McCutcheon Collection)

route crossing, but by 1953, the company according to advertising records began operating a regular service from Southampton to Canada (Halifax) and the US (New York) with different call combinations at Cobh, Dublin and Belfast. Bremerhaven was the origination of the new Atlantic route service as the company sensed a business opportunity with westbound migrant trade as the West Germans had yet to return to the market. Pride of the Greek Line fleet was the 23,000-ton liner *Olympia* - the first and only new build for the company - entering service in October 1953.[94]

There was a certain degree of prestige involved with the setting up of a named boat train since *Olympia*, a thoroughly modern and good-looking vessel (considered in some British shipping line circles to be rather brash), offered totally segregated first and tourist-class passenger sections, and perhaps, a throwback to the floating palace arrangements of the early twentieth century. The ship, however, was not fitted with stabilisers, and was later re-assigned duties after a number of rough crossings to calmer Mediterranean waters

Greek Line joined the Southampton named boat train express business in May 1954. Recorded at West Byfleet on 7 May 1963, the boat train is headed by a British Railways Standard Class 5MT no. 73118. It is a more unusual example of mainline boat train workings, indicating traffic on this particular nine-carriage train was lighter and did not warrant prestige Pacific class motive power. In the second Greek Line photograph from September 1963, West Country Class locomotive no. 34009 Lyme Regis is seen crossing Canute Road at Southampton Docks with a special boat train working. Lyme Regis in its re-built form looks to be turned out rather well and would remain on steam duties until October 1966 until she was withdrawn. (*Above and below*: Colour Rail)

operating between Piraeus and New York. *Neptunia*, *Columbia* and *Canberra* were smaller, elderly old-school ships operating on the Atlantic Ferry and considered as ideal vessels with the company pitching its business on the settler trade with regular sailings from Liverpool (and Southampton from) £50.00. TSS *Colombia* and *New York* sailed on the Canadian Trade from Liverpool to Quebec and Montreal calling at Belfast for emigrant business. By the early 1960s, Greek Line joined a plethora of shipping lines cruising in and out of British waters. Unfortunately, their 20,000-ton *Lakonia* was destined to become an ill-fated liner making headline news when she caught fire off Madeira in December 1963 and sinking with the loss of 128 lives. Sister ship, *Arkadia*, originally launched in 1931, brought many survivors back to Tilbury. This ship was eventually taken out of cruise business in December 1966. Progressively the company spent most of its time in the sector until the shipping line folded 1975.

Arosa Line was a later addition to the bank of the port's shipping lines and in 1955 issued the prestige of a named boat train. The company's main ships were the *Arosa Sun* and *Arosa Star* operating with UK and Ireland agents, J.D. Hewitt & Co, based at 109 Jermyn Street, London SW1. Hewitt's advertised the company's main Canadian routes extensively across regional press. Apart from the line's regular service, some journeys commenced in Bremerhaven with a main Southampton, Montreal and Quebec crossing. In the summer of 1955, the company inaugurated a new route from Southampton to Halifax and New York. *Arosa Sky* was promoted as a 20,000-ton vessel with extensive air-conditioning which at the time was still a relatively new phenomenon. Advertising extolled the ship's outside cabins - many amidships - with attractive public rooms, high-class cuisine and good facilities for children. First-class accommodation was available on all the company's liners, but the main push was towards tourist-class passengers pitched with excellent accommodation facilities and a trans-Atlantic crossing priced from £50.00. Perhaps as a sign of things to come, the Canadian route was changed in 1956 to St. Johns with a direct railway link to Montreal. Unfortunately, the business ran into financial difficulties, and the relationship with Southampton and the specialist boat trains ending prematurely around September 1958. Despite Arosa's problems, Italian line, Sitmar, was also became a latecomer to the named boat train business in 1960.

Post-war Sitmar Line took over two old American aircraft carriers, stripping them, and turning them into sumptuous one-class ships taking emigrants, on charter to Australia and New Zealand. The company, by the late 1950s, positioned itself as Sitmar Line of Genoa, operating a comparatively small fleet of single-class air-conditioned and low economy liners. In June 1956 their *Castel Felice* liner provided Canadian services from Greenock to Quebec and Montreal. From the mid-1960s Sitmar found a niche on the North Atlantic operating new low fare sailings from Southampton-New York aboard the same 12,000-ton vessel. Yet the company's main commercial focus was for intending Antipodean emigrant passengers, particularly from the north-east of England, Scotland and Northern Ireland hard hit by the closure of traditional industries and targeted in shipping line promotion. It was a format that worked well with regular Southampton sailings as the same regional advertising approaches were still employed ten years later.

In January 1968, Sitmar acquired Cunard's *Carinthia* and *Sylvania* liner pair providing accommodation for up to 1,600 passengers for

Being coaled at Eastleigh, Battle of Britain Class locomotive no. 34087, 145 Squadron sporting the Sitmar Line badging is being made ready for boat train duties. Boat train headboards were stored at the front of the Eastleigh steam shed in an old coach body. An undated photograph, 145 Squadron was re-built in December 1960 and performed duties on Southern Region until electrification in July 1967. Given its rather dilapidated state, it suggests the photograph was recorded towards the end of the locomotive's career. (Colour Rail)

service between Britain, Australia and New Zealand. By April 1970, the company began converting the vessels in Italian yards for their own purposes at a cost of some £14 million with respective renaming of *Fairland* (later *Fairsea*) and *Fairwind*. During the same year Tenerife and South African ports joined the list of Sitmar's line voyage itineraries, pitching the shipping line up against the well-entrenched Union Castle and P&O operations but with newly designed one-class vessels such as the *Fairsky* and *Fairstar* which was the former Bibby Lines emigrant vessel *Oxfordshire* converted for her new role at a cost of £2.3 million. In November 1971 Sitmar announced a merger of their marketing interests moving marketing, sales and ships' clearance business in to a new jointly owned venture operation with Shaw Savill Lines branded as Sea Travel Centres. In 1971 the company introduced Panama Canal sailings to and from New Zealand and, tackled the family reunion market that had not moved to the air at the time. However, the company recognized its blue-collar customer community. Advertising in the *Daily Mirror* was typical of the media they selected for their campaigns with a copy approach exploring the mystique of overseas travel coupled with the essentials of home such regular bingo sessions on board their ships:

> There's so much to enjoy when you sail SITMAR. All sailings are one-class, and if worried about currency, that means that you can enjoy everything that a SITMAR voyage provides – Fabulous food, Top class entertainment, Full air conditioning. Plus, those lazy days sunbathing round the pool, making new friends and discussing the next port of call. If worried about currency, remember, all purchases made on ship are in sterling and at shipboard prices! Value for money, you can't beat it - your own floating hotel taking you to your destination, calling at places which most of us have only dreamt of.

Despite having a traditional customer base Sitmar though was innovative introducing new international culinary themes for guests described them in promotion as 'festive food ships'. Even in the 1970s shipping lines such as Sitmar still played to the still relatively low cost of longer sea passages which was balanced against the quickness and more expensive nature of air travel. One particular voyage was required for *Fairstar's* winter cruise repositioning and the newly discovered mass-tourism cruise market in which Australia and New Zealand would assume such a prominent destination role but also as a cruise tourism generating market. *Fairstar* had also entered the British cruise market the previous year with a series of fourteen-day cruises from Southampton to both the Mediterranean and the Atlantic Islands. The vessel was particularly well-equipped with a swimming pool, cinema, casino, gymnasium, lounges, seven bars, lots of deck space and with Italian ownership, guaranteeing a mix of traditional and more exotic Continental style cuisine. Some 80 per cent of her cabin space had en suite showers and toilets. For the 1974 summer season, Sitmar came up with a completely new set of home port cruise itineraries described in advertising as 'eleven dazzling cruises'.

Two British shipping lines P&O and Orient Lines that had had long-held relationships with the port – the firms actually merged in 1960 under the P&O – Orient Lines marque which was

Recorded at Eastleigh, West Country Class locomotive no. 34022 Exmoor looks well-groomed for an outing for one of P&O's premier liners. The photograph taken on 6 August 1961, suggests the railway authorities placed considerable attention towards servicing the passenger needs of this venerable British shipping line institution. Exmoor was another of the bank of the re-built Pacifics that saw out their days in July 1967. The new and colourful condition of the *Oriana* named board suggests (at this stage) it has been well-looked after in its Eastleigh storage. (Colour Rail)

later shortened to P&O - did not feature in this list although the new company's flagship vessels *Oriana* and *Canberra* in 1961 were bestowed with named titles for the company's cruising and Australia duties.

By 1961 the newly merged shipping line were positioning themselves for premium business by marketing first-class return fares to Australia for £290.00.[95] Other former corn-coloured hull Orient Lines ships – a set of three post-war constructions – were connected to Southampton. *Orcades* used the port for Mediterranean cruises in the early 1950s whilst sister-ships *Oronsay* and *Orsova* operated from the UK on the Australian passenger routes. P&O also had an extensive post-war reconstruction programme to make good-war-time losses forming part of a strategy to build larger but faster vessels operating on the Australia service. Before the amalgamation of the two shipping lines, and notwithstanding both London and Southampton operating centres, boat trains never

Ready for a Waterloo departure, West Country Class locomotive no. 34041 Wilton, still in its original Spam Can form, is steaming up at Nine Elms. Recorded on 25 July 1965, Wilton was one of those West Countries that remained in un-rebuilt construction until withdrawn in January 1966 and probably accounts for the locomotive and the *Canberra* headboard's rather abandoned state. (Colour Rail)

carried named titles. Despite undoubted and successful cruising developments taking place throughout the 1960s, the combined P&O operation had excess capacity as passengers deserted the sea for the air with far quicker aircraft services to Australia. In 1967 the chairman reported to the AGM that P&O had 'to face up to the fact that fleet of 11 passenger vessels has more accommodation to sell than any hotel group in the country'.[96]

Trans-Atlantic travel also changed dramatically during later years as ideas of glamour and romance of combined rail and ocean travel disappeared with the mass transit airliner. The original *Queens* saw out their days replaced by Cunard's new flagship *QE2* who spent more of her sea time on cruise duties than New York line voyages. There was less reliance on public transport and the named boat train became less important as travellers turned their attention to the car and individual transport to and from Southampton Docks. By 1967 steam locomotive hauling of even the most important boat trains was at best very intermittent, and indeed, the rare appearance

Right at the end of named boat trains, steam traction could always be guaranteed to garner considerable public attention in this 1967 shot. A *Cunarder*, alongside the *Queen Mary* at Southampton's Ocean Terminal, awaits instructions to proceed out to the dock's gates. The boat train is headed by an old Southern unshakable no. 34090 Sir Eustace Missenden in re-built form and probably very shortly before finally being withdrawn from service in July 1967. (Colour Rail)

of a *Cunarder* or *Statesman* headed boat train progressively lapsed from the following year. Even before this, the placing of locomotive and carriage roof boards was something that gradually fell out of favour with most of British Railway's regional management structure. The practice of headboards attached to replacement diesels ceased, and a sad reflection of British Rail's modernist corporate ideology.

Despite the introduction in 1966 of the Queen Elizabeth II passenger terminal – firmly fixed on the car as the primary means of transport – *Ocean Liner* boat trains were now the last link in the grand tradition of luxury liners. By the mid-1970s the vast majority of them would slowly make their final journeys to breakers and scrap yards around the world, ending a glorious era that lasted for the best part of ninety years. The dockyard lines and the mainline connection to the Ocean Terminal lasted for some time but were eventually ripped up.

Plymouth Millbay: GWR and British Railways Western Region Ocean Mails boat trains

For much of the second half of the nineteenth century, and as recent as the 1960s, it was an exceptionally important port of call for mail and passenger traffic. It was, however, never regarded by shipping lines as a home station which in many ways is ironic since Plymouth, like Portsmouth, had always enjoyed the security of a large Royal Naval presence. The docks at Millbay had been joined to the rest of the Great Western's network by the South Devon Railway since 1850 and was specified as the Ocean Mail Port to handle British Government mail contracts. The GWR over time developed first-hand experience running fast and efficient boat train services – known as Ocean Liner Expresses – collecting and delivering both passengers and mail with an assortment of carriages and vans for sorting mail and specialist bullion stock whilst attracting the attentions of the world's leading shipping lines. Aside these attributes Plymouth also enjoyed an ideal position situated at the mouth of the English Channel acting as a conduit to other north European liner ports; the English ports of Southampton, Dover and London, Boulogne, Cherbourg and Le Havre in France, Antwerp in Belgium, the Dutch ports of Rotterdam and Amsterdam and Bremen and Hamburg on the North German coast. This cemented Plymouth's access to the Channel stimulating additional American and European passenger and mail traffic as the port benefited from half a day's steaming time over Southampton and a day over London and Liverpool. The development of Southampton as Britain's premier liner port ironically worked to Plymouth's advantage (particularly as Fishguard fell out of favour at the end of the Great War) as it was the first eastward point for the all-important Atlantic mail drop as well as other shipping originating from all corners of the globe.

Up until 1910 there had been significant competition for Plymouth boat train business before the LSWR bowed out having been badly bruised. GWR and LSWR's competing West Country services had been involved in many skirmishes over the years, as an ever-expanding merchant marine presented new freight, mail and passenger conveyance opportunities. The 1870s saw the opening of the Suez Canal, and a corresponding growth in trans-Atlantic shipping representing a sustained period of expansion for Plymouth and its handling of burgeoning worldwide ocean mail business. There had been several commercial tussles between the two railway companies but, perhaps, none was more graphic than the headlong engagement GWR and LSWR had with each other as they looked towards the spoils of blossoming port of call passenger liner business. By 1878 the GWR not only owned the Millbay Docks entrance but controlled the entire mainline from Paddington to Plymouth and the docks.[97] To meet liners, initially subject to tides, the first six-wheeled GWR sleeping cars appeared on the route in 1877. By 1881 they had been replaced by eight-wheeled narrow body corridor stock (so that they could be easily adapted for standard gauge running in due course) which contained six double-berth compartments with three lavatories, a pantry and considered to be 'far superior to anything on offer by the London & North Western Railway or the Great Northern Railway'.[98]

This lay the groundwork for future GWR boat train and ocean mail operations as by the next year the company could run express trains into the docks area adjacent to East Quay with its passenger waiting rooms. By the end of the 1890s there were considerable improvements at Millbay to enhance travelling experiences prompted by LSWR's Stonehouse Pool developments. Some railway writers have considered the GWR was rather smug in its treatment of passengers, and facilities availed to them in late-Victorian times; the company only to be rocked out of its complacency by its near neighbour the LSWR. This appears to be a consistent theme across many railway companies at the time with many loath to improve the quality of passenger journeys only forced into practical improvements through competitive pressures. The GWR had grown accustomed to regular revenue streams from Plymouth mail and bullion traffic, but to be fair to the organisation, a considerable level of capital and management time was invested in the conversion to standard gauge aligning all its carriages, locomotives and operations to the reduced width. But by the end of the century, the GWR was in a far better shape to fashion more comfortable and speedier rail travel. As shall be seen the company had its eyes on the prosperous American visitor market adapting a whole series of integrated and smart travel offerings considered quite revolutionary at the time. Curiously, the Great Western never took the opportunity of branding its own boat trains for American tourists in a way both the LNWR and LSWR did.

In 1906 When the company was promoting the new main line to the west of England, GWR took the time to include a number of visiting German journalists who were in London on a special train to Plymouth. As part of the occasion the party was then entertained to a trip around the Sound on one of company's tenders; no doubt the opportunity was not lost by GWR officials to emphasise the importance of new German trans-Atlantic liners calling at the port on eastbound crossings.[99] The GWR and LSWR were competing aggressively to secure trans-Atlantic passengers departing and landing at Plymouth Sound. From the 1890s the two companies offered dedicated quality boat trains often running with just five or six carriages catering for an upscale clientele. The LSWR set was a pretty luxurious affair although the company had experimented with Pullman cars on the Southampton and Bournemouth lines since the 1890s, but not on the West of England line. Despite the introduction of dedicated stock, LSWR's serious challenge to GWR's supremacy on the Plymouth routes ended by the end of the first decade of the 1900s. Effectively, the company had seen off their competitors assault maintaining lucrative bullion and mail contracts and conveying prosperous passengers wishing to disembark liners at the earliest possible opportunity. Up until that point the two companies had fought hard to maintain their respective liner traffic shares over the different routes to Plymouth. However, the competitive nature of the spat ended when the LSWR *Ocean Special* crashed at speed in Salisbury. Plymouth liner traffic by 1910 was left to GWR whilst LSWR turned its attentions to developing its own Southampton patch.

It was now a case accepting GWR's 'comfortable' carriage stock (though not necessarily truly luxury), or otherwise continuing on board ship to Southampton where LSWR's American boat trains would whisk one off to London. The problem was not all trans-Atlantic liners heading further east stopped at the port with some passengers having to make-do with tender transfers off the Isle of Wight. Yet it was not all bad on Great Western boat trains. The company had a new generation of modern-looking elliptical Toplight carriages, new dining cars with separate first-class sections separated by the kitchen car, and it took control of LSWR's prestige sleepers. All of these could be employed on Plymouth *Ocean Mails Special* boat trains depending on first-class passenger volume making the disembarkation on to the company's tenders in Millbay Sound. So, it was the number of passengers who determined the boat train's composition, its look, feel and facilities offered which might vary from a few passengers to several hundred international travellers.

The 1920s and 1930s were a golden era for steam hauled railway travel, but also a highly productive period for passenger shipping firms and GWR's own Plymouth *Ocean Liner* workings. The liner reigned supreme whether for line-voyages or for the fast-growing inter-war cruise market. First-class provision on ships remained exceptionally strong and in order to cater for this demand, railway companies responded to the needs of prosperous passengers by building new much admired and fast ocean express boat trains transporting travellers (and lucrative mail traffic) rapidly to and from London. Joint promotion between railway and shipping companies ensured joined-up prestige luxury train services enabling first-class passengers disembarking great ocean liners to reach London in the shortest time possible. These arrangements were not entirely new. Cunard and White Star Line had been providing their passengers with these types of facilities for the best part of forty years. During the period with much increased passenger liner volumes, Great Western Railway and Southern Railway still participated in a few commercial tussles to attract an increasing cohort of valuable customers. The Great Western had its Fishguard Harbour white elephant, technical running rights into Southampton Docks where port access was only achieved via a rather circuitous and comparatively slow route, and regular, though relatively small-scale, passenger volumes at Avonmouth, Bristol. Passenger liners also called at Welsh ports of call which formed part of GWR's home patch. United States Line's *George Washington* was the largest liner to have used Queen Alexandra Dock in Cardiff in 1928. The *Derby Daily Telegraph* noted 'a special boat train is being run today at 2.30 pm by the Great Western Railway from Paddington to Cardiff, in connection with the sailing of the Canadian Pacific SS *Montrose* on her initial trip, from the great Welsh port to Canada. Other sailings have been arranged for May 4 and May 27 and the United States liner SS *George Washington*, will again land American passengers at Cardiff this year'.[100] Cardiff was two hours and forty minutes by express boat train from London competing well for international passenger shipping line traffic with Avonmouth.

With little home port activity by the end of the 1920s, the Great Western decided to concentrate its efforts on developing services to cater for liners stopping at Plymouth. Whilst taking longer to reach London, it still saved passengers a minimum of six hours steaming time over Southampton docking. Where was demand coming from? Plymouth had always been an important port of call landing mail and passengers and according to writer Alan Kittridge between the years of 1921 and 1928, Plymouth's annual liner calls almost doubled to 708 with the figure peaking in 1930 as the port received 788 liner calls of which 682 were for homeward bound arrivals.[101] GWR's official position of business volumes was slightly less.[102] Many of the North Atlantic calls in the 1920s were for intermediate liners including Germany's NDL ships (an association with Plymouth that had begun in 1904 for their medium sized fleet), *Columbus*, *Stuttgart* and *München*, smaller United States Lines ships that made regular eastbound Plymouth calls, Red Star's *Belgenland* and CGT French Line who possessed a raft of superb liners like their exciting and grandly fashioned *L'Atlantique* very much in the stylistic visions of the *Île de* France. In addition, as well as their express liners *Paris* and *France* all offered high quality culinary provision designed to attract American travellers who did not take to US-owned vessels caught up with alcohol prohibition. After all, crossing the Atlantic was perceived as a celebration.

By the late 1920s, France was beating a path towards a lucrative American customer base who wanted a gallic travelling experience and convenient British landings by promoting in their marketing literature the slogan: 'Plymouth direct to New York as the route that cuts off the corner!'[103] Plymouth was conveniently located to land London bound tourist passengers providing CGT French Line and their European shipping counterparts; dropping off in the Sound for travellers wanting a British itinerary and then progressing to

Continental destinations with the balance of passengers. Whilst these vessels enjoyed first-class provision the real game changer in the luxury segment came with a new generation of large luxury liners or the super-liners, they were soon set to be called. With regular Plymouth calling, Holland America Line introduced *Statendam* in May 1929 followed later in the year by NDL's Art Deco styled 50,000-ton super ship *Bremen*. During the 1930s the United States entered the fray with two moderate-sized 24,000-ton sister liners *Manhattan* and *Washington*. Maritime historian William Miller suggests the vessels were 'considered by some to be America's ultimate and even grandest liners and proudly carried the flag in the fiercely competitive North Atlantic trade, sailing in competition against the likes of Cunard, the French Line, Holland America and Hapag-Lloyd'.[104] When *Manhattan* arrived at Plymouth on 30 April 1935 kicking off the American trans-Atlantic holiday season, some 400 US passengers landed boarding three separate GWR Paddington boat trains.[105] Plymouth Sound was proclaimed as the 'Gateway into England from the Atlantic Ocean' by the GWR appealing to American visitors to 'Land at Plymouth'.[106] Railway historian Dr Alan Bennett noted the city was 'the first port of call for many of the prestigious trans-Atlantic shipping companies in the inter-war era, Plymouth was the railhead for vast numbers of American tourists eager to get to London to embark upon their various pilgrimages'.[107]

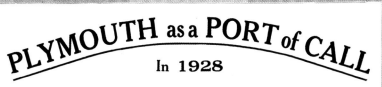

PLYMOUTH as a PORT of CALL

In 1928

653 HOMEWARD-BOUND OCEAN LINERS CALLED
representing
25 IMPORTANT SHIPPING LINES with SAILINGS between BRITAIN and ALL PARTS of the WORLD.

35,766 PASSENGERS LANDED, most of whom travelled by SPECIAL or ORDINARY GREAT WESTERN RAILWAY EXPRESS TRAINS to LONDON, SAVING at least ONE DAY compared with the SEA JOURNEY up CHANNEL.

OVERSEAS TRAVELLERS for all parts of GREAT BRITAIN, NORTHERN and MID-EUROPE should LAND at PLYMOUTH.

THE GREAT WESTERN RAILWAY EXPRESS TRAIN SERVICES offer UNEQUALLED FACILITIES for RAPID TRANSIT to LONDON, BRISTOL, BIRMINGHAM, LIVERPOOL, MANCHESTER, SHEFFIELD, LEEDS, GLASGOW, ABERDEEN, EDINBURGH, NEWCASTLE-ON-TYNE and EAST COAST PORTS with STEAMSHIP CONNECTIONS to CONTINENTAL PORTS.

Write to the Superintendent of the Line, Great Western Railway, Paddington Station, London, W.2, for all travel information.

Certainly, a numbers game with an almost obligatory Plymouth mail drop, it is little wonder many passengers took the opportunity to use the port to either board or land from liners. The mail drop guaranteed an awaiting *Ocean Mails Special* with corresponding passenger carriages. Facilities at the station head were not too bad either even if there were delays (not unheard of) to GWR boat trains or ship tenders. (Illustrated London News Ltd/ Mary Evans)

As soon as passengers had arrived from liner tenders and had negotiated customs, they were free to board the boat train. Carriages would have been moved by shunter into the closed area of the of East Quay's docks station. This photograph taken on 1 May 1931 shows a hive of activity as passengers (their luggage having already been transferred on to specialist baggage vans or brake coaches), made their way on to awaiting first and third-class carriages. One of the peculiarities of the East Quay docks set up was the lack of station platforms as passengers had to board coaches by way of wooden steps. In the second photograph, a GWR Castle Class locomotive is waiting for mail sacks to be loaded by conveyor on to the Ocean Mails vans from the Sir Walter Raleigh tender. Mail vans would be carried at the front of the combined mail/boat train. Typically, carriages featured in the above shot would be under the station roof as pictured at the rear of the of the train. (*Above left*: Associated British Ports Collection/Southampton City Museums; *Above right*: Alan Kittridge/Douglass Hoppins Collection)

Given the quality visitor flow, the Great Western quickly responded to ferrying well-off customers to London in record times. By focusing its attentions on Plymouth, which always had a strong Anglo-American appeal, the capital could be reached in around four hours by rail, and a major attractor instead of staying on ship for the best part of another day. Departing Plymouth boat trains hauled by King and Castle Class locomotives represented some of the country's most powerful examples of steam traction at the time.

In 1929 following discussions with the Pullman Company, special high-speed dedicated Pullman boat trains were put on running between Plymouth and Paddington. Seven Pullman cars were delivered to GWR and used within the formation of its prestige *Plymouth Ocean Liner* workings.[108] Yet the foundation stone between the Great Western and Pullman was not built on solid ground as in September 1930, the company decided to end its temporary relationship with the Pullman Company by pulling the recently launched *Torbay Pullman* service and Pullman boat train provision.

By 1931 the Great Western had produced its own equivalent high-quality carriage stock introducing new Super Saloon coaches for Plymouth boat trains. GWR was now able to service America's nouveau-riche used to comfort, quality, service, and most importantly speed (especially those from the business community and fellow travellers on a tight visiting schedule) with typical Great Western style and panache. Of all the Big Four railway companies the GWR had an inherent brand advantage in so far as its name had not changed at grouping but, more importantly, the company's name was known to Americans largely as a result of the sustained and consistent marketing investment made by the company over the years in securing US visitor traffic. Bennett describes the considerable efforts the Great Western made selling itself to the American market in the inter-war years providing the company with several bites of the cherry; early landing, the south-west destination itself (very popular with Americans), and Plymouth Super Saloons heading off to Paddington in record times.[109] Likewise, GWR guru Peter Semmens commented 'During

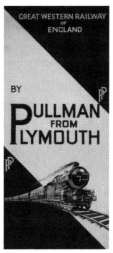

The ***Plymouth*** *Ocean Mail Pullman* is seen here alongside platform 8 of Paddington station in November 1929. The use of gleaming new Pullman cars on Great Western proved to be a short-lived experiment as the company subsequently decided to replace Pullman with their own luxurious stock. The second image features the inside spread of a GWR pamphlet promoting Pullman boat train services produced in 1929 and targeted particularly at prosperous and time-conscious US travellers. The American market was one the company understood well with travel representatives operating in New York from the turn of the twentieth century. As part of the strategy to attract visitors to England, GWR also produced joint publicity material in conjunction with Southern Railway. (*Above*: STEAM, Great Western Trust Collection, Southern Railway Publicity, *Overleaf*: Great Western Trust Collection)

ENGLAND
via PLYMOUTH

LAND AT PLYMOUTH AND SAVE A DAY! This is the slogan of many thousands of overseas travellers who have experienced the advantage of travelling via Plymouth. They make the journey from Plymouth to London in a sixty-miles-an-hour express train instead of prolonging the sea voyage. The time-saving boon which the Plymouth route affords is apparent. Substituting speedy train travel for a continued sea voyage up the English Channel with the possibility of sea-fog and other delays, London is reached in just **4 hours** by Great Western Railway.

Luxurious Pullman Car Special Boat Trains are run from Plymouth Docks to London (Paddington Station) for the day arrivals of principal liners at Plymouth, including:

Cunard Line - -	S.S. "Mauretania."
French Line - -	S.S. "Ile de France."
	S.S. "Paris."
	S.S. "France."
Holland America Line -	S.S. "Statendam."
	S.S. "Rotterdam."
United States Line -	S.S. "George Washington."
	S.S. "America."

For the added convenience of passengers, tickets may be obtained from the Pursers on board these Steamers between New York and Plymouth to cover all charges which need be incurred for disembarking and entraining at Plymouth—viz., labour charges, etc., at the Docks, conveyance of passengers and a reasonable amount of baggage and reserved seat in Pullman Car Special Train to London. The cost of these inclusive tickets is—1st Class, 61/- ($14.85) Adults; 35/6 ($8.65) Children.

In the case of Liners reaching Plymouth at night Special Sleeping Car trains are run to London, private berth and "couchette" sleeping accommodation being provided. The supplementary charge for a sleeping car berth is 15/- ($3.65) additional to the 1st Class fare.

Passengers not requiring Pullman Car Reserved accommodation or Sleeping Berth may obtain tickets on board the Liners inclusive of Dock Dues and journey to London by Boat Special Trains at the following fares:—

1st Class - 51/- ($12.42). 3rd Class - 32/2 ($7.83).

(Dollar figures calculated at 4.87 to the £1 Sterling current rate of exchange).

SKETCH MAP of the GREAT WESTERN RAILWAY of ENGLAND.
Route of PULLMAN CAR OCEAN BOAT EXPRESSES, PLYMOUTH to LONDON, shewn in Red
226 miles in 4 hours

REFERENCE

- Great Western Railway Main Lines
- Great Western Railway Branch Lines
- Lines over which G.W.R. has running powers
- Railways with which G.W.R. run in conjunction

THE GREAT WESTERN RAILWAY, in its 8,000 miles of track traverses the finest river, valley, mountain, woodland and pastoral scenery in the British Isles, and serving, as it does, so many places which are linked with Anglo-American history and literature, offers unique attractions to the visitor from the United States. Its connections extend as far north as Chester, Birkenhead, Liverpool and Manchester. It passes through the Shakespeare Country and picturesque Western Midlands; North, Central and South Wales; the Valleys of the Dee, Wye, Usk and the Severn; the Counties watered by the River Thames; and of course, as its name implies, through those beautiful West of England Counties, Somerset, Dorset, Devon and Cornwall. At least twenty-one Cathedrals may be visited by its various lines. In a word—to travel on the Great Western Railway is the surest means of seeing the best that England and Wales has to offer, and by landing at Plymouth, travellers substitute a mile a minute in the train for a considerable journey by sea to a more distant port.

the grouping it was the GWR which put some remarkable running with boat trains from Millbay to Paddington, and its finest rolling stock was to be built for such services in the 1930s.'[110] In defining the company's carriage stock Jenkinson noted they were 'redolent of confidence, authority and prestige in their dimension and luxurious interiors'. Opulent carriages, the Super Saloons most certainly were 'probably the grandest vehicles built for general service' and 'unashamedly up-market and aimed at the high-class clientele of the trans-Atlantic liners.[111]

The Super Saloons (and the later Centenary Stock) were the company's 1930s flagship coaches designed to showcase premier workings.[112] Collett used approaches with distinctive and definitive designing rivalling other major railway companies of the period as both LMS and LNER were making such incisive strides in coach design, comfort and riding quality.

Super Saloons were named after immediate royal family members, whose special permission had to be sought; in reality the Prince of Wales was seen aboard White Star line's finest trans-Atlantic vessels at the time and would have had no problem with any recommendation. The weight of the Super Saloons also caused problems in the numbers of carriages that could be worked in any

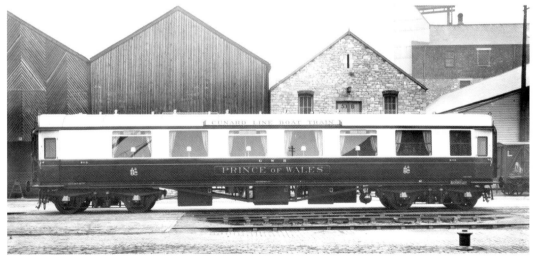

Prince of Wales was one of the luxurious named carriages of GWR's Super Saloon set. A first-class supplement was payable with the stock specifically designed to attract well-to-do patrons stepping off ocean liners at Plymouth. Anything Pullman could do, GWR felt they could do better, and this seemed to be the company's Swindon mantra. Their launch, unfortunately, coincided with the arrival of the depression years of the early 1930s and a dearth of income generating US passengers affecting most luxury train operators across Europe at the time. (STEAM)

given journey, and with additional restrictions on route workings elsewhere within the Great Western network. A total of eight separate bow ended railway coaches with running numbers 9111 to 9118 were constructed to the maximum loading gauge on the Great Western route. They were grand affairs and often described as the most luxurious carriages ever built by the company. They were fitted out in true Pullman style with interiors of light-coloured walnut, interior sliding doors with burr veneered panelling and an open style of thirty well-upholstered free-moving chairs; these were very heavy and did not move once the train was moving. The Super Saloons would be a welcome sight for hard-pressed prosperous passengers who might have endured a difficult Atlantic crossing. Yet due to their weight, the dedicated Plymouth boat trains never operated with more than five Super Saloons and two full brake luggage coaches helping to preserve an appearance of exclusivity. As with Pullman services, passengers were charged an additional premium of ten shillings each way on top of the first-class fare.

The Plymouth Super Saloon boat train carriages were fitted with brackets on the side of the roofs to support Ocean Special coach boards and for individual shipping lines like 'Cunard Line Boat Train' and 'French Line via Plymouth'. CGT French Line ships *Paris* and *France* had returned to Plymouth in 1922 whilst two years later the *De Grasse* was introduced on the New York service together with several smaller vessels calling in both directions on Caribbean routes. The Great Western maintained a tight grip on Anglo-French business so no small wonder the stock should be used for special occasions such as the company's maiden voyage of their new liner *Colombie* in 1931. Although Cunard and White Star Line operated their premier ships out of Southampton, Cunard would use the Great Western Plymouth route as and when required, especially with bad weather delaying Atlantic crossings or where vessels, from time to time, encountered mechanical problems. Boat trains could be involved in hilarious episodes. The *Western Daily Press* reported on one such occasion in November 1933 regarding the travails of a US traveller who missed his Plymouth connection:

> An American visitor to the country, a Mr Wise, arrived at Paddington Station, yesterday, to discover that he had missed, by a few seconds, the 3.30 p.m. special from Paddington to Plymouth, which connected with the French liner *Champlain*. Mr Wise not to be outdone, entered into negotiations with the

Whatever the social class of passengers arriving or departing from Plymouth, they would funnel into GWR's station waiting room. The company undertook a makeover of facilities at the enlarged shore-based waiting rooms situated at the base of the Pier Hotel. They created a certain degree of elegance when they were completely refurbished showing a simple décor design, bright and stylish, and in stark contrast to the heavy, Victorian interiors of before making it popular with the many American travellers. With awaiting boat trains once, passengers had emerged from the customs halls, Plymouth's facilities accommodated up to 170 passengers in one go. (Associated British Ports Collection/Southampton City Museums)

company and decided to catch the 4.30 train to Plymouth. It was arranged that the train should be specially wired from signal box to signal box that there should be no delay on the journey. But this train arrived at Plymouth at 10.14 and the *Champlain* left the dock a few minutes after 10, Mr Wise, however, took no chance and commissioned a speed boat to await him at the dock in order that he might chase the liner.[113]

Many non-Southampton based liners continued to use Plymouth as a port of call. On eastward crossings GWR's plush boat trains provided onward fast connection and access. Yet several factors led to comparatively short lives for their intended use. The first few years of the decade saw passenger volumes decrease due to the depression and its lag effect on confidence, shipping lines adopted slower speed policies to reduce fuel bills (particularly on Atlantic runs where a competitive market operated) together with a gradual relocation by shipping firms to using Southampton as the main UK passenger port. As Rex Pope observed: 'International travel, especially that of Americans, remained depressed throughout the

1930s.'[114] Consequently, Plymouth boat trains often comprised just two or three Super Saloon carriages as first-class traffic declined rendering the service uneconomic, forcing GWR to look for alternative uses for its specialist carriage stock. However, the Super Saloons size impaired their use over many Great Western and shared line routes. From a tourism perspective they were simply not practical for GWR's popular land tours pitched at up market patrons. The Great Western had made serious investment but the emergence of Southampton as the nation's home port meant the Super Saloons venture never made serious returns for the company. In many ways, they were regarded as white elephants with the company scrambling to find other revenue earning streams. Five of the original carriage stock, fortunately, have made it into preservation.

The one part of the Plymouth boat train operation that made money from the early part of the twentieth century was the *Ocean Mails Specials* driven by the volume of ships from all over the world landing mail. When GWR and LSWR boat train competition ended in 1910, the fast transit of international mail bags increasingly became the crucial feature of GWR's operations which also went on to include government mail contracts at Bristol and Fishguard. The focus changed somewhat as boat trains became mail trains with passenger accommodation rather than passenger trains that carried mail. Plymouth landings were convenience led and not luxury led (GWR's traditional rational), leading to a position where prosperous passengers had to make a trade-off for many years, until the company smelt the coffee of customer change in the mid-1920s and the rapid change of thinking.

Into the nationalised era British Rail's Western Region operated boat trains to Plymouth up until the early 1960s when liner trade suddenly declined irrevocably as the result of jet aircraft replacing liners as the primary means of international travel. The focus in the first half of the 1950s continued to be on boat trains running with both mail baggage vans as well as passenger carriages as record numbers of mailbags were handled. This proved to be short-lived as new mail contracts were gradually awarded to airlines rather than shipping lines. Whilst a mix of different types of ships continued to arrive, on 16 November 1961 Plymouth received its last trans-Atlantic superliner port of call visit. The end of an era and the Ocean Special boat trains was imminent.

As soon as the tender arrived with both passengers and mail, it was all hands-on deck so to speak to ensure mails were unloaded and on to GWR's Ocean Mail vans as quickly and efficiently as possible. The manual loading of mail bags by large numbers of dockers gave way to a more efficient system when an electric conveyor belt was introduced in 1927 equipped with its own landing stage next to Millbay's Princess Royal Pier. Most mail was destined for Paddington, although an adapted mail van could be employed and slipped at Bedminster for mail to Bristol and the north of the country. Similarly, Ocean Mails traffic was handled in a similar manner with Bristol Avonmouth's regular West Indian banana boat arrivals. (*Above and below*: Alan Kittridge/Douglass Hoppins Collection)

Plymouth Stonehouse: LSWR American boat trains

Along with Great Western, there is also the obvious story of LSWR's involvement running Plymouth boat trains. From the commencement of the modern shipping era, the company was determined to compete head on with GWR for passenger liner traffic. LSWR's acquisition of the port of Southampton in 1892 saw significant expansion of maritime facilities, but it would be several years before this all bedded down. In the intervening period there was an adjustment to the port's traffic as increasingly British, American and European shipping companies began using Plymouth as a port of call. It must be remembered at the tail end of the Victorian period Britain's ports were all vying for supremacy with competing interests and all jostling for position. In 1893 the LSWR decided to invest with new port capacity building a railway terminus at Ocean Quay on Stonehouse Quay, Plymouth to support increasing liner traffic. This included sumptuous first-class *American Eagle Express* coaches built to aid the development of Southampton for trans-Atlantic passengers. This internal corridor and lavatory stock were also applied to Plymouth ocean liner boat trains as well as utilising the new station set up for their existing Jersey and St. Malo English Channel crossings. GWR because of its Ocean Mail Port designation handling British Government mail contracts, had mail traffic and the first passenger pickings coming off liners, but the American Line opportunity alerted LSWR to the potential share of passenger business. In early December 1903, a telegram issued by the company in New York made known its intentions. 'It is officially announced that the American Line steamers running from New York to Southampton will from January land mails and passengers at Plymouth and Cherbourg.'[115] Not that the Great Western would easily hand over business to its great competitor. On Christmas Eve, the company announced its plans for the Devon port's working relationship with the American Line:

> Mr J.C. Inglis, the general manager of the Great Western Railway, authorises the papers to state that his company has received instructions from the Postmaster-General and the American Line respectively to make arrangements for the conveyance of passengers and mails which are expected to arrive at Plymouth in the New Year.

The Dartmouth & South Hams Chronicle commented:

> This settles a question which has excited some interest ever since
> the American Line decided to make Plymouth their English port
> of call for their homeward-bound steamers. Messrs Curry and
> Spence, representing the line some time ago visited Plymouth
> to ascertain for themselves the nature of accommodation the
> two railways could for dealing with new traffic. Extensions and
> improvements at Richmond Walk, Devonport seemed to indicate
> that the L. and S.W.R. Company were making a bid for it.[116]

A compromise split the spoils – GWR Ocean Mails traffic and
LSWR passengers – the latter decision of little surprise, given the
company's long-term Southampton relationship with American
Line. As Peter Semmens duly observed, 'Back in the 1900s the
LSWR had worked the passengers to London off the trans-Atlantic
liners calling at Plymouth, leaving the mails to GWR to handle, but
that was in the days of the 'Great Way Round.'[117] Notwithstanding,
the upgrading of LSWR's Ocean Quay was considered a sound
move by the company justifying it decision to invest at its own
expense. The new facilities included a 350-foot island platform
with two well-furnished waiting rooms and buffet, baggage hall,
Customs inspection rooms together with railway enquiry, ticket
and telegraph offices. The island platforms included rail lines
on either side of the building allowing passenger boat trains on
one side and baggage and any mails on the other. In 1907 the
platform roof was extended allowing two *Ocean Special* trains to
accommodate passengers embarking or disembarking from its
own tender ready to ferry or return them from liners moored in
Plymouth Sound.[118] At the time, LSWR required passengers to
buy their own tickets for tender passenger landings bringing them
ashore from liners rather than GWR's practice of getting shipping
lines to invoice them directly and then swallowing costs internally;
a business decision the LSWR was later to change by waiving fees.

In 1903 West of England services were accelerated considerably.
The LSWR would use its L12 Class locomotives designed for express
passenger work hauling the ocean specials. On the Salisbury to
Exeter line they were rostered at Nine Elms, Salisbury and Exmouth
Junction where they shared ocean-liner duties with the S11 class.
In the same year, the valued American Line decided to call at

In an effort not to be completely outdone by LNWR's prestige Liverpool stock, LSWR provided bespoke carriage sets for its Plymouth *American Boat Express*. Drinks and snacks were provided by attentive staff to passengers. From 1901 the upgrading of *American Eagle* allowed passengers to make their way to a separate dining car where high class meals were provided which for American travellers mirrored Pullman conventions with practices, they were totally familiar with. (STEAM)

Plymouth on east bound crossings with the company's *St. Louis* arriving on 9 April 1904.

First-class passengers would receive meals in exclusive compartments. In 1907 the company felt it had to provide a more satisfactory service for prestige American passengers who were disembarked from steamers in the early morning. To accommodate early morning arrivals or departures and especially prestigious White Star customers who might use Plymouth, LSWR built its famous high-quality 56-foot long sleeping cars which contained seven single and two double compartments which were said to be exquisitely adorned with brass bedsteads and bed knobs.[119] Whilst this was an obvious luxury travel enhancement for weary passengers, they were not to everyone's tastes. By Edwardian times hand washbasins became a common feature in British sleeping cars, but it would take a further thirty-years or so for showers to be introduced to LNER first-class sleeping compartments – an on-board facility the US passenger had enjoyed for many years. Despite LSWR's investment, the service proved to be unsuccessful. The coaching stock was eventually sold to GWR as the company withdrew from running Plymouth boat trains. By railway grouping LSWR had no sleeping cars to call its own; the position only changing with the introduction of the specialist Wagon-Lits *Night Ferry* sleeping cars in 1936.

Like Liverpool Riverside, it was all about speed with liner and railway transfers. In the case of Plymouth LSWR encountered stiff GWR competition for prestigious boat train traffic. However, by 1903 West of England services were hastened. Whilst the two railway companies would try and create solus passenger arrangements with shipping lines, they would nonetheless at times compete for the same liner business. Both companies speeded up tender and Customs transfer arrangements. Passengers could be whipped away on their London bound journeys in less than an hour after liners arrived at Plymouth Sound. But it was on the rails that the real competition between the two companies began as they sprinted towards their respective London terminuses. GWR ultimately gained the upper hand, courtesy of new fast locomotive classes such *City of Truro* recording the first train in the world to travel at 100 mph and the opening of the new Castle Cary direct route to the west of England that considerably enhanced Paddington journey times. However, it was the fatal accident at Salisbury on 1 July 1906 that ended GWR and LSWR's 'London Races' for liner traffic. At best this disaster was described as 'spirited competition between the companies' whilst others took a more caustic analysis describing the races as 'ruthless and dangerous'.[120] The wreck of the Stonehouse American boat train was widely reported since it was carrying forty-two first-class passengers from the US liner *New York*.[121] Three *American Eagle* vehicles were destroyed in the crash, ironically happening on the same day as the GWR made its new West Country route announcement. It was important news but relegated to run of page reporting as newspaper coverage concentrated on the aftermath of the express train leaving the rails that left twenty-seven people dead.

Whilst the races might have been over, LSWR carried on with Plymouth liner trade launching a new tender *Atlanta* in May 1907 to cater for White Star passengers. LSWR made considerable media noise in supporting their major partner who had transferred their premier trans-Atlantic liners to Southampton. *The Sketch* reported the tender 'will transfer passengers and baggage to the Ocean Quay station, where a corridor dining-car train will be in readiness to leave direct for London (Waterloo Station). The same arrangements will be carried out for each of the steamships arriving at Plymouth on following weeks. All inward steamers after calling at Plymouth will proceed at once to Southampton, via Cherbourg, passengers being conveyed by special train from Cherbourg to Paris, and from Southampton to London.'[122] Despite these initiatives this was finally to no avail as on 13 May 1910 the LSWR conceded Plymouth liner traffic to its arch competitor. Passenger volumes varied and it appears LSWR never made money on its Plymouth Stonehouse boat trains deprived as it was of potential American Line mail traffic income (handled exclusively by GWR) to underwrite services. Very simply, the company could never rely on sufficient customers in a hurry to reach London.[123] The two companies finally signed a multifaceted West Country railway agreement which resulted in Ocean Quay closing the following year.[124] To the observer this may seem a trifle odd, but as background it must be remembered serious board-level discussions between the respective chairman had taken place regarding the potential sale of the LSWR to the GWR. The LSWR's financial performance relative to that of the Great Western had been underwhelming in the previous five years leading to investor disquiet.[125] LSWR's boat train traffic was now left to Southampton.

Bristol Avonmouth: GWR and British Railways Western Region Ocean Mails boat trains

Interaction by railway companies with shipping lines was something far from new. Since the 1840s the Great Western had positioned itself for a pivotal role in developing liner traffic to North America. Brunel had always declared that he saw the line from London to Bristol merely as a staging post to New York. Bristol's docks unfortunately, were always too small hampering the city's aspirations in the early days to become a prestigious passenger liner port. Bristol tried very hard but never received official British government recognition as an emigrant port. A new deep-water facility was constructed at Avonmouth, to the north-west of Bristol in 1877 providing shipping lines with access to the growing markets of the Mediterranean and the Americas. In that year, a rail link between the national system and the dock station was developed for freight traffic. Despite the launching of passenger services on 1 September 1885, dreams of a major passenger liner terminal at Bristol dissipated, scuppered by Liverpool's growing dominance. Bristol by the turn of the twentieth century was anxious to secure a proportion of trans-Atlantic liner as well as West Indian shipping business as a result of new port developments taking place down-stream at Avonmouth. An embryonic relationship between Bristol, Jamaica and the Caribbean were re-established after trade had declined significantly after the ending of slavery on West Indian islands.

A fledgling Imperial Direct Line from 1901 ran white-hulled refrigerated hold steamships (a technological development of the 1890s) from Avonmouth and the West Indies. These vessels were specially designed for the banana trade. Unripen bananas could be brought in bulk up the Bristol Channel in specially refrigerated cargo-liners that possessed modest passenger accommodation. Four new vessels were built using Bristol as the terminal port. The *Port Morant* was the smallest ship at 2,900 tons in 1901 with accommodation for forty-one first-class and fifteen second-class passengers. The three other ships, the *Port Royal*, the *Port Maria* and the *Port Antonio* were larger at over 4,000 tons with accommodation for one hundred first-class and fifty second-class passengers. The groundwork for a flourishing combined passenger and cargo operation was now in hand. With a fast-developing Port of Bristol infrastructure, GWR (and Midland Railway) could then ensure rapid distribution of perishable stock (whilst it was still ripening) in special developed fruit vans. Within ten years and with the aid of a government subsidy, the value of the trade had expanded significantly with business almost trebling in the Edwardian period. The exotic banana suddenly became big business and a staple part of everyday food. At first passengers who disembarked from cargo-liners had to make-do with an adapted jetty on the outside of the old Avonmouth Dock before vessels moved on to the main part of the dock to unload their cargos. Whilst the new banana business stream was welcome, Bristol's denizens – the Merchant Venturers – considered the city was falling behind other British ports still harbouring illusions of gaining a foothold on passenger liner trade. As *The Sphere* newspaper reported 'Bristol was really the kernel of adventure. Was it not from there that John Cabot and his daring sons started in the spring of 1496 and discovered Cape Breton Island and Nova Scotia?'[126] This continued throughout the first half of the seventeenth century as Bristol's mercantile buccaneers sought to develop viable opportunities with the new lands of the Americas. Men such as Martin Pring, an English explorer and expedition leader set sail from Bristol in 1603 to assess the commercial potential of present-day areas of the north-Eastern Seaboard and islands such as Martha's Vineyard, and in so doing, established a long-term relationship between the city and the region. By 1901 changes were afoot. *The Sphere* newspaper reported: 'By a big majority on a general poll of the inhabitants Bristol has now decided to spend nearly £2,000,000 on harbour accommodation.'[127]

Avonmouth's port facilities were extended with the building of the Royal Edward Dock opened by the King on 10 July 1908. In a rare example of commercial insight, the dock's entrance gates were extended so they could technically accommodate Cunard's express liners even though the GWR's Fishguard plans were well developed at the time. And there was considerable competition for the Canadian Trade as White Star's brand-new intermediate liners *Laurentic* and *Megantic* were built specifically for this fast-developing market, but within a few short years the dynamics of the Atlantic Ferry had changed as the Royal Edward Dock was now too small for Olympic class sized vessels.[128] Whilst the largest liners were scheduled for Southampton, Bristol considered its new Avonmouth facilities could capitalise on medium-sized cargo-liner opportunities. *The Sphere* reported on the developments of the past forty years which had transformed the area with 230 acres of land for industrial development mostly reclaimed from the River Avon. Added to this was a new railway infrastructure linking both the old and new docks with Bristol.[129] Within two years dedicated railway passenger facilities were built for the blossoming liner trade. Out-and-out boat trains now became a matter of course.

Notwithstanding Atlantic Ferry developments, Avonmouth's notable success with West Indian banana and passenger business raised its awareness amongst many shipping lines using a combination of other British ports. Traffic was made up of a profitable combination of perishable fruit, passengers and mail for the West Indies. By the time a titled Great Western boat train had appeared in 1909, the West Indies, as has been discussed, became an important warm-weather winter and cruise destination for wealthy citizens anxious to avoid the harshness of the British winter. From 1912, Imperial's parent company Elders & Fyffes took over the banana trade with new ships capable of bringing back thousands

The recently completed wooden construction docks station and passenger terminal built by the Port of Bristol Authority (PBA) in 1910 looks impressive enough having provided Canadian Northern Railway with a range of facilities they required for their recently launched Royal Line shipping business. This put Bristol and its port at Avonmouth on the Canadian trade map, affording international passengers a totally integrated travelling experience. The covered platform concourse was just a stone's throw from the ship which would be moored alongside in Royal Edward Dock. The spacious facilities in the customs hall, baggage examination rooms and open-plan parcels office provided travellers with a relaxed environment. Interestingly, the booking office contained ticketing arrangements for both Great Western and Midland railway systems and joint Bristol Temple Meads arrangements. By this time GWR had built a new single-track connecting route from Stoke Gifford, north of Bristol, to Holesworth Junction at Avonmouth. The PBA's new passenger terminal was now within 120 miles of London, and quick, comparing favourably with a Waterloo and Southampton Docks run. One ocean liner special in July 1910 carrying passengers and mail connecting with RMS *Port Kingston's* arrival at the Royal Edward passenger terminal is reported to have reached Paddington in just over two hours. GWR's Temple Meads network not only provided quick access to London, but also to Birmingham and Birkenhead, Wales and the south-west of England. Likewise, Midland Railway's transport connections to the rest of country came into view. Routes to Scotland and the north of the country were now reachable in hours. (*Above and below*: Bristol Museums P.B.A. Collection)

of bananas stems together with up to 200 fare paying passengers. The Bristolian banana trade became a long-lasting relationship only concluding in 1967.

Whilst the Canadian Pacific had piloted some services to St. Johns from Bristol Avonmouth from around 1907 it was not mainstream. But in 1910 the port was selected as a home port for the new Canadian Northern Steamship Company which had entered the trans-Atlantic liner industry with a new operation branded as the 'Royal Line'. *The Sketch* sounded:

> Bristol has been selected by the Canadian Northern Railway Company as the port on the British side for their new steamship service between Canada and England. The Port of Bristol possesses some of the finest docks in the country, and in the matter of railway facilities, it is particularly well served, situated as it is in the centre of main routes to and from the north, south east, and west, and being within two hours' journey of London.[130]

One mystery that seems to have grabbed many railway researchers is the lack of knowledge surrounding Great Western's *West Indian Boat Train*. Photographed at Swindon in 1909, the train's static shot shows it hauled by 4-4-2 Atlantic Class Albion. However, by not including the latest carriage stock, suggests the GWR service was not entirely in the same league as LSWR and LNWR's *American boat trains*, or indeed the company's own Plymouth ocean liner business. More likely, it was intended to support the Jamaican banana export trade with Bristol Avonmouth's famous 'White Ships' now carrying significant numbers of first and second-class passenger accommodation as well as an important West Indian mail contract. (STEAM)

Avonmouth was now on the Atlantic Ferry map with regular Canadian passenger liner sailings; a move cemented by Bristol's long-term historic ties with the country's maritime provinces. In March of that year, the Canadian National Railway went on a charm offensive with West Country press extolling is commercial competency since the organisation had been created towards the end of the Victorian era.[131] The company now had two large (and expensive liners even by Edwardian excesses), *Cairo* and *Heliopolis* which were originally commissioned by the Egyptian Mail Steamship Company to operate on the Marseille and Alexandria route. The ships delivered in November 1907 and February 1908 respectively spent a year operating in the Mediterranean's warmer climes, before the Egyptian Mail Steamship Company went bust in 1909 as a result of well-entrenched competition from other shipping lines including P&O. After both ships had been laid up in Marseille, they were acquired by the Canadian Northern Steamship Company, (a subsidiary of the Canadian Northern Railway) and converted for cold water operation. The ships were pretty luxurious affairs having been built for a first-class passenger. Fletcher noted a trend on Canadian passenger shipping business where many ships were adapted with only second and third-class specifications but not so with the Royal Liners, who quickly acquired a first-class clientele following of who's who in Canadian politics and society. Notwithstanding, renamed as *Royal Edward* and *Royal George*; their second-class apartments, according to Fletcher, were equal to the first-class of a few years ago.[132] It probably helped that the Royal Liners were original designed as single first-class specification vessels and were considered the most luxurious running to Canada. *The Cheltenham Looker-On* concluded:

> There is something distinctive in all the three classes of travel. First-class passengers, for instance, may rent what may well be treated ocean flats, these apartments being models of all that could possibly be desired in comfort and convenience. At a lower rate, the accommodation provided for second-class passengers is the very finest obtainable, while the third-class is quite unrivalled.[133]

The quality of third-class accommodation ensured a rapid stream of female clients particularly those from the domestic service sector heading for new lives and opportunities in the vast country. Despite the affordability of Atlantic trips not everyone was intent paying the fortnightly Canadian passage. In June 1911 the *Hartland and West Country Chronicle* reported thirty-six stowaways were found on the *Royal George*. The trip did not do them much good as they were detained with the Dominion authorities who refused to accept them and forced to work their way back to Bristol on the ship as firemen.[134] *Royal Edward* and *Royal George* made regular sailings from Bristol from late April 1910 initially to Quebec. A Canadian boat train was there to meet the ship as the Canadian Northern Railway system inaugurated its first express through service from Quebec to Toronto. The train was made up of thirteen splendidly equipped cars, carrying over 500 passengers. In promotion, the company said its future regular boat trains would be run from Quebec with through tickets obtainable to all parts of Canada, affording unsurpassed service from Great Britain. For the four years up until the Great War, the Bristol Canadian route was extended to include Quebec City and Montreal in the summer and Halifax in the winter. The ships, although fast and achieving record transit times between Bristol and Canada, were not ideal for wintertime trans-Atlantic operations acquiring a nickname of the '*Rolling Georges*'.

Whilst Bristol could not match Liverpool and Southampton for liner traffic, passenger business was still refreshing for shipping lines and Great Western and the Midland Railway alike. From 1910 regular Avonmouth boat trains to the port were a well-known sight. Regional press shipping notices were full of steamship line advertisements. Dominion Line had set up a Bristol office at Welsh Back, Elder Dempster and Co's similarly had set up an office in Bristol whilst their Imperial Line had initiated an extra call to Bermuda. In addition, there were specialist travel firms organising the thousands of free Canadian homesteads and emigration services to Australia and New Zealand.[135] By December 1914, with the *Rolling Georges* acquired by the government for use as troopships, Canadian Northern had put on alternative vessels for regular duty between Bristol and Halifax, the Standard Line had steamers operating from the port, Australia and New Zealand were catered for with direct services from Avonmouth, the Charles Hill organisation established the Bristol City Line with a freight and passenger service to New York, whilst Dominion Line ran Royal Mail steamers to Quebec and Montreal with an additional service to Portland, Maine.[136] Not an unhealthy volume of boat train activity but this was to be transformed with Avonmouth based troop movements in the coming war years.

The first images of the Canadian Northern liner *Royal Edward*, arriving at the Royal Edward Dock, Avonmouth from Quebec and Montreal is recorded on 29 April 1910. The liner was able to come straight into the dock without anchoring. Aboard her were about 360 passengers, including some of the members of a Bristol commercial delegation that had been touring the Dominion with a view to improving trade relations. Sources say they came back very enthusiastic with one member going as far to say that Bristol now had the opportunity of recovering her position as the second port in the kingdom. Later in the summer on 22 September's morning tide, *Royal Edward* made the fastest eastward passage on record, and a possible daily service of liners to and from Canada was suggested as a future development. The first consignment of Canadian peaches was brought by the Royal steamers, for distribution to Bristol, Cardiff and Birmingham. The experiment was carried out by the Department of Agriculture, Ottawa, and from it, it was believed, the line could build up considerable fruit trade through Bristol.

Considerable planning went into developing the Royal Edward Dock infrastructure equipping it with a passenger terminal containing a custom hall, waiting rooms and a docks station with railway platforms on the south side of the entrance lock. Whilst never possessing the luxurious facilities international travellers might find at Southampton and Liverpool Riverside, they were nonetheless effective but in bad windswept weather, they were prone to the elements sweeping off the Bristol Channel. Luggage, however, would be moved swiftly and efficiently into the passenger terminal and awaiting Great Western boat trains as these passengers observed looking on from one of Royal Line's vessels around 1912. (*Above left*: J&C McCutcheon Collection; *Above right and above*: Bristol Museums P.B.A. Collection)

Royal Line, in its promotion promised, for those willing to make the move to Canada, exciting opportunities attracting thousands of families, including many Bristolians.[137] A concerted flow of West Country emigration led local observers to suggest the region was drained of its of its vitality. The Great War put pay to Bristol's regular Canadian passenger business as Royal Line vessels were requisitioned by the British government. In August 1915 *Royal Edward*, having survived ramming an iceberg off Cape Race at the end of May 1914, surrendered to a torpedo from German submarine UB-14, whilst *Royal George* was later sold with the rest of the Northern Steamship fleet to Cunard. Bristol Avonmouth joined Cunard's roster of ports in November 1917 with a Bristol and New York crossing as well as the Canadian route connecting with the company's Northern Railway system.[138] Advertising continued up until May 1918, but Cunard's relationship with Bristol, nevertheless, was not to last.

Apart from Elders & Fyffes West Indian business, there were other Avonmouth boat trains with regular steamship passengers bound for Rangoon and India with Henderson and Bibby Lines services, together with the Federal Line from Australia and New Zealand. By the early 1920s, the PBA, despite the loss of its Royal Line ships, continued its Dominion emigrant traffic relationship with Canadian Pacific operations. The same company also provided occasional cruises to and from Bristol to the West Indies. Bristol City Lines had introduced a new service to Norfolk, Virginia, Elder Fyffes West Indian traffic was as busy as ever whilst parent Elder-Dempster also brought other Empire emigrant services out of Avonmouth.[139]

Overseas traffic was also seen from other shipping lines such as Bibby Lines' motor cargo-liner *Cheshire*. In November 1927 the vessel, with a capacity for 300 first-class passengers, on the Rangoon run returned to Bristol. Henderson Lines small cargo-liner vessels, on similar routes, used Avonmouth from October 1928. Yet despite these developments, the port's principal relationship was with Elders & Fyffes and their famous white liveried banana boats. These vessels provided the main passenger-carrying capacity during the inter-war years and developed an established market niche. In 1929 the *Western Daily Press* reported on a double departure of two liners sailing together noting:

A special boat train from Temple Meads brought the passengers from both liners – 75 for the *Ariguiani*, and 35 for the *Motagua*. They arrived at the Royal Edward Dock Station about two pm, embarkation taking place immediately following arrival. Passengers by the *Ariguani* included Mr C.C. Gerahty, the new Attorney-General for Trinidad, Sir Alec and Lady Bannerman, and the Bishop of Honduras. The *Ariguani* left the entrance locks about 3.30 pm and was followed shortly afterwards by the *Motagua*. Both liners will be back at the outer docks with fruit for Christmas, the *Motagua* being due on December 18th, and the *Ariguani* on December 22nd.[140]

The White Ships cemented a strong relationship with Bristol life. In May 1930 the Fyffes liner *Carare*, moored in the Royal Edward Dock, hosted what was described as a brilliant ball in support of aid for the Bristol Children's Hospital. By 1935, the shipping line was rebranded as Fyffes Line in advertising whilst the company's vessels were of a first-class specification with outside rooms only.[141] Commercial banana importation grew considerably as well as Avonmouth's share of the traffic. Dedicated banana handling terminals were constructed featuring state of the art mechanical equipment designed for the rapid transfer of bananas onto steam-heated vans on the quayside. Fruit vans attached to fast mainline GWR express train services became a familiar feature of

Royal Line's advertising proclaimed their ships were the fastest to Canada. Bristol crossings were packed with passengers as the company advertised its Atlantic steamship services in upmarket press and through a network of British and French affiliate offices. On one occasion in May 1910, three separate boat train movements were required to bring around 1,000 passengers sailing aboard *Royal Edward*. An unclimbable fence had to be erected on the south side of the lock to Royal Edward Dock, rendered necessary by sheer numbers of people wishing to visit the port to see the Royal liners. Mail trains were kept busy. One *Royal Edward* departure on 28 June 1911 was accompanied by a record shipment 678 mail bags brought to Bristol from all parts of the country. (*Left*: Jacqueline Wadsworth Collection; *Overleaf*: Illustrated London News Ltd/ Mary Evans)

railway life in the first half of the twentieth century. Cargo-liner banana business required Avonmouth boat trains, although rarely on the scale of the services required at Southampton, where individual boat train formations could bring up to several hundred passengers at a time. As a result, the banana boat train was a typically modest affair normally consisting of several carriages, one at least for Paddington and the others for alternative destinations together with baggage and mail vans. The normal procedure was for a GWR locomotive to pick up the boat train (taking over from PBA's locomotives), and then head towards Bristol Temple Meads station where boat train carriages were attached to other services for onward transmission. Writers Colin Maggs and Maurice Hawthorne take up the story:

> At the southern end of Royal Edward Dock, transit buildings either side of the Junction Cut included 'R' and 'S' sheds on the west side. The latter included passenger, baggage and medical facilities for the embarkation of emigrants prior to the vessel moving up to the locks at the dock exit, where first class passengers boarded at Royal Edward passenger station. In the opposite direction, banana boats from the Caribbean, which also conveyed passengers, would work through the port in a similar fashion, dropping off first class passengers at the lock gates and then called at 'S' shed, before moving to the old docks via Junction Cut to unload the fruit. Mail would also come off here and be loaded into 'XP'-rated railway box vans, which were shunted over to Avonmouth Dock station and then added to the rear of a passenger service to reach Bristol.[142]

By the end of the 1920s, Bristol City Lines fleet of cargo-liners, always listed in the press as part of larger liner movements, ensured the city was linked by regular sailings to New York maintaining a route that lasted until the early 1960s.

Although commercial overtones were always present at Avonmouth, first-class passengers could always expect a certain degree of pampering which was particularly apparent in the inter-war cruise market. P&O introduced a number of new Strath-named liners - *Strathnaver, Strathaird, Stratheden, Strathmore* and *Strathallan* in the 1930s for the UK, India and Australia mail runs. These white-hulled painted ships were also ideal for warm-weather cruising. Whilst other ports were used, the facilities at Bristol

The Bristol Channel's navigational and tidal pitfalls hindered Avonmouth's progress as a viable alternative to Liverpool and Southampton, but the port played a pivotal role in the First World War and by the 1920s had developed as a major commercial axis with Elders & Fyffes banana trade. By this time, the company's white painted cargo-liners were a common sight at Avonmouth for the best part of a quarter of a century, as the port played a crucial role in the UK's importation of bananas. By 1925 the banana trade amounted to around 160,000 tons annually, the vast majority originating from Jamaica, Central America and Columbia. The adjacent boat train, hauled by one of the PBA's 0-6-0 Peckett Class works locomotives, indicates the banana boats were still a key source of passenger-carrying traffic at the time. The second set of images show the inter-war years as the heyday of Avonmouth's passenger and London Ocean Mails business with the port handling regular liner traffic. The main docks station and passenger terminal was business like, but certainly not like GWR's Plymouth Ocean Quay facilities, allowed passengers to locate their luggage which was arranged in alphabetical order before boarding the boat train on the station platform and departure to Temple Mead. (*Above*: Bristol Museums P.B.A. Collection)

Avonmouth attracted the company and customers especially for Baltic cruises. In July 1935 Bristol joined the ranks as a home cruise port. The *Western Daily Press* reported on developments:

> A floating palace of 22,300 tons gross, her white hull surmounted by eight decks, topped with three delicate buff funnels, the P. & O. liner *Strathnaver* glided into the Royal Edward entrance locks at Avonmouth yesterday morning. From the many points of vantage on her superstructure nearly 1,000 bronzed cruise passengers from the sun-bathed waters of the Mediterranean looked down on the large crowd of spectators which has assembled to see the arrival of the largest cruise liner which has been dealt with at Avonmouth.

It was a scene the PBA hoped to see replicated on many occasions with an accompanying infrastructure all-ready for the next cruise. The passenger terminal and the boat train also played their part. The report carried on:

> Once the baggage was ashore and sorted in the clearing sheds, the work of the disembarkation commenced. From the gangways fore and aft the passengers streamed in to the Royal Edward passenger station, and the necessary formalities in the Customs Sheds were got through expeditiously. There were ample postal facilities in the station waiting room, and telegrams and written messages were promptly despatched. Then the booking clerks had a busy time and presently the platform was filled with passengers and luggage. All rapidly disappeared into the waiting specials for London and the Midlands, there was the shriek of locomotive whistles and the well filled dining specials were away on their journeys.[143]

Another similar vessel *Strathmore* returned to Bristol the following year. Other P&O ships doing the inter-war cruise rounds included *Viceroy of India* and *Ranpura* built in the previous decade. All possessed considerable open deck spacing providing passengers with a range of on-board activities as well as just lapping up the sun in a leisurely manner. Bristol had delivered the business and forward sales for 1936 was brisk. Messrs Thos. Cook and Son, Ltd, their Bristol office located in Baldwin Street, stated 'that the P. and O. cruises finishing at Avonmouth and starting from Bristol's port are again proving very popular'. They advised intending passengers should book at once.[144]

Seen here at Avonmouth's docks station and passenger terminal adjacent to the Royal Edward Dock, P&O liner *Strathmore*, completed in 1935 on cruise duty judging by the sheer number of quality cars parked alongside the liner. The 1930s were the first point in time where a variety of different forms of motorized vehicles – cars and the charabanc – as well as the traditional boat train brought passengers to and from ports. *Strathmore* operated many long-haul sailings from its main liner berth at Tilbury but also from Bristol Avonmouth. (Bristol Museums P.B.A. Collection)

Post-war British Railways Western Region boat trains continued to operate to Bristol Avonmouth until the mid-1960s. Bristol's sea trade links with the Far East had been strengthened since the early 1950s. In January 1965, *The Liverpool Echo and Evening Express* noted:

> The largest passenger liner to call at Avonmouth since the wartime troopships disembarked 300 passengers yesterday. She is the 11,255-ton Anchor Line ship, *Caledonia*, with passengers from Bombay, Karachi and Gibraltar. This is the first time Anchor Line, based on Liverpool, have used Avonmouth as a terminal port.[145]

However, all sea passenger traffic started to decline in the 1960s as a result of the growing popularity and convenience of long-haul air travel. Bristol's West Indian, New York and Canadian route relationships was no different. Even though, the proposed development of Portbury was wrapped up as a liner port expansion to rival Liverpool and Southampton in 1966, it was more about the 'container revolution' and a convenient axis point for West Midlands exports.[146]

Around the turn of the twenty-first century, British and Irish ports saw a rapid re-emergence of passenger activity with substantial growth in the British cruise tourism market. Bristol Avonmouth, like many other ports in the past traditionally connected to boat train movements, witnessed a remarkable renaissance of operations. However, all vestiges of the Royal Edward Dock passenger station disappeared many years ago with rail-passenger access only achieved via the two-platform suburban Avonmouth railway station on the Severn Beach line.

The blood and custard liveried boat train carriages arriving at S Shed on Avonmouth Dock's estate was taken on 17 April 1962. Hauled by the PBA's S11 tank locomotive, the train is approaching the passenger platform ramp which can just be seen. The ship to the left is Elders & Fyffes *TSS Camito*, typical of post-war combination cargo/liners with their vast refrigerated holds on banana and fruit traffic duty. The Fyffes line *Camito* operated out of both Avonmouth and Southampton on Barbados, Trinidad and Jamaica West Indian routes until being retired in 1973. The second image shows a busy departure hall. Not recorded if this was an arrival or departure within the self-contained passenger terminal at S Shed, with its inclusive waiting area, baggage store and immigration and customs areas, however, the winter months of 1962–63 were severe. Passengers appear pretty well wrapped up for dealing with the British weather in coats, hats and scarves providing a period snapshot of early-1960s social life. Activity around the Post Office cabin (with its January calendar) and the British Railways booking office suggests the boat train might have been quite busy even though the era is drawing to a rapid conclusion. (*Above left*: M.B. Warburton/Gerald Nichols; *Above right*: Bristol Museums P.B.A. Collection)

PBA Corporation 0-6-0ST works locomotive is ready to pull out the last ever boat train from Avonmouth Old Yard on 26 August 1964. The maroon liveried three carriage boat train is made up of a Hawkesworth full brake and first and second-class coaches and would have been delivered to Bristol on the rear of a Paddington train and then taken over by ex-GWR 0-6-0PT tank locomotive (seen here adjacent to the Gloucester Road crossing box) on the edge of the Corporation's dock lines with Peckett Class No S11 taking over the last leg of the journey. In the second photograph the train makes its way past R shed on the Royal Edward Dock's south side, where red and black funnelled Clan Line cargo ships are discharging their refrigerated meat cargo into awaiting cold stores, to meet with TSS *Camito* performing the final boat train ritual which apart from war-years has lasted over fifty years. (*Above and below*: David J. Cross/Gerald Nichols)

Fishguard Harbour: GWR Ocean Mails boat trains

On Great Western's expansive territory, new facilities were completed in west Wales at Fishguard, where the company had grand designs not just on cross-channel business, but on emerging, prestigious and profitable ocean liner work that combined both passenger and Ocean Mails traffic. Cargo business did not form part of the equation as ocean vessels were serviced by tenders. Booth Line's RMS *Lanfranc*, launched in 1906 and a casualty of war as a hospital ship in 1917, was the first liner to arrive at GWR's new harbour on 2 April 1908. According to the *Manchester Courier*, the vessel 'was the first ocean liner to make Fishguard a port of call for ocean liners, arrived there yesterday for the second time from the Brazils, and landed a number of passengers, and, as on previous occasions, the transfer to the Great Western trains of the passengers and their luggage was performed in a remarkably expeditious manner'.[147]

GWR was in a position to mount an attack on several fronts; the company had a nascent boat train operation servicing mid-sized liners at Bristol, it maintained its regular port of call mail service and passenger contracts with liners anchoring in Plymouth Sound, but also had the prospect running new services into its port at Fishguard. The company placed considerable effort to influence shipping lines by moving some of their Plymouth based tender fleet *Smeaton* and *Sir Francis Drake* to Fishguard in 1909. Whilst the journeys from liners to the quay side was rapid, the GWR wanted to impress first-class passengers. The newly constructed *Sir Francis Drake* tender incorporated comfortable upholstered seating in a lady's saloon positioned at the rear of vessels.[148] In addition, the GWR processed mail traffic at Fishguard, and even set up a temporary Post Office desk on its tenders so that passengers could send letters for immediate sorting and onward dispatch in the shortest possible time. Alongside, new carriage stock and very well-appointed first-class dining saloons were introduced to commemorate the arrival at Fishguard of RMS *Mauretania* on 30 August 1909. GWR was galvanised to supporting the Cunard decision to use the port for eastbound calls. Maritime writer Alan Kittridge suggests on balance 'Cunard evidently felt they were losing business to IMM and the Channel Route.'[149] *Campania* in early 1910 was one of Cunard's visiting liners but serviced by *Pembroke*, a relic of 1880 and the largest and last GWR paddle steamer. It was designed and built to carry a combination of passengers, cargo,

The Cunard Line poster produced by Odin Rosenvinge is credited from 1914 representing a cementing of the relationship between GWR and the shipping line. Despite the considerable investment in port infrastructure, it took time for the railway to cultivate the shipping conglomerate who had trialled the port as early as August 1906. However, it was not until 1909 that Cunard started using the new port regularly with up to eight liner crossings per month. The company's response was almost most certainly driven by competitive pressures leveraged by White Star and other IMM registered shipping lines using English Channel routes. Fishguard at least offered the chance to land mails earlier; for some commercial organisations, this increasingly became a vital component of twentieth-century business life. The 'Cunard Line New Express Route' pamphlet is targeted at American London and continent bound travellers anxious to reach their desired destinations as soon as possible. Speedy doubled-headed locomotive boat trains provided the opportunity of avoiding Liverpool completely; thus, arriving in the capital earlier, and indeed with planned through boat trains to Dover, the chance to reach European capitals many hours ahead. (*Left*: NRM/SSPL; *Below*: J&C McCutcheon Collection)

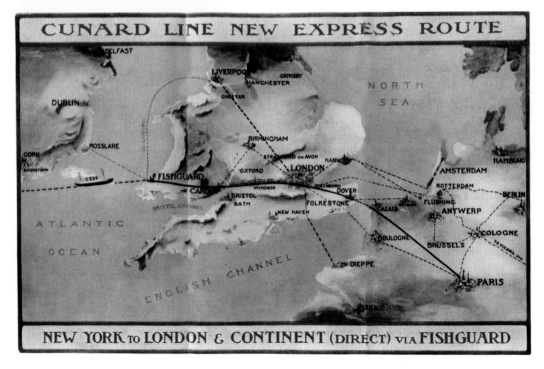

The number of passengers aboard smaller liners (and GWR's new generation of cross-channel steamers) did not always require double-headed boat train expresses as this photograph demonstrates. The single locomotive hauling shows Bulldog Class no. 3381 *Maine* departing from Fishguard Harbour on 2 May 1908 with an up Ocean Express service to Paddington from the recently completed railway terminal. The railway facilities and the condition of the pristine boat train suggests they were probably tidied up for the official photographer. (Great Western Trust Collection)

cattle and horses on the old Milford-Waterford route, but brought out of slumber and converted for tendering on Fishguard's new mail and passenger operation. This turned out to be a bit of a red herring as the port's new ocean liner experiment was not ultimately successful; Pembroke being sold in 1916.[150]

As part of the harbour try-out, promotion was very much on GWR's mind as the company issued a set of sepia collotype cards to commemorate Cunard liner arrivals as well as commissioning a poster by Alec Fraser showcasing the terminal station, the Fishguard Bay Hotel with one of the new GWR steamers leaving port together with an image of the *Mauretania* beyond the breakwater.[151] Cunard's two flagship vessels *Mauretania* and *Lusitania* used Fishguard for eastbound New York return calls up until the Great War; *Lusitania* was the last of the company's super-liners to call at the port on 14 September 1914, a little over a month after the outbreak of hostilities and never to return.[152] Yet the sporadic use of the port by leading shipping lines meant high-quality boat train dining car stock was mainly used for Plymouth Millbay duties.

GWR's first *Mauretania Special* boat train departure from Fishguard on 30 August 1909 was a significant event attracting many dignitaries and crowds of onlookers. The ocean liner special passenger train was hauled by no. 3402 *Halifax* as the lead engine recorded with either no. 4108 *Gardenia* or no. 4108 *Hotspur* shown leaving Fishguard. Double-headed trains hauled heavy first-class ocean expresses to and from Paddington in under five hours. This scene was copied by an illustrator in the second postcard image but incorporating a certain degree of artistic licence as the footbridge and onlookers were lost. Servicing the new liner port required the Great Western to provide three to four special boat trains depending on the number of passengers with improved carriage stock provided in each direction for each liner movement. Fortunately, the company was at the forefront of designing and building innovative and powerful 4-4-0 and 4-4-2 class design locomotives. Investment in more potent traction was driven by a healthy income stream based on mail and passenger traffic to accommodate the many new liners (particularly German and Dutch) using Plymouth. Although GWR's Fishguard boat trains would beat LNWR's Liverpool Riverside services, first-class passengers were increasingly disinclined to make longer rail journeys and despite GWR's subtle overtures is perhaps one of the reasons why Cunard ultimately choose not to relocate its premier New York services to Fishguard on a permanent basis. (*Above and opposite above*: J&C McCutcheon Collection; *Opposite below*: Great Western Trust Collection)

Having displaced LSWR at Devonport, the GWR introduced powerful new 4-6-0 locomotives for hauling Cunard ocean traffic that was to become renowned for comfort and speed.[153]

The port of Fishguard was used for trans-Atlantic steamer traffic up until 1914 but as the fateful year arrived, marked a turning point in the port's fortunes. When the smoke of war cleared and regular international shipping resumed, Fishguard Bay was to lose permanently its former liner business to the English Channel ports. Whilst Cunard had regularly supported Fishguard in the years before the Great War, it could be argued the port's fate as a major liner terminal was sealed by White Star's decision to relocate its premier Atlantic liners at Southampton. Weekly outward services connected Britain to New York via Cherbourg and Queenstown, and with regular eastbound returns calling at Plymouth landing both mail and passengers. Mike Hitches in his book *Rails to Rosslare* summed up the position commendably:

> Once the war was over, the GWR still retained hopes that trans-Atlantic liners would return to Fishguard and even turned down the possibility that the harbour could become the major importer of oil. The Anglo-Persian Oil Company approached GWR with a proposal to establish an oil refinery at Fishguard and negotiations took place in January 1915 but soon foundered because the railway company still had dreams of the return of ocean liner traffic.[154]

Post-war, the world changed forever with Cunard also moving its largest liners to Southampton. As a result, Fishguard was left out in the cold, handling boat trains for the morsels of Irish cross-channel services and occasional foreign-owned liners, but never, ever destined to achieve its full passenger liner business potential it was designed for.

Notes

Introduction

1. Roberts, p. 177.
2. Roberts, p. 362.
3. *Pall Mall Gazette*, 2 July 1906, p. 7.
4. *The Tyrone Courier*, 30 July 1908, p. 6; *Belfast News-Letter*, 25 July 1908, p. 5.
5. Crane.
6. Davenport-Hines, pp. 28, 29, 141.
7. Fletcher, pp. 272, 273.
8. Fletcher, p. xiii.
9. French Riviera Supplement to *The Bystander*, 30 November 1904, p. 573.
10. Mullen and Munson, p. xiii.
11. RAIL 410/600, *LNWR Officers' Committee Minute Book*, 39712, 17 July 1900.
12. *Railway Magazine*, March 1908, p. 259.
13. *Railway Magazine*, August 1914, p. 103.
14. Figes, p. 368.
15. Wolmar and Solomon, pp. 217, 221.
16. Faulkner and Williams, p. 172.
17. Fletcher, p. 275.
18. Ford, pp. 45, 46.
19. Fletcher, p. 236.
20. Fletcher, p. 236.
21. Gould in Chadwick, pp. 230-1.
22. Bryan (2017), p. 39.
23. Gould in Chadwick, p. 231.
24. Edwards, p. 7.
25. Bradley (2015), p. 130.
26. *Liverpool Echo*, 3 November 1977, p. 8.
27. *Belfast News-Letter*, 29 July 1955, p. 6.
28. *The Sunderland Echo*, 16 November 1954, p. 7.
29. *The Stage*, 13 April 1899, p. 14.
30. *The Shipley Times and Express*, 3 April 1914, p. 9.
31. *Northampton Evening Telegraph*, 27 March 1939, p. 1.

32. McDougall and Gardiner, p. 78.
33. *The Manchester Courier*, 27 September 1907, p. 8.
34. *The Northern Whig*, 22 September 1911, p. 10.
35. *Coventry Evening Telegraph*, 4 October 1956, p. 19.
36. *The Cornishman*, 20 May 1909, p. 8.
37. *Daily Herald*, 16 May 1955, p. 8.
38. Fletcher, p. 281.
39. Mullen and Munson, p. 8.
40. *The Daily Telegraph*, 19 June 1907, p. 4.
41. Mullen and Munson, p. 23.
42. Booker, p. ix.
43. Mullen and Munson, p. 123.
44. Booker, pp. 119, 121.
45. Reed, pp. 17, 24.
46. Norddeutsche Lloyd, p. 37.

Chapter 1
1. Crane.
2. Reed, p. 1.
3. Forwood, p. 39.
4. Matthews, p. 37.
5. Fletcher, p. 241, 242.
6. Walton, p. 7.
7. Fletcher, p. 144.
8. Bryan (2017), p. 37.
9. *Railway Magazine*, November 1897, p. 392.
10. Faulkner and Williams, p. 187.
11. *The Western Daily Mercury*, 26 January 1912, p. 1.
12. Davenport-Hines, pp. 98, 99.
13. *The Globe*, 12 December 1902, p. 3.
14. Reed, p. 10.
15. McDougall and Gardiner, pp. 7, 8.
16. *The Globe*, 15 July 1912, p. 9.
17. *The Bystander*, 24 August 1910, p. 366.
18. *The Morning Post*, 5 June 1908.
19. *The Tyrone Courier*, 30 July 1908. p. 6; *Belfast News-Letter*, 25 July 1908, p. 5.
20. *The Derby Daily Telegraph*, I October 1902, p. 1.
21. *The Globe*, 12 December 1902, p. 3.
22. Fletcher, p. 138.
23. *The Sphere*, 27 May 1939, p. 343.
24. Heffer (2017), p. 179.

25. Mullen and Munson, p. 8.
26. Mullen and Munson, p. 2.
27. *The Clifton Society*, 19 July 1906, p. 7; Mullen and Munson, p. xiv.
28. *The Sketch*, 8 April 1908, p. 420.
29. Mullen and Munson, pp. 147, 190.
30. Mullen and Munson, p. 193.
31. Mullen and Munson, p. 57.
32. Mullen and Munson, pp. 61, 106.
33. *The Clifton Society*, 19 July 1906, p. 7.
34. 'A Bolt to the Blue', French Riviera Supplement in *The Bystander*, 14 January 1914, p. 79.
35. Martin (2017), p. 34.
36. Norddeutsche Lloyd, p. 37.
37. Twain, p. 183.
38. Gould in Chadwick, p. 135.
39. Rideing in Chadwick, p. 216.
40. Figes, pp. 40, 43.
41. Mullen and Munson, p. 253.
42. Tungate (2018), p. 32.
43. *Gloucestershire Echo*, 2 May 1907.
44. Haresnape, pp. 66, 67; Ford, p. 9.
45. Wragg, p. 104.
46. Shin, p. 189.
47. Davenport-Hines, p. 136.
48. *The Bystander*, 14 January 1914, p. xvi; Brendon, pp. 185, 260.
49. Booker, p. 122.
50. Hannavy, p. 8; Booker, p. 122.
51. Brendon, p. 260.
52. Booker, p. 122.
53. Matthews, pp. 5, 6, 7, 35.
54. Smith, p. xii.
55. Matthews, p. 38.
56. *The Illustrated Sporting and Dramatic News*, 11 May 1901, p. 398.
57. Fletcher, p. 235.
58. *Railway Magazine*, August 1897, pp. 128, 140.
59. For further exploration see Cannadine (1990); Cannadine (1994); Heffer (2017).
60. *The Exeter and Plymouth Gazette Daily Telegram*, 12 July 1881.
61. *The Western Times*, 14 August 1890, p. 3.
62. *The Aberdeen Daily Journal*, 19 September 1905, p. 9; *Manchester Courier and Lancashire General Advertiser*, 14 September 1905, p. 6.
63. *The Daily Telegraph*, 10 June 1907, p. 11.

64. Brendon, p. 245.
65. Figes, p. 40.
66. Greenway, p. 8.
67. Mullen and Munson, p. 157.
68. Figes, p. 219.
69. Greenway, pp. 42, 46; Figes, p. 219.
70. Greenway, p. 8.
71. *The Scotsman*, 27 July 1978, p. 1.
72. Pigott, p. 36.
73. Bucknall, p. 76; Pigott, p. 76.
74. *Railway Magazine*, July 1897 p. 97.
75. *The Globe*, 22 May 1876; *The Globe*, 27 May 1878.
76. Greenway, p. 47.
77. Greenway, p. 53.
78. *The Sketch*, 23 December 1896 p. 326.
79. Greenway, pp. 53, 56.
80. Bucknall, p. 79; Haresnape, pp. 65, 66, 67.
81. *The Folkstone Herald*, 25 November 1899, p. 7.
82. Bucknall, p. 62.
83. Mullen and Munson, p. 160; Haresnape, p. 58; *Manchester Courier and Lancashire General Advertiser*, 19 April 1892, p. 6.
84. Bucknall, p. 20.
85. *The Dover Express*, 18 October 1895.
86. Bucknall, p. 21.
87. *Dover Express*, 21 April 1905, p. 8.
88. Ford, p. 43.
89. Bucknall, p. 127.
90. French Riviera Supplement to *The Bystander*, 30 November 1904, p. 568.
91. St. John Thomas and Whitehouse (1988), p. 66.
92. Mullen and Munson, p. 31.
93. Greenway, p. 35.
94. Greenway, p. 50; Mullen and Munson, p. 14.
95. Greenway, p. 60.
96. *The Sketch*, 19 December 1900, p. 354.
97. Mullen and Munson, p. 65.
98. *Railway Magazine*, October 1897, p. 313.
99. *Railway Magazine*, July 1914, p. 24.
100. *The Tatler*, No. 614, 2 April 1913.
101. *Railway Magazine*, July 1914, p. 25.
102. *Railway Magazine*, May 1907, pp. 411, 412.

103. *Railway Magazine*, July 1914, p. 25.
104. Wolmar and Soloman, p. 76.
105. Greenway, p. 8.
106. Greenway, p. 67.
107. *The Bournemouth Guardian*, 30 June 1894.
108. *The Jersey Weekly Press and Independent*, 7 July 1894, p. 4.
109. *Railway Magazine*, July 1914, pp. 27, 28.
110. Simmons, p. 217.
111. Herbert, pp. 65, 93, 130.
112. Herbert, p. 136.
113. Duff, pp. 209, 217.
114. Duff, p. 210.
115. *Railway Magazine*, July 1914, p. 28.
116. *Railway Magazine*, July 1914, p. 30.
117. Perkin, p. 232.
118. Mullen and Munson, p. 57.
119. Bucknall, p. 137.
120. *The Yorkshire Post*, 2 July 1925, p. 11.
121. *The Cornish Telegraph*, 26 September 1895, p. 1.
122. Jackson, pp. 35, 99.
123. *Jersey Evening Post*, 8 March 2015.
124. Greenway, p. 58.
125. Jackson, p. 35.
126. Greenway, p. 73.
127. *Isle of Wight Times*, 16 September 1897, p. 1.
128. Jackson, p. 39.
129. Jackson, p. 39.
130. *St. James's Gazette*, 2 July 1901, p. 6.
131. Greenway, p. 67.
132. Kittridge, p. 29.
133. Bennett, pp. 72, 73.
134. Bennett, p. 76.
135. Wilson, p. 67.
136. Figes, p. 236.
137. Mullen and Munson, p. 189.

Chapter 2

1. Martin, p. 38.
2. Walton, p. 1.
3. Mullay (1994), p. 18.
4. Boyd, p. 61.

5. Brendon, pp. 266, 267; Williamson, pp. 26, 121.
6. Brendon, p. 267.
7. Brendon, p. 274.
8. Brendon, p. 270.
9. *The Sphere*, 21 November 1925, p. 255.
10. Perkin, p. 231; Pimlott, p. 187.
11. Mullen and Munson, p. 246.
12. Mullen and Munson, p. 82.
13. Mullen and Munson, p. 77.
14. Pimlott, pp. 201, 207, 209.
15. Matthews, p. 2.
16. *The Sheffield Evening Telegraph and Star*, 12 December 1893, p. 2; *The Nottingham Daily Express*, 2 December 1893, p. 5.
17. Mullen and Munson, p. 75.
18. *The Sphere*, 25 July 1914, p. vii.
19. *The Sphere*, 23 August 1924, p. 222.
20. *The Bystander*, 4 November 1925, p. xiv.
21. *The Sphere*, 12 June 1926, p. xx.
22. Mullen and Munson, p. 237.
23. *The Sphere*, 30 September 1933.
24. Mullen and Munson, pp. 200, 201.
25. Bucknall, p. 143.
26. *The Sphere*, September 1936.
27. Pimlott, p. 263.
28. Danielson, p. 91.
29. Alsop, p. 304.
30. Baldwin, pp. 122,123.
31. Kidner, p. 85.
32. *The Sphere*, 2 June 1928, p. 462.
33. *The Evening News*, 28 August 1924, p. 1.
34. Alsop, pp. 315, 316.
35. *The Portadown Times*, 2 May 1930.
36. Bray, p. 171.
37. *The Bystander*, 22 March 1939.
38. Greenway, p. 127.
39. Jackson, p. 52.

Chapter 3
1. *The Sketch*, 9 February 1955.
2. *The Sketch*, 23 February 1955, p. 111.
3. Greenway, p.145.

4. Greenway, pp. 152, 153.
5. *The Sketch*, 1 January 1958, p. 42.
6. Woodley, pp. 100, 138.
7. *Dundee Courier*, 2 August 1952, p. 3.
8. Peel. pp. 72, 92; Winkworth, pp. 80, 89.
9. Greenway, p. 165.

Chapter 4
1. Jackson, p. 59; Peel, p. 92.

Chapter 5
1. Mullen and Munson, p. 310.
2. Mullen and Munson, p. 83.
3. *The Manchester Evening News*, 10 February 1894.
4. Mullen and Munson, p. 194.
5. *The Illustrated Sporting and Dramatic News*, 6 November 1897, p. 378.
6. *The Sketch*, 11 July 1894, p. 577.
7. *Railway Magazine*, December 1897, p. 542.
8. *The Sphere*, 30 December 1922, p. 346.
9. *The Globe*, 2 January 1897, p. 8.
10. *The Illustrated Sporting and Dramatic News*, 5 November 1904, p. 392.
11. Tungate (2018), p. 48.
12. Mullen and Munson, p. 317.
13. Caro, p. 15.
14. Caro, p. 348.
15. *The Illustrated Sporting and Dramatic News*, 5 November 1904, p. 392.
16. Wolmar and Soloman, p. 66.
17. Quinzio, p. 71.
18. Pimlott, pp. 187, 199.
19. Mullen and Munson, p. 67.
20. James, p. 3.
21. Pimlott, p. 199.
22. Perkin, p. 232.
23. Ring, p. 83.
24. Pimlott, p. 199.
25. Brendon, p. 129.
26. *Railway Magazine*, January 1899, p. 67.
27. Mullen and Munson, p. 254.

28. Mullen and Munson, p. 243.
29. James, p. 363.
30. Graves and Hodge, p. 34.
31. James, p. 363.
32. McKibbin, p. 23.
33. French Riviera Supplement to *The Bystander*, 30 November 1904, p. 581.
34. Pimlott, p. 199.
35. Mullen and Munson, p. 249.
36. French Riviera Supplement to *The Bystander*, 30 November 1904, p. 581.
37. Mullen and Munson, p. 318.
38. Perkin, p. 231; Ring, p. 31.
39. Cannadine, pp. 331, 332.
40. Lovell, pp. 160, 161, 162, 164; Ring, p. 130.
41. Brendon, p. 272.
42. Pimlott, p. 199.
43. McKibbin, p. 15.
44. Ring, pp. 67, 70; Duff, pp. 248, 262.
45. *Railway Magazine*, December 1897, p. 542.
46. Mullen and Munson, p. 309.
47. French Riviera Supplement to *The Bystander*, 30 November 1904, p. 568.
48. *The Globe*, 22 February 1872, p. 8.
49. Greenway, p. 74.
50. Pimlott, p. 71.
51. *Clifton Society*, 1 January 1891, p. 13.
52. *The Illustrated Sporting and Dramatic News*, 6 November 1897, p. 378.
53. *Railway Magazine*, December 1897, p. 540.
54. *Railway Magazine*, January 1899, p. 67.
55. *Railway Magazine*, January 1899, p. 60.
56. *The Sketch*, 21 January 1903, p. 38.
57. *The Sketch*, 22 November 1905, p. 194.
58. Simmons, pp. 216, 217.
59. Forsyth, pp. 10, 83.
60. *Railway Magazine*, July 1914, p. 25.
61. *The Sketch*, 19 October 1910, p. 35.
62. *The Bystander*, 14 January 1914, p. xvi.
63. Mullen and Munson, pp. 99, 101.
64. *The Bystander*, 14 January 1914, p. xvi.

65. Behrend, p. 88.
66. Graves and Hodge, pp. 34, 35; Pugh, p. 237.
67. Graves and Hodge, p. 39.
68. *The Western Daily Press*, 1 May 1922, p. 5.
69. Brendon, p. 263.
70. McKibbin, p. 27.
71. Lovell, p. 82.
72. *The Scotsman*, 14 December 1926, p. 7.
73. Boyd, p. 31.
74. Bucknall, p. 140.
75. Ring, pp. 2, 3.
76. *The Bystander*, 22 November 1922, p. 518.
77. *The Bystander*, 22 November 1922, p. 517.
78. Gardiner, p. 614.
79. Lovell, p. 128; Ring, p. 3.
80. Martin (2017), p. 45.
81. *The Bystander*, 21 November 1923, p. 558.
82. *The Bystander*, 19 December 1923, p. 917.
83. *The Bystander*, 20 November 1929, pp. 413, 414.
84. McKibbin, pp. 4, 9.
85. Lovell, pp. 119, 121; Ring, p. 117.
86. Mullen and Munson, p. 64.
87. Ring, p. 123.
88. Lovell, pp. 128, 136, 181; Ring, p. 3.
89. Mullen and Munson, p. 201.
90. Quinzio, p. 109.
91. McDonald, (2012), p. 52.
92. *The Sphere*, 30 September 1933.
93. Behrend, p. 99.
94. Graves and Hodge, p. 38.
95. Perkin (1989), p. 237.
96. Perkin (1989), p. 235.
97. Pugh, pp. 217, 219.
98. McDonald, pp. 46, 48.
99. Martin Gilbert (1982), Mary Penman journal. Winston S. Churchill, *Companion Volume V, Part 3: The Coming of War, 1936–1939*, pp. 1337, 3852; Churchill Archives, Churchill College, Cambridge University.
100. Ring, p. 106.
101. Lovell, p. 83; Brendon, p. 260; Pimlott, pp. 262, 263.
102. Pugh, p. 237.

103. Gardiner, p. 614.
104. Cannadine, p. 343.
105. Lovell, p. 2; Ring, p. 108.
106. *The Bystander*, 20 March 1929, p. 574.
107. *The Bystander*, 20 November 1929, p. 422.
108. *The Sketch*, 16 September 1931, p. xii.
109. *The Sphere*, 5 January 1935.
110. *The Yorkshire Post*, 2 March 1931.
111. *The Sphere*, 5 January 1935, 'Travel Notes of the Week'.
112. Lovell, p. 201.
113. Lovell, p. 202.
114. Martin, p. 43.
115. *Railway Magazine*, July 1986, pp. 427, 429.
116. Elliot, p. 24.
117. Bucknall, p. 140.
118. St. John Thomas and Whitehouse (1988), p. 7.
119. Bucknall, p. 146.
120. Jarvis, pp. 2, 3, 6.
121. Danielson, p. 13.
122. Greenway, p. 144.
123. Danielson, p. 13.
124. Hartill, p. 11.
125. *Coventry Evening Telegraph*, 8 October 1952, p. 2.
126. *The Birmingham Post*, 23 November 1952, p. 5.
127. *The Western Mail*, 11 October 1954, p. 7.
128. *Daily Mirror*, 26 October 1957, p. 20.
129. *The Sphere*, 18 June 1960, p. 496.
130. *Daily Mirror*, 3 January 1955, p. 10.
131. Martin, p. 49.
132. *The Sketch*, 5 June 1929, p. xxxvi.
133. Martin Gilbert, ed. (1982), Winston S. Churchill, *Companion Volume V, Part 3:, The Coming of War, 1936–1939*, pp. 1353.
134. Jenkinson (1996), p. 509.
135. de Winter Hebron, p. 77.
136. St. John Thomas and Whitehouse (1988), p. 73.
137. *The Scotsman*, 13 October 1936, p. 6.
138. *The Yorkshire Post*, 13 October 1936, p. 8; *The Dover Express and East Kent News*, 16 October 1936, p. 9.
139. *Belfast News-Letter*, 14 October 1936, p. 9.
140. *The Dover Express and East Kent News*, 18 December 1936, p. 6.
141. Danielson, p. 90.

142. Behrend and Buchanan, p. 15.
143. *Railway Magazine*, October 2017, p. 21.
144. *The Sphere*, 12 September 1936, p. 437.
145. Danielson, p. 91.
146. Williams (2015), p. 41.
147. Morel, p. 177.
148. Morel, p. 149.
149. Morel, p. 177.
150. *The Times*, 15 December 1951, p. 6.
151. Morel, p. 72; Behrend and Buchanan, p. 62; Winkworth, pp. 209, 210; Williams (2015), p. 43. George Behrend, acknowledged as one of the best authorities on the history and operations of Wagons Lits, alluded to this particular *Night Ferry* episode. He may have got his timings incorrect since a 1954 visit has been challenged by researchers. In Martin Gilbert's biography – Vol. VIII, 'Never Despair', 1945–65 – there is no reference to a visit to Paris in 1954 however impromptu, or a moment at which this might have been possible. Churchill's biographer Martin Gilbert is fastidious at documenting his whereabouts at any given week. During 1954 Churchill seems to have been caught up in domestic politics, especially the ongoing question of his retirement, and a visit to the USA in June/July although Clementine Churchill having spent the summer in France without him might have provided the opportunity for a spontaneous and brief visit.
152. Bucknall, p. 155.
153. Haresnape, p. 150.
154. Winkworth, p. 212.
155. *The Railway Magazine*, February 1950, pp. 75, 78.
156. Lovell, p. 3.
157. Lovell, p. 226.
158. McKibbin, p. 41.
159. Brendon, p. 281.
160. Ring, pp. 168, 169.
161. Lovell, pp. 230, 263.
162. Ring, pp. 161, 162.
163. Ring, p. 162.
164. Ring, p. 162.
165. Ring. p. 191.
166. Ring, p. 214.

Chapter 6

1. Forwood, p. 93.
2. *The Liverpool Daily Post and Mercury*, 22 November 1906, p. 11.
3. Holmes, p. 23.
4. Holmes, p. 19.
5. *The Sketch*, 16 May 1894, p. 153.
6. *The Sketch*, 16 May 1894, p. 153.
7. *Railway Magazine*, January 1898, p. 26.
8. Bradley, p. 480; Bray, p. 88.
9. *The Liverpool Mercury*, 11 July 1895, p. 7.
10. *Western Morning News*, 14 October 1895, p. 5; *Berkshire Chronicle*, 17 October 1896, p. 3.
11. Reed, p. 39.
12. *Railway Magazine*, January 1898, p. 27.
13. *Railway Magazine*, September 1897. pp. 195, 196.
14. *Railway Magazine*, January 1898, p. 26.
15. *The Railway Magazine*, June 1950, p. 373.
16. Hendry, p. 4.
17. *The Morning Post*, 26 July 1907, p. 8.
18. Fletcher, p. 238.
19. Baker, p. 75.
20. *Sevenoaks Chronicle and Kentish Advertiser*, 24 September 1909, p. 7.
21. *Yorkshire Post and Leeds Intelligencer*, 26 October 1907, p. 8.
22. Fletcher, p. 137.
23. Jenkinson, p. 229.
24. Haresnape, p. 100.
25. *Railway Magazine*, November 1907, p. 437.
26. *Railway Magazine*, December 1907, p. 533; *Railway Magazine*, January 1908, pp. 78, 79.
27. *The Daily News*, 27 July 1907.
28. *The Morning Post*, 26 July 1907, p. 8.
29. *The Standard*, 9 September 1907, p. 5.
30. *The Sketch*, 16 October 1901, pp. 520, 521.
31. Jenkinson, p. 230.
32. Reed, p. 31.
33. *Birmingham Gazette*, 5 July 1928.
34. Reed, pp. 23, 24; Kidner, p. 67.
35. *Portsmouth Evening News*, 18 July 1930.
36. *Liverpool Echo*, 25 August 1938, p. 12.
37. *The Sketch*, 22 June 1927; *The Bystander*, 30 April 1930.
38. *The Railway Magazine*, November 1971, pp. 590, 592.

39. *Aberdeen Press and Journal*, 28 July 1930.
40. Turner (2013), Faulkner and Williams, pp. 172, 173; Baker, p. 75.
41. Reed, p. 3.
42. *The Daily Telegraph*, 31 May 1904, p. 9.
43. *The Daily Telegraph*, 31 May 1904, p. 9.
44. *The Shipping Gazette and Lloyds List*, 10 June 1907, p. 8.
45. *The Daily Telegraph*, 10 June 1907, p. 11.
46. *The Northern Whig*, 14 December 1905, p. 11.
47. Baker, p. 61.
48. *The Illustrated London News*, 19 July 1902, p. 96.
49. *The Shipping Gazette and Lloyds List*, 22 May 1909, p. 10.
50. Faulkner and Williams, p. 172.
51. Turner blog 1.
52. Pigott, pp. 75, 96.
53. *The Sketch*, 1 May 1907, p. 94.
54. *The Manchester Courier*, 16 August 1907, p. 6.
55. *Eastern Daily Press*, 23 May 1907, p. 5.
56. Turner blog 2.
57. Baker, p. 77.
58. Davenport-Hines, p. 15.
59. Davenport-Hines, p. 15.
60. Baker, p. 77.
61. Walton, p. 4.
62. *The Western Mail*, 22 December 1920, p. 3.
63. *Cambridge Daily News*, 28 August 1939, p. 1.
64. Haresnape, p. 59.
65. Robertson, p. 5.
66. Gardiner, p. 615; Pugh, p. 237; Shepherd and Shepherd, p. 27.
67. *The Sphere*, 31 December 1932, p. 557.
68. *The Sphere*, 27 April 1929, p. 198.
69. *The Illustrated London News*, 1 February 1929, pp. 29, 30.
70. *Railway Magazine*, May 1928, p. 422.
71. *Derby Evening Telegraph*, 10 June 1937, p. 8.
72. Gardiner, p. 22.
73. Simmons, p. 217.
74. Elliot, pp. 32, 34.
75. *The Western Morning News*, 27 April 1937, p. 11.
76. Phipp, p. 42.
77. Phipp, p. 43.
78. Dawson, pp. 41, 42.
79. Dawson, p. 42.

80. *The Birmingham Post*, 20 June 1939, p. 15.
81. Dawson, p. 45.
82. Kidner, p. 67; Dawson, p. 71; Ford, pp. 111, 112.
83. Phipp, p. 86.
84. Miller (2012), p. 39.
85. Miller (2015), p. 85.
86. Rieger, pp. 179, 180.
87. Kittridge, pp. 99, 116.
88. Miller (2010), pp. 42, 84
89. *The Railway Magazine*, September 1950, p. 577.
90. Bryan (2017), p. 35.
91. *The Sphere*, 15 December 1956, p. 465.
92. *The Birmingham Post*, 11 November 1960, p. 11.
93. *The Sphere*, 18 June 1960, p. 496.
94. Miller (2016), p. 42.
95. *Birmingham Daily Post*, 13 August 1960.
96. Fenton, p. 80.
97. Kittridge, p. 15.
98. Maggs, p. 89; Haresnape, p. 55.
99. *Clifton Society*, 5 July 1906, p. 7.
100. *Derby Daily Telegraph*, 6 April 1929, p. 10.
101. Kittridge, p. 79.
102. *The Illustrated London News*, 15 June 1929, p.vi.
103. Kittridge, p. 65.
104. Miller (2012), p. 29.
105. *The Western Morning News and Daily Gazette*, 30 April 1935, p. 9.
106. Bennett, p. 52.
107. Bennett, p. 53.
108. Robertson, p. 5.
109. Bennett, pp. 49, 63.
110. Semmens p. 43.
111. Jenkinson (1996), p. 480.
112. Bryan (2013), pp. 122, 126.
113. *The Western Daily Press and Bristol Mirror*, 2 November 1933, p. 8.
114. Pope (2001), p. 69.
115. *The Sheffield Evening Telegraph*, 5 December 1903, p. 3.
116. *The Dartmouth & South Hams Chronicle*, 25 December 1903.
117. Semmens (1985), p. 43.
118. Kittridge, p. 34; Faulkner and Williams p. 172.
119. Faulkner and Williams, p. 167.
120. Kittridge, p. 42; Baker, p. 77.

121. *The Sphere*, 7 July 1906, p. 7.
122. *The Sketch*, 1 May 1907, p. 94.
123. Faulkner and Williams, p. 164.
124. Kittridge, p. 42.
125. Bennett, p. 5.
126. *The Sphere*, 2 March 1901, p. 218.
127. *The Sphere*, 2 March 1901, p. 218.
128. Fletcher, p. 69.
129. *The Sphere*, 11 July 1908, p. 31.
130. *The Sketch*, 23 March 1910, p. 11.
131. *Western Daily Press*, 23 March 1910, p. 7.
132. Fletcher, p. 264.
133. *The Cheltenham Looker-On*, 14 May 1910, p. 20.
134. *The Hartland and West Country Chronicle*, No. 177.
135. *Western Daily Press*, 1 March 1910, p. 4.
136. *Western Daily Press*, 15 December 1914, p. 1.
137. Wadsworth, pp. 7, 8.
138. *Liverpool Post & Mercury*, 20 November 1917, p. 1; *Liverpool Daily Post*, 24 November 1917, p. 1.
139. *Western Daily Press*, 29 April 1921, p. 5.
140. *Western Daily Press*, 15 November 1929, p. 11.
141. *The Scotsman*, 21 November 1935, p. 1.
142. *Steam Days*, June 2018, p. 47.
143. *Western Daily Press*, 20 July 1935, p. 5.
144. *Western Daily Press and Bristol Mirror*, 4 March 1936, p. 4.
145. *The Liverpool Echo and Evening Express*, 28 January 1965, p. 3.
146. *The Birmingham Post*, 24 October 1966, p. 9.
147. *Manchester Courier*, 3 June 1908, p. 3.
148. Kittridge, pp. 39, 43.
149. Kittridge, p. 41.
150. Jackson, pp. 141, 144.
151. Bray, p. 44; Wilson, p. 67.
152. Hitches p. 26.
153. *Railway Magazine*, July 1912, p. 59.
154. Hitches, p. 26.

Select Bibliography

Alsop, J., *The Official Railway Postcard Book*, John Alsop, 1987

Baker, M., *The Waterloo to Weymouth Line: Waterloo - Weymouth*, Patrick Stephens, 1987

Baldwin, J., *L.B.S.C.R. Brighton Atlantics*, Pen & Sword Transport, 2017

Baxter, J., *French Riviera, and its Artists, Literature, Love, and Life on the Côte d'Azur*, Museyon, 2015

Bennett, A., *The Great Western Railway and the Celebration of Englishness*, PhD dissertation in Railway Studies, University of York, Railway Studies Institute, 2000

Bennett, A., *Great Western Lines & Landscapes: Business and Pleasure, Heritage and History*, Runpast Publishing, 2002

Behrend, G., *History of Trains De Luxe: From the Orient Express to the HST*, Transport Publishing Company, 1977

Behrend. G., and Buchanan, G., *Night Ferry*, St. Martin, Jersey Artists Ltd., 1985

Booker, J., *Travellers' Money*, Alan Sutton Publishing, 1994

Boyd, J., *Travellers in the Third Reich: The Rise of Fascism through the Eyes of Everyday People*, Elliott and Thompson, 2017

Bradley, S., *The Railways: Nation, Network & People*, Profile Books, 2015

Brendon, P., *Thomas Cook: 150 Years of Popular Tourism*, Secker & Warburg, 1991

Bray, M., *Railway Picture Postcards*, Moorland Publishing, 1986

Bryan, T., *Britain's Heritage: Express Trains*, Amberley, 2017

Bucknall, R., *Boat Trains and Channel Packets: The English Short Sea Routes*, Vincent Stuart Limited, 1957

Burton, A., *The Orient Express: The History of the World's Most Luxurious Train 1883–Present Day*, Amber Books, 2018

Cannadine, D., *The Decline and Fall of the British Aristocracy*, Yale University Press, 1990

Cannadine, D., *Aspects of Aristocracy: Grandeur and Decline in Modern Britain*, Yale University Press, 1994

Cannadine, D., *Class in Britain*, Yale University Press, 1998

Carle, N., S. Shaw, and S. Shaw, eds. *Edwardian Culture: Beyond the Garden Party*, Routledge, 2018

Caro, I., *Paris to the Past: Traveling through French History by Train*, W.W. Norton & Company, Inc, 2011

Collard, I., *The British Cruise Ship: An Illustrated History 1844–1939*, Amberley, 2013

Cookridge, E., *Orient Express; The Life and Times of the World's Most Famous Train*, Penguin Books, 1978

Danielson, R., *Railway Ships and Packet Ports*, Twelveheads Press, 2007

Davenport-Hines, R., *Titanic Lives: Migrants and Millionaires, Conmen and Crew*, Harper Collins, 2012

Dawson, L., *Fabulous Flying Boats: A History of the World's Passenger Flying Boats*, Pen & Sword, 2013

de Winter Hebron, C., *Dining at Speed: A Celebration of 125 Years of Railway Catering*, Silver Link Publishing, 2004

Drummond, I., *Southern Rails On Southampton Docks: Including the Industrial Lines of Southampton*, Holne Publishing, 2013

Duff, D., *Victoria Travels: Journeys of Queen Victoria between 1830 and 1900*, Frederick Muller Ltd., 1970

Edwards, M., *Blood on the Tracks: Railway Mysteries*, The British Library, 2018

Elliott, C., E. and Duvoskeldt, *Night Ferry/Ferry Boat de Nuit 1936–1980*, International Railway Preservation Society, 2011

Elliot, J., *On and Off the Rails*, George Allen & Unwin, 1982

Faulkner, J., and R. Williams, *The LSWR in the Twentieth Century*, David & Charles, 1988

Fenton, R., *The World's Merchant Ships, Images and Impressions: The Paintings of Robert Lloyd*, Ships in Focus Publications, 2005

Figes, O., *The Europeans: Three Lives and the Making of a Cosmopolitan Culture*, Penguin Random House, 2019

Fletcher, R., *Travelling Palaces: Luxury in Passenger Steamships*, Sir Isaac Pitman & Sons Ltd, 1913

Forsyth, R., *Irish Sea Shipping Publicised*, Tempus, 2002

Forwood, W., *Reminiscences of a Liverpool Shipowner, 1850–1920*, Henry Young & Sons, Limited, 1920

Ford, A., *The Golden Arrow: Pullman Profile No 5*, Crécy Publishing, 2018

Furness, R., *Poster to Poster Railway Journeys in Art: Vol. 4 The Eastern Counties*, JDF & Associates Ltd., 2011

Furness, R., *Poster to Poster Railway Journeys in Art: Vol. 5 London and the South East*, JDF & Associates Ltd., 2012

Furness, R., *Poster to Poster Railway Journeys in Art: Vol. 7 The Glorious South-West*, JDF & Associates Ltd., 2014

Fryer, C., *British Pullman Trains: A Tribute to all Britain's Steam, Diesel and Electric Pullman Services*, Silver Link Publishing, 1992

Gardiner, J., *The Thirties: An Intimate History*, Harper Press, 2010

Gilbert, M., *Winston S. Churchill, Companion Volume V, Part 3, The Coming of War, 1936–1939*, Heinemann, 1982

Gosling, L., *Holidays and High Society: The Golden Age of Travel*, The History Press, 2019

Gould, J., in F. Chadwick, *Ocean Steamships: A Popular Account of Their Construction, Development, Management and Appliances*, Charles Scribner's Sons, 1891

Graves, R., and A. Hodge, *The Long Weekend: A Social History of Great Britain 1918–1939*, Cardinal, 1940.

Greenway, A., *Cross Channel and Short Sea Ferries: An Illustrated History*, Seaforth Publishing, Pen & Sword Books, 2014

Hannavy, J., *The Victorian and Edwardian Tourist*, Shire Publications, 2012

Haresnape, B., *Pullman: Travelling in Style*, Ian Allan, 1987

Hartill, J., *British Railway Shipping 1948–1984: A Nationalised Success Story*, MA by Research, University of York, The Institute of Railway Studies, 2014

Hendry, R., *British Railway Coaching Stock in Colour: For the Modeller and Historian*, Midland - Ian Allan Publishing, 2002

Herbert, R., *Monet on the Normandy Coast: Tourism and Painting, 1867–1886*, Yale University Press, 1994

Heffer, S., *High Minds: The Victorians and the Birth of Modern Britain*, The Random House Group, 2014

Heffer, S., *The Age of Decadence: Britain 1880 to 1914*, Random House Books, 2017

Wendell Holmes, O., *One Hundred Days in Europe:The Works of Oliver Wendell Holmes Part Ten*, Houghton, Mifflin and Company, 1887

Hitches, M., *Rails to Rosslare: The GWR Mail Route to Ireland*, Amberley, 2010

Jackson, B., *Weymouth to the Channel Islands: A Great Western Railway Shipping History*, Oakwood Press, 2002

James, H., *Travels with Henry James*, Nation Books, 2016

Jarvis, P., *British Airways: 100 Years of Aviation Posters*, Amberley, 2018

Jenkinson, D., *British Railway Carriages of the 20th Century: Volume 1: The End of an Era, 1901–22*, Guild Publishing, 1988

Jenkinson, D., *The History of British Railway Carriages 1900–1953*, The Pendragon Partnership, 1996

Kidner, R., *Pullman Trains in Britain*, The Oakwood Press, 1998

King, M., *An Illustrated history of Southern Coaches*, Oxford Publishing Co., 2003

Kittridge, A., *Plymouth: Ocean Liner Port of Call*, Twelveheads Press, 1993

Lovell, M., *The Riviera Set, 1920–1960: The Golden Years of Glamour and Excess*, Little, Brown, 2016

McCutcheon, C., *Port of Southampton in the 60s & 70s*, Amberely, 2009

McCutcheon, J., and C. McCutcheon, *Titanic & Her Sisters: A Postcard History*, Amberely, 2014

McDonald, F., *Britain in the 1920s*, Pen & Sword Books, 2012

McDougall, R., and G. Gardiner, *Trans-Atlantic Liners in Picture Postcards*, Ian Allan Publishing, 2004

Ross McKibbin, R., *Classes and Cultures: England 1918–1951*, Oxford University Press, 2000

McManus, B., *Our Little English Cousin*, L.C. Page and Company, 1908

McManus, B., *The American Woman Abroad*, Dodd, Mead and Company, 1911

Maggs, C., *A History of the Great Western Railway*, Amberley, 2013

Martin, A., *Belles & Whistles*, Profile Books, 2014

Martin, A., *Night Trains: The Rise and Fall of the Sleeper*, Profile Books, 2017

Matthews, N., *Victorians & Edwardian Abroad: The Beginnings of the Modern Holiday*, Pen & Sword History, 2016

Miller, W., *Great British Passenger Ships*, The History Press, 2010

Miller, W., *Great American Passenger Ships*, The History Press, 2012

Molyneaux, T., and K. Robertson, *The Heyday of Eastleigh and its Locomotives*, Ian Allan Publishing, 2005

Morel, J., *Pullman*, David & Charles, 1983

Mullay, A., *Streamlined Steam: Britain's 1930s Luxury Expresses*, David & Charles, 1994

Mullen, R., and J. Munson, *'The Smell of the Continent': The British Discover Europe*, Macmillan, 2009

Norddeutsche Lloyd, *Across the Atlantic: From New York to Southampton, Havre and Bremen*, Company published travel material, 1879, Digital reprint, Forgotten Books, 2016

Peel, D., *Locomotive Headboards: The Complete Story*, The History Press, 2006

Perkin, H., *The Age of the Railway: A Social History of 19th Century Britain*, 1976, reprint, Edward Evererett Root, Publishers, 2016

Perkin, H., *The Rise of Professional Society: England since 1880*, Routledge, 1989

Phipp, M., *Flying Boats of the Solent and Poole*, Amberley, 2013

Piggott, N., *The Encyclopaedia of Titled Trains: The Ultimate Directory of Great Britain's Named Expresses*, Mortons Media Group, 2012

Pimlott, J., *The Englishman's Holiday: A Social History*, Faber and Faber, 1947

Pope, R., 'Railway Companies and Resort Hotels between the Wars', *The Journal of Transport History*, 22(1), 62-73, 2001

Pugh, M., *We Danced All Night: A Social History of Britain between the Wars*, Vintage Random House, 2009

Quinzio, J., *Food on the Rails: The Golden Era of Railroad Dining*, Rowman & Littlefield, 2014

Reed, C., *Gateway to the West: A History of Riverside Station Liverpool*, MD & HB - LNWR, Premier Portfolio No. 10, London & North Western Railway Society, 1992

Rideing, W. in F. Chadwick, *Ocean Steamships: A Popular Account of Their Construction, Development, Management and Appliances*, Charles Scribner's Sons, 1891

Rieger, B., *Technology and the Culture of Modernity in Britain and Germany 1890–1945*, Cambridge University Press, 2005

Ring, J., *Riviera: The Rise and Rise of the Côte D'Azur*, John Murray Publishers, 2004

Roberts, A., *Churchill: Walking with Destiny*, Penguin Random House, 2018

Robertson, K., *In the Tracks of the 'Bournemouth Belle'*, Crécy Publishing Limited, 2016

St. John Thomas, D., and P. Whitehouse, *SR 150: A Century and a Half of the Southern Railway*, David & Charles Publishers, 1988

Semmens, P., *The Heyday of GWR Train Services*, David & Charles, 1990

Semmens, P., *History of the Great Western Railway 1. Consolidation 1923–29*, George Allen & Unwin, 1985

Shepherd, J., and J. Shepherd, *1920s Britain*, Shire Publications, 2010

Shin, H., 'The Art of Advertising Railways: Organisation and Coordination in Britain's Railway Marketing, 1860–1910', *Business History*, 56(2) 187-213, 2014

Simmons, J., 'Railways, Hotels, and Tourism in Great Britain 1839–1914', *Journal of Contemporary History*, 19, 201-222, 1984

Smith, W., *A Yorkshireman's Trip to the United States and Canada*, Longmans, Green and Co., 1892

Stevens-Stratton, S., *Bulleid Coaches in 4mm Scale*, Ian Allan Ltd., 1983

Tungate, M., *The Escape Industry: How Iconic and Innovative Brands Built the Travel Business*, Kogan Page, 2018

Turner, D., *Victorian and Edwardian Railway Travel*, Shire Publications, 2013

Turner, D., *Extract of LSWR Hampshire Record Office, 104A02/A3/03, Traffic Committee Minute Book, Minute 373*, 27th September 1893

Turner, D., *Managing the 'Royal Road': The London and South Western Railway 1870–1911*, PhD dissertation, University of York, Institute of Railway Studies, 2013

Twain, M., *The Innocents Abroad*, Penguin Books 1869 (reprinted as first edition, 2002)

Wadsworth, J., *Bristol in the Great War*, Pen & Sword Military, 2014

Walton, J., 'Power, Speed and Glamour: The Naming of Express Steam Locomotives in Inter-war Britain', *The Journal of Transport History*, 26(2), 1-19, 2005

Williams, M., *The Trains Now Departed*, Penguin Random House UK, 2015

Williamson, A., *The Golden Age of Travel: The Romantic Years of Tourism in Images from the Thomas Cook Archives*, Thomas Cook Group, 1998

Wilson, R.B., *Go Great Western: A History of GWR Publicity*, David & Charles, 1970

Winkworth, D., *Southern Titled Trains*, David & Charles, 1988

Wolmar, C., and B. Solomon, *The Golden Age of European Railways*, Pen & Sword Transport, 2013

Woodley, C., *History of British European Airways 1946–1972*, Pen & Sword Aviation, 2016

Wooler, N., *Dinner in the Diner: The History of Railway Catering*, David & Charles, 1987

Newspapers and Periodicals

Aberdeen Daily Journal
Aberdeen Press and Journal
Belfast News-Letter
Berkshire Chronicle
Birmingham Gazette

Birmingham Post
Bournemouth Guardian
Bystander
Cambridge Daily News
Cheltenham Looker-On
Clifton Society
Cornish Telegraph
Cornishman
Coventry Evening Telegraph
Daily Herald
Daily Mirror
Daily News
Daily Telegraph
Dartmouth & South Hams Chronicle
Derby Daily Telegraph
Derby Evening Telegraph
Dover Express
Dover Express and East Kent News
Dundee Courier
Eastern Daily Press
Evening News
Exeter and Plymouth Gazette Daily Telegram
Folkstone Herald
Globe
Hartland and West Country Chronicle
Illustrated Sporting and Dramatic News
Isle of Wight Times
Jersey Evening Post
Jersey Weekly Press and Independent
Liverpool Daily Post
Liverpool Daily Post and Mercury
Liverpool Echo
Liverpool Echo and Evening Express
Liverpool Mercury
Liverpool Post & Mercury
Manchester Courier
Manchester Courier and Lancashire General Advertiser
Manchester Evening News
Morning Post
Norddeutsche Lloyd
Northampton Evening Telegraph

Northern Whig
Nottingham Daily Express
Pall Mall Gazette
Portadown Times
Portsmouth Evening News
RAIL 410/600, LNWR Officers' Committee Minute Book
Railway Magazine
Railway Wonders of the World
St. James's Gazette
Scotsman
Sevenoaks Chronicle and Kentish Advertiser
Sheffield Evening Telegraph
Sheffield Evening Telegraph and Star
Shipping Gazette and Lloyds List
Shipley Times and Express
Sketch
Sphere
Stage
Standard
Steam Days
Sunderland Echo
Tatler
Tatler and Bystander
Times
Tyrone Courier
Wagon-Lits Diffusion
Western Daily Mercury
Western Daily Press
Western Daily Press and Bristol Mirror
Western Mail
Western Morning News
Western Morning News and Daily Gazette
Western Times
Yorkshire Post
Yorkshire Post and Leeds Intelligencer

Web sites

Crane, S., *The Scotch Express*, 1899. https://public.wsu. edu/~campbelld/crane/scotch.htm, accessed 24 February 2018
Illustrated Guide to, and Popular History of, the Channel Islands, https://jerseyeveningpost.com/news/2015/03/08/a-guide

book-from-the-1880s-offers-fascinating-insight-into-jerseys-tourism-history/, accessed 24 May 2019

Railway Wonders of the World, https://www.railwaywonder softheworld.com/folkestone_flyer.html, accessed 31 July 2018

Train of Dreams, http://traindesreves.com/en/, accessed 2 August 2017

David Turner (2012), 'The Railway Company Do Not Want': The L&SWR's Purchase of the Southampton Docks, http://turniprail. blogspot.co.uk/2012/02/railway-company-do-not-want-it-l. html, accessed 30 May 2017

David Turner (2012), 'Titanic' and the London and South Western Railway: An Intimate Relationship, http://turniprail.blogspot. co.uk/2012/04/titanic-and-london-and-south-western.html, accessed 30 May 2017

Wagon-Lits Diffusion, Gestion des marques et des droits Compagnie Internationale des Wagons-Lits (CIWL) et PLM cars, http://www. wagons-lits-diffusion.com/en/album/ciwl-plans-archives/, accessed 2 August 2017

Index